Daniel-Rops

SACRED
HISTORY

Translated by

K. MADGE

LONGMANS, GREEN AND CO.
New York · 1949

LONGMANS, GREEN AND CO., INC.
55 FIFTH AVENUE, NEW YORK 3

SACRED HISTORY

COPYRIGHT · 1949
BY LONGMANS. GREEN & CO., INC.

FIRST EDITION

Printed in the United States of America
Montauk Book Mfg. Co., Inc., New York

CONTENTS

PART ONE: THE PATRIARCHS

v

PART TWO: MOSES AND CANAAN

LIST OF MAPS

PART ONE

THE PATRIARCHS

I

ABRAHAM'S MISSION

A T UR,[1] IN SHINAR, a local capital of the Lower Euphrates,
about four thousand years ago, a man called Abram was
visited by God and, without hesitation, believed the
promise: "I will make of thee a great nation, and I will bless thee,
and make thy name great" (Genesis XII:2).

This is the point of departure assigned in the Bible to the whole
historical development of which the people of Israel were both
the agent and the witness. It is an event of an essentially mystical
order, no less mysterious in its essence and no less tangible in its
results than was, for example, the mission of Joan of Arc for
France. That a small Bedouin clan, nomads wandering, like many
others, across plains and steppes, should be the source of a
destiny so fraught with significance, the distant heirs of the
Patriarchs were to understand as a fact that cannot be explained
by the logic of history; it is explainable only as the will of God.

Never, during two thousand years, was this mystical event
called in question. In the worst moments of distress, in their most
misguided hours, the remote descendants of the inspired man
called to mind the promise in order to be comforted, or to repent.
"Your father Abraham," Christ said, "rejoiced to see my day." On
the Patriarch's act of faith, three great religions were established:
Judaism, Christianity and Islam. That far-reaching event, the setting out of a clan from Ur towards the hills of Harran, is a great
moment in history, and if we no longer believe, as Renan did, that
Abraham is the fabulous "Pater Orcham" of Ovid's *Metamor-
phoses*, he still remains, according to the sacred name that he was
later to bear, Abraham, "the father of a multitude of men."

[1]All place-names referred to in the text are to be found on the maps. *See*
the MAP OF THE FERTILE CRESCENT, p. 7.

3

Concise as are the phrases of Genesis in which the event is described, they are sufficient for us to divine, in Abram's decision, the outcome of a religious drama. Terah, his father, was an idolater. "They served other gods," Joshua said later (Joshua xxiv:2); no doubt the moon-god Nannar-Sin that excavated carvings represent in the form of one of those bearded princes whose beard and hair, carved in dark blue stone, have a strangely metallic look. This was the god of the luminous Asiatic night, and the crescent beside him a Euphrates barge with pointed prow, in which he voyaged towards the sky. From this lunar cult, from Mesopotamian polytheism, Abram resolved to break away, when he heard the nameless God bid him: "Get thee out of thy country, and from thy kindred, and from thy father's house" (Gen. xii:1). At the time of Judith, when the Assyrian Holofernes asked for information about Israel, he was told that this people had abandoned the religion of its forefathers, who honoured a number of gods; that they worshipped the one God of heaven, who ordered them to leave the country of the Chaldees and to go and live in Canaan (Judith v:8–9). The metaphysical mission of this race, by which monotheism was to be established in the world, is already implicit in the act of this man, who set out towards the north.

He did not go alone. This religious reformer convinced his family. His wife Sarai went with him; and he also persuaded his old father Terah to set out for an unknown country at the command of an unknown God, and the old man, as though to sever all links that attached him to the life he was leaving, took with him his grandson Lot, the child of a son recently dead. How did he convince them? We do not know. The East has great confidence in those who claim to be inspired by God. Israel believed in many prophets, and among another Semite people Mahomet, who received the angelic order, "Preach to your neighbours! Proclaim the one God!" after many efforts succeeded finally in getting a hearing. One may well wonder whether, in the departure of that entire clan, we must not also see other factors at work: a puritanical reaction, which might well be felt by nomads, at the wealth and corruption of cities; nostalgia for the free life of tents, whose memory was still fresh for them; and perhaps also the effects of one of those violent earthquakes so frequent in Mesopotamia.

For that inspired migration that at one time must have seemed strange and almost incomprehensible, almost on the farthest indistinct horizon of history, we now can see in a very precise setting, integrated with a whole series of events which date back more than fifteen hundred years before that time, as an incident, among others, of those displacements of peoples of which the country between the two rivers was often the scene. As, under the clay deposits, the meticulous excavations of the archaeologists discover, layer by layer, the moving record of civilizations, we can situate that episode more exactly in the course of centuries and civilizations. A mystical event, indeed, but also an historical event, the vocation of Abraham can only be understood in terms of that Mesopotamia whose traditions, so many thousand of years old, have passed, by way of the Bible, into the memory of the entire white race.

MESOPOTAMIA, CRUCIBLE OF NATIONS

When, about the year 2000 B.C., Abram left Ur, Mesopotamia had already a history dating back for at least fifteen hundred years. She was one of those two lighthouses that seem, in these beginnings of the Western world, to shine alone in the shadows of unformed barbarity. The other was Egypt, another plain of fertile land where water nourishes vegetation and where the patient effort of generations gave to society its first foundations. Outside these two favoured regions, it seems as though there was nothing but confused rumours and anarchies, with the single exception of Crete where, in a small island, the most perfect of all civilizations was coming into being.

But if we properly understand the principles that grouped men in these plains of great rivers at the period when agriculture was emerging as the basic occupation—elsewhere the same thing happened; in the Yangtze basin in China, or the Ganges basin in

India—it is clear that a similar development determined the history of the land of the Nile and that of Mesopotamia. Egypt is a long valley bordered with cliffs, which the river, rising with astonishing regularity, fills every spring: from this results for that land, whose fertility is continually renewed, a stability which its history seems to reflect. Moreover, although in contact with Asia and bordering on Africa, Egypt is only a corridor to the extent to which she deems it desirable to be so; she has never been an invasion route. In the country of the Tigris and the Euphrates, it was far otherwise.

Between the Persian gulf and the Mediterranean there is, on the map, a group of plains flanked by a trapeze of high land. On the east it is dominated by the forbidding border of the Iranian plateau; the Zagros Mountains, the Anti-Taurus and the Armenian ranges form an impressive barrier in the north; to reach the Mediterranean the Lebanon or the mountains of Palestine must be crossed.

In the heart of this country, six or seven times as large as France, burns one of the most terrible deserts in the world. Uninterrupted, though varying in geographical appearance, it stretches endlessly towards the south, as far as the red sands of Dahna, and beyond to the stormy desert of Hadramaut. But bordering this brazier, nature has accorded man a fringe of fertile land. This is the Fertile Crescent: a river delta, the pastures of northern Syria, and the plains of the Orontes and of the Jordan.

Mesopotamia comprises the western and largest part of these favoured regions. As its name (given by the Greeks) implies, it is the region of the two rivers, between-two-rivers. If Egypt is, as Herodotus calls it, the "gift of the Nile," Mesopotamia is, one might say, a gift of the Tigris and the Euphrates, but a gift often revoked, often contested.

Although both arise in the Armenian ranges, these two rivers are very different in character. The Tigris has steep banks, a rapid current, and its flood, beginning in March, reaches its height on June 15th; when it overflows, it feeds, too often, only swamps. The Euphrates has less water and, on the border of the desert,

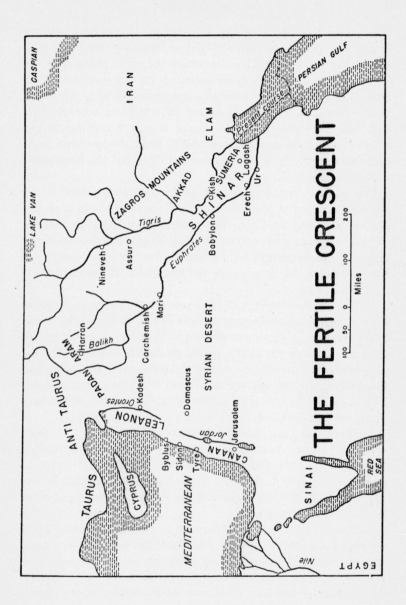

THE FERTILE CRESCENT

often dries up. Its flooding is later and more gradual, and extends more regularly over its low banks. And this beneficent inundation explains why nearly all the towns are situated near them. But even the Euphrates cannot be compared with the Nile. Much of the fertile soil remains beyond the high-water mark of the flooding, and in order to create those "eternal waters" of which Hammurabi, contemporary with Abraham, speaks, immense labour and a system of canals and embankments is necessary; that whole system of irrigation that the men of four thousand years ago practised with such skill and whose abandonment brought the country into the distress in which it lay for half a century.[2]

Nevertheless in comparison with the desert, that desert where man is "consumed by heat by day and cold by night" (Gen. xxx:40), Mesopotamia gives the impression of being a garden. Here wheat and barley almost certainly had their origin. Here, if the supply of water does not fail, three harvests can be gathered from the soil. Here the date palm grows to perfection. The country produces confections, honey, wine and many kinds of textiles. Sesame yields an oil with a nutty flavour; the fig-tree bears fruits so exquisite that they were offered to the gods; the vine produces an excellent wine, and the tamarisk exudes a sugary gum. One can understand only too well the strength of the attraction of these favoured lands for their neighbours.

For this is the drama of Mesopotamia, and with it, of all the Fertile Cresent. These rich lands are a perpetual temptation to the nomads of the desert, forever threatened by drought. And as if that internal danger were not enough, there is also the covetousness of all the mountain peoples of Elam, Iran, the Upper Tigris and the Anti-Taurus mountains, for whom these lowlands are at once a corridor and a granary ready for pillage. There has never been a time when migrations starting from the desert and converging towards the plains or coming down from the surrounding

[2] One sees (*see* map: THE FERTILE CRESCENT) that the two rivers do not join, as they do today, in the Shatt-al-Arab. During four thousand years the alluvial deposits have extended the coast line enormously and the delta is now in common. At the time of Abraham, Ur was near the sea-coast; it is now more than 125 miles inland.

mountains have not mingled in that crucible of races and civilizations. Egypt, disturbed only once or twice by invasion, has never
been long in resuming the course of her stable destiny; Mesopotamia bears the imprint of all her conquerors.

THE CIVILIZATIONS OF MESOPOTAMIA

The first civilization that Mesopotamia was to know was the
product of a very remarkable race, the Sumerians. Where they
came from no one knows—Afghanistan, or Baluchistan, perhaps,
some five thousand years ago. About the year 3500 B.C. they
were well settled in the lands of the Lower Euphrates that the
Bible calls Shinar. They were certainly not Semitic. We have
only to consider the round, smooth-skinned face, with a prominent but short nose, of Gudea, a typical Sumerian of the twenty-
fifth century B.C. of whom the Louvre has eleven statues; or, in
the British Museum, the unforgettable features of Queen Shub-Ad
who died at Ur fifty-five hundred years ago, whose nostrils, sensual lips and wide eyes seem on the point of living again, and
who, strangely crowned in metallic foliage, still incarnates the
eternal temptation and the mystery of woman.

These Sumerians were the founders of civilization throughout
Mesopotamia. It was they who initiated methods of irrigation,
agriculture and building, the great religious myths, the principles
of law. More than one of the fundamental themes of our own
thought has its roots in the earth of Sumeria. It has been said
that they played, for the lands of the Euphrates, the same rôle
as the Latin race in the elaboration of occidental societies. But,
unlike Rome, Sumeria never had the idea of unifying the country.
Each city, Ur, Lagash, Erech, was a tiny state ruled by a petty
king, or *patesi*, vicar of the local god. Wars between these cities
were all too frequent. Neighbours profited by them; hence the
first wave of assaults from the desert upon the Fertile Crescent.
These newcomers were undoubtedly Semites. Their noses were
aquiline and their hair crisped. For many centuries they occupied
the land of Akkad on the Middle Euphrates; they were held in
respect because of the power of their *patesi* and their civilization

was a poor imitation of that of the Sumerians. But about the year 3000 B.C. they attacked. For the next two centuries there was a great Semitic expansion. At about the time when the great Pyramids were being built in Egypt, the King of Akkad, Sargon the Elder, a gardener who had risen to be a general, conquered the little Sumerian princes and defended himself from all threats of invasion from the mountains by campaigns in Elam, and then turning to the west, he advanced as far as the Mediterranean where he washed his arms and conquered the "Cedars of Lebanon and the mountain of silver," the Tagus. This Semitic expansion of the twenty-seventh century left its historic traces almost everywhere; the Phoenicians are no doubt one of its branches, and we find Semitic colonies dating from this epoch even in the heart of Asia Minor, in Cappadocia.

But this conquest was never stabilized. The available forces were insufficient; scarcely had the conquerors (who did not leave an army of occupation) departed, than they had to come back to deal with revolts. Naram-Sin, grandson of Sargon, spent his reign in this way. And the Akkadian Empire was so unstable that we find, not long after, the first invasion from the mountains of those mysterious peoples, the Guti, whose arrival disturbed Mesopotamia to such an extent that the Sumerians won back their independence and, in about 2500 B.C., in his capital at Lagash, Gudea rose to be a powerful sovereign.

At the time of the birth of Abram, therefore, Mesopotamia presented a mosaic of little states, some Sumerian, others of Akkadian origin, more or less hostile, without any political unity, but all having reached about the same level of civilization under Sumerian influence. Of this civilization we learn more year by year. A hundred years ago Emile Botta, French Consul at Mosul, had the idea of excavating the mounds that are scattered over the plain, and what prodigious horizons were opened by his discoveries! No doubt countless forgotten things still lie buried, awaiting the happy chance that may bring them to light; the method of oblique photography, invented by Father Poidebard, reveals more and more sites to be explored. Recently, where the caravan-route crosses the Euphrates, a French party which has been excavating since 1934 has uncovered the palace of Mari, occupying an area of five acres, with temples and a tower of many stories, and innumerable museum specimens. Although the site of Agadé, the capital of the great Sargon, has not yet been discovered, we can now study on the site excavated at Ur the birthplace of Abram. Since 1922 important work has been going on there, and today five hundred years of history have been laid bare before our eyes. The tower of the temple, emerging from the sand where it lay buried, reveals its vast foundations. A whole checker-board of houses surrounds it; and in London, Philadelphia and Bagdad, we can admire today the fabulous treasures of Ur: the wrought swords of kings, the bronze helmets of soldiers, the golden goblet that lay against the teeth of a woman's skeleton when it was discovered, a work of art of amazing beauty.

The migration of Abram that our fathers imagined as occurring at the very beginning of civilization is now seen as a relatively late event in the succession of Mesopotamian history, and it is evident that many of the traditions of the Terahites were of Sumerian origin, and that the events and customs to which Abram referred are those with which he was familiar at Ur in his early years.

The city, in his day, was the city of bricks that archaeologists have discovered. The only building material available in the country is clay, baked or dried in the sun. Imported stone was reserved for statues of the gods and for the tables of the laws of the kingdom. The houses were built in long meandering streets, with blind walls; according to the custom still followed in the East, private life was concealed, and only to be seen in the central "patio" with its white, rough-cast terraces, a fig-tree in the corner of the court; the houses of modern Iraq have preserved the same pattern as those of four thousand years ago. But Abram was to preserve the memory of the house that he left to follow God. In the vestibule, the hands and feet of any guest would be washed in a small basin or gutter carved out for this purpose; and when he received the three strangers under the oaks of Mamre, he therefore said to them: "Let a little water, I pray you, be fetched, and wash your feet" (Gen. xviii:4).

What he rejected in leaving Ur was not only the comfort and luxury of a city, beautiful encrusted furnishings, silk hangings, embroidered garments, jewels and perfumes, but also the meticulous bureaucracy whose archives fill the brick libraries, and which had been imposed by the *patesi* of Sumeria for nearly a thousand years upon their subjects—a kind of state control to which the archaic Hebrew temperament was always to be hostile. He rejected a religion of many gods, or natural forces: Enlil, the air; Anu, the sky; Enki, the fecund water, were the idols to whom honey, wine and cakes made with dates were offered. And perhaps also he wished to escape from certain customs which religion appears to have imposed.

For, in this highly civilized society, a horrible fact disconcerts us: human sacrifice was practised. For the honour of gods and kings, victims were claimed. In the burial grounds of Ur, the excavators have found a horrifying spectacle: about the bodies of kings, covered with pearls, gold, lapis and agate, are buried twenty-five, fifty, seventy-four sacrificed servants. Among them are men and women, officers, domestics, even a muleteer with his beasts, lined up as if on parade. No trace of violence is to be found on their bodies. These victims must have been done to death with poison. Renan says that Abram's glory lies in the substitution that he made in the sacrifices of a ram for a man; the discoveries at Ur lead us to think that there is some truth in this view.

HAMMURABI, CONTEMPORARY OF ABRAM

But a particular historical event may have had a more direct influence on the destiny of the inspired man. The twenty-second century, that is to say, the century before that into which Abram was born, was marked by great events of whose course we are only now beginning to have some idea: the appearance, in history, of the Aryans. Coming from a region that it is not easy to identify—probably the continental isthmus that stretches from the Baltic to the Caspian and which was perhaps at this time already for them only one stage in their immense displacement—impelled by motives even more obscure (want of food, change of climate, or perhaps spontaneous imperialism)—masses of men, speaking almost the same language, poured southward. In about the year 2150 B.C. the migration reached the borders of Mesopotamia, Asia Minor, and Iran; we meet these people under the name of Hittites, Kassites and Mitannians. Another branch moved towards Europe; the Achaeans installed themselves in the Greek peninsula a hundred years later. At this time, displacements of masses of people in distant countries did not yet trouble the ancient civilizations. In the oasis of the Nile the Pharaohs of the Thebaid, having re-established order after the strange social crisis that brought down the ancient empire, were occupied with the magnificent development which characterized Egypt under the Senusret Dynasty. In the shelter of his island, Minos, King of Crete, was building the first palaces of Phaistos and Knossos. His tables were served with superb egg-shell china. It was not until two or three centuries later that these stable kingdoms were to be rudely shaken by the Aryan tidal wave. But Mesopotamia, nearer to the countries from which these barbarians were advancing, was already feeling the first shock.

The great wave of Semitic expansion of Sargon's empire towards the Mediterranean now, as it were, ebbed back again. From the country of the Amorites (now Syria) came other waves. Perhaps under Aryan pressure their chiefs, of whom one at least was a great leader, had some conception of the peril and sought to establish a Mesopotamian unity in order to resist it.

The attempt of Hammurabi, greatest of these Amorite kings, is a curious one.[3] For a century without interruption, his ancestors had proceeded to raise themselves to power at the expense of the petty kings of Akkad and Sumeria. Hammurabi came to the throne about the year 2000 B.C., continued the work, and carried

[3] A chart at the end of this book indicates the chief events in other civilizations contemporary with the history of Israel.

it much farther. His aim was to unify all these peoples and to
give them both an outer and an inner organic entity. He brought
about a religious revolution, dispossessed the ancient gods, and
installed a supreme idol, Marduk. His city, Babylon, was to be
the capital of all the lands of the Euphrates. And, in the fortieth
year of his reign, he had carved in stone his "decisions of equity,"
a code still preserved in the Louvre, and which was the summary
of the ancient Sumerian traditions which he set out to impose
on his subjects.

This attempt had something Napoleonic about it. At once conqueror and lawgiver, this Hammurabi was one of the greatest
figures of his epoch. Did he succeed in his aims? Not entirely,
for this artificial unity could not resist the attacks of the Aryans
who, a hundred years later, sacked Babylon. Nevertheless, the
language of Babylon was henceforth to be the diplomatic language in use from Asia Minor as far as Egypt, and Amorite
influence impressed itself deeply upon the history of civilization.
But this prodigious attempt certainly encountered fierce resistance. The full list of cities sacked by Hammurabi would be long.
Mari was never to rise again. And when, the great conqueror
being near to death, Ur attempted to revolt, its walls were razed
to the ground and its population carried into captivity by the
son of the despot.

To what extent was Abram's decision to leave the country
where he had lived due to that insupportable political tyranny,
that totalitarianism? In order to convince Terah in his old age
that it was better to go, Abram must have had good reasons to
point to in the policy of the king of Babylon. And who knows
whether the attempt to impose religious unity in the cult of the
idol Marduk did not finally decide the man who carried in his
heart the certainty of the one God?

THE CLAN OF TERAH ON THE MOVE

In a society whose complexity is now becoming clear to us,
what place was held by the little clan of Terah whose historical
significance was to be so great? Certainly it was Amorite in origin.

Ezekiel, accusing Jerusalem, was to say, "Your father was an Amorite!" But the impression that we gain from reading the eleventh and twelfth chapters of Genesis is that this group of men must have been in some sense apart. Were they a family who had but recently arrived? A community still retaining strong traditions of the period when the Semites camped in tents in the desert? In North Africa there is a tribe, the Mozabites, who practise a sort of Moslem protestantism, who live in this way, occasionally settling in towns of the coast but always in the end setting out again towards the pentapolis of Gardaia. The Jews retain the memory of a tradition according to which they would seem to have served as mercenaries and merchants in Babylon before the departure for Canaan.

In any case, Abram decided to leave Ur. Like his remote ancestors he took the road again. Asia has witnessed, from China to the Bosporus, many more considerable migrations! In these great spaces, it is as though men were blown hither and thither by the wind, like the sand-hills. Among all these waves moving within the Mesopotamian basin, Abram's clan appears only as a ripple. To form an idea of this displacement, we have but to see one of those caravans that one meets on the routes of Syria, with its train of rocking camels, stretching for hundreds and hundreds of yards, or one of those encampments of black tents, "black but comely," as it says in the Song of Songs, that the nomads of Palmyra still set up in our own time.

What route did that migration follow? The Bible tells us: from Ur to Harran, that is, from south to north up the Euphrates.[4] Harran is situated in the range of hills that comes before the Anti-Taurus range, from which flows a tributary of the Euphrates, the

---

[4] It is to be noted that certain historians, among them one of considerable authority, M. Lods, do not accept the commonly accepted tradition according to which the Ur of the Bible is identified with the Ur of Sumeria. These point out that since, in the account of the earliest origins of the race, Noah's ark came to ground in Armenia, which is in the north, not in the south, we must look to this district as the point of departure of the Terahites, and he affirms that the names of the ancestors of Abraham "seem to be dotted along the direct route from Armenia to Canaan." At all events, Harran was a stage in this route.

Balikh. All this region forms an important route; Turks and Cru-saders fought in it for Edessa. It must have been one of those places where caravans rested; in order to cross the Fertile Crescent, as the desert is virtually impassable, it is almost impos-sible not to go through Harran. It must have been a sort of Babylonian trading centre, where merchandise was exchanged, and also myths, and ideas. The great Prophet Balaam, much later, was said to have come from there (Numbers xxiii:7). For the choice of that city there may have been religious reasons: for the same god was worshipped there as at Ur, the moon-god.

It was in any case a country likely to attract a nomad with his flocks and herds. Fairly well watered with some rain and by mountain streams, there is grass. In spring the flora is even abundant; white marguerites, crimson tulips, and yellow crocuses form a speckled carpet. Caper-trees sway their mauve tufts, and tall flower stalks of rose-coloured blossoms spring up everywhere. This fragrant steppe-land is already dry in May, but flocks can always find some pasture. Harran, in the hollow of its hills, was then no doubt as it is now, a little town of brick houses, lime-washed, whose tiny domes (for every house is domed) look like a collection of billiard-balls.

Their stay in Harran had a profound influence on the history of the Terahites. Through the period of the Patriarchs, this coun-try of Aram-Narahaim, or Padan-aram, was to be the real fatherland. They used to go back to find wives among those members of the tribe who had remained there. Rebekah and Rachel came from here. And when, long after, the Israelites spoke of their ancestry among themselves, they used to begin with the words, "A wanderer from Syria was my father . . ." (Deuter-onomy xxvi:5). At all the crossroads of their history, we find these wandering tribes; their name indicates the great tide of which the Terahites were only a little wave; they were to spread far, and over a long period, and their language was to be, finally, dominant in the Syrian-Palestine area, the language spoken by Jesus. The period at Harran was, no doubt, spent in the manner of "Syrian wanderers" outside the city gates, in a temporary encampment.

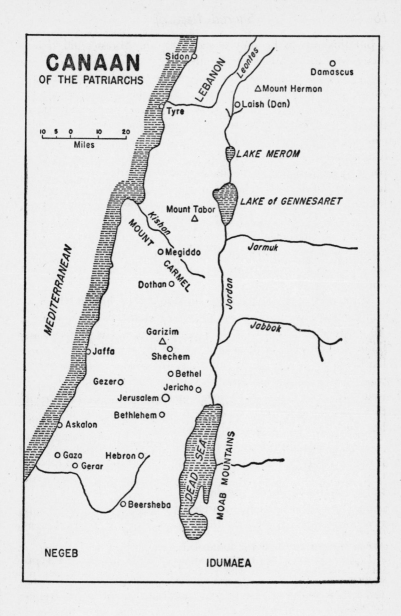

But this was to be only a stage. Terah, Abram's old father, died. Now the head of the family, the inspired "patriarch," set out again, knowing that he had not yet reached the country where the destiny of his people was to be accomplished. He made towards the south, the land of Canaan, the other point of the Fertile Crescent. There was nothing illogical in this. This country between Syria and Palestine has at all times throughout history been a corridor. From north to south, invasions have passed over it; it is the inevitable route from the Mediterranean to the Euphrates. The clan of Abram, like many other nomads, followed their flocks from pasture to pasture. The Canaanites, few in number, occupied only their fortified cities, and never dreamed of interfering with these migrations. This first entry into Canaan is not described: the Bible makes no mention of any contact with its inhabitants, or of any battle. But it records a fact important in another way.

At Shechem,[5] where the ridge of Mount Garizim (to which we will have frequent occasion to refer) descends to the plain, Abram received from God the confirmation of His promise, and the definition of it in the words, "Unto thy seed will I give this land" (Gen. xii:7). From this time, the destiny of this people was to be bound to that country. Canaan now became "the promised land." But it was to be seven or eight hundred years before these nomads settled there: there is no record of any other race having taken so long to establish themselves.

After a pause "to the east of Bethel, on the mountain," Abram's people went from one encampment to another until they reached the southern extremity of Palestine, the Negeb, whose grim solitude stretches from the mountains of Judah to Sinai.[6] Famine came upon them here. In such circumstances the invariable solution for nomads is to lead their flocks to pasture on the rich

---

[5] *See* Map: CANAAN OF THE PATRIARCHS, p. 17.

[6] Some historians think that this movement of the Terahites towards the south was contemporaneous with a displacement of sedentary peoples from Syria and Upper Mesopotamia. This was the origin of certain races that we find in Palestine on the return from Egypt in the time of Joshua, the Horites, the Perizzites, etc. (*See* below pp. 31 and 138.)

plains; this difference in fertility between adjacent areas is one of the main causes of Asiatic migrations. Not far away lay Egypt, rich, inexhaustible. And although the social structure of the Kingdom of the Pharaohs was infinitely more closed than that of Canaan, this fact did not prevent wandering tribes from insinuating themselves into it. At about this period, a tomb of the Twelfth Dynasty shows us a whole Bedouin caravan in the land of the Nile—men, women, children and their asses—and the text informs us that a certain Ibsha and his clan had given the officials of Egypt some trouble. The agricultural people of the Algerian coast regarded with no less anxiety the descent of these nomads of the high plateaux, threatening their ripening crops.

It was during the stay in Egypt that an incident took place that was to recur several times during the early history of the Israelites. It throws light on the physical appearance of these Semites, and on the conception of sin they had at that time. Pharaoh, having observed the beauty of Sarai, took her. Abram, who feared that he would be regarded as an obstacle and made away with, gave out that she was his sister. (This was not altogether false, she was in fact his half-sister.) As the king's favourite, Sarai gave her "brother" many gifts. But Pharaoh, without knowing it, was an adulterer; God smote him: sin is a sort of malady, whose results may infect one's children. Horrified, Pharaoh gave back Sarai, and banished the whole clan from the country without other punishment. One thinks in reading this story of those gypsy women on the outskirts of our own towns, whose beauty is at once fascinating and vaguely sinister, and of the obscure dread that these wandering people inspire.[7]

At all events, the stay in Egypt must have been of short duration, and left no such mark on Abram's people as did the longer period from Joseph to Moses. Of the two great civilizations that were to form Israel, so far only one, that of the Euphrates, had

---

' Even so, a question is suggested: How was Sarai able to inflame such passions? She was at that time sixty-five years old. This enigma is closely related to others—the longevity of the Patriarchs and their astonishing fecundity. It is evident that the Biblical narrator intends to indicate in this a divine purpose, a rare prerogative extended by God to His chosen people.

left its trace. Abram and his people returned to Canaan, to Bethel. They still lived in tents as before; the incidents that occurred at this period were those of a nomadic life.

There was an attribution of pasture between two divisions of the clan. Abram's flocks had multiplied since the stay in Egypt, and Lot, his nephew, who had accompanied Abram during the whole migration, had also many of his own. "The land was not able to bear them, that they might dwell together." There were quarrels between the herdsmen of Abram and Lot. A division was agreed upon. Lot travelled towards the Lower Jordan, at that time as rich as Egypt itself, a veritable garden, for the catastrophe that was to destroy Sodom and Gomorrah had not yet taken place. Abram moved his tents to the north, into a wooded country of trees and brushwood, to the oaks of Mamre not far from Hebron.

There was also a typical "*razzia*" and "counter-*razzia*." The region of the Dead Sea was at that time governed by five petty kings who owed some sort of allegiance to more powerful sovereigns in Mesopotamia. From one side of the Fertile Crescent to the other, there was thus exercised a sort of centralizing authority. Dissatisfied with their Canaanite vassals, the kings of the Euphrates planned a punitive expedition. It has been suggested that Hammurabi was one of the four leaders of this expedition— Amraphel, King of Shinar—who must have had with him Sumerian Elamites, and even Hittite allies, that is, forces from Asia Minor. Abram's clan was not involved in this affair, but it seems that having suppressed their vassals, Amraphel and his allies carried off, among the deported populations, Lot and his people. Hearing of this, Abram planned a counter-attack. He armed his men— 318 of them—perhaps also collected allies, and followed the tracks of the victorious caravan. At Dan, just as the Mesopotamians were about to leave Palestine, no longer fearing anything, Abram attacked by night, recaptured Lot and his people and drove off the enemy towards Damascus.

There was nothing, to be sure, in this nomadic existence that was out of the ordinary. The tribes of Transjordania and Palmyra lived in most respects a very similar life. But this small clan was different from the others. Events occurred again and again to recall the promise, the mystical gift. When Abram returned, after his victory, to the ordinary site of his encampment, a man came towards him and blessed him, bringing him bread and wine, and addressing him in these words: "Blessed be Abram of the most high God, possessor of heaven and earth." This was Melchizedek, a mysterious personage, about whom we know nothing, "without father, without mother, without descent, having neither beginning of days, nor end of life," as St. Paul said, but "made like unto the Son of God" by his name, which signifies king of justice, and whose town, Salem, signifies peace, and is no other, as Egyptian documents prove, than Jerusalem. A prophetic coincidence, and a new sign from God.

THE COVENANT

Did Melchizedek know that the decisive hour for Abram was near? A new period was beginning in the life of the Patriarch, in which God was to multiply proofs. This man, no longer young, was tormented at heart by a fearful doubt: the posterity promised him, how could it ever come into being, since he had not even a son, and since all the evidence seemed to prove beyond doubt that Sarai was sterile? But God heard his complaint, and renewed his promise. "Look now toward heaven and tell the stars, if thou be able to number them: and he said unto him, so shall thy seed be." Abram hesitated to believe, but God insisted. A veritable drama took place in the mind of the visionary, "a horror of great darkness." The thing that he was asked to believe seemed so impossible. But God was precise. Not only joy and fruitfulness lay in store for these future men who were to be the children of Abram: before they should inherit the promised land, they were to suffer as slaves in a strange country. But they would be born, and would possess the land "from the river of Egypt unto the great river, the river Euphrates." Abram believed at last.

His wife Sarai was more sceptical; but, being practical, she found a solution. The old Sumerian law, as it was formulated at this very time in the code of Hammurabi, made provision for the case of childless wives. The husband could ask his wife to choose one of her servants, to give him children. Sarai, therefore, gave Abram an Egyptian slave, Hagar, and Hagar conceived. But the concubine, filled with pride, scorned the legitimate though sterile wife. The jurists of Hammurabi, good psychologists, foresaw this possibility which cannot have been uncommon: the wife had the right to chastise the proud slave, as Sarai did, evidently rather too harshly. This might have led to the loss of all Abram's hopes, for Hagar fled to the desert, where a pregnant woman might well have died. Without the intervention of the Angel of the Lord, this would have been the end. But Hagar returned to the encampment, and shortly afterwards bore Ishmael. Abram learned that God could give a son to a man eighty-six years old.

Thirteen years passed. Abram would soon be a hundred years old. Ishmael must be the promised heir. But God visited His faithful servant yet again and His word was clearer than ever. He no longer promised only that a nation should be born of him, nor that this nation should possess the land of Canaan; if Abram "walked before God and was perfect" a covenant would be established between his people and the Almighty. That spiritual grace that Melchizedek, "a priest of the Most High," had laid upon Abram, God himself confirmed. A veritable treaty was established between the Unseen and the Patriarch, which imposed conditions on both sides.

In exchange for the special protection that he was to receive, Abram must submit to two conditions. The first was to change his name, which, amongst all primitive races, and especially in the East, is a matter of considerable importance; the name does more than designate or describe; it creates and maintains. Instead of Abram, in which perhaps there was some etymological trace of a Sumerian god, he was to bear the name of Abraham, which signifies "father of many nations." And in order to prove that Sarai too had not failed, and that she was to be associated with the destiny of her husband, she received the name of Sarah, which conveys a meaning of pre-eminence, something like "your highness."

The second condition imposed by God is yet more strange. He required that Abram should consent to be circumcised, together with all his clan. One sees in this the resurgence of one of the most ancient rites of humanity. We find it in almost all parts of the world, and at all periods. In pre-Columbian America and Polynesia circumcision was practised. So it was among Egyptians, and it was perhaps from them that Abram learned of it. Its origin is very obscure. Herodotus attributes it to motives of cleanliness. Others think that it is to be explained on purely physiological grounds. Some see in it a relic of ancient blood sacrifices or religious mutilations. There are races of African Negroes who perform it also on their women. In any case, circumcision was to take on considerable importance in the tradition of the descendants of Abram. Seen simply as a ritual, it was to become a sort of initiation, without which no one could be of the Chosen Race, and in this respect one can even say that it became one of the issues on which the universalism of Christianity was to overthrow the old exclusive Judaism. It is the sign of the Covenant, the painful mark of submission to the will of God; the rite is not enough: "circumcision," says Deuteronomy, "is of the heart" (Deut. x:16; xxx:6).

The Covenant was established. Abraham was circumcised, and all the men of his house with him. God rewarded them. One of the most beautiful passages in the Book of Genesis describes this new visit of God; all the light of an Eastern day seems to shine through it, with all the promise of a marvellous future. Abraham was seated at the door of his tent, in the heat. The oaks of Mamre gave a dappled shadow. Abraham dreamed, or dozed. Suddenly, raising his head he saw three strangers before him. He hastened towards his guests. Water was sent for to wash their feet. Sarah prepared cakes. Tender veal was set to simmer in the best butter. In every visitor, the noblest oriental traditions taught men to see a messenger from the gods; but these three visitors at Mamre were God Himself and two of His angels. The Most High treated the Patriarch as a friend, and became a guest under his roof. And He announced good news. Sarah herself was to bear a son. Did she doubt it? She laughed secretly—"After I am waxed old shall I have pleasure, my lord being old also?" "Is anything too hard for the Lord?" the visitor replied. The pre-destined man and the supreme master are on an equal footing, in marvellous simplicity.

From his host, his confidant, God did not conceal the fact that in coming, for a moment, to Mamre, He had also another motive. The bringer of happy tidings was also the bearer of punishment. Sodom and Gomorrah had drawn down terrible threats upon themselves. Their immorality had decided God to destroy them. Abraham protested. Destroy them entirely? But since God is a just God, is it just to destroy the innocent along with the guilty? If there were a few just men in the cities, would not God spare them? The angels of the Lord departed to the two cities. There they were treated shamefully. The people of Sodom and Gomor-rah had indeed customs that called for punishment. It came in terrible form. "A rain of dense fire fell upon the city with con-tinuous violence, again and again. The fields were burned, the pastures, and the budding groves. Burned were the forests of the hills, the trunks of the trees consumed to the very roots. The stables, the horses, the fortresses and public buildings all were burned. The populous cities became tombs, and when the flames had devoured all that remained on the ground they penetrated into the very soil, making it sterile." Thus the Alexandrian his-torian, Philo, described it in the year 20 B.C.

Is this drama borne out by documents other than the Bible? Was it suggested by the spectacle of the Dead Sea landscape, by the water heavy with salt and bitumen, whose surface, with its metallic reflections, extends along the length of the purple cliffs of Moab? It is certain that all that country is volcanic. In this valley a mineral odour clings, an odour of death. But the Bible insists in more places than one on the beauty, the fertility of this country before the cataclysm, and archaeologists think that it is proved that, about the year 2000 B.C., the region was in-habited and cultivated. The ruins of the shameful city would have been submerged by the rising of the sea-level.

Only the clan of Lot escaped from the catastrophe, because he showed humanity in the midst of these ferocious populations, and received the angels of the Lord. He was able to escape, through the rain of fire. But his wife, returning to see the terrible spectacle, was suffocated by poisonous gases, and a salt deposit covered her. We can still find in that sinister country whitish obelisks that resemble statues, great shrouded forms, petrified by the terror of God.

THE FINAL TEST

Was the promise at last to be realized? Abraham might well have doubted it, for when he went down to the plain of Gerar to pasture his flocks there, the king of the country, Abimelech, carried off Sarah. The same episode as with Pharaoh was repeated,[8] which seems the more surprising as the wife of the Patriarch had long passed her eightieth year. The biblical narrator no doubt wished to prove yet again how God protected the fruit of Sarah's womb, for Abimelech gave her back promptly, and it was her husband's child that she soon afterwards conceived.

The waiting at last was over. Great was the joy in the tents of the Terahites. That child, miraculously born, brought with him the guarantee that the divine promise would be fulfilled. And that happiness is recorded in the name given to the new-born son, who was named Isaac, which expresses the idea of happiness, of mirth. "Who would have said unto Abraham," Sarah exulted, "that Sarah should have given children suck? For I have borne him a son in his old age."

The child grew. An incident troubled the clan for a time. Sarah and Hagar, the wife and the concubine, were on worse terms than ever. And the wife, looking to the future, already thought of the heritage of Abraham; the son of the Egyptian must not be in a position to dispute the claim with her own son. Again she demanded that the slave and her child should be sent away. Abraham was troubled; the laws of Hammurabi did not authorize such cruelty except in the case of an insolent concubine, and Sarah had no more grievances to produce against Hagar. But to

---

[8] The critics trace these two episodes to two sources which suggests that we have here two accounts of the same incident, localized in different districts.

Ishmael also a great destiny was promised. God told the father of this, whereupon he let him go, with his mother. They made their way towards the desert of the south. There a great peril threatened them. The goat-skin flask was empty, and there was no water. The lad was near to death, but again the Angel of the Lord appeared; a well was near them, which they had not seen. Thus the descendants of Ishmael, the Arabs of the desert, know that they too have received the promise, and that the will of God Himself has made them a great nation.

A worse danger, however, threatened Isaac, who remained in his father's tents. The Patriarch was to be tried one last time. The voice of God came: "Abraham!" He replied, "Behold here I am." And God said: "Take now thy son, thine only son Isaac, whom thou lovest, and get thee into the land of Moriah, and offer him there for a burnt offering upon one of the mountains which I will tell thee of" (Gen. XXII:21). Now, as formerly at Ur, Abraham did not question the command to give up everything, or ever contemplate disobeying this terrible command. He saddled his ass, cut wood for the holocaust, and, calling his son, set out.

This episode, bewildering from so many aspects, is one in which the thread that links Christian symbolism to the most ancient traditions is most clearly apparent. That son against whom the hand of his own father raised the knife has always been the prototype of another victim. The parallelism is still more evident if, as certain authorities believe, the mountain in Moriah [9] is the hill on which, long afterwards, Solomon built the Temple: only a valley would then separate the pyre raised for Isaac and the gibbet raised for Jesus.

Historically, the episode falls into a perspective that today is quite clear: the custom of sacrificing the first-born. This was a very ancient custom, and the inhabitants of Canaan certainly practised it. In the high country of Gaza, one of the centres of the Canaanite cult, numbers of jars containing the skeletons of young infants have been discovered, almost all of them less than eight days old. Was this barbarous custom preserved in Phoenicia and Carthage under other forms up to a much later period, Semitic or

[9] Others think rather of Sinai.

pre-Semitic? It was regarded as the most effective of all propiti-
atory rites. When a house was built, the horrible "sacrifice of the
foundation" was often performed; many of these little skeletons
have been found. At Megiddo, the body of a young girl of fifteen
is cemented into the stones of the foundations of a well.

What thoughts disturbed the Patriarch as he climbed the hill
indicated for the holocaust, and when the young victim himself
said to him, in his innocence, "Behold the fire and the wood, but
where is the lamb for a burnt offering?" (Gen. xxii:7). It was
only a trial. The Angel of the Lord withheld the knife, ready to
pierce the neck of Isaac. "And Abraham lifted up his eyes, and
looked, and behold behind him a ram caught in a thicket by his
horns: and Abraham went and took the ram, and offered him
up for a burnt offering in the stead of his son." And archaeology,
throwing fresh light on that sublime narrative of a new vision—
or perhaps posing a new problem—shows us, among the objects
found in the tombs of Ur, a ram caught in a bush by his horns.
Have we here again an ancient Sumerian tradition? The sign of
a change of the religious conscience, the refusal of a human sacrifice? This historical fact is less precise than its moral significance: the entire submission of the predestined man to the will
of the Most High.

ABRAHAM'S END

Abraham had now completed his witness. Nothing remained
for him but to await death, which came, however, very slowly,
for it was fitting that this perfect servant of God should die ripe
in years. The clan now lived in the south, near the wells of Ber-
sheba, the use of which King Abimelech, in a solemn treaty, had
granted to the Terahites. But, among all the pasture lands, that
dearest to the old man's heart was that region of brushwood and
small oaks where the three divine visitors had appeared to him
in the heat of the day. The clan climbed again to Hebron, and
there the life of the Patriarch ended.

Of these long years of old age the Bible tells us nothing. We
only know that he married his son, according to his promise, and
that his wife died. A problem arose at that time. These nomads

were strangers among the population of Canaan; where should the last resting-place of Sarah be? In the country of Sumeria, the family would certainly have had its private vault, like those uncovered by the excavations. It would no doubt have been beneath the court of the house, or even below one of the rooms on the ground-floor. The dead were laid in these vaults side by side, wound in straw matting, with dishes of food beside them, and a goblet from which to drink. But Ur was too far away, and, in nomadic tents, what did tombs signify? Abraham therefore adopted the funeral customs of the land of Canaan, which was to make use of unoccupied caves. Such a cave he bought from a Hittite king installed in the district, and Sarah was buried there. Later, having reached the age of a hundred and seventy-five years, the Patriarch was buried beside her. This was the cave of Machpelah, opposite Mamre, on which today one of the most venerated mosques of Islam stands. It remained the burial-ground of the Terahites and, if the cave were to be unsealed, perhaps we should find there the bones of the great Patriarch, with those of Isaac and the mummy of Jacob.

Before his death, Abraham had clearly stated that, among his numerous sons, only one was to inherit the prerogatives of an heir. The children of his concubines were to receive only maintenance. This is according to the law of Sumeria. The man to whom God Himself had twice given life, invested with the mission by this decree, became the new leader of the chosen people. After the death of Abraham, God blessed his son Isaac (Gen. xxv:11). The providential history continued.[10]

[10] In order to situate the story of Abraham in history, we have adopted the traditional chronology, which is also favoured by Mgr. Ricciotti. But some historians, following the findings of archaeology, are inclined to think that the great Aramaic tide, of which the Hebrews are but one wave, rolled into Palestine in 1700 B.C. at the time of the Hyksos Dynasty in Egypt. (*See* below, p. 45.)

On this hypothesis, the patriarchal period would be of shorter duration, by perhaps a century and a half, that is to say, four normal generations. This immediately raises the problem of the longevity of the Patriarchs attested by the Bible. (For this theory, *see* R. P. R. de Vaux, "Le Palestine et la Transjordanie au 11e millénaire et les origines israélites," in *Zeitschrift für die alttestamentliche wissenschaft,* 3–4, 1938.)

II

THE PATRIARCHAL LIFE

THREE CENTURIES IN TENTS

THE DEATH OF ABRAHAM in no way altered the life of the clan. As in the days of its founder, his children, his grandchildren, and all his descendants for three centuries led the life of nomads, moving as the requirements of pasturage dictated, living in Bedouin tents. The mere fact of these wanderings is a shock to our modern Western habits of thought; apart from the gypsies, we know no rootless tribes; to be homeless is, in our ancient agricultural counties, an offence. The East, with its steppes, has not this idea that life should necessarily be fixed. No one would see anything strange in the sons of Abraham wandering from Shechem to Gerar, from one watering place to another in the Negeb. Besides, the political situation in Palestine during those three centuries gives yet another clue to the great freedom that was enjoyed by a nomadic people.

Situated as it was, Canaan was inevitably disturbed by the two greatest powers of the time, the Egyptian and Mesopotamian Empires. From the south or from the north, for three thousand years (if the only ancient historical record is to be believed), successive waves of invaders fought and sometimes struck a balance of power on that soil. At one time a battlefield, at another a protectorate, it happened on at least two occasions that this little country found itself suspended between its two powerful neighbours, enjoying a sort of anarchic liberty. The centuries of the Patriarch coincided with one of these interludes.

Until the time of Abraham, domination had come from the East. From Sargon to Hammurabi, there is a long list of these Mesopotamian masters of Canaan. The Babylonian language and the cuneiform alphabet were then in official use in Palestine and

Syria. Egypt had certainly, from time to time, attempted to intervene in these regions; in the twenty-fifth century B.C., the great
Pharaoh Pepi I (a contemporary of the Sumerian Gudea) had
made a serious expedition into Canaan. But the Egyptians were
interested principally in the coast, and above all in the great
Phoenician port of Byblos which, in exchange for Egyptian
papyrus, exported to Egypt wood and resin for the coffins of
mummies. Already in about 2800 B.C., Mykerinos, builder of one
of the great Pyramids, was sending presents to the Semitic god
of Byblos!

Canaan's Mesopotamian tutelage came to an end during the
lifetime of Abraham. After being heavily defeated in a raid by
these same Hittites who came down from the Anti-Taurus mountains, the great empire of Hammurabi was weakened. Babylon
was sacked, and its gods led into captivity. The local kings revolted against the capital. Soon after this, coming down from the
Zagros mountains, the Kassites fell upon the plains and took possession of Babylon. They reigned there for seven centuries, semi-
barbarians who gradually assimilated the old civilization, their
supremacy continually contested by attacks from the neighbouring mountaineers.

Egypt made no attempt to take advantage of the opportunity
to install her empire in Palestine. Nevertheless she had already
at this time, by the nineteenth and twentieth centuries B.C.,
great sovereigns in the Amenemhets and Senusrets of the Twelfth
Dynasty, whose famous deeds were, much later, recorded by the
Greeks in the heroic legend of Sesostris. But these great kings
were occupied in subduing Nubia, and advancing the frontier of
their own kingdoms by some 250 miles, as far as the second
cataract of the Nile. They confined themselves to installing a
viceroy at Byblos, to trading with the Canaanites, and went no
further. After them came the confused and troubled dynasties
designated by the numbers Thirteenth and Fourteenth! Nefer-
hotep, with his young girl's face, and Nehasi, with his negroid
head, were incapable of doing great things in politics. When the
tide of the Hyksos poured in, Egypt was submerged by it.

Therefore during the three centuries of the Patriarchs, Canaan remained without a ruler. It was easy to encamp there with flocks and herds, for no one showed any surprise to see yet another race installed in a country that already supported so many. The population of Palestine at this time was a jig-saw puzzle. There were, together with later races, the descendants of the most ancient men of the Stone Age, numerous in prehistoric times, and those Horims, Anakims, Emims, Zuzims, Zamzummims mentioned in the Bible, and the Rephaims, whose name means, simply, "the dead." There were descendants of the ancient Sumerian race, perhaps the Perizzites, villagers, agricultural people. There were, most important of all, the successive layers of Semites who, in the course of centuries, had scoured the country, from the time of the Akkadians of Sargon's period to the Babylonians of Hammurabi's. One can roughly distinguish the Canaanites, who seem to have been the most powerful, and the Amorites, more or less confined to the north. There were also, here and there, settlements of Hittites, like those from whom Abraham purchased the cave of Machpelah, the first comers of a growing infiltration. On the coast, the population was perhaps even more mixed: Phoenicians, closely related to the Canaanites, Cretans, who came to buy corn and who had established a sort of consulate, and those Philistines who were later to assume so much importance, but who at this time were nothing more than the Aegean precursors of future Aryan waves. Finally, there were in the interior the tribes of whom the descendants of Abraham themselves say that they were their own kin—Edomites, Moabites, and Ammonites, wanderers like themselves, but more towards the edge of the desert.

The power—if the word can properly be applied to these petty rulers—must have been in the hands of local kings, whose dominion was limited to their own townships and a few acres of fields. The cities were well defended; their walls were thick and further defended by a glacis and the multiple traces of their surrounding defences already bears witness to a developed knowledge of the art of war. Within these defences, the houses were jumbled together with no plan, not unlike those of the Sumerians, but poorer, with terraced roofs or bee-hive domes, with a hole for ventilation. Away from these townships, the nomads had all the freedom they could desire; provided that they did not lay waste the fields, or raid caravans, they were free to pasture their flocks. Thus the descendants of old Terah lived for three centuries.

A PROUD ARISTOCRACY

Whoever has met, in the East, whether in the Sahara or on the Syrian steppes, one of these tribes who still live in tents, knows the pride, the calm and dignified scorn with which these nomads look down on the fixed populations. In reading the biblical narrative, we feel very strongly that the men of the clan of the Patriarchs had that same proud reserve. They did not show that systematic aggressiveness toward the people of the country that we find some centuries later, when they returned from Egypt under Moses. Indeed they were not sufficiently strong for the occasion to arise. But clearly they kept them at a distance. They maintained courteous relations with the princes of the territories on which they encamped, and traded with the citizens. But they remained "strangers," as Moses said (Exodus vi:4).

It was certainly not by chance that, in their traditions, they tell how Noah cursed Ham, the son lacking in respect, the ancestor of Canaan. "Cursed be Canaan; a servant of servants shall he be unto his brethren" (Gen. ix:25). Shopkeepers, lackeys— that is more or less the way in which nomads still regard the people of the towns to this day.

And they lost no occasion of sneering even at the other tribes living a similar life, but not of their own blood. It is amusing to notice how the biblical text loses no occasion of telling a discreditable story of some other clan. The Moabites and the Edomites are related to Abraham certainly. But look how they behave! Lot's double incest with his two daughters on a drunken evening! Far from flattering!

This exclusiveness certainly cut off the men of the clan from neighbouring populations. They had a very clear sense of their superiority, of their difference. As inheritors of the promise, they were proud. What was their name at this time? Abraham is called by the name of "Hebrew" (Gen. xiv:13), which may be used to signify "son of Heber," a descendant of Noah, ancestor of the Patriarchs, as well as in its more general sense of wanderer, or nomad, the equivalent of the Arab "bedouin." But it seems clear that the term was inclusive of more than the Terahite clan. Later the biblical text makes a distinction between "Hebrews" and "Israelites," the latter being a subdivision of the former. The qualifying term of *Israel* occurs first in the story of Jacob, the time at which, it would seem, the group reached its maximum degree of self-consciousness.

Thus the Terahites appear to us as an aristocracy, in the truest sense of the word, one of those privileged minorities that play a much more important part in the world than their members alone would seem to justify. One can find analogous cases of powerful minorities in ancient history. We can point to examples among the Hyksos and the Hittites. The case of Sparta is well known. But, unlike so many instances, force is not the explanation of the reason why the later history of the Semites in Canaan came to be identified with that small clan. Their domination was spiritual. It had its origin in their certitude of their mission. Moreover, the important thing, for them, was their direct, legitimate descent from Abraham, the inspired man.

ISAAC AND REBEKAH AND THEIR SONS

Before his death, the great Patriarch had made such dispositions as would ensure that the purity of the race should be adequately preserved. It was necessary to make certain that the young Isaac should not be seduced by some woman of those mixed races of Canaan; therefore Abraham himself arranged his marriage. The oldest of his servants was given instructions to go to the home-country, Padan-aram, where a part of the clan had remained. Indeed there had recently been news of Nahor, a brother of Abraham, the head of a large family. The servant was to find among them a wife for his young master.

This is the exquisite scene, so evocative in its detail, whose charm Poussin has captured. The servant came to Nahor's house. His camels knelt down near the wells. A young girl came up, her water-pot on her shoulder. The messenger asked for water to drink; she "hastened to let down her pitcher upon her hand," offered him the water, and, when he had drunk, remembered the camels and returned to the well to draw water for them also. To whom could the gold ring and bracelets of betrothal more fittingly be given than to this lovely maiden? The will of God was in it, for she was, in fact, Rebekah, grand-daughter of Nahor.

The character of Isaac is the least clearly defined in the gallery of the Patriarchs; he is indistinct, a pale shadow of his father. The only important events that concern him seem to belong rather to the life of Abraham. Rebekah, like Sarah, was sterile, and gave her husband sons only when he was approaching sixty. And Abimelech, treating the daughter-in-law as he had the mother, carried off Rebekah to his harem, believing her to be Isaac's sister, but hastened to restore her when he discovered their true relationship.

Nevertheless, two important events are recorded in his story. One marks an important change in the economic life of the Terahites: "Then Isaac sowed in that land, and received in the same year an hundredfold" (Gen. xxvi:12). For the first time the nomads devoted some of their time to agriculture—prelude to their future settlement.

The other is the famous rivalry between the sons of Isaac, which shows more clearly than anything the supremacy of one part of the clan over all others—that part that had preserved its racial purity, and which was to remain the repository of the divine gifts. When Rebekah became pregnant, she bore twins, and "the children struggled together within her." This was a sign, God told her, that two hostile races should descend from them, "the one people shall be stronger than the other people; and the older shall serve the younger." The first-born was "Edom," that is, red and hairy. He was named Esau. But the second must have been better looking, for his mother showed a marked preference for him. He was given an auspicious name, a name with a hidden meaning; for as he was born holding his brother by the heel, he was called Jacob, "foot-holder." But to hold anyone by the heel is to trip him up, to supplant him. Rebekah indicated in this way the one who, according to the promise, should rule the other: Jacob, "the supplanter."

This incident was fully confirmed. When he grew up, Esau made his home in a country "shaggy" like himself, a wooded country (not that it takes very much, in these bare lands, to earn the name, even today, of *Jebel Cheir*, the wooded mountain). This region is known by its descriptive name of "the red country," Edom. It is Idumaea, beloved of poets. There he lived as a huntsman, and, no doubt, more or less as a robber. In these southern steppes, raids were of common occurrence. But though his posterity may have been numerous, they have little historical importance. They play a minor rôle, while Jacob is the ancestor of the priests of the chosen people. "Jacob the supplanter" had indeed supplanted his elder brother.

For it must not be forgotten that Esau was the elder, and both the material and the spiritual prerogatives attaching to this title were so considerable that, when twins were born, the midwife would fix a red thread round the arm of the first-born. That is why Jacob planned to possess himself of the privileges of the first-born. Unlike his brother, he was not one of those men who "live by the sword," but peaceably, guarding his flocks, and planting corn and vegetables about his tents. As a matter of fact the way in which he won the birthright leads us to admire rather his astuteness than his charity or his candour. One day when Esau returned exhausted from hunting, he begged his brother to give him a plate of tasty lentils. Jacob shamelessly took advantage of the situation and only consented to feed the hungry hunter in exchange for his right of inheritance. Later, to this legal transaction, he gave a sacred character by receiving, by a deception, the blessing of his blind father. Rebekah, more partial than ever, had covered the hands of her favourite with goatskin, to resemble the hairy skin of her first-born.

The anecdote in itself, if it is not remarkable for its morality, has a great deal of that salty quality that the Greeks admired in Odysseus; and it shows that the nomads recognized that subtle intelligence triumphs over brute force. But it has a deeper meaning. What is the reason for that preference of one son over another, one posterity rather than another? There can be no doubt that the explanation lies in those verses in which the Bible tells us that Esau had married Hittite and Canaanite women, thus disobeying the fundamental faith of the clan, and introducing foreign blood into the race. These alliances had been "a grief of mind unto Isaac and Rebekah." Jacob, on the contrary, was to be the son through whom the legitimate descent of the race was to continue.

JACOB WRESTLES WITH GOD

What clearly proves that this was the essential point is that from the very hour at which he decided to go in search of a wife of pure race, God unmistakably confirmed Jacob as the repository of the Promise. Rebekah had declared feelingly that she was "weary of her life because of the daughters of Heth"; one is reminded of the anger of a practising Jew whose son wishes to marry a Christian. Jacob, obedient, set out for Padan-aram.

On the way, one night as he slept on the ground, a stone for his pillow, a dream came to him. A great ladder joined heaven and earth; above it was God, and God spoke to him. He confirmed the promises made to his ancestor and even gave details. Indeed his posterity should be "as the dust of the earth." Indeed they should possess the land, but, what was more, wherever they should be, a particular providence would watch over his descendants. Waking, the traveller was still filled with the divine presence; following an ancient custom of the country, he raised a stone to commemorate the event, a menhir we would say, a *massebah* in the Hebrew tongue. Henceforth this place was to be blessed, and was later Bethel, the home of the Saviour. And Jacob swore that if God would protect him during his journey, he would remain faithful to Him.

In the country of Harran lived Laban, his maternal uncle. He had two daughters, Leah and Rachel. The younger was beautiful and, from the moment he first saw her at the springs, bringing her sheep to drink, Jacob loved her; and Leah was tender-eyed. When the young man wished to marry Rachel, Laban tricked him into marrying Leah first. A shrewd father! He even made the young man serve him gratis. Jacob remained with Laban for twenty years. By his two wives, and two of their servants, he had many children; eleven sons, born to him, were the fathers of the Tribes of Israel, together with one other, Benjamin, the youngest. But if Laban was cunning, Jacob was more so. By various means, more astute than honest, the shepherd so arranged matters as to increase his personal flock. In particular there is a memorable episode in which Jacob arranges to have all the striped and spotted beasts—those of least value—given him by way of salary, and afterwards arranged by a novel method that large numbers of them should have speckles and stripes.

The situation between uncle and nephew became so tense that Jacob decided to flee. His whole caravan made a night-flitting with his wives, concubines, children and cattle. Laban learned of their departure the next day, and declared that the *teraphim*, or domestic idols, that he conserved with religious care according to the ancient usage of Shinar, had also disappeared. He set out in pursuit, resolved to have an explanation. As a matter of fact, the matter passed off satisfactorily. The two men were reconciled; as for the *teraphim* they were never discovered: Rachel had hidden them in the saddle of her camel, and was sitting on them. And Jacob went on his way southwards, towards the land of Canaan.

It was then that the impressive scene took place from which Jacob emerged transformed, from which the chosen people were to receive their name. This man, returning to his native land after an absence of twenty years, became filled with a growing anxiety. What would he find there? The brother whom, long ago, he had supplanted, would he tolerate the return of Jacob to the camp, with his rich flocks from Padan-aram? Had he not good reason to fear the attack of that sturdy brigand, of whose approach, with four hundred men, he had already been warned? He had sent large presents to his brother. Would they appease him? Jacob advanced, increasingly on his guard. He spent the night at the ford of Jabbok. The encounter was imminent.

There are in men's lives moments when the tension of events mysteriously corresponds with the inner tension of the soul. With Jacob it was not simply a matter of safeguarding his goods. The torment of his mind had another reason: what awaited him at Padan-aram? Ought he to have remained for twenty years in a strange land? As heir of the Promise, why was he returning so late to his country? Would God still keep faith with him? And as for himself, the returning exile, was he still worthy? Every attempt to explain in human terms this enigmatic episode must be inadequate and paltry. It is only in the sight of God, within the broken heart, that the ultimate truth is to be known, the wrestling with the angel. In the small hours of the night just before the dawn, alone, he underwent that spiritual conflict "as fierce as the battling of men," as one poet says, this naked encounter with the powers of destiny that Delacroix has immortalized in his painting.

When dawn came, Jacob realized that the danger had passed. The combat left him exhausted, and wounded in the joint of his thigh. But he had won. He had even induced the invisible power to bless him, thus confirming his mission, and the adversary had said to him, "Thy name shall be called no more Jacob but Israel, for as a prince thou hast power with God and with men, and hast prevailed."

Thus Israel, the posterity of the wrestler of the night, was to struggle in order to safeguard their convictions, in darkness, constraining God.

ISRAEL AND THE PATRIARCHAL LIFE

These spiritual battles were the struggles of a new birth. All that in Jacob was of doubtful worth, his attachment to riches, all the turmoil of passions and failings of character, seem to have been abolished for ever by that breath of the spirit. From this time, he followed in the steps of his fathers, and became a Patriarch, like Isaac, like Abraham, and his sense of his mission was apparent in all his actions.

The first sign of divine protection accorded him was that the encounter with Esau passed off well. The brothers were reconciled, and Jacob's clan returned to its old life, that of the Terahites for two generations. He set up his tents first in the plain of Shechem, but a brutal incident with the people of the town obliged him to move. The son of the local king dishonoured one of Jacob's daughters, Dinah. He offered to marry her, but the brothers of the injured girl would not agree to this. The marriage would in itself have been a defilement, a stain on the purity of the race. By a ruse they took possession of the town, where they carried out a terrible slaughter. The clan was forced to move.

Israel first encamped at Bethel, then in the hills of the south. There, where later Bethlehem was to stand, Rachel, pregnant once again, bore a last son, the founder of the twelfth tribe; but this birth was to cost her her life, and divining this in advance, she named the child "Ben-oni," "the son of my sorrow." An ill-omened name! Jacob changed it, and this latest-born son was called Benjamin, "the son of righteousness," an auspicious name. The clan then moved to Hebron, to the oaks of Mamre; there they found the aged Isaac, who was only awaiting this return in order to die.

Bethel and Mamre, the two places of the promise, of the visitation of the spirit! The life of the Patriarch was from now on associated with these two places. At Bethel, where he had made his vow of fidelity, he worked a sort of religious conversion on his people. In Harran, many of the clan had acquired various Mesopotamian customs, the cult of the *teraphim*, the wearing of amulets and earrings. A purge was imposed. These objects of idolatry were buried at the foot of an oak, and there was raised an altar in gratitude to the one God. At Mamre, Jacob found his old father, and when Isaac had died, ripe in years, at the age of a hundred and eighty, and when in his turn he had been laid in the family vault at Machpelah, it only remained for "Israel" to enjoy his long old age in that regular, peaceful existence whose tranquil majesty is described by the word "patriarchal."

These nomadic traditions were to haunt the memory of Israel when this people had become a nation. The Book of Job, to take one perfect example, borrows its images from that source. It seemed later to this people, established as citizens and labourers, that life had been purer in the days when they lived as wandering shepherds, perhaps because in those days they had been less attached to worldly possessions, and enjoyed a more perfect liberty. We must not consider that life from the standpoint to which the civilization of towns has accustomed us. Far as it is from our modern conception of comfort, we can recognize its great attraction and its grandeur. Even now, in the Syrian desert, the tents of chieftains, tents with six pickets, divided in the middle by the curtain that partitions off the women's quarters, are both comfortable and splendid. Rugs spread on the ground make a soft couch, and in the simple hole and the three stones that remain as the only trace of the camp when the caravan moves on delicious food is cooked.

There is freedom. It is a matter only of an hour or two to set up a camp wherever one wishes, or to take it up again. Their wealth is moveable, consisting not in land, but in heads of cattle, goats and sheep. For transport, asses are used, not like the wretched donkeys of Algeria, but fine beasts, rather like small mules, with silver-grey coats, and astonishingly sturdy. The camel is a mark of luxury. A few beasts yield almost all the necessaries of life. Cultivation round the camp is a mere trifle. Meat is rarely eaten, for to kill a beast is to destroy capital; milk, butter, and fruits are their staple foods. And their clothes are made of goats' hair, as are their tents, their black tents.

Towards the great civilized bureaucratic societies, the nomads of Israel maintained the same attitude as we found among the Terahites of Ur; they felt their attraction, like the attraction of sin, but their attitude was above all one of horror. The idea of counting men and making a census of them, always seemed to them in the nature of an attack on man's personal dignity. They were unwilling to serve a master. Their chief was their father; there was no distinction between the authority that comes from ties of blood and weight of experience, and political authority and both were exercised with great wisdom. This sentiment, so quickly lost by people of the towns, by members of excessively organized states, the sense of solidarity and mutual responsibility, is very strong in the patriarchal family. Dinah's brothers avenged the honour of the clan, and would listen to no excuses. And underlying all rebellions and quarrels (and polygamy tended to divide the family into factions that were often in rivalry) there existed an ideal of community. For that, too, Israel retained a nostalgia. Even more than of the tribe, one can say of the patriarchal family, in Renan's words, that it was "a school of pride, respect, and mutual loyalty." This picture has become enhanced by tradition, but its image is significant, both as a model and as a regret.

THE STORY OF JOSEPH

It was an episode of nomadic life that gave rise to the story of Joseph that is, as literature, one of the most beautiful in the Bible. It is written in the form of a story, but with so much vividness in the depiction of the characters and of their surroundings that it cannot be other than a historical document (Gen. xxxvii–l). For these nomads the problem that came before all others was the finding of pasture and water for their flocks. If grass failed, it became urgently necessary to find new pastures; the drying up of the water supply meant disaster. Then they must have recourse to drastic measures, migration to more fertile regions, perhaps the elimination of superfluous mouths.

Joseph was Jacob's favourite son, the son of Rachel, the wife he had loved so much. The others were jealous on account of this preference and the young man certainly gave occasion for arousing his brothers' antagonism. Did he not tell his dreams, in which he always figured in the most favourable light? At one time he was a sheaf of corn in a field, that all the other sheaves saluted with reverence; at another time he was in the sky, where sun, moon and eleven stars bowed down to him. Jacob, grown old, while he reproved the lad for his chatter, knowing the mystery of the divine will, pondered these things in his heart.

One day, while the elder brothers were leading their flocks near Shechem, Jacob sent the youngest with news: the wells were dry. Joseph only overtook his brothers at Dothan, still farther to the north. It was a wild place, and the sons of Jacob were tough customers. "Here comes the dreamer," they said to each other. And they decided to settle accounts with him. Reuben, the eldest, interceded. Not that he was much more moral than the others; not long before he had created a scandal in the camp by seducing one of his father's concubines, but perhaps he hesitated to burden his conscience with another crime. He therefore suggested to the others that they should put Joseph in one of the dry wells; an unkind joke, but nothing more. But in his absence a caravan of Arabs passed by. The brothers drew up the wretched boy from his prison, and sold him to the Ishmaelites, and in order to explain the disappearance of his darling to Jacob, brought him the boy's coat, covered with blood, as though a wild beast had devoured him.

The Ishmaelites were on their way to Egypt, their camels laden with spices and aromatics. They took Joseph with them and sold him to Potiphar, an official of the royal palace. But God had designs for the young man. All that Joseph did prospered, so much so that his master made him steward of his household and placed trust in him. But Joseph was handsome; Potiphar's wife observed this only too well. To her proposals, however, the young Hebrew answered with a refusal, giving reasons of the most honourable kind: he would not betray the confidence of his master; and he could not sin against God. Such exemplary chastity was by no means usual among these ardent Eastern peoples. At this very time—the Bible records the matter in cryptic terms—one of his brothers, Judah, was frequenting the temple of prostitutes who were to be found in the neighbourhood of the cities of Canaan.

Women find it hard to forgive a refusal of this kind. Furious, the wife accused Joseph: he had wished to seduce her, she had cried out, and he had fled; but she had evidence to convict him, the garment of the insolent man. Potiphar threw the supposedly offending servant into the royal prison. In his trial, Joseph remained calm and virtuous. The chief gaoler took an interest in him. Two of Pharaoh's servants, imprisoned for embezzlement, were put in Joseph's charge. One morning the two men were disturbed. "Why so sad today?" Joseph asked. "We have dreamed a dream," they said, "and there is no one here to interpret it." Among the gifts of great visionaries, that of interpreting dreams is fairly common. Joseph predicted what lay in store for each of them. The royal butler would return to favour, the royal baker would be hanged. And so it was.

It happened two years later that Pharaoh himself was troubled by a terrible nightmare. The butler bethought him of the young Hebrew in the prison. What the king had seen was disturbing and almost certainly premonitory. Seven fat cattle were feeding in a meadow, when seven others, meagre and ill-favoured, came up from the Nile and devoured them. Seven heads of corn appeared, full and heavy, and beside them were seven more, thin and blasted with the east wind, and the thin ears withered up the good. All the diviners of Egypt, who no doubt were afraid to tell Pharaoh of dire misfortunes, had failed to interpret the dreams. Joseph, with the courage of youth, took the bull by the horns. The meaning of the dream was clear. After seven good years, seven years of dire famine would come. And the event was near, for God had announced it twice. Only one course was possible—to store up reserves. And the diviner cleverly suggested that a Minister of Produce should be invested with full powers, a sort of dictator of supplies.

This was the beginning of a distinguished career. Under an absolute monarchy such things are possible, and the prisoner became vizier and, clothed in fine linen, a necklace of gold about his neck, and the royal signet on his finger, he set out to inspect the reserves. He was thirty years old. All happened as he had foretold. For seven years there were abundant crops and the minister set by enough from the harvests to constitute stocks. The lean years might come; from the royal granaries, corn was available, thanks to Joseph's foresight. His triumph was complete. He was happy, rich, and celebrated; the wife bestowed upon him by the king, a girl of noble birth, had borne him two children, Ephraim, "fertility," and Manasseh "who brings forgetfulness." But had he really forgotten?

Now, as always happened in times of famine, starving nomads arrived from the East. Among them came a delegation of ten men to buy food for a clan in Canaan. Joseph's heart was full: his dreams had come true; bowing before him like the sheaves and the stars of his dreams, he saw his own brothers; they did not recognize him. Joseph did not make himself known to them. He gave them corn, for he feared God. But in order to be sure that they were not spies such as he often had to deal with on that dangerous north-east frontier, he kept one of them as a hostage. When they returned, they were to bring the youngest of the family, Benjamin, and then he would return Simeon to them. The nomads left, troubled in their minds, the more so when, opening their sacks of corn, they found the very purses which they had left as payment with the vizier.

What were they to do? Should they come back to Egypt with Benjamin, the child, the consolation of his old father, Jacob? Leave Simeon in captivity? All this besides the severe famine. The sons of the Patriarch set out again, the child with them. In their trouble they must have remembered with remorse that other child whom they had disposed of long ago. On seeing his own mother's son, the little brother whom he could scarcely remember, Joseph was overcome, and, unable to restrain his tears, went away to weep in private. His reception of them might have opened the eyes of Jacob's sons; they ate in his company, he refused to take the money for the first purchases of food, and they left quite overcome. But before pardoning them and making himself known, he decided to impose a test. On the pretext of theft, he had Benjamin arrested. The criminal brothers of former times had made themselves responsible to the old Patriarch for the child's safe return, and now they were themselves struck where they had once been the aggressors.

The denouement was at hand. Judah pleaded on behalf of them all in the presence of the redoubtable minister. He spoke of the old father living in the country, whose death would be caused by the loss of his youngest son. He offered himself as a hostage, as a slave. This was enough. Joseph could no longer contain himself. He cried, "Cause every man to go out from me," and he said to his brothers: "I am Joseph your brother, whom you sold into Egypt. Now therefore be not grieved nor angry with yourselves, that ye sold me hither. For God did send me before you to preserve life." He embraced Benjamin and wept, and Benjamin embraced him also. He kissed all his brothers and wept as he embraced them. The scene is moving, and its human truthfulness is manifest. Now they must make haste and send for the old father. Ten asses and ten she-asses, loaded with the richest produce of Egypt were to be sent, and he was to come to the kingdom where his son was all-powerful.

EGYPT AND THE HYKSOS

That is the simple narrative. But does the history of Egypt, where it is supposed to have taken place, make it more plausible? Are the details that the biblical narrative takes from the civilization of the Nile confirmed by the study of Egyptology? The most sceptical critic is bound to answer this in the affirmative.

Joseph's Egyptian adventure can be dated with fair exactitude; it seems likely that it took place during the seventeenth century B.C.; the dates suggested vary between 1740 and 1630. At that time in the country of the Nile events occurred of which the chronology of the Pharaohs as well as the records of archaeology have preserved many traces.

The incapacity and weakness of the Twelfth and Fourteenth Dynasties had disastrous consequences for Egypt. Attacked on the Isthmus of Suez, the weak Pharaohs of this time, who must have installed themselves in the Delta to guard the frontier, were submerged in the great Asiatic wave. This invasion has been called by Manetho, the Egyptian historian of the third century B.C., the period of the Hyksos, a name which no doubt means "the shepherd kings," or "the desert chiefs." Victorious, they occupied all Lower Egypt. Two dynasties in the royal records certainly belong to these intruders.

Who were they? Their origin is not exactly known. Semites? The Jewish historian Josephus, eighteen centuries later, refers to them as "our ancestors," and adds "unless they were Arabs, as some say." The names of some of their leaders—Jacobel, Anatel, Khyan—confirm the hypothesis that they were a Semitic race. But from their statues, with their large round faces, thick noses, and prominent cheekbones, we hesitate to identify them with the elegant Arabs, or the Israelites with their fine aquiline profiles. It is more likely that in them we have a mixed race, a blend of all the elements of the Mesopotamian crucible, and perhaps other elements as well, coming from the mountains. The Hyksos must have constituted a military aristocracy leading an army of all sorts of hungry adventurers, destitute desert and mountain-dwellers, tempted by the prize of affluent Egypt.

The date when this formidable wave of invasion arrived—about 1800 B.C.—corresponds with other grave events with which we are already familiar: the Hittite attack in Babylon, and the Kassite conquest. It is therefore more than likely that this migration was the result—one of the results—of the movement of the Aryan hordes into Asia Minor. At the time the Mitannians, a mixed race of mountain people and Aryans, had established their empire on the Upper Tigris, and the Hittites, more to the west, had installed themselves and begun their expansion, from the old disrupted kingdoms came men full of the spirit of adventure. The Hyksos were not so much a race as a band, like those of the Renaissance, or of the Thirty Years War; they were condottieri, Colleone or Wallensteins.

Their victory had the dazzling character of those wars in which there exists a great difference in the quality of the arms of the two armies. Not only did the Hyksos bring with them horses trained for war, which were unknown in ancient Egypt, but their bronze weapons were incomparably superior to those of the Egyptians. What can a poor foot-soldier, practically naked, armed only with a spear and a bow, do against a warrior in chain-mail wielding a sharp scimitar, and worse, often mounted on a metal armoured chariot? The invasion was so brutal that Egypt retained a horror of Asiatics long after she had repelled them.

Were they then barbarians? So it has been thought until our own times. Recently this view has changed. Discoveries (in Jericho, in particular) show, during the period of their dominance, an authentic art, strongly naturalistic, that suggests a late rather than a primitive style. Maspero has suggested that it is possible that the great artistic revival of the second Theban period—that of the time of Tutankhamun, for example—with its subtle Asiatic and European influences, is perhaps indebted to the foreign leaven introduced and worked into the old Egyptian dough by the terrible hands of the "shepherd kings."

At the time of Jacob, therefore, the Hyksos reigned unchallenged in Egypt; and not only in Egypt, but also in Canaan.[1] An Hyksos named Khyan even founded an ephemeral empire that reached as far as the Tigris. In Palestine numbers of seals have been discovered, engraved with Hyksos names, one proudly inscribed, "The master of the country." The migration of the little clan of Israel and its establishment in Egypt must therefore be seen as part of the vast flood of a great migration of peoples. The capital of the "shepherd kings" was Avaris; for nomads coming

[1] At the same time, the Hittite Empire underwent a sudden relapse in every respect similar to that of Egypt. The records ceased abruptly and it was after two centuries of silence that the power of the kings of Khatti was reborn. (*See* below, p. 92.)

from the Isthmus of Suez, it was quite near. And that Asiatic Pharaoh, that conqueror who was a stranger in the land over which he ruled—perhaps Apopi, represented for us by an armed fist, brandishing an impressive scimitar—might well have been tempted to select, for a position of trust, an Asiatic like himself.

A DISRAELI [2] UNDER THE PHARAOHS

No one any longer calls in question the veracity of the Egyptian details of which the story of Joseph is full. The more extensive the discoveries in the field of Egyptology, the more accurate and drawn from real life the events and institutions described in this adventure are seen to be. Will there someday be found, on an Egyptian papyrus, the story of that strange rise to supreme power of a foreign vizier? The sarcophagus of another Semite has, in fact, been brought to light, evidently an Arab, who was a governor under a Hyksos Pharaoh.

The names mentioned in the biblical text have been recognized as really Egyptian. Zaphnath-Paaneah, the name given to Joseph by the Pharaoh, means "God has spoken"; his wife's name was Asenath, which means "belonging to the goddess Nath," a deity worshipped in the Delta, while Potiphar is a little distorted—"Pa-di-pa-Ra," the gift of the god Ra, the great god, protector of the Nile.

But, more generally, it is the fundamental theme of this story that corresponds to all that we know of Egypt, the Egypt of the past, and of all time. "Gift of the Nile," to use the epithet of the illustrious Herodotus, this marvellous country would be nothing more than a portion of the Sahara but for the river, "born in another world" as a hymn of the time of the Pharaohs says, "sent by God to nourish all the provinces." Today as the time of the flooding approaches, all those responsible for the distribution of the water are on the watch for the first signs. The appearance of a green tinge in the water, indicating that, far above, in the

---

[2] In making this comparison, we are not overlooking the fact that Disraeli belonged to a family of converts.

marshes of Bahr-el-Ghazal, the water is beginning to rise, is immediately broadcast. By about June 20th, the whole of Egypt has only one thought—the river. The river rises, and runs red, carrying fertile mud washed down from the Ethiopian ranges. The rising of the river as recorded by the "Nilometers" is observed with anxious interest. Will the watery god prove favourable? Will the river rise to the necessary level?

For in order that Egypt may live, a certain height of water is necessary. Then, with great labour, the precious liquid is drawn up by means of the *shadouf*, the old-fashioned pumping apparatus, or of the wooden noria, the *sakieh* whose plaintive melody, endlessly repeated, fills the Egyptian night. But there is no remedy against an insufficient flood. Pliny, with Roman conciseness, sums up the situation in these words: "Twelve cubits of water, famine; thirteen, sufficiency; fourteen, happiness; fifteen, security; sixteen, abundance." This is why the celebrated statue in the Vatican Museum shows the Nile surrounded by sixteen children. Today, it is estimated that a depth of twenty-four feet and four inches is indispensable; this corresponds to a supply of ninety thousand cubic metres.

The years of the "lean kine" correspond to a period of drought. The history of Egypt is not without instances of this kind. An inscription believed to be very old, the "pillar of the seven years of famine" speaks of one such period of misfortune. "For seven years the Nile has not risen; corn has failed, and the fields are dry. The dead are no longer shrouded for burial; children weep, the young fail in strength, and the old despair; all, with feeble limbs and folded arms, are bowed and prostrate." Such trials the Nile has many times imposed upon Egypt: during the Twelfth Dynasty, again in the Seventeenth, once during the Roman occupation, and in our own era, from 1064 to 1071, and again in the twelfth century. It is therefore certain that the story of Joseph refers to some specific climatic reality. As to the symbol of the cows, it refers, no doubt, to the sacred cows of the goddess Isis-Hathor, of which one was kept in each of the seven provinces.

For this unavoidable misfortune, the Bible indicates that the

Pharaoh felt himself to be personally responsible. This again is an accurate detail. The masters of Egypt, powerful as they were, were always secretly afraid of the domesticated nation from whom they drew their wealth. The history of the Pharaohs includes several real social revolutions: one of these brought the ancient empire to an end. The fellahs, patient, tireless workers, asked only one thing of their rulers: assurance of enough bread. Bonaparte, with penetrating insight, observed that the Nile imposes a strict government. "Under a good administration," he said, "the Nile gains on the desert. Under a bad, the desert gains on the Nile." Joseph was the ideal minister, the man who providentially saved a foreign Pharaoh, alarmed at the possibility of a revolt, from a singularly dangerous predicament. His fortune is entirely explained by this fact.

All the details that we know about this success are no less characteristic and exact. The Pharaoh that the Bible describes, so sure of himself and full of majesty, was certainly a mere descendant of the usurpers. But we know that the Hyksos Dynasties regarded themselves as in all respects authentic Pharaohs, and wore the *pschent*, the double crown, white for the south and red for the north, symbol of the two regions of Egypt. When Joseph was summoned into the royal presence, he shaved himself (Gen. xli:14); his Asiatic beard would have been an insult to the king's majesty, for, according to Egyptian etiquette, only the Pharaoh wore a beard, the sign of power; often, in fact, it was a false beard. The necklace that was hung about his neck as a sign of his elevation was something more than a mark of power; these jewels were, for the Egyptians, the equivalent of the gods who defended the breast from all evil, and the gold from which they were made, the symbol of indestructibility, worn by the Pharaoh himself; sometimes necklets of beads, stars and animals, sometimes heavy pectorals of red jasper, green felspar and lapis-lazuli.

The office conferred upon Joseph is exactly that which, in Islam, is designated by the title of vizier. Egypt under the Pharoahs was a superlatively bureaucratic state in which thousands of officials exercised a control, implacable to the minutest degree, over the poorer classes. There were officials for all tasks and all eventualities, from heads of districts to tax-gatherers, solidly assisted by Negro toughs, and between these extremes such desirable sinecures as those of Inspector of the Queen's Baths, and wig-maker and barber to the King. In this perfected officialdom Joseph occupied a privileged position. "Director of Orders" and "Chief Minister of the Nile" are titles that have been found; Joseph no doubt bore them. He seems to have fulfilled exactly the definitions of the function of vizier given by a Pharaoh of the same period in the following instructions: "You are to see that all is done according to the law, and that every man has his due. You are to be just, and to send no plaintiff away without a hearing. Let your audience chamber be known as the room of Double Justice." The vizier had certain prerogatives: fine clothes of white linen, a wife of high rank. He rode in a royal chariot, one of those chariots that the Hyksos had brought into use. And when he went out, couriers went before him crying, "*Abhrekh!*" as in the *Thousand and One Nights* they cried, "On your knees!" when the Caliph appeared.

But what is even more remarkable than the material details that establish the story in the chronology of Egyptian history, is the psychological veracity of the biblical narrative. Is not this young Israelite, full of finesse, attractive to women, persuasive with men, using all his charm in order to further his career, the forerunner of those Jewish men of affairs who have risen to power in Christian communities? He is a Disraeli, with a Pharaoh as Queen Victoria. He combines in himself sound qualities and useful faults: a balance between imagination and prudence, moderation even in passion, a sense of affairs, the serene pride of intelligence, maintained by the certitude of a high destiny.

For he never forgot that, as the son of Jacob, he was the heir of the Promise. The attitude of chaste morality that we find in him has a very clear significance when we consider the sexual licence fashionable in the Egypt of the Pharaohs. The passion of Potiphar's wife for this handsome young man seems to have been nothing out of the ordinary in the country of the Nile. "The Story of the Two Brothers" describes a little later a similar incident. And a poem has been found in which a mature woman says to a boy, "Come with me to the bath. My vest of royal linen shall flatter your desires." The Pharaohs and the great men of the kingdom had immense harems; Rameses II had a hundred and eleven sons and fifty-nine daughters; and if the queens had not the same privileges, they found, if Pindar is to be believed, numerous consolations. It is all the more remarkable to find, in this milieu, the young Joseph remaining pure and, when married, living a life of domestic dignity. This reserve has a significance; in Egypt these Patriarchs remained God's chosen.

JOSEPH INSTALLS HIS BROTHERS

Need it be said that the end of the story of Joseph seems to be no less true to history and to psychology? How well one knows these Iraelites who during the course of centuries, having succeeded in one of the western countries, send for their family, living in the ancestral ghetto? Joseph found under the Pharaoh a land where his family could establish themselves; they arrived one and all with their sons, their wives, their flocks and their old father, now a hundred and thirty years old. Because of Joseph, the Pharaoh welcomed them, and Jacob blessed him. Saved from famine, the children of Israel set foot in the land of Egypt; there they remained for a long time. But already one can divine one of the reasons which, much later, made them insupportable to the Pharaohs and the fellahs alike: the Bible informs us that in fact Joseph, in exchange for the corn that he had stored, purchased the land, the goods, and even the persons of many Egyptians. It was no doubt on behalf of the Pharaoh that Joseph worked: was he likely to be any more popular on that account?

Jacob meanwhile was drawing near to death. He had named Joseph as his successor, and adopted Ephraim and Manasseh. He had solemnly blessed all his children in a long incantation in which each of the twelve tribes was later to recognize its origin and to read its destiny. (The most outstanding glories seem to be promised to Judah.) Then he died. And his sons carried him in a sumptuous caravan to lay him to rest at Machpelah in the family vault beside his fathers, according to his wish. Reconciled with his brothers, Joseph ruled the clan after him and lived in peace and prosperity to see his grandchildren and great-grandchildren. He died at the age of a hundred and ten.

These two successive deaths were the occasion of a revealing detail. Joseph "commanded his servants the physicians to embalm his father," and this task took forty days; when he died in his turn, he was embalmed and also placed "in a coffin." This was an Egyptian custom adopted by the Israelites, described by Herodotus: "The embalmers drew out the brain through the nostrils, made an incision in the belly with an obsidian, removed the intestines and washed them in palm wine. Then the body is salted, laid in nitre, and afterwards wound in bandages," and placed in a wooden sarcophagus imitating the form of the human body. Abraham and Isaac must have been buried with no such preparation, perhaps in the crouched attitude adopted in the burial of their dead by the ancient Canaanites, the posture of the child in the mother's womb. These embalmings are a significant sign; in addition to the influences originating in Mesopotamian antiquity, the chosen people are to undergo others in the course of their long sojourn in the land of the Nile.

III

FAITH AND TRADITION

HISTORY OR STORY?

THIS EPIC OF THE PATRIARCHS, that closes with the death of Joseph, is presented to us in the Holy Scriptures as a page of history and it is a matter of faith for Christians to accept this text. The localities in which it is situated, and the many coincidences that we find, make it seem credible. But it might still be a historical romance, skilfully framed in a background carefully studied by a narrator who was master of his subject. Is it nothing more than that? Certainly we cannot hope to give, in the present state of knowledge on these distant periods, those precise details that are expected when we are concerned with more recent times; history is always hard to write even when it concerns recent events; when the facts in question cannot be deciphered except in the light of contradictory hypotheses, his muse is ever ready to aid and abet the historian led astray by logic.

Nothing is more dangerous than to claim to explain too far facts that remain scarcely explicable, and to define what is, in its very essence, indefinite. One can suggest approximate dates for the history of the Patriarchs; these vary from one authority to another. It is of no importance whether Abraham lived between 2000 and 1900 B.C., as some suppose, or between 2160 and 1958 B.C., as is stated by others. Based on a whole series of logical deductions founded on correlations with the royal chronology of Egypt, and cuneiform tablets, supported by the evidence of fragments of pottery, these dates remain mere surmises, and one can only smile when one chronology affirms with serene gravity that the departure from Ur took place in the year 2010 B.C. and that Joseph was sold by his brothers in 1645! Modesty compels us to

admit that all dates before the seventh century B.C. are hypothetical.

But apart from the dates, what of the people and the facts?
This matter has long been open to dispute. For some this story
has only the value of a symbol; a theme of religious thought
could be expressed in this form in the course of centuries. Abraham would be a moon god whose voyage from east to west re-
produced the celestial migration, and his twelve distant descendants, the sons of Jacob, would be the months. For others the
Patriarchs are the epic heroes of the Israelites at the time of their
formation as a race. In the same way as we speak of Uncle Sam
for the United States, John Bull for England, and Marianne for
the Third Republic. The names would suggest anecdotes! For
example, Israel, by a play upon the words, Jacob's striving with
God. There are other critics, again, who allow the existence of
real men named Abraham, Isaac, Jacob, and Joseph, but who say
that around these true facts of history legends have grown up.
Here again we are in the field of hypothesis, and no theory carries
sufficient conviction for the discussions of the biblical text to be
closed, in the absence of further evidence from the field of archaeology.

But it is a very narrow conception of history that sees it as the
mere science of facts. There is a human verity that is persuasive,
even in the absence of documentation. And this verity shines
from every page of the whole epic of the Patriarchs, Abraham,
Jacob and Joseph (Isaac less), revealing them as being profoundly alive men who have left their mark on their times, who
have engaged the destiny of their people. Each has his own
character, his individual way of behaving, and even his own
passions. The spiritual change in Jacob after the great crisis of
Jabbok carries all the conviction of a conversion; and a portrait
of Joseph, in his career in Egypt, is drawn for us by means of a
marvellous psychological analysis.

Amongst these psychological traits, one stands out clearly. It is
the one from which unfolds, ultimately, the whole history of the
people born of Abraham. This trait had been so clearly marked

in the character of these Patriarchs that, century after century, men of their race were to strive to keep alive in themselves the same virtue. For we cannot separate this epic from the development that came afterwards. The history of Israel is a progressive history that has a clear meaning and corresponds to an intention. The conviction of being the chosen people was to be, throughout the years, the motive of all their actions; and on what does that conviction rest, if not on the affirmation a thousand times reiterated that the Patriarchs were the repositories of the Promise, that they lived in the presence of God?

MYSTICS OF ACTION

These great Patriarchs appear to us, in fact, as mystics of action. If a man may be called a mystic who tries to realize in his life the will and the presence of God—"It is no longer I, but Christ liveth in me," as St. Paul says—Abraham and Jacob, these inspired men, were certainly mystics. All the Patriarchs were in that relationship of sublime familiarity with God that we find, in another period, in St. Joan of Arc or St. Francis of Assisi. Realists they were, like all the great mystics, "men and women of outstanding common sense," as Bergson says; capable of acting in the military and political spheres when necessary, but referring always to the divine intention without the mediation of any priest, practically without any rites, in a direct relationship continually renewed. Mystics, certainly, but mystics of action; they are not isolated and ascetic contemplatives; it is their life that bears witness, their life that is in itself both prayer and contemplation. Their very acts praise God.

Never does the narrator of this history of the Patriarchs miss an opportunity for underlining the intervention of God in the conduct of events. All that is inexplicable is attributed to Him, and frequently men, all unawares, accomplish His designs. From Him comes happiness, fertility, long life. He rewards, but also punishes, towns like Sodom and Gomorrah, or men like Onan. Merciful, he hears the prayers of the just and comforts Jacob in his desolation. This power of God is ever-present. It may manifest itself in a dream, a vision, or under those angelic forms that seem to be the visible images of the invisible that man cannot behold directly: charisms and visions of the great mystics, like those experienced by St. Bernard, St. Teresa of Avila, St. Mary of the Incarnation and many others.

Between man and God, strict relations were established, called in the Bible the "Covenant." This is a veritable pact, concluded with precise ceremonial borrowed from the customs of the time. The maker of the sacrifice cuts a victim in half, and passes between the two halves. The Patriarchs, in their own name and that of their people, engage themselves, but in exchange feel themselves to be under the protection and guidance of God.

It is a wonderful thing, this confidence that they all manifest in the supreme Power, a confidant and friend. On all occasions the sacred name is uttered, and prayer rises to men's lips. They consult God, call upon Him as a witness; to bless in His name is a sacramental, irrevocable act. The divine presence literally is everywhere in that patriarchal religion that, across the distance of four thousand years, seems to us so living, so close to the eternal needs of the soul.

There are few rites, few doctrines in this mystical life; nomadic existence does not lend itself to complicated ceremonial; it would be difficult to transport a temple on camels. The Patriarch is himself the priest; he officiates when a sacrifice is to be offered or an oblation or prayer made to God. The religious practices that we find are those that many peoples have practised in their early days. They go up to the high places in order to implore the supreme Power, in order to be, as it were, more completely alone in that Presence, or nearer to it. The noblest mountains of Palestine still bear the traces of these cults—Carmel, majestic Hermon—and altars of cupped-out stone have been found that are perhaps the same as that to which Abraham led Isaac. Sometimes, also, they raised stones according to an extremely ancient custom, the same as that practised in our own countries by the neolithic builders of dolmans and menhirs; these were the *mas-sebah*, the sacred steles, an impressive alignment of which has been discovered at Gaza. They also accorded respect to noble trees and flowing water; evergreen oaks and springs play an important role in all these narratives.

But these simple rites, originating no doubt in a secular tradition, were purified in their adoption by the Patriarchs. The fetishism found in the Canaanite and Mesopotamian religions they clearly discarded: if Rachel had the *teraphim*, her husband knew nothing of it. The horrible human sacrifices of Sumeria, long practised also by the Phoenicians, we find expressly rejected. Nor do we find any trace of the magic that vitiated the otherwise noble contemporary Egyptian religion. And even if we cannot judge the sexual morality of the time of the Patriarchs by our own standards, it is nevertheless clear that licence and excess and all violations of the laws of nature were repugnant to them, and seemed to them things condemned by God. Hammurabi, at the same period, set forth his great attempt at theological unification as the simple fruit of ancestral experience; and a little later, when the Pharaoh Amenophis IV carried out his revolution in mysticism, the only authority he invoked was his own. In Israel, everything was a reflection of the will of an all-powerful God, of the Most High.

THE ONE GOD

This God whom Israel served from this early period is the One God—is, in fact, God. There is no possible doubt of the strictly monotheistic character of that patriarchal religion, and here we touch upon the greatest mystery of that history. The people born of Abraham appeared, in the course of the centuries, at a certain point in time, in order to teach men—or perhaps remind them—of the cult of the One. All their subsequent development arises from this.

The Patriarchs designated the supreme divinity by several words, none of which can be called an actual name, in the sense in which Osiris or Athena are names.[1] For to name is, in itself, to impose a limitation. God is *El*, a very ancient syllable of the Semitic languages, near to the Babylonian *Illu* and the Arab *Allah*. What exactly does it mean? Perhaps "the first," or, more likely "the power," that by which all is born and lives, the breath that animates the created world. It is a highly metaphysical conception, as far removed from idolatry as it is possible to be: and the term *Elohim* is grammatically a plural, but is commonly employed as a singular, in order to express the multiplicity of power.

There is no trace of polytheism in the patriarchal tradition, and even many indications that prove an explicit monotheism. When, for example, Laban swears "by the God of Nahor," that is to say by a Mesopotamian divinity, Jacob replied by invoking the One God. And all the attempts made by certain critics to unearth a Pantheon from this Unity are but feeble. The Patriarchs sometimes qualified the Deity as *El-Olam*, "the eternal God"; *El-Roi*, "God of vision"; *El-Shaddai*, "the God who acts"; or by other designations that commemorate some historical event, as *El-Bethel*, "the God of Bethel," "God of Jacob's dream," or by attributive names, like "the Terror of Isaac," or "the Rock of Israel." There is no more evidence of polytheism in this than in the Catholic custom of designating the Virgin Mary by the names of her shrines, her apparitions, or her qualities; no one has ever supposed that Our Lady of Chartres, the Virgin of Salette, and the *Regina Cœli* are three different entities.

We may well wonder that this nomadic tribe, whose customs were so unlike our own, these men separated from us by four thousand years, had such a high and pure conception of God. "The Almighty, He whom we cannot attain," He was to be called in the Book of Job. This was already the idea held by the nomads.

---

[1] In Genesis we find the name Yahweh employed concurrently with the divine terms of *El, Elohim, Eloah,* etc. But Exodus explicitly states that this name dates from Moses. In the earlier writings, the use of this name is an anachronism for which an editor of later date is responsible, comparable with that by which a historian might speak of the Latin *Lutetia* as "Paris." One can even distinguish in Genesis two juxtaposed versions, in one of which God is called *Yahweh*, and in the other, *El* or *Elohim*.

El, Elohim, all the mystery of God is in these terms, a metaphysical idea which has given life to Western civilization. Renan never said anything more true than his affirmation that "from the remotest times, the Semite shepherd has carried on his brow the seal of the absolute God."

With regard to this monotheism, two questions present themselves. First of all, is it the religious conception of the Patriarchs themselves that is presented to us in the first books of the Bible? Might it not be a conventional conception, projected into the past by the authors of the book at a later date? But we can point to many differences between the religious forms of the patriarchal epoch and those of later times. If they did in this way modify the conceptions of the past, would they not have inserted into the history of the origins all the essentials of the beliefs and customs of their own times?

The other question opens much wider perspectives. This monotheism, whence did it come? Renan, in a well-known passage, affirms that it was a spontaneous creation by the Hebrews or perhaps the Semites, resulting directly from their nomadic life. "The desert is monotheist; sublime in its immense uniformity, it first revealed to man the idea of the Infinite." This is the application to the domain of religion of the theory of environment favoured by Taine. In fact, the study of the religious customs of the nomadic Semites—for example the Arabs before Mahomet—does not confirm this view and, on the contrary, reveals an abundant crop of polytheistic beliefs. No one today regards as valid this naive application of historical materialism to the origin of a metaphysical belief.

Did this monotheism that later imposed itself on the whole world arise solely then from the will of Abraham, from the revelation made to him? Or did the Patriarch rather rediscover, in a sense, under the accumulated dust of superimposed rites and customs, the authentic tradition, that which dated from the origin of man? Many theories have been built around this hypothesis, which have the appearance rather of charming speculations than of demonstrations. One invokes a natural bent in the human soul, which even among savages tends to the conception of a great being, just and good. Others point out curious coincidences. When, for example, Aeschylus says of Zeus, "He is the air, the heaven and the earth, the universe, and that which is beyond the universe," is he not speaking of an unique God? Renouf, the translator of the Egyptian *Book of the Dead,* assures us that "Five thousand years ago in the valley of the Nile, the religious hymn began with the recognition of the Unity of God." And an English Assyriologist affirms that, with the Sumerians as with the Semites, "monotheism preceded polytheism and the belief in good and evil spirits." [2]

The grandiose image of a humanity that knew God at the beginning of time, and later was separated from Him in the fallen state, and later slowly rediscovered Him by an immense effort, corresponds faily closely to the account which Genesis gives of the origins of man. Abraham, according to this view, and his people after him, would have recovered a fidelity lost by other races. This detracts nothing from his worth or from the originality of his mission. But it opens for us perspectives so vast that they bewilder us, glimpses that excite our imaginations. What evidence do the ancient traditions preserved by the people of Israel bring to bear on these theories of the Creation and the earliest period of the human race?

THE POEM OF CREATION

"In the beginning God created the heaven and the earth . . ." These are the opening words of the Book of Books and there is no theme of human invention that has served to fertilize the imagination to the same extent as have these first eleven chapters of Genesis. Christian morality has its source in them; the conception that millions of human beings have held and now hold of their destiny, the psychological explanation of our interior misery, the hope that sustains us, all that most clearly dis-

[2] Stephen Herbert Langdon, *Semitic* [mythology]. (Mythology of all races, vol. v), Oxford: Jones, Marshall, 1931.

tinguishes us perhaps, comes from these pages; suppress them and a whole immense field of art is abolished. Therefore it is scarcely surprising that so many attempts have been made to explain their mysteries, to check the statements given by means of the records of archaeology and the hypotheses of human history.

In such a field, extreme caution must be observed. It can no longer be denied that points of contact may have been established between the biblical text and the findings in certain fields of research. This tradition, which grew up in a Mesopotamian environment, certainly derives a number of features from this source. But it is unwarrantable to carry these affirmations too far, and to regard as proofs what are often only distant analogies, whether for the purpose of denying all originality to the biblical text or of establishing it too precisely on a historical basis.

The first verses of this cosmogony have the beauty of poetry. In describing the Creation, it is as though our old familiar words took on again their primitive meaning and their force. Dante himself could not have improved upon the image, "The earth was without form, and void; darkness was upon the face of the deep, and the Spirit of God moved upon the face of the waters." The God who manifests Himself in this opening of the book is clearly the same God as the Patriarchs invoked, the uncreated Creator from whom all things proceed, and who Himself proceeds from nothing. He is the organizing spirit by whose means chaos is ordered; in the same say, He was to be seen as the God of Justice, against whom all disorder is an offence.

Attempts have been made to correlate this cosmogony with others—a Babylonian poem, for example, which treats of the same subject; but there are few resemblances. In Egypt there would have been certain conceptions that admitted the existence of a god anterior to everything, who had raised up the world at his command; but these ideas belong to the school of Hermopolis, which is so long after the time of the Patriarchs that we must speak rather of coincidence than of influence. The "sources" of the first chapter of Genesis are still unknown.

God created the earth; He divided light from darkness; He
divided the waters from the firmament; He parted the sea from
the dry land, and beneath the newly risen sun He caused green
plants to germinate; in the sky He placed the stars; on the earth
and in the water animal life began; such were the first five days;
on the sixth, God created man after all the rest, as if the final
achievement of His work before taking His rest.

The creation of man is no less full of admirable symbols. The
being in which the divine work found its completion, the highest
achievement in the whole of Genesis, is likewise the miserable
creature that we recognize in ourselves. Pascal's two extremes
are already operative: "Misery the end of greatness, and greatness of misery." Man is made from "the dust of the ground."
Adam is literally the son of the "Adamah," the soil, the rich
black alluvial soil of the land of the great rivers whence all life
came. This is certainly a very ancient conception; in Egypt also,
Tem, the first man, was born of the soil. But what the tradition
of Israel adds is that Adam is created in the image of God, after
His likeness, and that he is the lord of all creatures. The conception of a being promised an exceptional destiny, depository of
the divine image, is there already, plainly manifest. When Michelangelo in one of his finest works shows, in the Sistine
Chapel, God creating man by touching his hand, it is that same
familiarity, that tenderness of the father for his child, that is
expressed. The Christian world and, even when it forgets the
fact, all Western civilization, carries within itself the certitude
of that parentage.

Man was not created alone. God gave him a companion, the
wife described in a remarkable play upon words. She is born of
the very flesh of man, "bone of his bones and flesh of his flesh,"
and is therefore called *Ishah* (woman), because she is made from
the man *Ish*, the male.[3] Thus, distinct in sex but fully equal,
man and woman are united in the same destiny. With Adam,
born of the earth, is associated Eve, the mother of his children.

---

[3] It is perhaps of interest to note that in Sumerian the same word, *Ti*,
means both "life" and "rib." Cf. Gen. II: 21, "and he took one of his ribs."

Nothing could be more concise or yet more noble than that brief description of the first pair. A whole psychology, and the whole Western sexual morality, are its fruits.

Has history traced these two remote ancestors to their source? It is highly doubtful. Some authorities have claimed to have read their names in the forms Aiou and Hawwa, in the work of the Phoenician scribe Sanchuniathon, and perhaps on some Egyptian tablets found at El Amarna. An Akkadian seal of before 3000 B.C. represents two personages, a woman and a man (the latter horned), on each side of a tree; the conclusion that this represented the original pair was hastily reached. But more convincing than the historical evidence in giving veracity to the text is its psychological truth, the picture of Adam and Eve confronting one another in a state of innocence. They are happy together. But sin comes into their lives, and all is disordered. The crime passes to their children. The human drama begins, with its inner evil and sorrow.

PARADISE LOST

The whole theme of original sin, a dogma in which is contained one of the deepest mysteries of man and of human life, bears the mark of the most profound verity. In it every man finds his own drama, his hopes, his fears, and his destiny. Adam and Eve lived in the garden of delights, among trees, "good for food and pleasant to the eyes," in familiarity with the animals, to which man had given names, which, according to the ancient conception, established his power over them. And naked in each other's presence without shame, they knew in nature as in themselves only peace. Thus in each of us lingers that high dream of an age of gold, better and purer than our own, in which all men lived in a harmonious world, where nothing was infected, ineluctably, with the malady of death; that dream of Paradise that so many painters have attempted to evoke, and that continually haunts the minds of the poets from Dante and Milton to Rimbaud.

The state of innocence comes to an end through man's fault. In the midst of the garden are planted trees, admirably named

the tree of life and the tree of knowledge of good and evil. God
has forbidden men to eat their fruit. The whole biblical narrative
it too well known to dwell upon: under the symbolism of the
serpent and the apple, in the story of the temptation of Eve, we
discern something that is still a great human reality—sin. Where
it penetrates, it is as though something is corrupted and faded,
there is a sense of separation; a sense of disintegration comes into
play, that brings the thought of death. This theme is so profoundly human that many religions have varying versions of it.
It is the basis of the dualism of Iran, one of the expressions of the
religious thought of Aryan antiquity, in which life is presented as
a combat between the god of good and the god of evil, between
whom man must continually make his choice. In Egypt, *The
Book of the Dead* is impregnated with similar concepts; the dead
man who comes before the judge of the dead must reject "the
maternal taint" and say, "Heart of my birth, heart that I had on
earth, do not rise in witness against me before the divine powers;
do not weigh in the balance!" The accuser of man, he who drives
him from Paradise, is at once God and his own heart, that heart
that best knows both his fault and his distress. Adam and Eve
driven from Paradise are, in these distant sources of Western
tradition, the dramatic image of the human condition.

From this time, all is out of joint. The peace of Paradise is
destroyed. Eve has "gotten a man from the Lord," a son; and
afterwards another is born to her. Cain's attack on Abel is the
first symptom of that disaccord into which humanity has come
since the Fall, the first war. In it, one can detect traces of the conflict that must have existed between the settled races and the
shepherds; as a nomadic race, the Hebrews give their preference
to the shepherd Abel over the farmer Cain; God accepts the
offerings of the one, rejects those of the other. One might even
speculate as to whether here we have not an allusion to the conflicts provoked in neolithic times by the invention of metal arms:
the descendants of Cain were smiths, and we still can find, in the
deserts of Syria, tribes of armourers, who are shunned and generally held in suspicion as practisers of black magic.

From Cain and another son, Seth, "the substitute" for Abel, the Bible traces the descent of the human race. Herein we find one of the most curious points of contact with the ancient traditions of Babylon. The first men are represented as having enjoyed a longevity far greater than is known today. "All the days that Adam lived were nine hundred and thirty"; Seth, nine hundred and twelve; Enos, nine hundred and five; Cain, nine hundred and ten; Mahalaleel, eight hundred and ninety-five years, and so on until the time of Noah, Methuselah bearing the record of nine hundred and sixty-nine years. Then the account of the Deluge interrupts the normal course of human development, and when the new genealogy, derived from Noah, is taken up, longevity is far less and continually decreases—six hundred years for Shem, two hundred and five for Terah.

This has clearly a meaning. The narrator wishes to suggest a diminution of vitality in the human race. To have a very long life is seen as the mark of divine protection; therefore the Patriarch lived for more than a hundred years. But the farther we are removed from the time of Paradise, the shorter life becomes, as though the fire kindled by God were slowly dying away. It is strange to consider that, in the Mesopotamian tradition, we find an entirely similar intention. It is said that the kings of the earliest dynasties lived for a fantastic number of years, twenty thousand and seventy thousand. Then came the Deluge, after which man's longevity, which was still astonishing but less (about a thousand years), steadily decreased to a modest hundred. We have here a symbol which surely calls for comment from the sciences both of medicine and of theology.

THE FLOOD

The episode of the Flood is, of all the Book of Genesis, the one most fully borne out by the findings of archaeology; so much so that with an enthusiasm that is perhaps excessive some Anglo-Saxon professors have not hesitated to declare it to be "historically proved." Reduced to its essentials, the account is as follows: God, considering the wickedness of man, repents of having given him life, and resolves to suppress his breed by drowning; but on this earth, "corrupt before God and filled with violence," Noah, a just and righteous man, found grace in the eyes of the Eternal. Counselled by God, he built a vessel and painted it with pitch—the Ark. He took refuge in it with his family and a pair of each species of animals. Then were "all the fountains of the deep broken up and the windows of heaven were opened. And the rain was upon the earth forty days and forty nights." Humanity was destroyed: men were re-born of the just Noah when the deluge ceased and the Ark came to rest on Mount Ararat, whence the dove, sent out to explore, had brought back an olive-branch.

Now it is upon a precise event, climatic and geographical, that this episode rests. Is there any trace of it to be found in the lands of Mesopotamia? If these rivers suffer from great droughts, so likewise they are subject to excessive floods; the Nile has known many such. But the text of the Bible would seem to indicate a phenomenon of a quite exceptional character. In 1929 two archaeological parties, one at Ur and one at Kish, made a singular discovery. Having removed beds formed of pottery and debris, they found a layer of clay perfectly smooth and homogeneous. The workmen declared that the bed of the river had been reached, but continuing to dig, after four feet ten and one-half inches of clay the archaeologists were surprising to find pottery reappearing, more archaic and of a finer quality. The clay deposit constituted therefore a definite break in the sequence of time.

One can imagine the speculations suggested by such a discovery. The physical explanation of the fact remains profoundly obscure. It seems scarcely possible that a deposit of four feet ten and one-half inches of clay was formed by the rivers alone, even aided by exceptional rains. Certain bold speculators have ventured to attribute to the Deluge those great geological phenomena which shook the whole earth at the end of the tertiary period in connection with the most recent upheavals of the mountain ranges. There was at that time a universal Mediterranean, the Thetys, that encircled the globe, and of which the Black Sea and the Caspian remain as fragments. The Deluge was a great tidal wave of the sea, and we may observe that the Bible seems to locate the event in the region of the Caucasus, for the Ark came to land on Mount Ararat in Armenia. These are merely bold guesses. All that can be said with certainty is that, geologically, a deluge in this Mesopotamian region is not only possible but probable.

But the Deluge, as the Bible describes it, seems to have been more widespread. And one cannot avoid thinking of all those deluges that we find in the traditions of so many races, that of Deucalion in the Hellenic mythology, that found in the Vedas of India, and even those that appear as the basis of pre-Columbian legends of America or in Lithuania. Obviously the question remains an open one, and the meaning of these similarities remains obscure.

There is a more precise parallel, and one of considerable significance, with the Mesopotamian tradition. The most famous epic of Babylon describes one of the old legendary kings, Gilgamesh, a Sumerian Hercules and Samson, demi-god and hero of many exploits. We may see him in the Louvre, represented in bas-relief, stifling a lion by crushing him to his chest with only one arm. This poem—which dates from before Hammurabi—had in the Mesopotamian world the same vogue as had the Odyssey and the Iliad in Greece; numerous versions of it are known, and even a translation into the Hittite language. The eleventh of the twelve tablets that constitute the epic is a detailed account of the Deluge. Gilgamesh, who has been to visit "the master of life," learns from him this ancient history. In many points the Babylonian text corresponds with that of the Bible.

We find the same theme of the divine Power resolved to punish humanity by destroying men by water. Here too a favoured man is warned, builds a ship, "takes into it the seed of all life," and finds refuge in it with his family. From the depths of the sky a black cloud arises; "the sluices of heaven are opened." In the Mesopotamian poem the cataclysm lasts only six days, after which the Ark comes to rest on a high mountain; the birds are sent out on reconnaissance: "The crow set out, to see whether the waters were drying; he ate, paddled, croaked, and never came back." The saved man set foot again on the earth and offered a sacrifice to the Divinity.

The resemblance is too striking to be attributed to chance. Precise details in the two texts are of the same origin, which they clearly derive from an identical source: the form of the ship is the same, a vessel with decks; bitumen is mentioned in both accounts; the narrative is on the same lines. The existence of a Mesopotamian tradition on a cataclysm that threatened to destroy humanity is beyond question, but we cannot deduce from this that the Deluge described was of world-wide extent.

If we must abandon the attempt to date the Deluge by means of documents other than the Bible—it took place in 5000 B.C. according to some, 3500 B.C. according to others—it remains nevertheless a fact retained in history. Perhaps it really terminated a legendary age, and inaugurated the times of which we have precise knowledge. A very obscure passage in the Bible seems to suggest this (Gen.: beginning of chapter VI). It is said that before the cataclysm giants lived on earth, born of the union of the "sons of God" with the daughters of men. "The same became mighty men which were of old, men of renown." Was Gilgamesh one of their number? But here again we are in the realm of dreams and imagination.

THE TOWER OF BABEL

The Deluge seems to have had a redemptive value, for God, when His vengeance was accomplished, promised Noah that He would not repeat it. He knows well that "the imagination of man's heart is evil from his youth," but He will refrain from carrying out on that account such an exemplary punishment. Henceforth all is to be normal on the earth, "seedtime and harvest, and cold and heat, and summer and winter, and day and night shall not cease." Relations of confidence were established between God and man and, as the first concession of the eternal promise, a covenant was made whose image was the consoling rainbow.

Henceforth humanity resumed its life and multiplied. Noah had three sons, Shem, Ham, and Japhet. The favourite was Shem, for he was the most respectful; when, taken off his guard by the hitherto unknown drink produced by the newly introduced vine, his father became drunk, Shem had decently covered his nakedness, while Ham had mocked him. Therefore Ham was cursed in his posterity, while Shem was to become the ancestor of the Semites, the race from which sprang the chosen people.

The Bible insists on the original unity of the entire human race. It even specifically says that in those happy times "the whole earth was of one language and of one speech." As, in the matter of an original universal monotheism, it is impossible to know whether we have here the expression of a sharp regret at the division of men or the memory of some very ancient tradition. History records a number of these great phenomena of dispersion, like that which divided the Aryan mass into a number of separate elements, carrying some into India, others to Gaul. Something of this kind is suggested by the text of Genesis.

The races born of the two sons of Noah were not to remain united. Journeying from the east towards the plain of Shinar (Gen. XI:2), they settled there, and built a tower of bricks, cemented with bitumen, so high that it seemed to defy God. The Almighty cut short this sacrilegious undertaking. He confused their languages; henceforth disunited, the races dispersed over the earth.

Is any historical reality to be traced in this new episode? Is the descent of the races towards Shinar a memory of the remote times when the Sumerians first installed themselves in Mesopotamia? The discovery of the technique of making brick, the use of which we have already observed in the Fertile Crescent, is clearly indicated in the biblical text. As for the Tower of Babel, we have found plenty of examples. It is the *Zikkurat*, the terraced Babylonian pyramid. At Ur, there is such a rectangular construction, of 211 feet and 3 inches by 139 feet and 9 inches; the inner structure is of raw bricks, the exterior of baked bricks. This monument consists of terraces built in stories of decreasing area; the first is

32 feet and 6 inches in height, the second and third 6½ feet and 8 feet and 1½ inches, the fourth 13 feet. Herodotus describes the *Zikkurat* as follows: "A massive tower upon which another rises, on this second, another again, and so on, sometimes up to eight. In the highest tower there is a shrine, containing a great and richly appointed bed, and a golden table. There are no statues, and no one spends the night there, except a woman of the country whom the god himself chooses from amongst all her companions." Ramps made it possible to climb to the summit, and, as these were steep, a railing was provided in the middle of the ramp.

The religious significance of this monument remains obscure. Was it a kind of observatory from which Mesopotamian astronomers, whose knowledge was remarkable, observed the nocturnal sky? It also clearly contained a symbol; perhaps an image of the earth, as it was then conceived; or a sacred mountain, the trace of one of the ancient cults of the High Places. (It is likely that each terrace was laid out in gardens.) The stories were probably painted, the lowest white, the highest red; the high chapel had blue tiles; this may have represented the underworld, the earth, and the sky respectively. But it is certain these grandiose monuments had, for the people of Sumeria and Akkad, a significance of pride. We know the names by which they were called. At Babel— that is Babylon, "the gate of god"—the temples built by the command of Hammurabi were called "house of the haughty brow" and "house that upholds the earth." That is the equivalent of the biblical term for a tower "whose top may reach unto heaven."

Here again we find the mark of an eternal psychology. "The spirit of pride has dispersed the languages," Saint Augustine was later to say. It is self-intoxication, the will to power, that divides men and creates impassable barriers; together with a metaphysical and a moral meaning, the old text contains a political theory. Here also we find a trait of racial psychology; the nomads of the clan of Terah, who decided to leave Ur and the civilization of the cities, surely saw in the *Zikkurat* that archetype of great undertakings, the image of all that they mistrusted and all from which they wished to fly: polytheist idolatry, the immoral luxury of the great cities, human masses marshalled under the baton of bureaucratic states. Thus ancient traditions substantiate this ancient history and corroborate the mystical event of Abraham's vocation.

THE COMMON BASIS AND THE NEW ELEMENT

Thus it is beyond question today that the books in which the Bible describes to us the remote origins of man are drawn from a common source from which many Mesopotamian traditions are also drawn. These resemblances serve to eliminate the mythological theory formerly in favour. The time has passed when rationalist criticisms claim to have explained the mystery of Genesis by invoking a solar myth and the faculty for inventing fables with which primitive races are gifted.

We see no reason why the fact that Genesis is the Hebrew expression of a tradition conserved in Mesopotamia should lessen its value. If the facts are true, why should they not have been known before the descendants of Abraham had the idea of giving them form as a narrative? In fact, it is satisfying and reassuring to suppose that in ancient Sumeria they were already speaking of the triumph of the Light over Chaos, and that, as the Babylonian priest Berossus recorded three centuries before our era, they explained the creation of man by saying that the blood of a god had animated a body of clay. But two further questions arise: what was the origin of this common source? and what was the original contribution of Israel?

The Bible has, undoubtedly, drawn upon elements anterior to the arrival of the Semites in Mesopotamia. In the same way as the laws and customs followed by Abraham and the men of the patriarchal period, closely resembling the laws and customs codified by Hammurabi, bear the Sumerian imprint, their religious traditions are strongly marked with pre-Semitic elements. The Bible was to be, through the Book of Genesis, the Hebrew chapter of the great body of cuneiform literature.

What is the source of that cuneiform basis itself? Here human knowledge can do no more than indicate the presence of an uncharted region, in'o which as yet only a few very tentative explorations have been made. Some authorities believe that we must look for its distant origin beyond Iran to a region between the Caucasus, Russian Turkestan and Central Asia, where originated hieroglyphic writing, to which Sumerian writing is related. This common source would not be an absolute point of origin, but already the product of a long process of human thought. Similarly, as our knowledge of the origins of the Ayran race increases, the more it seems that there is a rich past, a language already perfected for several thousands of years, whose origin was likewise perhaps in that same region of Central Asia, the veritable fountain-head of races. Sir Flinders Petrie, the celebrated English archaeologist, has even based a curious deduction upon this supposition. In the Egyptian *Book of the Dead* it is said that the sun rises over the mountains of Baku and sets behind Tamanu. Now Baku and the peninsula of Taman are the two extremities of the Caucasus. Is it possible that those lakes of fire described in the *Book of the Dead* are the sheets of petrol of the Caspian? [4]

If we take the statements of Genesis literally, not only the common origin of the human race but also the geographical course of its dispersion is clearly indicated. The race of Shem went towards the south, that of Ham, south-west, and that of Japhet, westwards; that is, the first towards Arabia, the second towards Syria, Egypt and Africa (the Hebrews were later to call Egypt the "land of Misraim," a son of Ham), and the third towards Europe. All races can therefore claim a part in these traditions of their origin, since they date from before the dispersion. And the coincidences which anti-religious critics have used as a weapon seem rather to be proofs of their veracity. But the implications of these coincidences should not be exaggerated. As yet no single account as complete and coherent as that given in the Bible has been found. We have shown that, for many points (the creation of Adam and Eve, for example), no other is known to exist. And above all, anyone who reads without prejudice the

[4] It is to be noted that Mount Ararat, where Noah's ark came to land, is in the same region.

story of Genesis side by side with the cuneiform documents, interesting as these are, will see clearly that there is a great gulf between them.

The originality of the biblical cosmogony lies, in the first place, in its rigid monotheism. In the account of the Deluge, for example, the Mesopotamian text is polytheist, full of gods whose intervention hastened the cataclysm, or who lamented it, feeling themselves also threatened; whereas Genesis attributes everything to the One God. It is the same in every case. The Babylonian cosmogonists attribute different roles to Enlil, Marduk, to the moon-god, to any number of powers; in the Bible, the "Spirit of God" is alone responsible. It is as though the descendants of the Patriarchs in borrowing the elements of the narrative from ancient sources (Sumerian or Asiatic?) had purged them of their idolatry and restored the single God. This confirms all that the story of Abraham tells us of his mission, as he received it and as his people were to preserve it after him.

A second element of originality is of equal importance. This cosmogony is already a matter of history. From the first, the image of the seven days of the Creation, in showing the divine task as being accomplished in stages, suggests that the world has in its distant beginnings a principle of progress, an advance towards the future, a destiny to fulfil. Other accounts of the beginning, that of the Greeks, for example, give the impression that human society has remained fixed in a state of regret for the Golden Age. Genesis holds the promise of a future; its necessary fulfilment is the vocation of the sons of Shem, the special task assigned to them by God.

And that cosmogony itself holds but a tiny place in the great whole. Here is yet another element of originality, one that characterizes the whole Bible, which is a history, the most ancient of histories, the story of human events: man is the essential thing. The relevance of the psychology herein revealed has a meaning that is not so much theological and metaphysical as moral and mystical; the Bible is a book whose scale is that of man. It is not in nature, in appearances, that Israel was to seek for God, but in the human person, to the point of revealing the perfect image, the Son of Man, the Son of God.

THE INHERITED TRADITION

Abraham's departure, in answer to the call of God, the life in tents in the land of Canaan, the relations between the Patriarchs and the Almighty, and finally the astonishing success of Joseph, were all traditions of recent origin that the Israelites handed down from father to son, during their life in the land of Egypt. They also handed down the much more remote traditions that explained the origin of the earth and of man, the drama of life, the conflict of good and evil, the origin of races. A final question presents itself: how were these traditions preserved?

We have seen too clearly how strongly Mesopotamian influence has affected the Bible to refuse to admit that the whole may well have been transmitted in written form. For at least a thousand years before Abraham, the people of Shinar had known the art of writing. By turn, following a traditional evolution, their writing had been pictographic, that is, figurative, each symbol representing an object; later, ideographic, the sign no longer corresponding to an object, but to an idea; gradually stylized, it became syllabic; later the alphabet came into being. At the time of Abraham, we are no longer at the stage of archaic writing whose awkwardness is exemplified in the inscribed clay cakes of Tello or in the first pharaoic inscriptions. Hammurabi had written his laws on stone, and the whole Babylonian world employed widely at that time the already perfected writing known as cuneiform.

On tablets of baked clay of varying size (some as large as quartos, others rather like small pocket note-books), the scribe printed with a stylus whose trace, like a nail, left a *cuneus*. This writing was used for many purposes: personal letters, business letters, circulars, tables of calculation. In order to give authority to the writing, the scribe added his seal, a stamp in the form of a small cylinder, on which was engraved some religious emblem, and the name of its owner. When the brick was written on, or dried, it was slipped onto a rod, with others, or, if it was in the form of a letter, placed in a clay envelope and sealed.

This process met with great success. It was to be used from the time of the Hittite Empire from Asia Minor, and from what is now Russian Turkestan, to Egypt, where the Pharaohs received a large diplomatic correspondence on clay. It had the advantage of being indelible, but there were great disadvantages in the use of such a heavy material. Translated into cuneiform, the Books of Genesis would weigh a hundredweight. It is therefore highly doubtful whether in their migration the Terahites would have carried numbers of these heavy tablets. The fact that writing was in current use proves that the tradition may have been based on a precise documentation. But it is likely that this was not the form in which it was commonly transmitted.

Our twentieth-century Western habits, for centuries accustomed to the current script, light paper, and more recently, to printing, make it difficult for us to conceive the transmission of facts by other means than those of writing. In many nations it is otherwise. Memory has long been regarded as the safest means. Among the Greeks, the Homeric poems were recited long before they were written down. In Egypt, in the archives of the Pharaohs, we find a letter from an official to the king which says, "At the same time as this letter, I am sending a messenger who knows it by heart." Among the Jews, the immense Talmud was recited for generations, and the Koran of Mahomet was conserved by an oral tradition, "recited" or "chanted," not read.

In the black tents in the land of Mamre, and later in the small white houses of the Delta, it was by word of mouth, from the ancestral guardians of the national tradition, that the distant descendants of Abraham conserved their history. Later, when that tradition was fixed—still long before it was set down fully in writing—they attributed the authorship to the man through whom their history entered into its second great phase—Moses.

PART TWO

MOSES AND CANAAN

I

A LEADER OF MEN

ISRAEL IN EGYPT

"I DIE; and God will surely visit you, and bring you out of this land into the land which he sware to Abraham, to Isaac, and to Jacob" (Gen. L:24). Egypt was to be no more than a halt. Nevertheless the prophecy seemed slow in fulfilment. Many generations passed. "And the children of Israel were fruitful, and increased abundantly, and multiplied, and waxed exceedingly mighty; and the land was filled with them" (Exod. I:7).

The Israelites were settled in "the land of Goshen," "the country of Rameses," or "the fields of Tanis," [1] according to various texts in the Bible. This does not identify the region exactly. But it certainly refers to the undulating plain that stretches from the Delta to the bitter lakes. Tanis is not far from them, and may have been the Avaris of the Hyksos. Rameses II established his capital in this region; roughly it was the valley of the Wadi Tamilat, a frontier region where it seems natural that a Pharaoh who had come from Asia should have installed wandering Asiatic tribes. The pasture lands made it possible to raise abundant livestock, and crops must have grown with little trouble around the tents. Half nomad, half settled, the children of Israel enjoyed a pleasant life. The fine Egyptian onions long remained in their memory as a nostalgic regret.

Abruptly, all was changed. "Now there arose up a new king over Egypt, which knew not Joseph" (Exod. I:8). The services rendered by the great vizier no longer protected his descendants. Their rapid increase in numbers was alarming. The persecution began.

Here an historic event stands out—the war of independence

[1] See MAP: SINAI, p. 83.

waged by the Theban Pharaohs of the Seventeenth Dynasty against the "pastoral kings." A local prince, Seqenenrê the Brave, raised a revolt in Upper Egypt. The Asiatics, taken by surprise, were shaken, but they rallied. A fierce struggle commenced in which three Theban kings were to be killed. After fifty years the liberation was achieved, Avaris taken, and the "Asiatic pest" driven back to its own country, and even a raid on Palestine was carried out in order to complete the route of the Hyksos. As friends of the shepherd kings, the sons of Israel were inevitably suspect in the eyes of the Egyptians. They must have remained prudently neutral, but they were nonetheless associated with the "hateful Asiatic foreigners" and, their protectors being gone, suffered accordingly.

At first the persecution took the moderate form of a labour conscription. Great building operations were always going on in the land of the Nile. Many foreigners—Babylonians, Trojans, Negroes, served the Pharaohs as manual labourers. We see the fierce nomads compelled to make bricks. A mural painting at Thebes shows us what this terrible labour involved. In the burning heat of the day, under the whip of taskmasters, they filled rush baskets with clay, mixed with this earth finely chopped straw, filled the moulds, and finally laid out thousands of bricks in line under the hot sun.

But in this there was nothing worse than humiliation and fatigue. Several decades later, matters became worse. The Egyptians, in a wave of nationalism and imperialism, set about eliminating all alien elements. The Pharaoh first had the idea of ordering the midwives to kill at birth all the male children of the Israelites. This attempt having failed, he ordered all the new-born of the hated people to be thrown into the Nile. The chosen race seemed to be doomed to extermination. It was at this time that Moses appeared.

THE LIBERATOR

The story of Moses opens charmingly. Humans love their great men to have an unusual beginning; the great Sargon and Gilga-

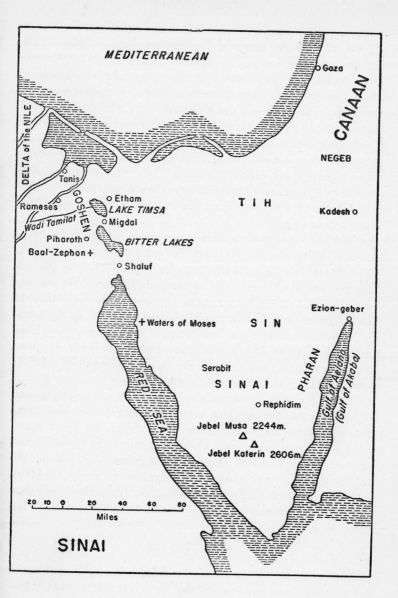

MEDITERRANEAN

Gaza

CANAAN

DELTA of the NILE

NEGEB

Tanis

Rameses

GOSHEN

Etham

LAKE TIMSA

Wadi Tamilat

Migdal

T I H

Kadesh

Piharoth

BITTER LAKES

Baal-Zephon +

Shaluf

Waters of Moses

S I N

Ezion-geber

Serabit

S I N A I

PHARAN

Gulf of Aqaba (Gulf of Akaba)

Rephidim

Jebel Musa 2244m.

△
△

Jebel Katerin 2606m.

RED SEA

20 10 0   20   40   60   80

Miles

SINAI

mesh are also said to have owed their lives to God's special protection, as later did Bacchus, Perseus, Romulus and Sigurd. The biblical narrative contains no mystery, but it is full of poetry. A woman of Israel had lacked the courage to drown her new-born child. She watched by the spot where Pharaoh's daughter came to bathe, and there exposed the tiny infant in a floating cradle. The princess was touched at the sight of the frail creature, took the child, and named it "saved from the waters," Moses. She then looked for a nurse. Was there any in the neighbourhood? One offered her service, and was accepted—the child's own mother, who seems to have managed things remarkably well.

It is a significant fact that the future liberator of Israel began his career among those whom he was later to oppose. He was "learned in all the wisdom of the Egyptians" (Acts vii:22), and knew all their weaknesses. Later Philip of Macedonia was to retain from his childhood in Hellas memories that were to help him to defeat the Greeks. Vercingetorix, before his revolt, was an officer allied to the Romans, who dined with Caesar; and the black Napoleon of San Domingo, Toussaint L'Ouverture, before fighting them to the death, had been in the service of the whites. The personality of Moses seems to us neither as simple nor as lifelike as that of Joseph. He is, above all, the man with a vocation; powerful, majestic as Michelangelo has depicted him in St. Peter's, his brow pierced with two shafts of supernatural light, but at the same time dark in his magician's arts, and upheld by the holy violence of a just cause.

He might, like Joseph, have made his fortune at the Pharaoh's court, at the price of some betrayal. One thinks of those Jews who in their desire for success passionately disown their race. Moses chose his mission in preference to his career. That thirst for justice that burned on the lips of the prophets is already ardent in the first of their number. He had gone out "unto his brethren," toiling in the building-yards of Pharaoh. "And he spied an Egyptian smiting an Hebrew, one of his brethren. And he looked this way and that way, and when he saw that there was no man, he slew the Egyptian, and hid him in the sand" (Exod. ii:11-12). Protected though he was, the assassination of an official of public works could not be overlooked, and "Pharaoh sought to slay Moses."

The land of Midian, whither he fled for safety, was just beyond the frontier. North of the Gulf of Akaba, there now stretches a bare plain. In antiquity it was more populous; ruins of aqueducts and dams have been found; and in the time of Solomon the gold of Ophir was unloaded there. The population was Semitic, descendants of Abraham and one of his concubines; a priest of the country, Jethro, who had seven daughters, gave one to the exile as wife. As the father of a family, and as a shepherd, Moses was now a happy man. But in the desert, in the solitude, the civilized courtier re-awoke. The blood of his race flowed in his veins. And as his brothers in Egypt, in the extremity of their servitude cried out to God, the Almighty heard their complaint. "God remembered his covenant with Abraham, with Isaac, and with Jacob. And God looked upon the children of Israel," and "had respect unto them" (Exod. II:24–25).

The role confided to the ancient Patriarch in the revelation of Ur was taken up by Moses. One day as he wandered with his flocks in those great solitudes of the south, he had a strange vision. A bush was on fire yet not consumed; dazzling as the yellow flame of plants impregnated with salt, that brightness was like a presence—it was indeed a presence, it was God. Hiding his face, and having removed his sandals, Moses listened. He, and no other, was charged with the task of freeing his people from oppression. "Who am I," said Moses, "that I should be called to such a task? I am slow of speech and what sign shall I show to my brethren?"

Proofs? These: The stick that Moses carried would change into a serpent, and again become wood. His hand would become leprous and clean again, before his eyes. And as for a sign, God gave him one beyond all question: He taught him His ineffable name as though to promise that He, the inaccessible, was at hand to help him. Moses obeyed. He returned to Egypt, though not without a last conflict of soul, recalling the nocturnal combat of

Jacob. By these manifest signs, the people recognized that he came from God. He was eighty years of age.

To lead Israel out of Egypt was by no means easy. The Pharaoh detested Asiatics, but he needed labourers. Aided by his brother Aaron, whom God gave him to assist him, the inspired man attempted to obtain permission for the departure. He encountered the king's refusal. There remained force. Not in vain had God given him miraculous powers: in that land of magic, a magician would be heard. The wrath of the Almighty should fall on Egypt!

In turn, ten plagues arose. The kindly Joseph had averted distress from the borders of the Nile; the burning prophet summoned it. The waters of the Nile were turned to blood, so unwholesome that the fish in them died; frogs infested the whole country, even to the royal bed. Mosquitoes, numerous as grains of sand, made life unbearable. Then came other insects, beetles, as if in a nightmare; an epidemic killed all the cattle, from camels to sheep; sores broke out on the skins of men. Hail laid low the crops, and locusts completed the devastation; last of all, day and night, darkness plunged the country into terror. Was this enough? Nine times Pharaoh promised, in his fear, to let Israel go, and then withdrew his promise. Then came the last trial.

These ten "plagues" are presented in the Bible as miraculous. It matters little that "water turned to blood" suggests the flood of the Nile which is as a matter of fact red and unwholesome as it begins to rise; that swarms of insects and frogs are frequent when the flood rises high; that locusts are a common cause of trouble, those great mauve and yellow locusts that St. John the Baptist lived on in the desert. The demoniacal shadows may have been caused by clouds of sand carried by the wind, the deadly *khamsin*, and festering sores are not rare in the East. It remains true that such a series of miseries has the value of a sign. In that mounting series of catastrophes the whole of Egypt saw "the finger of God."

The tenth plague was the worst, and also the most mysterious. The Lord was to pass during the night, and kill all the first-born of the Egyptians. Would He distinguish the children of Israel? Yes, for each family at evening, ready for departure, dressed for the journey, was to slay a lamb. Having renounced the raised bread of the cities, they were to wait. On the door, they were to make a sign with the blood of their victim which, like Abraham's ram, was to ransom the life of the children of God. In the same way, at the present time in Syria, in order to protect a guest, a mark is traced in blood on his cloak and on the neck of his horse or mule. Easter is born, the feast of the Passover: Israel was to commemorate it year by year, in memory of the night when the power of death "passed over" and constrained brutal force to give place to the Will of God.

A PROBLEM OF DATES

The people of Israel are about to leave Egypt. History here raises endless problems. Does the meticulous record of the Pharaoh's government retain any mention of the settlement and subsequent Exodus? Who was that tyrannical king, or, which amounts to the same thing, how long did Joseph's descendants remain in the land of Goshen?

No Egyptian document mentions the Israelites. We have abundant proofs of the presence on the Nile of nomadic Semites; a bas-relief shows a thick-lipped African and an Asiatic with a hooked nose bound back to back; the sceptre of Tutankhamun represents, reversed like the two figures on a playing-card, a Negro and a Semite, the double peril to the crown. But this state of affairs existed at the time of Abraham and did not come to an end with the Exodus. And does it refer to Joseph's descendants?

Later, when the biblical tradition became known throughout the East, legends grew up. Manetho, the Egyptian historian, related that the Israelites were the "lepers" who were isolated near the bitter lakes, and who, after the defeat of the Hyksos, revolted and fled; which is but a literal reading of the expression "the Asiatic leprosy" used to describe everything that recalled the shepherd kings.

An interesting suggestion has been provided by the discovery at El Amarna of tablets recording the presence in Egypt of people called the *Habiru*. Were these the Hebrews? There can be little doubt of it. Father de Vaux [2] concludes that these were certainly nomadic Semites belonging to the great Aramaic wave. But the name *Habiru* occurs almost everywhere, as far as Hittite Asia Minor, and although it is certain that the Israelites formed part of that ethnic group, we have no reason to believe that all the *Habiru* were the descendants of Joseph. The discovery at El Amarna has therefore only a limited value.

There are, however, traces of the presence of Israelites, if not in Egypt, at least in southern Palestine, in a stele created by the Pharaoh Mineptah in the thirteenth century B.C. He enumerates the nations that he has conquered—Canaan, Askalon, Gaza—and he ends, "Israel is destroyed and has no more seed." This is the first mention of that name in the biblical text. It confirms the existence of the posterity of Jacob. But, in order to understand its exact meaning, we would have to know the date of the Exodus, and here our knowledge is purely hypothetical.

Can we fix this date by establishing the duration of the sojourn in Egypt? Our Bible states that they remained there 430 years, but the Greek version of the Septuagint, compiled in the third century B.C. at Alexandria, includes in that figure the period of the Patriarchs, reducing the Egyptian period by almost half. Other methods of calculation are equally imprecise: counting back, for example, from a date that is more or less established, in the reign of Solomon, and adding up the length of time implicit in the text. Recently, evidence has been drawn from the excavations at Jericho, the first stronghold taken by Israel in Palestine: are there traces there of that destruction, comparable to those at Troy in which it is believed that the fire kindled by Agamemnon has left its mark? The question remains open.

Does the history of Egypt allow us to fix the date by identifying the persecutor? Not very precisely, for the Egyptologists do not agree on the method of establishing dates. Some adhere to the

[2] *See Note, p. 28.*

"long," others to the "short" method of chronology; at the period of the Exodus this would represent a discrepancy of some three or four hundred years. According as we adopt the one method or the other, the Exodus would have taken place about 1440 B.C. or about 1250 B.C. And the perspectives are very different. One thing is certain, that the departure of Moses took place some time after the expulsion of the Hyksos, during the period when Egypt under the Pharaohs of the Eighteenth and Nineteenth Dynasties,[3] had reached the height of her impressive power. Let us attempt to see the possible course of events in the light of each of these hypotheses.

By the longer computation, we have the Eighteenth Dynasty. After the rout of the Hyksos by the Pharaohs of the Seventeenth Dynasty, their successors realized that in order to avert similar catastrophes they must defeat Asia on her own ground. Through their contact with the Shepherd Kings, the Egyptians had perfected their military methods; they had divisions of chariots, their sol-

---

[3] TABLE OF THE EIGHTEENTH AND NINETEENTH DYNASTIES
OF THE PHARAOHS

(All these dates are approximate)

Eighteenth Dynasty:	Amasis	1580–60	
	Amenophis	1560–30	
	Tuthmosis I	1530–00	
	Tuthmosis II	⎫	
	Hatshepsut	⎬...1500–1450	
	Tuthmosis III	⎭	
	Amenophis II	1450–40	
	Tuthmosis IV	1420–10	
	Amenophis III	...1410–1375	
	Amenophis IV	...1375–60	(the revolutionary Pharaoh Ikhnaton)
Nineteenth Dynasty:	Tutankhamun	1360–50	
	Haremhab	1350–15	
	Rameses I	1315–14	
	Seti I	1314–1290	
	Rameses II	1290–25	
	Mineptah	1225–15	
	Amenmesse	⎫	
	Siptah	⎬.....1215–05	(followed by a period of anarchy)
	Seti II	⎭	

diers had better arms, javelins and swords, and instead of fighting naked wore head coverings and sometimes padded breastplates. About 1530 Tuthmosis I vanquished Syria, reached the Euphrates, and stupefied to find a river that flowed in the opposite direction to the Nile, engraved on a stele, "I have seen the returning water, flowing down as it flows back." After a pause, other campaigns were undertaken under Tuthmosis III, a magnificent conqueror We see the face of this man in the Museum at Cairo, full of intelligence and courage. He carried on victorious warfare for some twenty years, approximately from 1500 to 1480 B.C. Palestine and Syria were his protectorates; Cyprus and the Greek Islands paid him tribute. In the temple of Ammon at Karnak the list of his exploits covers about 119 square yards. After him came a decline. His son Amenophis II was a nonentity; and fifty years later the revolutionary Pharaoh Amenophis IV reversed the whole policy of Egypt, and invented a sort of pacifist universalism that allowed the power of the realm to undergo a terrible decline.

The Bible refers to two Pharaohs: the persecutor of Israel, and the Pharaoh of the Exodus. The first would have been Tuthmosis III, which would correspond with his nationalist policies. It would then have been under his feeble son Amenophis II that Moses would have led Israel out of Egypt between 1450 and 1420 B.C. On this hypothesis, we can even possibly identify "Pharaoh's daughter." On the death of Tuthmosis I the power was in the hands of a regent, who supplanted her half-brother and husband, the insignificant Tuthmosis II. This woman was Hatshepsut; she is represented on monuments bearing the royal pschent and the false beard; it was she who built the temple of Deir el Bahari, the "most high of the most high," whose columns have a Doric purity; it was she, likewise, who sent an expedition into the "land of Punt" (Eritrea and Somaliland), in search of perfumes. Was she the charitable girl who saved the little abandoned Israelite? Flavius Josephus, the Jewish historian, recounts that Moses, in his youth, had commanded an Egyptian army in a war in Nubia. The story would clearly be that Hatshepsut rescued and brought up Moses, and conferred high charges on him. When she died her son-in-law Tuthmosis III, who hated her (he had her name removed from monuments), drove out the late favourite and persecuted the Jews.

There are many objections to this attractive hypothesis. In the first place, why reduce the sojourn of Israel in Egypt? Is it likely that that proud people would have exaggerated the length of the time during which they were slaves? And, on the other hand, if the Exodus took place in about 1440 B.C., the Hebrews would have been in Palestine in the thirteenth century; how is it then that the Bible makes no mention of the dramatic events which took place there under the Nineteenth Dynasty?

After the political and religious crisis brought about by Amenophis IV, the revolutionary, the devout impiety of Ikhnaton,[4] a sincere, stupid man restored order. This was Tutankhamun, whose funeral treasures, discovered in 1922, made his name famous. A new dynasty now arose that returned to the offensive in Syria. Across this defensive outpost of Egypt, Seti I made several expeditions, as far as the Taurus mountains. His son was Rameses II. The destiny of this king, who was certainly remarkable, but by no means to the point of deserving to be the only Pharaoh whose name is known to the world, is a strange one. Everyone has seen the photograph of his mummy, that aged face whose expression of lucid energy embalming has not obliterated. One of his obelisks stands in the Place de la Concorde. Tall, graceful, and powerful, during the sixty-five years of his reign this king experienced everything that power and life can give.

Under dramatic circumstances, Rameses II saved Egypt. This was early in his reign, at Kadesh on the Orontes,[5] when he was twenty-five years of age. The danger came from those Hittites whom we have already observed on the move six or seven centuries earlier. This term, "Hittite," is a little puzzling, one of those biblical names that arouses conjecture. What is implied by "sons of Heth"? Who were these Hittites, or Hethites, from whom Abraham purchased the cave of Machpelah? The Greeks knew of

[4] *See* paragraph below.
[5] *See* map, p. 7.

these people only in legend, as the Amazons. A hundred years ago in 1830, the French archaeologist Charles Texier discovered, near the village of Boghazkeui in Turkey, about sixty-three miles to the south of Sinope, extensive ruins; no attention was paid to them. In 1893, Chantre and Boissier brought to light in the same region cuneiform tablets which they declared to be in an unknown language. Finally in 1906, Dr. Winckler, a German, came upon a mine of documents: 2500 tablets. In 1915 the Czech professor Hrozný began to read them and published a grammar. The Hittites made their appearance in history. Now we see in them an essential element of the ancient world of Asia Minor, fully civilized, from which sprang the roots of Greek civilization.

Their origin was Aryan. They arrived, apparently, from Europe by way of the Aegean. On their monuments they are often represented with straight noses continuous with their foreheads, like the Hellenes. Their language bears a certain resemblance to archaic Greek, as though both had been derived from a common source. Their political system was established on a hierarchy of petty kings under one supreme king, which curiously recalls that one whom the Homeric Greeks, in speaking of the siege of Troy, called the "King of Kings." Well-situated in the heart of Asia Minor, controlling the routes from the Mediterranean to the Fertile Crescent, owners of rich iron mines, which assured great power of arms for them, they subjected neighbouring peoples whom they civilized. For the nineteenth to the seventeenth centuries, they enjoyed a period of power and imperialist splendour. Their supreme king, who described himself as "my sun," had subjected the whole of Asia Minor and driven wedges as far as Babylon. A period of decline followed, corresponding to the Hyksos domination in Egypt, whose cause was clearly the same as that which subdued the Pharaohs. Re-established during the fourteenth century, the kings of "Hatti" resumed their program of conquest. One of them, Shuppululiumash, a sort of Hittite Louis XIV, profiting from the crises into which the mystic Ikhnaton had plunged Egypt, established his power throughout the whole of northern Syria. From 1360 to 1260, the capital of Asia

Minor, Khattus (now Boghazkeui), was the veritable centre of Eastern politics, the place in which the essential combinations of power were held together. There was a deadly conflict between this young race, in full tide of expansion, and the ancient kingdom of the Pharaohs.

The conflict broke out soon after Rameses II came into power. The old Hittite king, Muttalish, with thirty-five hundred chariots, laid a trap for the young and presumptuous Pharaoh. His army was split into two before Kadesh, and Rameses seemed doomed to perish. His personal courage and the Hittite love of pillage enabled him to turn the tide of battle. The outcome was indecisive, which was at least better than a disaster. Peace was signed, in a meticulous treaty written in the bureaucratic language of the times—Babylonian. Rameses even married a Hittite princess, and for posterity had himself represented as a victor in his fine chariot drawn by his two favourite mares, "Joy of the Goddesses" and "Glory of Thebes."

It seems unlikely that if the Hebrews had witnessed these events the Bible would not have made any mention of them. Furthermore, according to the shorter chronology, the Pharaoh who persecuted Israel would have been Rameses II. This agrees very well with what we know of his methods, of his desire to rid Egypt of all Asiatic influence, and above all of his great building undertakings. For Rameses II was a fanatical builder, an enthusiastic overseer. Not content to build, he confiscated and had his name written on the monuments left by his fathers; for speed, he often used sham effects, paintings made to look like sculpture, hollowed out moulds instead of relief. But Karnak and Luxor are full of his gigantic works. And in order to command the frontier of the isthmus, he built a new capital in the Delta, on the eastern side, a magnificent city for which he requisitioned labour from all available sources. It seems likely that this was the "City of Rameses" at which the Bible tells us the Israelites laboured; the bricks of their servitude created these enormous buildings.

On this hypothesis, we can no longer identify the "daughter of Pharaoh," but is it not more credible that she was one of those charming creatures whose likenesses the Nineteenth Dynasty has left us, a young girl with braided hair and subdued smile, who presses a lotus flower against her breast, rather than the imperious Hatshepsut? The Pharaoh of the Exodus would then be Mineph-tah, the thirtieth son of Rameses II; he came late to the throne (owing to his father's long life), and had great difficulties in Palestine and Syria, was compelled to send many expeditions there, and at last retreated on to African soil under the threat of the people of the coast. One can readily believe that Moses might have profited by this weakness. It is on these grounds that the date generally given for the Exodus is about 1225 B.C.[6]

THE EGYPTIAN INFLUENCE

A sojourn of several centuries in the country of the Nile could not fail to exercise a profound influence on the Israelites. And in fact, throughout the Bible, Egypt is ceaselessly evoked. But in most cases this is in terms of opprobrium. "The strength of Pharaoh be your shame," we read in the Prophet Isaiah (xxx:3), who further calls the Egyptians fools, consulters of magicians, idols and necromancers, trembling before the God of Israel (xix:1–25). The Egyptian imprint was something that the chosen people were to combat in themselves.

Moses himself had an Egyptian side, the most obscure element in his character—the super-normal gifts upon which the Holy Scripture insists. That "wisdom of Egypt" in which he was learned was perhaps that esoteric knowledge held in high regard on the borders of the Nile; a magician was called *rekh khetu*, "he who knows things." We see Moses engaged in a match of sortileges with the native sorcerers; in the *Contes Populaires d'Egypte* collected by Maspero, the magicians accomplish prodigies, such as dividing the waters of a river, cutting off a man's head and replacing it, giving life to a wax effigy of a crocodile, becoming

[6] Father de Vaux (*See* note above, p. 28) gives for the occupation of Canaan the second half of the thirteenth century, which would place the Exodus in the second half of the reign of Rameses II.

invisible, etc. The memory of these exploits is retained in the Greek tradition in the shape-shifting of Proteus, described by Homer.

Nevertheless the great difference between the thaumaturgy of Moses and the magic of Egypt is that the former was not designed to constrain God. The "professors" of the Nile sought by their secret means to attain divinity; the sinner even, who deserves to be condemned, can escape if he knows the formulae—an immoral inconsistency in a religion that contains, nevertheless, so much that is admirable. Moses, prophet of God, used his powers only in order to accomplish his mission.

It was evidently from Egypt that the Israelites borrowed the notion of a priestly caste. The priesthood constituted a real power under the Pharaohs themselves, sometimes against the Pharaohs. Assembled in wealthy colleges, politically very active (particularly the priests of Ammon), they were formidable upholders of the national tradition. The Levites were to play—sometimes to excess—the same role in the destiny of Israel. Moses belonged to the tribe of Levi that he dedicated to the service of God. Perhaps they had preserved the cult of the One God in its purest form; they would then have served as the nucleus about which the race of Israel was to crystallize.

For there is no doubt, in the case of the Exodus as with the migration of Ur, that the deepest causes of the migrations were matters of faith. Egypt was a country saturated in theology, a profoundly religious country. Too much so, indeed! Polytheism there took the strangest forms; a whole pantheon, in the guise of a menagerie, a whole fauna of deities, the falcon Horus, the goose Geb, the crocodile Sebek, the bull Apis, the hippopotamus, the vulture, the adder, besides all those gods half human half animal, with a woman's body and a cow's head, a lion's beard and a human face. Dominating that mythology was the far purer image of Osiris, the god who died to overcome death.

Religion occupied an important place in Egypt. The only monuments built to endure were temples—not palaces—and tombs. A century before Moses a strange incident occurred. A Pharaoh,

Amenophis IV, the most mysterious figure of all the dynasties, had attempted a revolution in the name of religion. The portraits reveal him as of the purest Egyptian type, with his large cranium and thin neck, which seemed to carry his too heavy head with difficulty. His eyes are obliquely set in his long face; and everything about him seems on fire with a strange passion. His wife, Nefertiti, who resembles him, has all the charm of a flower of decadence. Nevertheless this fragile pair attempted the most audacious revolution ever known in Egypt. In order to rid himself of the power of the priests of Ammon, Amenophis IV broke up their god, Ammon. He proclaimed another, Aton; he himself changed his name to Ikhnaton, "the favourite of Aton"; Thebes was abandoned as a capital, and farther away the revolutionary constructed a new city, "the horizon of Aton," that El Amarna where a complete set of his diplomatic archives has been discovered. All the customs of Egypt were overthrown; the property of Ammon was secularized, and his name chiselled off monuments. Art itself changed under foreign influence, Cretan no doubt; Ikhnaton substituted a ravishing realism for the traditional hieratic style.

This religious revolution was not to trouble for long the course of Egypt's destiny. Ikhnaton's own son-in-law, Tutankhamun, reverted to the accustomed gods; two dynasties later, the priests of Ammon were to supplant the Pharaohs and become kings. But the attempt shows to what extent religious verity counted in Egypt. If it is not certain that Ikhnaton had reached the conception of the single God, he at least conceived Aton as the supreme divinity, to whom all the others were subject. And he speaks of his god in such terms of love that no one who has any sense of mysticism can fail to be moved.[7]

It is natural that, even while holding itself apart, Israel should have felt the influence of this atmosphere charged with religiosity. Some of these influences are purely external; in the same way

[7] See A. Weigall, *Life and Times of Akhnaton, Pharaoh of Egypt*, London: Butterworth, 1933; and J. D. S. Pendlebury, *Tell el-Amarna*, London: Dickson, 1935.

that certain rites had been borrowed from Mesopotamia and Canaan, we find in the Mosaic religion certain traits of an Egyptian character. The Ark of the Covenant doubtless owed much to the sacred boats of Ammon that the priests of Egypt carried in religious ceremonies. The *Cherubim* were, in origin, men winged like falcons, imitated from the cult of Horus (later they took on an Assyrian appearance). The cultural ornaments of the Levites, robes and pectorals, are of Egyptian origin. All this is of little importance; what matters is the significance accorded to the rites.

There was a deeper influence also. It had its good side. There are parallels between the Commandments of Moses and the *Book of the Dead*; it is to the credit of the antique morality of Egypt that it made Israel become conscious of the law. There is a similar parallel between Psalm CIV of the Bible and Ikhnaton's hymn to his god; both speak of the mystical glory of the creator; there is nothing, however, to show in which direction the influence was exerted, and whether the revolutionary Pharaoh was not familiar with Israelite modes of thought. But besides these noble influences there were others which were less so. Idolatry pure and simple did undoubtedly contaminate the people of Israel during their long sojourn in the land of idols. The purity of the mission could only be safeguarded by rejecting all syncretisms, all compromises. The district in which the Israelites were installed was just such a corridor region as was likely to bring about a mingling of races and ideas; in his capital in the Delta, Rameses II had temples built to all sorts of gods, to Astarte, for example, the Asian goddess. To leave, to return to the desert, was to break free from these temptations to idolatry. Moses sternly compelled the people of God confided to him to do this.

THE DEPARTURE FOR THE DESERT

Moses has that grandeur without charm that characterizes all true leaders of men, of those who leave an indelible stamp on the heart of a nation. With him, the Bible tells us (Exod. XII:38), a cohort, a mass of people, departed. For forty years he kept them in the desert; and Goethe, who is amazed that a man of action should mark time for so long, fails to see that this is exactly the time it takes for a generation to die out, those accustomed to the amenities of Egypt, and for another, hardened in the desert, to grow up.

How many of these refugees were there? "Six hundred thousand on foot that were men, besides children" (Exod. xii:37). Elsewhere, "a great multitude of people" is mentioned. This seems a great many. The chance of supplying some two million people in the open desert for forty years would be a slender one. There has been discussion of the reading of the figure 600, and of the meaning of the word, "thousand." At the time of their first great military effort, the Israelites numbered only forty thousand. The particulars given in the Bible seem to suggest a figure of this order.

The Pharaoh, alarmed by the catastrophes called down on his country, decided to allow the Hebrews to leave. They left forthwith and at night! They fled, carrying what goods they could, clothes, bread that had not had time to rise, and, which is to be noted, Joseph's sarcophagus. They did not take the direct route which would have led them to Canaan along the coast. Besides passing over desert whose sands at times were perilous, it would have led them into the Holy Land by way of an even greater danger, the country occupied by the Philistines. They went, therefore, due east, towards Succoth, skirting the Wadi Tamilat. In this Exodus, many places mentioned with precision in the Bible have not been identified. Etham, the first halt, was perhaps near Lake Timsah.[8] Next, the great caravan made a bend and returned towards the south-west, in the direction of Phihahiroth, near Migdal, opposite Baal-Saphon (no doubt a temple of Asiatic divinities); this was God's order. He Himself was present and protected the travellers. He went before them "by day in a pillar of a cloud, to lead them the way; and by night in a pillar of fire, to give them light" (Exod. xiii:21). And the zig-zag was also His will, in order that His power should be made manifest. Pharaoh was

[8] *See* MAP OF SINAI, p. 83.

deceived, and believing that the Hebrews were lost in the desert, decided to take advantage of this to settle accounts with them.

At the time when the Israelites were on the eastern side of the bitter lakes, the king set out in pursuit of them with his chariots. "They were sore afraid: and the children of Israel cried out unto the Lord. And they said unto Moses, Because there were no graves in Egypt, hast thou taken us away to die in the wilderness?" (Exod. xiv:10–11). They added that they would have preferred servitude to the danger that now threatened them. Such reactions were to be frequent during the course of the Exodus; that rabble was continually on the verge of rebellion. But the leader remained calm: "Have no fear, the Lord shall fight for you!" The angel of God that went before them took his place behind. The pillar of cloud that led them took its place on the rear, dark on one side, lighting their way on the other. And all night the east wind, the breath of God, piled up the waters because Moses had stretched forth his powerful hand. Over the dry bed Israel set out while the waves, held back, formed a double barrier. Having seen this manoeuvre, the Egyptians came in pursuit; in their turn they entered the dry belt; but the wheels of their chariots stuck in the sand and mud; while they were trying to disengage them, Moses again made a gesture, and at dawn the sea, resuming its accustomed place, submerged the army of the Pharaoh.

Three thousand years ago, the branch of the Red Sea which ends on the beach of Suez stretched much farther north, communicating with the bitter lakes and perhaps with Lake Timsah. Kolzum, the port of embarkation for India during the Middle Ages, is today a ruin, six miles inland. "The Sea" of the Scripture may indeed have been one of the lakes now traversed by the Suez Canal. Over these shallow mudbanks the east wind that raises opaque clouds of dust—was the mysterious column such a cloud?—could likewise blow back the waters. It is true that the Arabian "sirocco," the *kadim*, begins suddenly, and as suddenly drops. Is not that great wind the breath of God?

In the joy of this spectacular miracle the Israelites acclaimed their leader and praised God; Miriam, the visionary, sister of Moses, danced to the music of their tambourines. Quickly encouraged, quickly despondent, people are always so. A leader of men can count neither on their gratitude nor their fidelity.

SINAI

The country into which the fugitives now penetrated is rather a dry steppe than a desert. It is not a country of sands like the great *erg* of the Sahara, nor like the stony *hammada*, the country of death. There are tufts of grey plants, sometimes even tamarisks. But in comparison with the pleasantness of Egypt, it was a severe test for the travellers! At Marah, the wells yielded only bitter water, like the magnesium pans of southern Algeria. Outcry from the people! The leader found certain plants which made the water palatable. Then food was scarce; murmurs again: "In Egypt we sat by the fleshpots and did eat bread to the full." The great leader must work miracle upon miracle. One evening quails flew down near the camp. Next day dew lay on the ground, and when it had dried, the ground was covered with "a small round thing, as small as the hoarfrost on the ground" (Exod. xvi:14). "What is it?" the crowd asked. "This is the bread which the Lord hath given you to eat!" Moses replied. This bread was manna, the divine food. "The manna was as coriander seed, and the colour thereof as the colour of bdellium"; ground and baked, "the taste of it was as the taste of fresh oil" (Numbers xi:7—8). The desert even now has secret sources of food for its initiates; in Syria, the *kema*, a whitish truffle with the flavour of an artichoke, leafless and rootless, swells up the ground; and all over the Arabian peninsula, the wood of a variety of tamarisk exudes a honey-like substance that the nomads call *man-es-sama*, "gift of heaven." The miraculous manna with which, for forty years, the Lord supplied His people must have been more sustaining. Hunger being overcome, thirst still had to be slaked, and, striking the rock with that staff which God had long ago placed in his hand, Moses caused living water to flow.

In addition to these natural difficulties, arose others. Bedouins attacked the caravan—the Amalekites, who must be fought. The engagement took place near Raphidim. From the height of a hill, Moses watched the battle, commanded by the people's future leader, Joshua. Praying to God, his staff raised, he drove back from afar off the onslaught of the enemy; when his arm was lowered, Amalek regained the ascendancy. But the victory remained with Israel—yet another proof of the divine protection! A yet more weighty attestation was to follow.

They had reached the foot of Mount Sinai. It was a strange place, of fantastic grandeur, worthy to be the site of God's revelation of His power. Blue granite and purple porphyry gave it the aspect of an apocalyptic world, where mineral alone reigned supreme. For months a rainless heat beat down that cracked the rocks into gigantic debris. Sometimes terrible storms, cracking the rocks to their very foundations, echoed from the walls of the ravines with the very voice of eternity. Nevertheless this lifeless place was not entirely unvisited; even today a monastery there holds in remembrance the revelation of Moses; and from the remotest antiquity the Pharaohs mined copper, malachite and precious stones there. Semitic tribes frequented it. The old moon-god Sin is perhaps the origin of the name of the country; and a divine image was venerated there, in which was blended, apparently, Ishtar of Akkad and Egyptian Isis, as "the goddess of turquoises," protectress of miners.

"There Israel camped before the mount." But the voice of the Eternal had summoned Moses to a new contemplation. "Thus shalt thou say to the house of Jacob . . .: ye have seen what I did unto the Egyptians, and how I bare you on eagle's wings and brought you unto myself. Now therefore, if ye will obey my voice indeed, and keep my covenant, then ye shall be a peculiar treasure unto me above all people: for all the earth is mine: and ye shall be unto me a kingdom of priests, and an holy nation" (Exod. xix:3–6). "And all the people answered together, and said, All the Lord hath spoken we will do."

Until this time, God had shown Himself to the inspired in the intimacy of friendship; now He was to appear in terror and power. Where are we to locate that "Horeb" whence came the sound of a superhuman trumpet? Several summits of over six thousand feet lay claim to the honour of the apparition; one of them is to this day known as the Jebel Musa, "Mount Moses." The whole range indeed might well inspire terror. The leader forbade anyone, on pain of death, to violate the divine solitude. Then he climbed amid the thunders and lightnings and a thick cloud on the mountain that was all smoky. Face to face with the Supreme Power, he heard the voice that dictated to him the Commandments, on which were to be founded the law of the people, "of priests and kings," the Decalogue. A mystical faith upheld him in this naked encounter; its light remained in his face, whose very skin shone.

"And all the people saw the thunderings, and the lightnings, and the noise of the trumpet, and the mountain smoking . . ." and they said to Moses, who had come down to them, "Speak thou with us and we will hear: but let not God speak with us, lest we die." And the inspired man replied, "Fear not: for God is come to prove you, and that His fear may be before your faces that ye sin not." And the Covenant was concluded with rites that recall those of their ancestors: an altar was built, and twelve *massebah*, or menhirs, were erected, as in former times, one for each tribe; victims were sacrificed, and the people pledged to fidelity. And Moses went up again, escorted by Aaron and seventy elders who likewise saw God.

For a second time, the leader of the people came down and now he wished, no doubt, to prove the people. He would go up again to the holy place, leaving his men to their own devices; the elders and Aaron were to direct them. He himself, in a final retreat of forty days and forty nights, resumed his listening to the divine voice; God dictated to him, with extreme minuteness, the rites and details of the law. Let the people keep themselves pure during this time! Let them be proved worthy!

But on his return, the leader was to learn that one can put small trust in the wisdom of the masses; the resolutions passed by assemblies of men seldom reflect the will of God.

"WRITE THIS!"

In all this portion of the biblical narrative, one cannot fail to observe a singular insistence on invoking the written testimony. Already after the battle of Rephidim, God had said to Moses, "Write this for a memorial in a book" (Exod. xvii:14). After the revelation of Sinai, He gave the same command, "Write thou these words!" (Exod. xxxiv:27). In Numbers, in Deuteronomy, in the Book of Joshua, we find the same indications. Everything suggests that the Israelites who later wrote down the tradition had in their hands very ancient texts.

But, for a people who had come from Egypt, where every temple wall, and even the humblest tombs, were covered with hieroglyphics, the fact of writing could not have been so remarkable as to require stressing in this way. This insistence surely corresponds to an intention. In 1905, Flinders Petrie, the English archaeologist, discovered in the very heart of Sinai, in that part of Serabit whence the Pharaohs used to receive their turquoises, curious inscriptions engraved on a sphinx, two statues of men and seven steles. They provoked much discussion. Were they drawings or letters? These signs seemed to suggest an alphabet, incomplete to be sure, but in which might be recognized, it was thought, a source of modern letters. Since then many discoveries have shown that the first beginnings from which our alphabet must have arisen belong to an even earlier period; some authorities say about 2000 B.C. Throughout the country between the Taurus mountains and Sinai, these ancient writings have been discovered; at Ras-Shamra, opposite the island of Cyprus, archaic Hebrew, dating from about 1450 B.C., written in a script of twenty-seven characers; at Lakhis, in southern Palestine, a monolith of the thirteenth century B.C. carries about its base an unmistakable alphabetic inscription.

In what does this invention consist? A system of twenty-five or thirty signs, capable of rendering all the subtleties of language, was substituted for the complicated writings—cuneiform and Babylonian, Egyptian or Hittite hieroglyphics—in use in Mesopotamia, in Asia Minor and on the Nile. The invention was made when men of genius discovered the possibility of reducing syllables into simple sounds. In the beginning they limited themselves to writing consonants, not vowels—and Hebrew was to bear the mark of that omission. Moreover, the letters were not clearly defined. At first there were eighty, later fifty, and finally thirty-six. Gradually perfected, this prodigious invention was to revolutionize the world of thought.

What was the origin of letters? We can easily trace our Latin characters to the Phoenician alphabet, for the Phoenicians, marvellous intermediaries of the Mediterranean world, were the propagators of this new method. But from what pictographic and syllabic system were borrowed the signs that have been isolated? Some incline to the view that they were the Egyptian hieroglyphics; others, the cuneiform; it is sometimes suggested that Crete was the origin, the kingdom of Minos whence it seems that so many elements of civilization were broadcast over the world. Perhaps the invention, as so often happens, was perfected in several places at the same time, according to different systems that the traders of Tyre and Sidon later systematized.

The fact that the most ancient specimens of the alphabet have been found in Sinai gives rise to strange speculation. From these inscriptions of Serabit, we have proof that a Semitic script of this kind was in existence in these countries to which Moses came Did the children of Israel, abandoning the written language of their late oppressors, adopt the new system? To the revelation of faith there would then be added an intellectual revelation; this is no more than a hypothesis, in the margin of a history fraught with so much significance.[9]

TEMPTATIONS AND REVOLTS

Moses was still on the mountain when God warned him. During his absence the people whom he had thought were faithful had fallen into idolatry. "A stiff-necked people," rebellious against

[9] It is to be noted that the Hellenistic historian Eupolemes affirms that Moses invented the alphabet. But he is full of errors and fantasies.

good principles, hardened in pride. The leader came down in haste, carrying the tables on which the law was written. In the plain, the camp was making merry, feasting and rejoicing. And in the midst of their tents arose their abject idol. Was it a cow, like the Egyptian Isis-Hathor? Or a bull like that which the hymns of Sumeria and Akkad describe as "pure and dazzling," that in Crete is honoured by picturesque games, and venerated alike in Cyprus, Rhodes and the country of the Hittites? Aaron, a man of weak faith, had given way to the appeals of the mob; for the immaterial, transcendent God, he substituted an idol, the golden calf; this strong beast better symbolized power than an abstraction coming out of the clouds and dispersing with them.

"Moses' anger waxed hot, and he cast the tables out of his hands, and brake them beneath the mount. And he took the calf which they had made and burned it in the fire, and ground it to powder, and strawed it upon the water, and made the children of Israel drink of it" (Exod. xxxII:19–20). This apostasy merited exemplary punishment. "Who is on the Lord's side?" cried the leader. And the Levites "gathered about him." The idolatrous rebellion was stamped out; three thousand men perished. This was the first serious crisis of the Exodus; but it was not to be the last.

Returned to their fidelity, the guilty people, pardoned, resumed their service of the Most High. God gave new tables of the Law. In order to house them they built the Ark of the Covenant, the holy coffer, which was to accompany the caravan. The Passover was celebrated on the anniversary of the flight from Egypt. And they set out again with renewed confidence towards the north, towards Canaan, in a long orderly procession, each banner under the command of a chief, the strength of the migrants sustained by prayer.

The desert of Paran, not far from the Gulf of Akaba, is severe. The complaining and the state of suppressed rebellion began again. Manna was no doubt delicious, but in the long run meagre fare. Empty stomachs turn readily to blasphemy. The Eternal Power answered their reproaches with punishments. On one occasion at Taberah, the tents took fire. On another, having in a bout of gluttony eaten high quails, the Israelites were attacked by a sort of eczema. Even of his own family, Moses was severely critical. Aaron and Miriam opposed him, and at Hazeroth the man of God cured his sister of leprosy with which God had punished her. Stage by stage, from one dramatic episode to another, the troop at last arrived at the oasis of Kadesh, and there set up their pickets.

Coming from the desert, this place seemed a very paradise. About a hundred and thirty miles long, with scrub-covered hills, it was not verdant like some of the oases of the Sahara; there one did not, as at Marakesh or Touggourt, see under the banded trembling palm leaves rich orange trees sheltering strawberry-plants and long beds of vegetables. The water was too scarce to support vegetation all over the oasis; but in the hollows many wells were bordered with fine turf and sometimes springs even ran out upon the grass. Fruit-trees grew, and irrigation made possible the cultivation of cereals. The rich grass that grew in spring, spangled with crocus flowers and small hyacinths, was a royal feast for the cattle accustomed to the dry scrub of the plains.

For more than thirty years the fugitive tribes remained settled here. Had they given up all hope of reaching the Promised Land, which now was not very far away? No, for early in their stay there, they had sent out spies into Canaan; but their reports had plunged everyone into despondency. Yes, it was a fine country, a land "flowing with milk and honey"; they brought back fruits with them and enormous grapes! But they must expect difficulties, for the cities seemed strong, and the inhabitants ready to defend them. To which others had added: The inhabitants? Monsters, giants, beside whom the children of Israel seemed like grasshoppers! The anxiety turned to despair and finally to panic. They cried, shouted and tried to stone Moses, to nominate a new leader to take them back to Egypt. Two of the spies protested, Joshua and Caleb, the best of them. The people were nevertheless on the verge of sedition. The anger of God broke forth. He threatened to destroy that race so stubbornly rebellious; Moses interceded, implored pardon. The pardon would be granted; very well, Israel should survive, but the guilty should never enter Canaan. They were to drag on in Kadesh, and only when that generation had passed should the conquest take place; Joshua and Caleb alone were to be spared.

Now the crowd went from one extreme to the other, as always! They would get out at once! They would march to attack Canaan! The rash attempt ended in defeat. The Palestinians repulsed the Israelite troops and pursued them as far as Sephat. The Israelites were compelled to install themselves in the oasis and submit to God's verdict.

The historical significance of the stay in Kadesh, of these rebellions and repressions, seems clear. All this evidently corresponded to the period during which Moses imposed on the people with his strong hand laws, an organization, dogmas. A rabble left Egypt; a nation entered Canaan. But this sojourn in Kadesh evokes something more than a period of severe discipline; it seems to be marked with opprobrium. The Scriptures are silent about these long years, although they are prolix on the theme of the departure. Much later the Prophet Amos, upbraiding the Israelites, reproaches them with their impieties: "Have ye offered unto me sacrifices and offerings in the wilderness forty years, O house of Israel?" (Amos v:25). It seems that even the rite of circumcision was abandoned during that time. In the midst of the desert and its austere virtues, the oasis stands for sin and its licences. Rebellious against God once more, and more gravely than in the days of the golden calf, had they sunk into the apathy of an easy life, or had they scattered, their national unity broken? We do not know. The authors of the book have drawn a veil over this inglorious page of history.

Had Moses himself, the man of God, the hero of faith, been able to stand firm in the midst of these temptations? Perhaps not entirely. What we suspect is very obscure. On a day of drought, in order to provide water for the people, he had struck the rock as before, but he had given way for a moment to doubt. He had said to the people, "Shall I succeed in drawing water from the rock?" and his rod was twice lowered. God, in order to punish him, had decreed that he himself should not enter the Promised Land. A hard punishment for a moment of human weakness. But those souls to whom God has given much have heavier obligations than ours, and their sins weigh more heavily than do those of common sinners.

TOWARDS CANAAN

Crises, rebellions, apostasies, all were finally resolved. Perhaps there was an external reason for the great gathering of strength with which the stay of Israel in Kadesh came to an end. The Pharaoh Minephtah made, at about this time, a fierce expedition into these lands, of which the Bible tells us nothing, but of which we learn from the famous stele,[10] that Israel was one of the victims. It was now necessary to make the resolution to attempt the emigration to Canaan. They set out once more.

Just to the north of Kadesh, the Edomites were solidly installed. They had already even a central organization under a king. Moses asked permission to pass through their lands; he would pay for water and keep strictly to the roads. But Edom was mistrustful at the prospect of seeing that immense horde crossing its pastures; and perhaps the descendants of Esau still felt some bitterness towards the sons of Jacob. They had to make a detour to the east; they skirted Canaan by Transjordania. A local king who attempted to prevent their passage was brushed aside. They coasted the Dead Sea, followed the heights that dominate it and reached the Arnon.

This was desert, still desert, always desert! Water failed, they were weary of manna. "Their souls loathed this light bread." Generations may pass, but human behaviour remains always the same. Famine quickly leads to revolts. Once more God had to punish. Serpents with venomous stings infested the camp. And once more the miracle-worker saved this incorrigible people. He placed the image of a serpent on a stake; whoever was bitten and who, in token of his faith, cast a suppliant look towards this symbol was healed. Excavations in Palestine have brought to light serpents

[10] *See* p. 88.

like that made by Moses; at Gaza, a bronze asp, contemporary with this incident, and elsewhere others in clay. We detect here one of those local influences to which the Israelites were so readily subject; the serpent was one of the totems of the country; five centuries later Hezekiah had to destroy that metal emblem, for the relic of Moses became an idol.

From the Arnon onwards there was war. The tribes inhabiting the regions across the Jordan were of Semitic origin, more or less closely related to the Hebrews. Those coming from the north, Ammonites, others from the south, Midianites, and others again more or less installed, Moabites. To all these, Israel appeared as a new arrival and undesirable. Moses had done well to adopt a policy of prudence and to seek to avoid conflict; these peoples united and adopted all possible means against the invading horde.

A king of Moab even called upon the invisible powers to stop the advance of Israel. In Padan-aram, a land steeped in religiosity, lived a magician, Balaam. He was summoned. This man knew and feared God. As he travelled southwards, an angel of the Lord barred his way. He did not see the angel, and tried to pass; but, as in fairy tales, animals perceive things that man does not discern, his she-ass had recognized the angel and refused to advance. Balaam beat her; and the she-ass opened her mouth and spoke. Enlightened by this miracle, the magician saw the angel. Wherever he was going he was not to speak words other than those that God would speak through him.

Cursing one's enemies was an ancient custom. Before coming to blows, the warriors of Homer cursed in this way, in a solemn manner, and in Egypt potteries have been found on which the Pharaohs inscribed the names of their adversaries, in order to break them by magic. The king of Moab installed the magician in a high place with the Israelite camp in view. Here he was to pronounce the words of execration! But God put into the mouth of the magician words far other than those that were looked for—a sequence of oracles on Israel, exalting her power and foretelling disaster for all her enemies.

Israel was also threatened by more secret dangers; men are always more in danger from their intimate complicities than from their worst enemies. In the land of Moab was practised one of those erotic cults of which the East has produced so many examples. About the temple of a local Baal, "Baal-peor"—from which we have the name Belphegor—Israel abandoned itself to debauchery among the temple prostitutes, and the daughters of Moab invited them to sacrifice to their gods (Numbers xxv:1). To root out idolatry from this people and give it a sense of its own greatness was certainly a superhuman task. Moses took action. A man of Israel who had gone so far as to bring a Midianite woman into the camp itself was killed on the spot when a spear, thrown by the great-nephew of the leader, pinned both him and his companion to the earth. And Moses hurled the chosen people into a war of extermination.

Each tribe raised a thousand men. The Midianites, taken by surprise, were defeated; their five sheiks were killed, immense booty was captured besides prisoners, both men and women, in thousands. Moses imposed a terrible measure. All the prisoners were killed, even the women—especially the women—for they had led Israel into infidelity. Only the children and virgins were spared. Even the booty was burned, as something irremediably tainted. This was the first example of these systematic destructions, the result of vows, of which the period of Joshua and the Judges was to know many examples.

The war against Midian resulted in the conquest of Transjordania as far as Jabbok. Israel now had excellent bases of attack from which to proceed to conquer Canaan. Moses' task was thus completed. He had now only to die, in obedience to God.

MOUNT NEBO

Among the mountains of Moab that dominate from a height of five thousand feet the deep gulley through which the Jordan flows into the Dead Sea, the Nebo stands out as one of the highest summits. From its peak one can see a great part of the plain, the yellow river that sparkles among willows and reeds, the mimosas on the hills, the city of Jericho. There Moses climbed to see from afar the land so greatly desired, on which he was never to set foot.

He had worked incessantly for the future, established the basis of a veritable code, planned the organization to be instituted after the conquest, the partition of land and cities. This code, the expression of the divine will, he had placed, with the tables of the Law, in the protection of the Ark. He had, finally, chanted a long canticle to the glory of the Most High, exalting His merits and His benefits, blessed the tribes of Israel, and laid his hands on Joshua, who was to succeed him.

"And Moses was an hundred and twenty years old when he died. His eye was not dim, nor his natural force abated." The Children of Israel mourned for thirty days. God Himself laid him in the earth—in spite of Satan who, according to a Jewish tradition, of which we find an echo in the Epistle of St. Jude, wished to dispute with Him the claim to the body of His great servant. "No man knoweth of his sepulchre unto this day" (Deuteronomy xxxiv:6).

II

THE LAW AND THE LAND

THE NATION OF ISRAEL

WE KNOW LITTLE of Moses the man, that powerful personality who is nevertheless overshadowed by his work. On the other hand, the historical and providential significance of his achievement is clear. The scattered tribes in the Delta had the sense of being members of the same race, but they were not a nation. Moses drew them together, made of them a federation, and led them towards a new country; he tightened the threads of national solidarity about a very high religious ideal.

This transition from anarchy to nationhood involved a hardening of customs and institutions. We are never again to find the tranquil sweetness of the patriarchal period. Renan, lamenting this, fails to see that the transformation was necessary. Moses in this way safeguarded the heirs of the Promise; left to themselves, the Hebrew tribes would have been lost; the "stiff-necked" nation was to safeguard its unity and survive.

Moses was the first of the great national leaders thrown up by the people, who expressed in his actions the meaning of their most secret purposes. He brought to light the foundation of all nationalism, the sense of collective discipline, administrative firmness, the love of a country and the faith that implants self-consciousness in the collective mind. It was from him, besides, that proceeded that intensity of life that for centuries animated Israel, and that transformed a grumbling and disorganized rabble, the survivors of the great exile, into the champions of the holy war.

We have seen him in a series of crises, establishing discipline. He never presented it as an end in itself. He never proclaimed the values of established order in a conservative sense; but rather,

as a revolutionary, he required order for the purposes of the task
to be performed, which disorder would have brought to nothing.
In everything he did he envisaged the future, and was pledged
to it.

The administrative organization rested with the tribes. There
were twelve of these, plus one, that of the Levites, who assumed
the religious functions and who were therefore scattered throughout the other tribes. The bond which united the members was
understood to be a blood-tie; each tribe claimed descent from one
of the sons of Jacob. As a matter of fact, the tribe was a federation
of those clans that lived near each other, numerous enough to
defend themselves in case of attack, but not too numerous for the
pastures that had to support them. Well-defined obligations
existed between the men who composed the tribe, chief among
which was that of the avenging of blood. If one of its members
was killed, an entire group regarded itself as having been attacked, and took up the vendetta. The exclusiveness of the tribes
took a long time to break down, but it gave rise to fertile emula-
tion and an admirable pride. Nothing could be more different
from the Egyptian fellah, conscript labourers forever ordered
about by officials, than the nomadic Israelites who would submit only to a leader whose prestige they recognized. A democratic
ideal existed, which was never to be lost. Moses himself had to
argue, persuade and punish his men. His whole purpose was to
maintain the bond between these twelve groups scattered across
the steppes. Several times he took the census, the "Numbers" of
the tribes; above all, he gave them those ideals that could best
preserve their unity, by engaging them in action.

JAHWEH

Moses is, in the Hebrew religious history, the man who revealed the *name* of God. In the encounter of the burning bush, he
had exclaimed, "Behold, when I come unto the children of Israel,
and shall say unto them, The God of your fathers hath sent me
unto you; and they shall say to me, What is his name? what shall
I say unto them?" (Exod. III:13). And, bold as the question was,

God did not conceal the answer. The importance of the event is not easily understood by the modern mind, but in antiquity men attributed a mysterious power to the name, an irresistible potency. We retain certain traces of this belief; we feel very strongly that a name describes a character; we speak of a Don Juan, or a Tartuffe; Balzac chose with great care the sounds that should designate his characters; and in the "Our Father" we still praise the name of God which, as the Commandment says, is not to be taken in vain.

In Mesopotamia and in Egypt the knowledge of a name was regarded as sacred. The ancient Greek philosophers even admitted that there is a connection between things and their names. To name is to call into existence. To know the name of a god is to have the power to invoke him. In the Egyptian legend of Isis we see the god Ra, stung by a serpent, begging the goddess-magician to cure him; and she first of all demands that he should give his name, the secret of his supreme power. Something that our society, desiccated by rationalism, refuses to understand is regarded in the ancient traditions as one of the spiritual foundations of humanity.

"And God said moreover unto Moses, *I am that I am:* and he said, Thus shalt thou say unto the children of Israel, *I am, . . .* the LORD GOD of your fathers, the God of Abraham, the God of Isaac, and the God of Jacob, hath sent me unto you: this is my name for ever, and this is my memorial unto all generations" (Exod. III:15–16). In speaking of Himself, God says, *I am*. When man speaks of Him, he must say, "He is." This latter is to be the name of God as we find it throughout the Bible. *He is* in archaic Hebrew is *Jahweh,* pronounced with the y-sound instead of J. Clement of Alexandria transcribes it so into Greek. As the Hebrew alphabet had no vowels, it was written by means of its four consonants YHWH. When in the Middle Ages the first Hebrew scholars attempted to read the divine tetragram, they speculated as to the vowels, and mistakenly concluded that they were those of another word, *Adonaï,* "the Lord," which is also used in the Bible to praise God. From this arose the inaccurate but solidly traditional reading of Jehovah, used in all our classics.

What is the meaning of that enigmatic formula, *I am that I am?* Countless pages have been written on the subject of those simple words. The study of grammar permits of two interpretations: *Jahweh* could signify "it is"—which expresses the metaphysical idea of the uncreated being, which exists in itself, which requires no thing and no person in order to be: the God of eternity. Or it can mean, "it makes to be," "it realises," that which creates, sustains, keeps promises, God the creator. The two interpretations are in fact linked and the tradition of Israel does not separate them.

At all events, the Bible clearly indicates that the knowledge of the divine name marks an advance. "I am Jahweh," God further said to Moses. "I appeared unto Abraham, unto Isaac, and unto Jacob by the name of El-Shaddai, but by my name of Jahweh was I not known to them" (Exod. vi:2–3). El-Shaddai was the God of power, the mysterious and incalculable power by which everything on earth is regulated. It is the Most High, the Almighty. Jahweh is something more, the same God, the God of the Patriarchs, but defined. One can but marvel at the metaphysical profundity that Moses attained to. In this sphere as in others, he led the chosen people into a new domain. And parallels that have been drawn from other religions of antiquity have but revealed the complete originality of Mosaic monotheism. When in Egypt the revolutionary Pharaoh Ikhnaton praised his god Aton, he knew him as the master of the world, as creator of men and creatures, as the orderer of all things and even as a moral reality "living in the heart of those who love him." But even this falls far short of the sublime vision by which Moses understands Jahweh.

It would be out of place to carry metaphysical analysis too far. Moses' contemporaries probably had only a vague intuition of the immense verities that were implied. But what is clearly important is the development that in the course of generations grew from it and which is implicit in the sacred tetragram. God is unique in His very nature, and not by the exclusive choice of a man or a nation, which differentiates Him absolutely from Hammurabi's

Marduk, or the Egyptian Aton. He is necessarily the God of the
Universe, of the whole of humanity, even if He is known and
served by a specific nation. And the virtues which in Him are
worshipped—bounty, justice, and benevolence—are the natural
attributes of His unique being, since every injustice, every
violence, is opposed to harmony and unity.

This supreme God, Israel recognized as its own. If we take
texts from the Bible relating to a much later period when national
organization had taken on a more rigid form, the basis of the
state that is invoked is still the same: the alliance between the
chosen people and Jahweh. This profound conviction cemented
the national unity. El-Elohim, the God of Abraham, had promised
to the Patriarchs that their posterity should become great and
that Canaan should be theirs. But in relation to Jahweh, Israel
was henceforth to feel itself bound in a more complete depend-
ence: they are the people whose mission is to bear witness to
Him and accomplish His works. Jahweh had singled them out
and, by a miracle, led them out of Egypt. Jahweh had shown
Himself on Sinai, and established the conditions upon which
His protection was to depend: He had repeated the promises of
the Elohim, and announced a glorious destiny. Moses penetrated
thus far in that revelation so magnificently evoked by the image
of the burning bush; and it is this doctrine that his personality
imposed.

Here again, we are struck by the human character of this
theology. Its point of departure is an event in history. Israel, unlike so many nations, does not claim any legendary descent from
God; the revelation took place at a moment of time and was
transmitted through a man. Hebraic humanism which is, together
with that of Athens and of Rome, one of three foundations of our
civilization, depends entirely upon this simple affirmation.

THE DECALOGUE

What is the text that God gave to Moses, that Decalogue inscribed on the tables of the Law? It is a treatise on morality of

the simplest and most natural kind. The Bible has conserved it in Chapter XX of Exodus and in Chapter V of Deuteronomy. There are slight differences of expression between the two passages, but no divergence. Four commandments define the duties towards God: "Thou shalt have no other gods before me; thou shalt not make unto thee any graven image; . . . thou shalt not take the name of the Lord thy God in vain; remember the Sabbath day to keep it holy." And six regulate the relationships of men towards each other. "Honour thy father and thy mother; thou shalt not kill; thou shalt not commit adultery; thou shalt not steal; thou shalt not bear false witness against thy neighbour; thou shalt not covet thy neighbour's goods."

Admirable simplicity! The whole of natural morality is summed up in this short treatise of ten lines; the highest forms of civilization have not in any respect improved upon it, and have at most enlarged its scope to that point of sublimity at which the accent is placed rather on the law of love than on these strict regulations—for love, in a single word, includes them all.[1]

Simple and human as it is, it is natural that the Decalogue should be compared with other treatises in which the same problems are discussed. Mesopotamia and Egypt had both, as we have seen, played a large part in the formation of the elect race. And Moses, learned in "the wisdom of Egypt," would undoubtedly have been familiar with the texts in which the ancient wisdom was recorded. In the land of the Nile, when a man died his soul went to be judged according to its deserts. Many painters have represented that scene in which Ma'at, the lady of Truth, weighs in a pair of scales the heart of the dead man, in the presence of Osiris, while the hideous she-beast Amait, "the Devourer," a cross between a crocodile and a hippopotamus, awaits the verdict ravenously. At that terrible moment the man recites a petition that is preserved for us in the *Book of the Dead*. In particular he says, "I have not dishonoured God, I have not stinted my offerings at the temple. I have not committed any in-

---

[1] The law of love is, however, already indicated in Leviticus xix.

justice, I have not killed men, I have told no lies. I have not committed fornication. I am pure! I am pure!" The resemblance is certainly striking. No less so is the similarity of the Babylonian ritual in which the priest puts questions like these: "Has he outraged any god? Did he hate his ancestors? Did he despise his father and mother? Has he spoken impure things, committed sinful actions? Has he been intimate with the wife of another man? Has he shed the blood of his neighbour? Has he stolen his garment? Has he said 'it is so' instead of 'it is not so'? Has his mouth affirmed what his heart denied?"

These resemblances prove nothing more than the universality of the Mosaic precepts. But the important thing is that the text was given by God, that it was in the nature of a revelation. Thus morality and religion are indissolubly blended in it. Whoever keeps his conscience aright is in communion with God. No doubt the morality of Moses and even more so the morality of his people had not yet attained the heights that we find in the Prophets, much less to the superhuman splendour of the Gospels, but the principle is already stated by which faith in God is associated with good conduct. The Mosaic law, the law of the Prophets, and Christianity are in a direct line. It is as remote from the magic of Egypt, for which the devout act is independent of all moral motives, as it is from those extreme Pharisees who later tended to isolate the practices of a cult to the point of inconsistency alike with conscience and with common sense.

To the Decalogue Moses added a number of decrees which together constitute the Book of the Covenant (in Exodus), and which was evidently also the inspiration of Deuteronomy. The Law of Israel, the Torah, was to be appealed to from the time of Moses to our own day. How well one can picture this great leader of men in his role of lawgiver! Seated before "the tent of meeting," guarded by Joshua, he heard all those who had a complaint to bring against another, or a question to be settled. Sometimes he would enter the tent and pray to Jahweh, who would answer him as a familiar friend. And from the inspired verdicts of the leader a jurisprudence took shape which was afterwards codified.

Here again, the basis was in no way original: we find many of the legislative rulings of Moses in Hammurabi's "decisions of equity," in the old customs of Sumeria and Babylon, in the laws of the Hittites; we gain the impression of dealing here with very ancient traditions of justice which were in force in the whole of Asia at an earlier period, laws already known to the Patriarchs.

In the Mosaic code, everything is envisaged; the position of slaves, blows and wounds, the violation of virgins, damage caused by animals, and a host of other matters! Evidently all this is the outcome of experience, of life itself. These unrelated items reflect the incidents of tribal life.[2] Severe, one is sometimes inclined to say; and the celebrated *Lex talionis* is always cited: ". . . life for life, eye for eye, tooth for tooth, hand for hand, foot for foot, burning for burning, wound for wound, stripe for stripe" (Exod. xxi:23–25). This was the part played by discipline, of which the "stiff-necked people" had much need. But of what rare delicacy, by contrast, are some of the other precepts? "You shall not afflict any widow or fatherless child. . . . If thou lend money to any of my people that is poor by thee, thou shalt not be to him as an usurer, neither shalt thou lay upon him usury, and when thou cuttest down thine harvest in thy field, and hast forgot a sheaf in the field, thou shalt not go again to fetch it; it shall be for the stranger, for the fatherless, and for the widow. . . . If thou buy an Hebrew servant, six years shall he serve: and in the seventh year he shall go out free, for nothing . . . and his wife with him . . . If thou take at all thy neighbour's raiment to pledge, thou shalt deliver it unto him by that the sun goeth down. . . . If thou see the ass of him that hateth thee lying under his burden, and wouldst forbear to help him, thou shalt surely help with him." In these precepts, is there not already the first dawning of the sweetness of the Gospel?

[2] Certain rites covering food, the manner of slaughtering beasts, and of cooking meat, "thou shalt not seethe the kid in his mother's milk," refer no doubt to very ancient practices, or to passing necessities. By giving excessive weight to them, Israel came at last to betray the spirit of the Law to the observance of only the letter.

Such a religion has small need of ritual. Its cult is simple. In reaction against the population of statues that encumbered the temples of the Pharaohs, Moses forbade the representation of God. An image for this still primitive people would constitute a perpetual temptation to regard Jahweh as limited, to identify Him with the object created by human hands. But in the same way as Catholics to this day venerate places at which the Virgin Mary has been seen, their cult was centred about these places where God had manifested Himself. The *Ark* is His "footstool"; when He revealed Himself within the canopy that sheltered the holy box, He appeared between the two cherubim which surmounted it. It was no more than a small casket, three feet in length and under two in breadth, of acacia wood decorated with gold. Rings were fixed to it through which were passed poles upon which it was carried. On its cover, a plaque indicated the place of the Divine Presence, and the only images that were permitted were the two cherubim, the servants that with their wings sheltered the Almighty. In this casket were the two tables on which God's law was inscribed, nothing else. It stood only for the divine protection; it was the Ark, the sign, and the receptacle of the Covenant.

The cult still retained much of the patriarchal simplicity. To God were offered the first fruits of the flocks and of the earth; sacrifices were offered just as in the times of the ancestors. There were, however, new elements. The sanctification of the Sabbath dated from the beginning of the Exodus, from the week in which God gave manna. On the sixth day, Moses ordered a double quantity to be gathered in order that the seventh day should be passed in rest and in returning thanks to Jahweh for His benefits. Three times a year, the people celebrated feasts: the most solemn of these was that of the Azymes, of the Passover, commemorating the time when Jahweh had led Israel out of Egypt, and of the unleavened bread that the people had eaten on that occasion.

But the most important innovation of the Mosaic epoch was

the institution of a priesthood. In the times of the Patriarchs, we find no intermediary between man and God. The more specialized national organization now required the cult to be committed into the hands of men set apart, and not left at the mercy of individual anarchy. The priests constituted a specialized caste, at once the jealous guardians of the Ark that they carried during the migration, sanctifiers and mediators before the Presence, judges learned in the law, sometimes, even as it were, consecrated police, responsible for the punishing of offences. The sumptuous vestments that they wore during ceremonies marked their sacred office: a robe of pleated linen; tunics of violet or crimson; high mitres or tiaras ornamented with a diadem, and on their breasts a heavy pectoral of "cunning workmanship" adorned with four rows of precious stones, of emerald, opal, onyx and amethyst, together with sapphire and diamond. One of their principal duties was to interrogate Jahweh on His intentions. An object not precisely dedefined, the *ephod-oracle*, sometimes a kind of box, sometimes a small plastron, served them for the purpose of casting divine lots, with inscribed bones, the *urim* and *thummim*, whose meanings they interpreted. In those priestly functions one tribe specialized—the tribe of Levi, to which Moses belonged. His brother Aaron was its first superior.

THE LAND OF CANAAN

When the people were on the march, "the cloud of Jahweh was upon the tabernacle by day, and fire was on it by night, in the sight of all the house of Israel" (Exod. xl:38). Thus they went forward, carrying their shrine. But they were not to remain nomadic for ever. Had not the promise made to the Patriarchs been renewed by Jahweh, even after the infidelities that He had pardoned?

Their great leader added a final element to the definitive constitution of his people. For it was he who began the fulfilment of the promise, by giving Israel a foothold on the borders of the Promised Land. Their ancestors had been strangers there. The twelve tribes made it their own, by divine right. No sentiment was better calculated than this imperialism to set the seal on their communal destiny.

Canaan is not a very large country. The Babylonians did not distinguish it from Amurru (Syria), of which it was part; the Greeks extended to the whole country the name which they gave to the coast, and called it the land of the Philistines, Palestine, the name which we retain. "From Dan to Beersheba," "from the sluices of Hammath to the river of Egypt" (Wadi of Sherba),[3] according to the expressions commonly used in the Bible, it extends for less than two hundred miles. In the north it is bounded by the Anti-Lebanon range, from which extends like a wedge the great Hermon massif, reaching a height of six thousand feet, snow-covered in winter. Towards the south, the plains of Palestine extend without a break into the great solitudes of Tih. If we do not include Transjordania, Canaan covers some 26,000 square miles, about half the area of Brittany. From the sea to the desert, the distance as the crow flies is only about sixty miles, and even less in the north; it is a fringe, a border, squeezed between the sand and the sea, the slender horn of the Fertile Crescent.

In this small space, however, nature has manifested herself under the most varying aspects. A plain, hills that try to be mountains, a gorge that penetrates into the very bowels of the earth, and finally a high glacis with an abrupt drop, in four parallel bands running from north to south, with variations of soil and climate creating subtle local differences.

The plain in early biblical times was as yet scarcely the Promised Land, being occupied, for the most part, by the Philistines. Nevertheless, it is the most favoured district, the Plain of Sharon, that Isaiah names as the type of riches; it is the centre, at the present time, round about Tel-Aviv, of the Zionist farms of lemons and grapefruit. Behind a straight sandy coastline bordered with dunes, where only the Bay of Haifa sheltered by Mount Carmel provides a suitable port, extends alluvial soil which

[3] *See* Map: Canaan of the Judges, p. 145.

requires only a little water in order to yield garden produce, in
the shade of palms. The sandstone hills that rise from the plain
are covered with vines. At the foot of the mountains, behind a
line of high country that calls to mind the cliffs of the Ile de
France or the Côte d'Or, the Sephelah, which Samson was later
to contest with the Philistines, extends as far as eye can see,
grey-green with olive trees.

Next come three steep gradients beyond which lies Palestine
proper. Over an area of some thirty miles stretch a group of
heights—"The Mountains of Judah," Mount Ephraim, Mount
Gerizim, Mount Tabor, the Bible proudly names them. These
names are not to be taken literally. In Flanders, the Hill of
Kemmel, three hundred feet high, is called a mountain. These
Palestinian mountains are, more exactly, high hills, sometimes
rounded at the summit, sometimes forming a striking relief against
the background of the little plains. Tabor is 1865 feet, Garizim
2864, and the highest peak in Canaan, the Jermak, is just over
3960 feet! Generally the country slopes gently from west to east,
but beyond the ridge, descends steeply towards the Jordan.[4]
Apart from the north-south ridge, the oblique ridge of Carmel
alone has any marked direction in the general confusion of
contours.

One might imagine that all these high lands would be alike;
but this is not the case. There are great differences between harsh
and austere Judea, monotonous as a rabbinical chant; varied

[4] *See* section of Palestine in diagram.

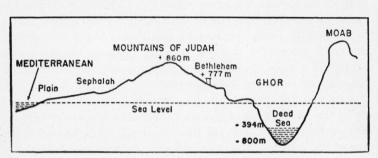

Samaria, where the contours stand in undulating relief, and the plains give "promise of corn"; gentle Galilee, where Christ lived His human life, at the foot of slopes covered with cypress.

Each of these three regions was to have, in the Sacred History, its place and its special significance. Judea, the dry land where water is often scarce, a country of scrub, thorns and teazles, was always to be disputed between the nomads and the settled population; defended by the fortresses of Hebron and Jerusalem, it was nevertheless in its wild isolation the place of refuge from strict orthodoxy, the district that was never settled. Samaria is a zone of communications. The heights descend into it; the plain of Esdrelon, from the Jordan towards the sea, is a perfect corridor. Tuthmosis III there fought a decisive battle at Megiddo, and Bonaparte was to pass that way. The fertile black soil, enriched with volcanic alluvium, like that of the Limagnes, produces corn and fruits; its hills are covered with sheep. A place of many contacts, of riches, and the Jews would add, of heresy and immorality. As for Galilee, broken up by valleys and hills, better watered and even today covered with forests on the mountains and, in the valleys, hundreds of little white hamlets, she earned from her situation on the frontier, as a district of many battles, the corridor of invasions and of mixed populations, her name of "Galilee of the Gentiles."

Looking west from the Mountains of Judah, we see, beyond the grey plateau and the green and yellow chequer-board of the plain, the Mediterranean sparkling in the sun; but looking towards the Levant, the scene is grand and sinister. A deep gorge opens its yawning lips—one of the strangest geographical freaks in the world. From the foot of the Taurus right into Africa, the earth, under the stress of contrary volcanic forces, is torn across like a piece of old cloth; this long fissure can be traced on the map by the steep depressions of the Red Sea, the lakes of Nyassa and Tanganyika, and by the enormous volcanos thrown up by the break in the earth's crust, Sinai, the Abyssinian heights, Kenya, Kilimanjaro. The rift through which the Jordan flows is one of the results of this great geological upheaval. The level of

the Dead Sea is 1300 feet below the sea level of the Mediterranean, and its depth is about 2640 feet. And this already seemed
so strange to the Israelites that the prophets Zachariah and
Ezekiel predicted that a day would come when the mountain
would be rent, and the waters of the Mediterranean, flooding the
plain, would fill the valley.

This *ghor*, this gorge whose width varies from one to twelve
miles, has played the part rather as a boundary than as a frontier
over which there was any contact. A lake of 150 miles in length
completely filled it at a not very far distant geographical epoch;
evaporation had reduced it to three smaller lakes, linked by the
Jordan as it descends from Hermon. "The waters of Merom" are
no more than a large tarn, bordered by bean-fields, where storks,
motionless on one pink leg, pounce on small fish among the reeds.
The valley slopes sharply; at Dan, the height is eighteen hundred
feet; Merom is almost at sea level. Seven miles lower down, the
Lake of Gennesaret is already over six hundred feet below sea
level. Actually one would not suspect this, among the gentle hills
where bougainvillia cover the white walls of the hamlets with a
violet mantle, where clear water reflects the snows of Hermon,
where every streamlet is fringed with oleanders between the corn-
fields. It is one of the most beautiful places in the whole of Palestine, as lovely as an Italian lake; Herod Antipas built there his
sumptuous capital Tiberias, so named in honour of his master,
Tiberius; Christ worked miracles there, stilled its waves, and on
its shores multiplied the loaves and the fishes, and drove the
herd of bewitched swine into its waters.

The gorge becomes still deeper. The valley sinks between white
limestone and red sandstone. The plain becomes dryer, almost
desert; at first fringed by tamarisk and mimosa, later bordered
only with alders; into this wilderness St. John the Baptist led his
followers. Lower still we reach the Dead Sea, sometimes like a
sheet of tin below the purple mountains of Moab, sometimes
opalescent turquoise, set in gold. That was the first sight of the
promised land that Moses' Hebrews ever knew, that heavy still
water, so saturated with salt and asphalt that no life can survive

in it, and that the human body floats in it; seascape of death and
cataclysm, this sheet of water is good only to produce bitumen
for mummies. One can imagine the horde of nomads, looking
from the plateau of Transjordania, across this sinister water to the
yellow hills of Judea, theirs already in faith and in desire.

Geography imposes a contradictory character on Canaan. It is
inevitably a corridor from the Nile to the Euphrates. But it is
difficult to pass through. The valley of the Jordan is by no means
an easy route; the highlands offer but a poor route, full of climbs
and descents; the real routes skirt the country by the coast and by
Transjordania (now followed by the Mecca railway), and the
oblique route from one side to the other across the plain of
Esdrelon, "the sea-route" from Haifa to Damascus. The history
of the chosen people therefore developed in comparative isolation.

It developed also in great disintegration. For this varied country so divided up naturally lends itself to oppositions between
rival groups; the exclusiveness of the tribes took full advantage
of this. It is not only in a supernatural sense that the destiny of
Israel is linked with Canaan.

"A LAND FLOWING WITH MILK AND HONEY"

Palestine, for many peoples, is to this day the "Holy Land," but
it is, besides, a pleasant country. By day, under a dazzling sun,
the sky and the plains compose themselves in masses of pure
colours, azure, ochre, and crude white; and at night, among blue
and silver shadows, one cannot say whether the diffused light is
reflected from the ground or comes from the stars that so thickly
spangle the sky. As in Greece, it requires but little to confer on
any place an incomparable grandeur; a cypress at the corner of a
wall, the shadow of a trellis in the yellow sunlight, a flight of
storks making for the Jordan. Spring is heavenly there. "For, lo,
the winter is past, the rain is over and gone; the flowers appear
on the earth; the time of the singing of birds is come, and the
voice of the turtle is heard in our land; the fig-tree putteth forth
her green figs, and the vines with the tender grape give a good

smell" (Song of Solomon II:11–13). Exquisite things appear at every step; even the driest rock shelters in a cleft a tuft of those red anemones with a black centre that are undoubtedly the "lilies of the field" of the Scripture, because they are compared to the lips of the beloved; and that so insignificant brownish moss, if you stoop to it and breathe its scent, is nard, one of the aromatics with which Mary Magdalene anointed the feet of Jesus Christ.

But beauty is not a sign of richness. A peasant from the Beauce, or a vine-dresser from Médoc transported into Judea would call these lands worthless. And yet the Bible insistently describes Canaan as a fabulous country "flowing with milk and honey," where all yields *foison* and increase. Oriental exaggeration? It has been suggested that since biblical times there has been a retrogression; in certain regions, Carmel, for example, that is now so barren, there are traces of woods, gardens and vineyards; for want of attention, the walls that kept the soil from washing down have fallen, all culture being brought to an end.

The summer is hot as in Greece and Algeria; in the month of August the temperature is at least 73° Fahrenheit and 113° has been recorded. In winter the weather can be very cold. It is a healthy climate, which makes men hardy; except on the Lower Jordan, fevers are rare. The sea-wind brings freshness even in summer; in the evenings the inhabitants go up on to their terraces, or into their gardens, to take the air, as God did in Paradise, so it is said in Genesis (III:8). It was that same sea-wind that winnowed Boaz' barley on the night when Ruth went to find him. But the beneficent influence of the Mediterranean is opposed by that of the desert; sometimes a savage wind blows from the great solitudes, carrying sand, freezing in winter, burning in summer; the breath of anger, "Jahweh's wind," that casts that leaden shadow that fell upon the earth at the hour when Jesus died.

But the great problem of the Mediterranean countries is not easily solved in Palestine: that of water. The Bible throughout attaches great importance to this "garden-spring, well of living waters, brook that flows from Lebanon"; the Song of Songs multiplies images in which the precious liquid is praised. There is no flood as in Egypt, or even in Shinar. In a sense, the proud nomads preferred, as it is put in Deuteronomy, not to water the land with their feet (xi:11), that is to say, not to have to turn the shadoof, the water-elevating apparatus. Canaan drinks only the "waters of heaven" but, in many districts, it drinks very little. Whereas Syria, more favoured, receives three feet of rainfall at Beyrout, Hermon receives scarcely more than four inches; the winter rainfall in Galilee and in Samaria is less than nine inches (it rains more in Paris); in Judea, six inches, and in the valley of the Jordan, barely four. If one further takes into account the enormous evaporation (a depth of half an inch of water evaporates each day from the Dead Sea, or about fifteen feet a year), these rains are clearly insufficient. The wells in the limestone are seldom unfailing; cisterns must be multiplied, and the "water of the heavens" hoarded jealously.

The vegetation has, therefore, on that thirsty soil, little chance of being luxurious. As we know it, it is very different from that familiar to the Hebrews of the Bible; many plants, familiar to us, were not introduced until much later: Barbary figs, agaves and even the *doura,* the commonest form of food in Palestine today, our maize. The forests which have now become bare through ill-advised deforestation could never have been dense: Aleppo pines, cypress, ilex, turpentine and carob trees, and in the far north, on the slopes of Hermon, those cedars of exquisite fragrance, so noble in appearance that they were compared to a regiment of young warriors. But if trees are rare, shrubs are abundant, as fragrant and various as in the Corsican *maquis;* myrtles, laurels, mastics, brooms and rock-roses, and liquorice, with an undergrowth of nard, thyme, marjoram and fennel.

Where water suffices, the earth lends itself readily to cultivation. The plains of Sharon and of Sephelah, of Esdrelon and of Tiberias are today exceedingly fertile. Wheat, barley, beans, lentils and sesame have been grown in Canaan from very early times, and its gardens have always yielded excellent fruits and wines. A son of Gideon, in an apologia, tells how in electing a king, the trees in turn offered the crown to the olive, the fig-tree and the vine (Judges IX). Oil, carefully extracted from olives, not too ripe; wine rendered fragrant to a degree by partly drying the grapes in the sun; figs preserved in pressed masses and served cut in shapes were common fare in Palestine. But there were still other useful trees—the palm, the almond and the sycamore, whose fruits were gathered as a flavouring; the walnut with its cool shadow, so welcome in summer.

Although an agricultural land in which Israel abandoned tents for houses, Canaan remained at the same time a pastoral country whose people were never wholly to abandon the shepherd's crook for the plough. For a long time, nomadic *douars* moved about the hills; shepherds tended their flocks, crook in hand, and all through the Bible we hear the echo of their four-stopped pipes. At night when the sheep were gathered into enclosures of dry stones, they remained on the watch, for bears, wolves, and even lions still roamed at large, ravaging the flocks. Cattle were rare, and were a sign of wealth; the common people all had a few sheep and goats. Asses were plentiful, and although the horse had been introduced by the Hyksos during their brief sojourn, it was used very little and only in war.

All this suggests modest comfort, but not wealth—at least to our Western minds. But this people who had for half a century been wandering in the desert must have cast longing eyes on this land of bread and wine and oil. "Milk and honey" is a nomadic phrase; much milk is drunk in the tents, and the Bedouin of the present time prizes his cordial sweetmeats. Once more the ancient law of Asia, by which the vagabonds of the desert attack the plains, was to operate. The Israelites were not to pause again until Canaan was theirs.

A COUNTRY FOR THE TAKING

Have we here a new proof of the divine protection? At the very moment when they attacked it, this country was literally to be had for the taking. It no longer belonged to any of the great neighbouring empires, and this second parenthesis in history [5]

[5] *See above* p. 30.

was to last for long enough to allow Israel to organize itself into a kingdom and take its stand as a state in the full sense. If the Exodus took place about 1225, there would be about 150 years between the first appearances of the Hebrews on the borders of Moab and the crowning of their first king, Saul (about 1040 B.C.). Now this period is marked throughout the Near East by important events, singularly fortunate for Israel, certain of which still condition our destiny.

Following the great battle of Kadesh, the Egyptian-Hittite treaty had established Syria and Palestine as a kind of buffer state divided into two spheres of influence. The Hittite control extended to the Upper Orontes; the Pharaoh dominated the south. This state of affairs was in itself favourable; when there are two masters, it is easy to play off one against the other. The petty kings of Canaan lost no opportunity of doing so.

But just at the time when Israel in the desert was coming into consciousness of her nationhood, these two masters themselves were to disappear from the Palestinian stage. The great event of the twelfth century B.C. was the entry of the Aryans into the Mediterranean scene. For seven hundred years their migrations had proceeded without intermission. They arrived in successive waves, each blotting out the established populations, even when these were of their own blood. In the same way that, on French soil, we were to see the Roman Aryans conquer the Gaulish Aryans, and themselves suffer the attack of the German Aryans, in the same way, in turn, the Hittite, Phrygian, Trojan, Achaian and Dorian waves poured over the shores of the Aegean: this thousand year migration is a terrifying and magnificent spectacle; has it indeed, even now, finally come to an end?

Crete was its first victim. In that small island, in its relative isolation, a civilization of rare beauty had grown up. Since Evans, in about 1900, brought to light the ruins of Knossos, that Cretan world has seemed so near to us that it is with difficulty that we remember thirty-five hundred years divide us from it. The face of a girl smiles from a little fresco, a roguish Parisian smile. The men in short trunks remind one of football players, and the women wear crinolines like the Empress Eugénie. Marvellously placed in the centre of the eastern Mediterranean, the priest-kings of Crete, the Minos, were able to establish a maritime empire that dominated the Aegean, exploited the copper of Cyprus and Rhodes, and traded in everything, everywhere. They made wise use of their enormous wealth; their palaces enjoyed a degree of comfort unknown to Louis XIV, running water in the bathrooms and modern sanitation. Their walls were decorated with charming frescoes. In these we see princes bathing in the waves, a cat stalking its prey among the leaves, a king walking, a lily in his hand.

In about 1400 B.C. a sudden catastrophe wiped out this exquisite civilization. At Knossos everyone was occupied as usual, a sculptor finishing a stone vase, masons preparing plaster, a jeweller setting a jewel; in the throne room, a ceremony was in progress. The attack was so sudden that everyone remained helpless just where he was. Fire consumed the beautiful palace. An Aryan fleet had landed on the island. Of Crete, all that survived in Greek civilization were names ending in "inth" (Jacinth, Corinth), some religious rites and two legends: in one of these, Minos is a just king who judges souls in the underworld, a memory of the equity that reigned in Crete under these enlightened monarchs; in the other, he was a ferocious being who in the recesses of his labyrinthine palace fed his pet monster, the Minotaur, on young Athenians whom he claimed each year—a memory, no doubt, of the period when the master of seas had levied, by means of his ships trading with the continent, a heavy tribute.

This wave of conquerors was the Achaian wave. They had installed themselves in Greece in the fifteenth century, erecting on high points of vantage or in the shelter of mountains their fortresses of Mycenae and Tiryns built of enormous blocks, and little by little imitating rather crudely the art of Crete; savage, feudal, forever engaged in fraticidal wars. Aeschylus and Sophocles have preserved for us their bloodstained stories. One can still see at the portals of one of their castles two angry lions that seem to roar for carnage, and in the museum of Athens the gold masks with which they used to adorn their dead retain an indescribable air of violence and savage grandeur.

Crete was not the only scene of their redoubtable exploits. All the islands of Greece were to see them appear. In Asia Minor, they and closely related tribes landed repeatedly. During the fifteenth and fourteenth centuries B.C. the Hittites were so strong that the newcomers could gain no foothold. During the thirteenth century they began to establish themselves on the coasts, and naturally no sooner were they installed than they had to defend themselves against new waves seeking a foothold in their turn. The Hittite tablets of Boghazkeui tell us of these raids of the "Akhaiwas" (Achaians), and it is even thought that the same names of Alexander, Atreus, Andrews, Eteocles that recur in Homer's *Iliad* are to be traced.

For the war of Troy is simply an episode in that confused history of the Aryan invasion. In search of new land, or as is more probable, anxious to gain control of the route which led to the corn of Russia, the Achaians joined under the leadership of Agamemnon in a destructive war against the Trojans, a people of Asia Minor, evidently Aryans like themselves, but who had been installed for some time near the Dardanelles. Historical coincidence: at the very moment at which Joshua was to lead his men to the conquest of the promised land, almost to the year, Odysseus was to introduce the perfidious horse into Troy.

Another episode in the same drama overthrew the Hittite empire. Another Aryan people, installed farther to the south, in Phrygia, attacked that great nation which had dominated Asia Minor for eight centuries. Had the Hittites lost their military qualities by intermarrying with the indigenous races? Did the invader possess better arms? Everything about this episode is mysterious, and the Greeks, for some unknown reason, taunted the King Mita, conqueror of the Hittites, with the name of Midas, who changed everything to gold, but to whom Apollo had given asses' ears as a punishment for having failed to appreciate his singing! If the details of these events have been lost, the essential fact is clear: from the beginning of the twelfth century B.C. there was no longer a Hittite empire; there remained only a federation of little states; the ancient vassals of "the great king," still proudly bearing the ancient name of "Hatti"; their centres were Aleppo in Syria and Karkemish on the Euphrates. They resisted for a long time Assyrian attacks, but were finally brought to ruin by Sargon II at the end of the seventh century B.C. But meanwhile they were not strong enough to establish their domination in Canaan.

On the Egyptian side the invasion was less violent than in Crete and Asia Minor; but the power of the Pharaohs nevertheless received a severe blow. Documents speak of these "people of the sea" who from the beginning of the thirteenth century B.C. began to make their appearance on the Delta. They came from a place that the Egyptians called "Kefti," evidently the same as the Bible calls "Caphtor," which it gives as the place from which the Philistines came. It was a heterogeneous assemblage of all the peoples who, at that time, were struggling for supremacy in the Aegean Sea. There were Trojans, Achaians, Phrygians, and many others, probably even Cretans. We cannot find a better parallel with their historic rule than that of the Normans. Like them, they arrived in light ships whose prows were ornamented with the head of a swan or some fantastic beast, drew up their ships on the shore, and made bold raids of pillage and destruction.

There can be no doubt that these pirates were Aryans. What the Egyptians tell us and what the Bible says about the Philistines coincides exactly with Homer's description of the Achaians: blond giants with long craniums, fair skin, blue eyes, blood-brothers of the Germans and the Celts. When the first bands made their appearance, Rameses II, who had defeated them without any trouble, had so much admired the bearing of these men that he had made them his personal bodyguard. But the situation rapidly became more serious. Minephtah had to wage hard battles with them, and after him Rameses III had to face a veritable tide of them. Twice in four years, he fought dire battles; he attempted to defeat the "people of the sea" in their own element. He succeeded in saving Egypt, but a great number of these pirates installed themselves on the southern coast of Canaan where they joined with the Aegeans who had had their trading-centres there since the Cretan domination. This mixed but pre-dominantly Aryan race constituted the Philistines, the enemies of Israel. Egypt thus found herself cut off from Canaan; in order to overcome this state of affairs, they would have had to repeat the stubborn effort of Tuthmosis III or Rameses II. But Rameses III was the last of the great Pharaohs. After him the kings of the Nile, whose officers of state were the priests of Amon, sank into de-cadence. A little later, while one dynasty reigned in the Delta, the clergy of Thebes proclaimed another, that of their own great pontiffs. The land of the gods was declining towards its ruin; nothing could arrest its inevitable destiny.

Canaan had therefore no need to fear a master either in the north or in the south. Was there danger from the east as in the time of Hammurabi? Not yet. The time of the third robber had not yet come. Three centuries later this third was to be Assyria, a name of blood. In the mountainous triangle of the Upper Tigris, a race of terrible warriors had installed themselves during the period of the Semitic invasions of 3000–2000 B.C. The country, which was a barren one, had kept them warlike. During the twenty-fifth century B.C. when Gudea reigned at Lagash, there were several important Assyrian kings. Later they seem to have been more or less subject to Babylon, and after that to have been overshadowed by the Mitannians and Hittites. But in the thir-teenth century B.C. their star began to rise. Shalmaneser became so powerful that his proximity was one of the reasons that decided the Hittites, after Kadesh, to make peace with Egypt. In the twelfth century appeared the first of the great conquerors of Asshur, Tiglath-Pileser I, who left in the temple of his capital the record of his forty-two victorious campaigns. We find him in turn in Armenia, in Kurdistan, checking Midas' Phrygians when, having conquered the Hittites, they advanced to the Euphrates; attack-ing Babylon where the Kassite Dynasty had recently fallen; and finally reaching the Mediterranean where he cut the fragrant cedars of Lebanon to use in building his temples. Would he impress his strong rule in the place of the weakening dynasties? Not as yet. Tiglath-Pileser's successors did not carry on his work. Canaan remained free for long enough to enable Israel to accomplish its destiny.

ENEMIES TO BE OVERCOME

This does not at all mean that the people of the Promise had not numerous enemies in their way. The Bible, indeed, enumerates so many that we cannot possibly mention all of them. But as a matter af fact, certain names refer only to very small tribes or clans. Altogether the situation was very much simpler than it had been five or six hundred years earlier when the Patriarchs had grazed their flocks in these same lands. Israel was to meet with three classes of enemies—the people who occupied Canaan proper; the various nomads who, according to the ancient custom, pressed in upon the frontiers from the desert; and the Philistines, established on the coast. After a few generations, the situation was even simpler, and by about 1000 B.C. there were only two rival races in Palestine—Philistines and Israelites. The Canaanites had been annihilated during the course of that double immigration.

The Philistines were those pirates, those "people of the sea" who, having been repulsed by Rameses III, fell back upon the southern coast of Palestine. Their ports were Ashdod, Askalon and Gaza. An allied tribe held Dor, near Carmel; but, not content with occupying the coast, they had penetrated inland and rich Sephelah was subject to them. On Egyptian frescoes, we recognize them instantly; tall, with straight noses following the line of their foreheads, fair skinned (while the Semites were painted the colour of brick), they are noticeable on account of a kind of felt cap pleated on the backs of their heads, fixed on by strings under the chin, and surmounted by an ornament of upright feathers, closely ranged, with a braid of bright colours. In peace, they wore a simple loincloth; in war, a cuirass of articulated strips of metal. They were heavily armed: a round shield, a long sword and two daggers, which they wielded in both hands at once. Such was the equipment of Goliath.

They were not, strictly speaking, barbarians, or at least not more so than their fierce cousins whom we admire under the names of Achilles and Odysseus. They had learned much from their contact with Crete and the civilization of Asia Minor. It is likely that they knew the use of iron before Israel. It is almost certain that a disk inscribed with strange signs found at Phaestos in Crete, resembling the game of "goose" and one of whose figures represents the famous feathered headdress, comes from their country. In this case, the Philistines were the inventors of printing, for the letters of this alphabet have been stamped in the clay by means of one stamp for each letter!

Israel had numerous contacts with them, and not always in warfare. If we are to judge from the story of Samson, the Philistine women had light virtue. These people seemed to merge very quickly with the native tribes, exactly as in Greece the Archaians intermarried with the primitive races; their religion was based on cults that were practised throughout the Fertile Crescent. It was perhaps through them, if Herodotus is to be believed, that the naked Semite goddess was to reach us as the charming Hellenic Aphrodite, born of the sea-foam.

The Philistines were to be the most redoubtable enemies of Israel, because they had good arms, chariots, and an efficient political organization (similar to the Greek "tyrannies"), and because they too were in process of expansion. But in the north, east and south, other dangers menaced the frontier of Canaan, from those Bedouins of Semitic origin who intermittently descended upon the fertile lands. From the north, the great Aramaic tide gathered at Damascus. Two waves advanced towards the south, in Transjordania the Ammonites and the Moabites; closely related to the Hebrews, they opposed them with a jealous hostility, while Israel held them in contempt on account of their idolatry; this antagonism was never to cease. In the south, Edom was never to forgive the sons of Jacob for the dish of lentils refused to Esau; these nomads on more than one occasion at-

tacked Israel, now become sedentary. Finally, in the extreme
south of Negeb, the Amalekites, robbers by profession, a mixed
race of unstable tribes, often made murderous raids northwards.

Such were the frontier races; but the interior must also be
subdued and its inhabitants conquered. All the peoples whom we
saw so split up in the time of the Patriarchs, the Canaanites, the
Ammonites, the Perizzites and the Jebusites, had merged during
six centuries. There still remained a jig-saw puzzle of little cities,
but the race had become homogeneous. The Bible refers to them
sometimes as Canaanites, sometimes as Ammonites. Their density
and their strength varied considerably in different districts; solid
in the plain of Esdrelon and Samaria, more scattered in Judea.
These Canaanites, whom the Israelites naturally did not paint in
flattering colours since they were their enemies, were in reality
more civilized than the rude tribes who were shortly to vanquish
them. They had for centuries been subject to Cretan and Egyptian
influences. In their little kingdoms, the women dressed in the
fashion of Knossos. They had alabaster vases in the Egyptian
style, or ornamented with flowers and marine animals in the
Cretan manner. The study of their pottery leaves no possibility of
doubt; the advent of Israel resulted in a rapid decadence; the
clay became coarser, and ill-fashioned; decoration was reduced
to lines. In order to possess beautiful objects, David and Solomon
had to buy them from the Phoenicians.

Israel was to defeat the Canaanites and conquer Canaan. But
the law formulated by Horace is no new thing: "Conquered
Greece subdued her fierce conqueror." In entering this country
the Hebrews found on every side, and in countless guises, the
well-known temptations. Canaanite idolatry had certain rites in
common with those practised by the people of God in the days
of the ancestors: monoliths or *massebahs,* and the cult of high
places. Later they gave up even these, to avoid the danger of
confusion with idolatrous rites, just as they gave up addressing
the Most High by the old Semitic term, *Baal,* in order not to
name the god of their enemies. We know that Canaanite religion
through the horrified condemnations levelled against it by the

Bible, and by the attraction that it exerted over the people of God. Against the *Ashera*, or totem-pole, similar to those which we find today among the black races of Africa, the followers of Jahweh waged a relentless war. They anathematized the bloody rites, human sacrifices, and obscene cults that gathered about the temples both men and women vowed to religious prostitution. The Canaanites must have been a deeply religious people, if we are to judge from the number of idols found in their ruins. The naked Semitic goddess occupied an important place. They worshipped Baal, the master, the lord of the soil, under many different aspects; the monstrous Moloch, thirsting for victims burned alive, who occupied first place in Phoenicia and Carthage, did not yet seem to be worshipped. Their goddess Astarte was the counterpart of the Babylonian Ishtar, the beneficent, who presides over the fertility of flocks and whose sexual character is associated with the impure rites practised in the temple precincts.

This Canaanite religion seems poor indeed in the light of the grandiose monotheism whose teaching the chosen people received in Sinai. But we must remember human weakness, and the very concrete satisfaction that it demands. And also the fact that for a race about to become peasant, that religion of divinized nature would seem more tangible than the cult of the transcendent Jahweh. Baal was much more easily accessible for purposes of invocation. The internal danger that had already been so grave in the desert was to increase by reason of the conquest and it was to last for a very long time.

The two tasks that confronted the chosen people, as they stood on the banks of the Jordan ready to attack, were to conquer the country and to keep themselves pure. What God offers, man must still merit through his fidelity and his courage. The battle for the land and for Jahweh had begun.

III

JOSHUA AND THE JUDGES

THE MILITARY EPIC OF ISRAEL

A GREAT JANGLING OF ARMS, shouting, massacres, burning cities and in the foreground acts of individual heroism; such is the new page of history that Israel was now about to write. In the Bible Joshua and Judges represent a veritable epic, which in many respects reminds us of the other war-epic of the same period that the Greeks handed down from father to son until it was recorded four centuries later as the *Iliad*. Modern wars have more hypocrisy about them; propaganda veils primitive hatred in lofty moralizations. Primitive people are more unaffected; these records positively exude holy hate.

This is not the most moving portion of the Holy Scriptures, although it is not without some passages of great beauty. But it throws light on the psychology of the race. It has all the energy and the illogicalness of impetuous youth; customs were brutal, and no scruples were allowed to stand in the way of the thirst for blood. One day Israel gives way to her instincts, and the next prostrates herself in humble penitence, acknowledging her fault; at one time she is carried away by enthusiasm, at another prostrated by despair; jealousy, egoism, guile, comradeship, fidelity—the contraries alternate. They were people in their infancy, in the throes of the struggle that was to determine not only their destiny but also the spiritual values that this destiny was to realize.

This violence has, moreover, its significance. In the first place, a military significance; a reputation for ferocity constitutes a force by inspiring fear; the Assyrians and the Carthaginians were to take it into account in their strategy. But, above all, a religious significance—Israel was at war with an impure people. Systematic destruction was a sacrifice that they offered to Jahweh, which was better at least than abandoning themselves to looting. Again and again we find this *herem* in which a city anathematized in the name of God is wiped out and not a man left alive and not a wall left standing, while everything in it, instead of being carried away, is burned. In the ruins of Jericho, destroyed by Joshua, the archaeologists have discovered the charred remains of lentils, onions, corn, food of all kinds, and all sorts of objects that the conquerors had not touched. It was an offering and at the same time a precaution against contamination of all kinds, and acceptable to God (Deuteronomy vii:2; xx:14. Joshua vii:11).

Nor must we exaggerate these holocausts. They were relatively few in number. And it is not unlikely that the biblical narrator has exaggerated their horror from pious motives and for literary effect. The Canaanites were not exterminated. There were sometimes more friendly relations between them and their conquerors. As for the massacre of captives, conquered kings hanged and mutilated, the ruses and treacheries that again and again recur, these were common to all accounts of primitive wars, always highly coloured and full of bloodthirsty humour. Homer describes similar things.

The war of conquest was a hard one. Israel, although superior to the Bedouin tribes, was not the equal of the Philistines, who had real arms. The Hebrew footsoldiers were often without lances or shields, as we learn from the Song of Deborah. They had no chariots. And even the forts of the Canaanites were of formidable strength; the Hyksos had taught them the art of building double walls, sometimes nearly four yards thick, and surrounded by a sloping glacis that gave the advantage to the archers; at Beisan and at Jericho *migdols* have been discovered, enormous dungeons in the centre of a whole complex of fortifications that gave protection to silos of corn; it is not surprising that simple nomads were often defeated by such defences. The warfare of Israel was to have the character of guerilla warfare, surprises and stratagems in the manner of Duguesclin, a war of skirmishes.

Courage was needed. This Israel did not lack, for the certitude of divine protection was with her. One day while Joshua was meditating on the shores of the Jordan, he raised his eyes and saw a man standing before him, sword in hand, "Art thou for us or for our adversaries?" he at once asked. "As captain of the host of the Lord am I now come," replied the mysterious stranger (Josh. v:13–14). Led by the angel of wrath, Israel knew that the victory was already hers, God willing it so.

JOSHUA

"Now after the death of Moses . . . the Lord spake unto Joshua the son of Nun, Moses' minister, saying, Moses my servant is dead; now therefore arise, go over this Jordan, thou, and all this people, unto the land which I do give to them, even to the children of Israel" (Josh. 1:1–2). Joshua had been the great chief's deputy, one of the two emissaries who had gone to spy out the promised land, the last survivor of the older generation. He took command, gathered provisions, and prepared his troops.

In the cities of Canaan and particularly in Jericho, the most threatened, the gathering of the nomads on the other side of the river was watched with suspicion. One day it was discovered that two Hebrews had succeeded in entering the city; they were thought to be hidden in one of the houses of ill-fame that backed on to the city walls. A search was sent there to look for them. "The men are no longer here," Rahab the courtesan told them. They hoped to overtake them at the ford over the Jordan—but in vain. In fact, the woman had hidden the spies on her roof and afterwards helped them to climb down by the wall. They had doubled back into the mountains in order to elude their pursuers. Rahab, who had engineered the victory of Israel, played her own hand. "Jahweh," she said, "has given you this country, I know, and I also know that you have anathematized this city. If I save you, promise that you will save me in my turn." The spies promised to do so. Rahab was to hang a red cord in her window and her house would be spared. This incident is revealing as showing the fear that Israel inspired and the kind of assistance that they could expect to find.

The camp was pitched before Jericho,[1] on the left bank. And Jahweh announced to Joshua that He would prove to the people that He had chosen him as the successor of the Leader. The first obstacle was the Jordan. In this lower valley, it is wide—nearly eighty yards across—but shallow, and as a rule fordable. But, "Jordan overfloweth all his banks at the time of harvest" (Josh. III:15). A miracle seemed necessary, of the kind vouchsafed at the crossing of the Red Sea. "The waters which came down from above stood and rose up upon an heap very far from the city Edom . . . and those that came down toward the sea, . . . failed, and were cut off: . . . And the priests that bare the ark of the covenant of the Lord stood firm on dry ground in the midst of Jordan, and all the Israelites passed over on dry ground" (Josh. III:16–17). The city Edom is presumably El-Damieh, sixteen miles upstream from Jericho. There the river flows between tall banks of clay, thirteen yards high, which easily subside. In 1927 as the result of an earth tremor they subsided and blocked the channel so that the flow was interrupted for twenty-one hours. The theory of an earthquake is not to be excluded. "Lord, when thou marchest out of the field of Edom," Deborah sang, "the earth trembled. . . ." And Psalm CXIV also says, "Jordan was driven back; the mountains skipped like rams, and the little hills like lambs."

On the right bank they paused to reform the column. In commemoration of the miracle, Joshua had a circle of stones erected, in the fashion of antiquity at Gilgal, an ancient Canaanite sanctuary. And to confirm the Covenant in blood, as God had commanded Jacob to do, all the men who had not been circumcised in the desert now underwent the rite. The Passover was celebrated, and on the following day the manna disappeared, as mysteriously as it had come. Israel no longer required it. From now on they lived on the produce of the land promised to them;

[1] *See* MAP: CANAAN OF THE JUDGES, p. 145.

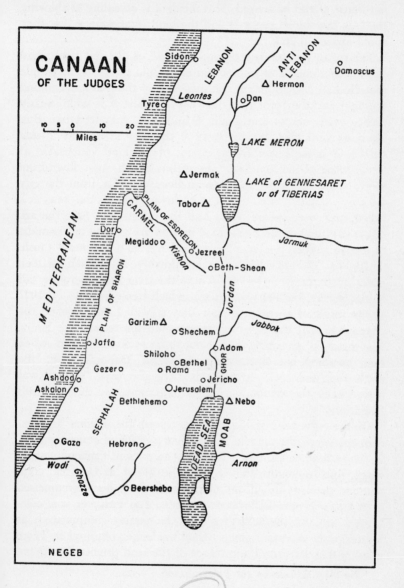

CANAAN
OF THE JUDGES

10 5 0   10   20
Miles

MEDITERRANEAN

Sidon

LEBANON

ANTI LEBANON

Damascus

Hermon

Leontes

Tyre

Dan

LAKE MEROM

Jermak

LAKE of GENNESARET
or of TIBERIAS

Tabor

PLAIN OF ESDRELON

CARMEL

Kishon

Dor

Megiddo

Jezreel

Jarmuk

PLAIN OF SHARON

Beth-Shean

Jordan

Garizim

Shechem

Jabbok

Jaffa

Shiloh

Bethel

Rama

Adom

GHOR

Gezer

Ashdod

Askalon

Jericho

Jerusalem

SEPHALAH

Bethlehem

Nebo

MOAB

DEAD SEA

Gaza

Hebron

Wadi Ghazze

Arnon

Beersheba

NEGEB

and to this day the tamarisks of Gilgal produce nothing but the pink snow of their own flowers.

On the edge of the *Ghor*, Jericho's high silhouette arose. Built on high ground and strongly fortified, it was an oasis in that arid country in which Christ was to fast for forty days. In the plain, barley grew; on the hill, there was only a greyish vegetation sprinkled with asphodels. Isolated shepherds, in white and brown striped garments, tended their sheep. "The city of palm-trees" was the more remarkable, lying as it did in this semi-desert Josephus, the Jewish historian, praises the excellence of its dates in their many varieties, the quality of its honey, gathered on the hills, its precious balm, its cypresses. "In calling this place divine, we shall not greatly err, for trees there are abundant, and of rare species. . . ." In winter the climate is so sunny that one can wear cotton clothes even when Judea is covered with snow. It is not surprising that there had grown up the developed civilization whose luxury has been brought to light by the excavator's spade.

Jericho, with its gates closed, trusting in the strength of its walls, waited until hunger should compel the nomads to depart. Joshua led the attack; it must have seemed quite absurd. But again a miracle occurred. By the order of God, the priests carried the Ark round the city, sounding a trumpet. On seven successive days this procession was repeated as we see it in the miniature of Fouquet, in all faith, the people following in religious silence. On the seventh day, at a given signal, from the seven thousand throats of the attackers came an immense shout. The walls collapsed, and the city was taken. One wonders if the blowing of the trumpets was not done to distract attention while mines were being laid. When the work was done, another signal was arranged to warn the sappers to get clear of the galleries, having first kindled dry wood to blow up the walls. But was the Israelite army not too primitive for such a piece of military engineering? Some think that an earthquake was responsible for this manifestation of the will of God.

The terrible *herem*, the religious anathema, descended on the unhappy city. Rahab alone was spared, the reward of her treason. An Israelite who had violated the sacred tabu and who returned with loot was stoned to death, together with his family and his flocks. Fear swept the entire country; we learn the first result. A Canaanite clan, the Gibeonites, sought alliance, and came over to the side of the Israelites. Upon which five cities allied themselves in order to break the advance of the invaders and turned on the Gibeonites who asked Joshua for aid. He came by night and made a surprise attack in the morning. This was a dazzling victory, so complete that the radiant memory of it was long cherished. Later, when the history of this time was written, the biblical historian drew upon a very ancient poem, composed not long after the battle, "The Book of the Just"; according to this record, Joshua "said in the sight of Israel, Sun, stand thou still upon Gibeon; and thou, Moon, in the valley of Ajalon. And the sun stood still,[2] and the moon stayed, until the people had avenged themselves upon their enemies" (Josh. x:13). The time seemed all too short for the exploitation of this success. As for the five allied kings, they fled for refuge to a cave, from which they were taken out, hanged, and replaced in the cave, dead.

Under such a leader, the conquest of Canaan proceeded apace. A series of rapid attacks and successful strategies gained Israel

[2] We are indebted to M. Jean Bosler, Director of the Marseilles Observatory, for a very interesting hypothesis bearing upon "the miracle of Joshua." The Bible records (Josh. x:11) that the Gideonites who fled before Israel were beaten by a hail of stones raining from the sky. Now these showers of meteorites are often accompanied by clear nights—the prolonging of twilight into the following dawn. Thus on June 30, 1908, a shower of meteorites, since famous, fell in Siberia, and was followed by a phenomenal prolongation of the day, noted by the French papers *before* the fall of meteorites in Siberia had become known. It is the presence of particles of dust in the stratosphere that thus abnormally prolongs the twilight. A similar phenomenon was observed during the eruption of Cracatoa in 1883, and also on other occasions. There must have been, at the time of Joshua's victory, an unusual prolongation of the daylight, which had, in practice, the same result as the sun standing still. Elsewhere, Flavius Josephus speaks of a "long day." The fall of stones from the sky and the standing still of the sun would therefore be parts of one and the same miracle, performed by God on behalf of Joshua. Science therefore entirely confirms the supernatural event.

many cities—Lachish, Hebron, Debir and many others. A raid towards the south brought them to the borders of Palestine. Another, towards the north, by a victory won near Lake Merom, broke up another coalition, and allowed Israel to reach Hermon. No doubt victory was still far from complete. The Canaanites held their positions in the centre of the country. Many more battles were to come, but God's promise had begun to be realized. Joshua decided, therefore, that the time had come to assign to each tribe the part that it should play in the war effort and also in the sharing of the land.

The tribes were thirteen in number, for each was descended from one of the twelve sons of Jacob; the two sons of Joseph, Ephraim and Manasseh, who had been adopted by the Patriarch, formed another tribe. The tribe of Levi, on account of its sacred function, received no land. The heart of the country, the zone of solid mountains, was given to Judah, called to a high destiny, and to the hardy hands of "the house of Joseph," Ephraim and Manasseh (part of this last tribe, finding it impossible to live on their land, went into Transjordania with Gad and Reuben). The others received the surrounding lands. The religious capital of the country was established at Shiloh, in Ephraim; there the Ark was deposited. There the people assembled on important occasions. But this new religious centre did not make the people forget the cherished site, dear to the memory of their ancestors, the Shechem of the Patriarchs. It was there that after its long journey Joseph's mummy, brought out of Egypt, was at last entombed. It was there that Joshua, grown old, gathered the people and reminded them of the providential significance of their history, and made them promise to observe the Covenant and raise, near those oaks at whose feet Jacob had buried the impious amulets, a memorial stone.

Joshua died at the age of a hundred and ten years. He was buried on Mount Ephraim, and in order to perpetuate the significance of the return to ancient observances that he had imposed, the stone knives with which he had circumcised his people were buried with him.

THE BOOK OF JUDGES

Two or three centuries succeeded the events which are known to us only partially. It is always the same warlike web from which, as in heroic tapestries, detached vigorous episodes stand out. But to establish a chronology, or to follow out a logical development, is a very difficult matter. The history of Israel here subdivides into as many separate histories as there are tribes.

Each of the group settled in Canaan must, for the sake of its members, accomplish the conquest of the zone assigned to it, and defend itself against those enemies who attacked it from all sides. In most cases the tribes attempted to act for themselves. Exclusiveness, stimulated yet more in the excitement of conquest, gave way rarely—and even then incompletely—to the necessity of cohesion. And this anarchy, regrettable as it may have been, corresponded so profoundly to the deepest instincts of these people, lately nomads, that the authors of the Book of Judges ended their work with these words, charged with regret: "In those days there was no king in Israel: every man did that which was right in his own eyes." In fact one of the interesting things about the period is that experience, very often tragic, was to show them that unity is strength, and the period came to an end with the great cry of a people clamouring for the authority of a king.

The complete settlement in Canaan was effected in a number of ways. War was one. But another was that patient infiltration in which the chosen people have always excelled: marriages with the women of the country, and also no doubt alliances with petty kings who took one clan or another into their service. This conquest led to very important results. The nomads became cultivators; they abandoned tents for houses. And at the same time, by mixing with local races, they underwent marked influences both in civilization, which these influences advanced, and in the religious order in which there were strong inducements to backsliding.

It is the latter aspect that the Bible most strongly stresses; indeed it is the one with which its record is chiefly concerned, because it proves the absolute power of God. Rather than a continuous history, the Book of Judges is a series of historical episodes constructed on roughly the same model. God has abandoned His people in the midst of idolatrous populations "to prove Israel by them, to know whether they would hearken unto the commandments of the Lord" (Judges iii:4). Israel succumbs to the temptation, serves false gods, "prostitutes herself." And then Jahweh brings an enemy to oppress them; but the people of the Covenant remember Him in their trouble, supplicate, implore; and God, merciful, sends them a leader, who delivers them. After which, the story recommences because, as Saint Augustine says, "in chastisements, men confess their faults; but when God rescues them, their tears are quickly dried."

These providential saviours are the Judges. In a tribe in the toils of enemy oppression an inspired man arises, who is faithful to the one God, who is indignant because of the betrayal of his comrades. The spirit "bloweth where it listeth"; it may be the noble chief of a clan, or the son of a prostitute, a hero notorious for his power, or a woman celebrated on account of her prophetic gifts. It is all one. The authority of that messenger of the Almighty never fails to impose itself. During the time of danger his authority is absolute, just as republican Rome was later to nominate for six months those dictators with twenty-four lictors who checked the enemy. As a rule, their task performed, these temporary leaders of Israel returned to their original rank, retaining only an immense moral prestige; a few, however, became practically kings of their tribes. On the day when that power became permanent and national, the monarchy was established.

"Judges" (in Hebrew, *shophêt*), corresponds exactly to the term *suffête* by which the Carthaginians, also Semites, designated their magistrates. The word means, "he who protects by means of justice." More than the sheikh of the tribe, but less than its sovereign, an intermediate form of authority in a transitional period, these picturesque heroes performed their task well—the task of protecting Israel against others, and also against herself.

DEBORAH THE PROPHETESS

In the plain of Esdrelon with its rich black alluvial soil, the tribe of Issachar had received its portion. But that country through which passed the route to the sea was coveted by all. The Canaanite kings, still powerful in this northern region, united in order to resist the inroads of the Israelites in their infiltration of the plain. Their chief, Sisera, had the routes guarded in the region of Haifa, in order to intercept the communications of the Hebrews. "The highways were unoccupied, and the travellers walked through byways" (Judges v:6). Then Deborah appeared on the scene.

The situation was unfavourable; arms were lacking. Most of the tribes were passing through a phase of discouragement, distressed at finding the conquest that they had thought would be so easy fraught with difficulties. But Deborah the Prophetess burned with holy ardour. She was celebrated in her own tribe for her wisdom; when she was seated under her palm-tree, people came often to ask her to settle difficult questions in dispute. She was known throughout Israel. And God bade her arise! Logic is not the only consideration in great events. Joan of Arc also mocked at reason.

The prophetess went to Barak, chief of a neighbouring tribe. He himself had been a prisoner in the hands of the Canaanites. Surely he would bestir himself to conquer them! He hesitated. He would only go into battle if the prophetess would accompany him, in order to be quite certain of God's intentions. Other tribes agreed to send detachments (not all, however—six, not counting the Levites, who did not take part in the coalition). The troops gathered on the slopes of Tabor: peasants, down-and-outs, a heroic rabble. In the plain of Kishon, near Megiddo, Sisera massed his war-chariots.

The day arrived on which Deborah was told by God that the time to act had come. It was raining. The torrent poured down. "Up," said the prophetess, "for this is the day in which the Lord hath delivered Sisera into thy hand!" But in order to punish the chief for his want of faith, she added that the enemy should not die at his hands, but by the hands of a woman.

Jahweh's storm favoured the Israelites. The clouds poured down their rain, and the soaked earth became unsuitable for the manoeuvres of chariots. Surprised by a double attack, one from in front, and the other in the rear, led by the tribe of Ephraim, the Canaanites weakened. Their troops lost ground, and the river carried down many corpses. Immediately, other groups, gaining courage, fell upon the fugitives. Sisera, attempting to return to his own country by way of the mountains, utterly exhausted, sought shelter in a nomadic douar. A woman recognized him, feigned to offer him shelter, and then, as he slept, in defiance of all the laws of hospitality, drove a nail into his temples, with such force that she fastened his head to the ground. The prophecy was fulfilled—Sisera had perished, shamefully, by the hand of a woman.

Deborah had delivered Israel. In honour of that victory a poet who had witnessed it composed a savage hymn, the "Song of Deborah," one of the most ancient texts in the Bible. This hymn first narrates the events, then pours insults on the tribes who did not take part in the battle, and finally sings the glory of the conquerors. The opening strophes are savage, spoken in the accents of wrath, echoing the clash of arms and the cries of the wounded. Then comes the flight and the pursuit. "Then were the horsehoofs broken by the means of the pransings, the pransings of their mighty ones." Finally, the ferocious poet imagines the mother of Sisera watching from her window for her son returning from war. "Why is his chariot so long in coming, why tarry the wheels of his chariots?" He had promised her the spoils of war, a coloured robe and two women at least for every warrior! This irony can be compared to that used by Aeschylus in the "Persians," or to that of the French ballad of Marlborough.

The drama is over. Peace once more reigns in the plains, and throughout the villages of Israel. "So let all thine enemies perish, o LORD: but let them that love him be as the sun when he goeth forth in his might."

GIDEON'S RAID

The Canaanite danger had been averted, but peace was still insecure. Another danger remained—from the Bedouins. The very success of Israel served to encourage wandering tribes to come to snatch a share in the prey. They came from great distances, from as far as Negeb, Midianites, Amalekites, for ever on the move and inspired by greed. The rich plain of Esdrelon was one of their chief objectives. The bandits came up through Transjordania, crossed the river near Lake Merom, and entered the coveted zone by the gateway into Jezreel. "As numerous as grasshoppers," they fell upon the ripe cornfield, and the fat beasts; in a few days the pillage was completed, and their camels loaded with booty set out again towards the east while Israel digested her anger.

One cannot say very much for the courage of the Israelites of that period. Deborah was no longer there to put courage into them. When the bandits were sighted, they hastily hid a little corn. But none of them contemplated standing to fight; in the tribe of Manasseh, a sheik, Joash, two of whose sons had been killed by the Bedouins, did not even attempt vengeance. It seems that settlement on the land had emasculated the soldiers of Joshua. This humiliation had its significance. God decreed it. It was the outcome of a betrayal, for idolatry was gaining ground; Joash himself had in his house an altar to Baal, and this Canaanite god was gaining ground among the people of Jahweh. Nevertheless, at the depth of their misfortune the unfaithful people remembered their God and "cried to Him"; and Jahweh raised up Gideon.

Gideon was another of the sons of Joash. "He threshed wheat by the winepress, to hide it from the Midianites" (Judges vi:11) when the angel appeared to him and said: "The Lord is with thee, thou mighty man of valour." Gideon was the more surprised as he had not thought of himself as a hero; he was a prudent, observant boy, who had no wish to expose himself to blows except with the minimum of risks. But the spirit of God carried him

beyond himself. One night he overturned the *achera*, the idolatrous altar, cut down the grove sacred to infidelity and used it
for firewood in the sacrifice of one of his father's young bulls in a
burnt offering to Jahweh. The next day there was great consterna-
tion. The people would have stoned the iconoclast, but Joash,
observing the inaction of the outraged deity, said with great good
sense, "Let Baal defend himself." In order to lead the people back
to the cult of the One God, the inspired youth raised an altar to
Jahweh; he heard the voice of the angel commanding him to
defeat the Midianites; his prudence gave place to courage. A new
leader had arisen in Israel.

Once more the Bedouins arrived to pillage. Guided by the
divine spirit, Gideon chose three hundred picked warriors, selected by a strange test—they were those who, coming to a brook,
lapped the water like dogs, and did not go down on their knees
like men. For the projected raid, savage dogs were needed. They
lay in wait for the enemy as, laden with booty, they set out again
towards the east. One night he placed his men in three groups.
Each soldier carried a trumpet and a torch concealed in an
earthenware pot. At a given signal, they all broke their pots,
raised their torches, and with a cry of, "The sword of the Lord
and of Gideon," the three hundred trumpets rudely aroused the
nomads from their sleep. Bedouin tribes are given to panic. They
fled. Gideon pursued them indefatigably. On the plateau of Gilead
his troop, exhausted, begged bread from the Israelites who in-
habited the towns there. They refused to help their kinsmen. No
matter. Gideon held to his bold course. A second time he surprised the nomads, fought them and captured two chiefs. His
victory was complete. He returned to Jezreel, having, as he returned, taken vengeance upon the indifferent Gileadites, killing
some and punishing others with thorns and briars from the
wilderness.

This bold campaign had important results. Gideon had avenged
the honour of his tribe. The two Bedouin sheiks had perished at
his hands. The danger from the bandits was overcome. His prestige was such that he was offered the royal crown—first symptom

of a desire new to Israel, for a centralized authority. Gideon was too astute to go as far as this. "I will not rule over you; neither shall my son rule over you; the Lord shall rule over you." But as a matter of fact, for the reminder of his life, he had all the prerogatives of royalty. Still a military leader, he was also within his own tribe, and even in Ephraim, a sort of pacific despot. He had great wealth, a considerable harem, and seventy-one sons. His glory was so firmly established in Israel that the Psalms preserve its memory, and the great Isaiah praises him.

This prudent man clearly realized that the time for a monarchy had not yet come. One of his sons, having assassinated sixty-nine of his brothers, had himself proclaimed king at Shechem. The only result of this was that he brought revolts upon himself, in one of which he was killed by a millstone that a woman dropped on his head from the city walls.

JEPHTHAH'S DAUGHTER

Incidents like those we have just seen—pitched battles, sudden attacks, pursuits—are repeated over and over again in the Book of Judges. We can number twelve "Judges," but many of them are known only by their names and a few lines. Every tribe must have had them; tradition has selected from among them all examples that illustrate the supernatural theme of the fault, the pardon, and the divine intervention.

The story of Jephthah takes us farther east, to the plateaux of Transjordania. This is a region of steppes but reasonably fertile, where there is sufficient grass to support numbers of cattle, and where stretches of volcanic soil are under cultivation. The ethnic situation was vastly complicated. The ancient Amorites, defeated by Moses, had still numbers of douars. The Moabites and the Ammonites kept chiefly to the pastures, but were strongly entrenched there. The Hebrew tribes of Gad, Reuben and eastern Manasseh occupied the cities. All these neighbouring peoples mixed, overlapped, intermarried and wrangled. And to complete the disorder, the great Aramaic wave was pouring in ceaselessly from the north.

Israel had her work cut out to defend that frontier. Othniel, a judge of Judah, had already stopped a raid of Aramaeans, who, no doubt driven from their Syrian lands by the People of the Sea, had penetrated as far as the extreme south of Canaan. An expedition coming down from the heights of Moab across the channel of the Jordan had succeeded in recapturing the region of the city of Jericho, which was occupied by the tribe of Benjamin: there arose a judge named Ehud, who had got rid of the Moabites and assassinated their king. He had had himself announced to this king as one sent by God, was received by him in his high chamber, and had planted a knife in his bowels with such force that "the haft went in after the blade, and the fat closed upon the blade."

In this country of the south, as in the north, idolatry was rife. Yet again the "children of Israel did evil in the sight of the Lord," and punishment was not long delayed. The Ammonites took from them rich pastures south of Jabbok. The tribes of Israel installed in Transjordania realized that action must be taken, but no man capable of taking command was forthcoming. At last they thought of Jephthah. He was a bastard, a good-for-nothing, the son of a prostitute. An outcast from society, he had made himself the leader of a desert band of outlaws who raided the townspeople and looted the caravans. God uses all kinds of men for His work. The desert had preserved the outlaw from the taint of polytheism; he served Jahweh, and Jahweh alone.

The delegation sent to him was not well received. "Did not ye hate me, and expel me out of my father's house? and why are ye come unto me now when ye are in distress?" (Judges xi:7). He made conditions—"If ye bring me home again to fight against the children of Ammon, . . . shall I be your head?" (Judges xi:9). A solemn agreement was prepared, in the name of Jahweh. Jephthah took the command.

At first he attempted to negotiate. Could an agreement not be reached as to the territorial boundaries? There was room enough for both Ammon and Israel. But the conversations came to nothing. Jephthah prepared for battle. But this religious man wished to have assurance that his God was with him. He made a vow to Jahweh: "If thou shalt without fail deliver the children of Ammon into mine hands, then it shall be that whatsoever cometh forth of the doors of my house to meet me, when I return in peace from the children of Ammon, shall surely be the LORD's, and I will offer it up for a burnt offering" (Judges XI:30–31). Then he went out against the enemy. An encircling movement enabled him to make a surprise attack; thrown back towards the south, the Ammonites were forced to seek refuge in the mountains of Moab. "And Jephthah came to Mizpeh unto his house and, behold, his daughter came out to meet him with timbrels and with dances: and she was his only child; beside her he had neither son nor daughter. And it came to pass, when he saw her, that he rent his clothes, and said, Alas, my daughter! thou hast brought me very low, and thou art one of them that trouble me: for I have opened my mouth unto the Lord, and I cannot go back. And she said unto him, My father, if thou hast opened thy mouth unto the Lord, do to me according to that which hath proceeded out of thy mouth . . . and she said unto her father, Let this thing be done for me: let me alone two months that I may go up and down upon the mountains and bewail my virginity, I and my fellows."

Tender hearts cannot but be wrung at the thought of that young victim who wept for sixty days, like Sophocles' Antigone, for the children that she would never bear, and who returned at the appointed time to offer herself to her father's knife. A gentler interpretation has been suggested: that only her virginity was consecrated to God, like that of a nun or a vestal. But history would bear out the literal interpretation to this terrible offering, considering the fact that Canaan practised these human sacrifices, and that the Phoenicians were to continue them long afterwards, and that a king of Moab sacrificed his son under similar circumstances. From this time, every year the daughters of Israel commemorated the sacrificed maiden by four days of prayers and lamentations.

Jephthah, for the remainder of his life, governed the land beyond the river; he even imposed his authority on Ephraim, the

proud "house of Joseph." [3] The one-time exile foreshadowed the
future kings of the chosen people and in particular David who,
like him, was to gather his strength in the solitude of the desert.

THE MIGHTY DEEDS OF SAMSON

These diverse incidents have brought us to the first half of the
eleventh century B.C. By this time the Canaanites had resigned
themselves to their lot as a conquered people, and, at least for the
time being, the desert nomads were under control. Another enemy
was to claim the attention of Israel, one so threatening that after
terrible crises the chosen race was to become aware of the extreme
urgency of national unity, and to organize a state. This enemy
was the Philistines.

Since Rameses III had thrown them out of Egypt, the Aryans
installed on the coast of Canaan had made steady progress. They
spread endlessly all round the mountain, penetrating into territories where the tribesmen of Judah were peacefully cultivating
their barley and into those where the tribe of Dan found itself
more and more closely beset by their invasion. What could be
done? Very little. Israel hated the Philistines as an alien race of
uncircumcised idolaters. But their ancient prudence compelled
them to recognize that, in the face of these men of powerful
stature, armed with solid iron swords, mounted in redoubtable
war chariots, the only wise course was to submit and wait for a
better opportunity. Pillaged, impoverished and subjected, the
Israelites dreamed of the time when they would be able to be
revenged. But the time was slow in coming. There were only individual exploits here and there; but messengers of deliverance are
praised the more highly in proportion to the fewness of their
numbers!

Already one Shamgar, armed with an ox-goad, had led a hard

[3] This conflict with Ephraim was marked by a curious episode. Having
defeated the Ephraimites, the followers of Jephthah lay in wait for them at
the ford over the Jordan. When a fugitive appeared, the Gileadite soldiers
asked him his tribe. And as Ephraim pronounced the letter "Sh" as "S",
they recognized them by making them pronounce the word *shibboleth*, and
killed them.

life of conflict with the Philistines. But the great figure of the anti-Philistine struggle was Samson, the very type of the popular hero, strong and also resourceful, who will slay a thousand enemies with the greatest ease but fall an easy victim to a woman. There is something of Hercules in him, something of Robin Hood, and of "le Grand Ferré." He was a true servant of Jahweh, fanatical in the righteous cause; but not to be expected to obey a strict moral code! Even while they were at war, Hebrews and Philistines very often intermarried. Delilah, the ravishing traitoress, is the very type of the charm of these deplorable unions.

In the tribe of Dan, a pious couple received a singular visit. A stranger met them in the fields and refused to give his name, which, he said, was ineffable. When they offered him refreshment he said, "You would do better to offer it to Jahweh!" And when the wood of the holocaust burned up, the nameless guest rose into the flames and vanished into the heavens. He had told the couple that the child expected by them would be blessed by God, to whom he was to be dedicated. As a sign of his consecration, he was never to shave his hair.

Samson, "the little Sun," grew. The seven locks of his hair were the assurance of his strength, given him by God. He became a giant, able to oppose the strongest of the Philistines. No one could stand against him; gentle at most times, he was capable of terrible rages, and at the same time inventive in expedients. Having fallen in love with a Philistine woman while hunting a lion in the plain of Timnath, he decided to marry her. On the day of the wedding, being warmed with wine, the guests played a game that was widespread among the primitive Aryans; they asked one another riddles. Samson's wife having told her blood-relations the answer to the riddle he asked, the great dunce of a hero lost his wager. However, this did not greatly trouble him, for in order to pay his bet he went to the neighbouring town, slew thirty Philistines, and with the booty settled his account. This incident created a certain coldness between Samson and the Philistines. But wishing to see his wife again, Samson returned to Timnath; she had married another man, one of the wedding guests! He revenged himself by a practical joke in the style of the time; he tied foxes together in pairs, each drawing a lighted firebrand, and let them loose among the cornfield of his enemies.

These attentions had the result that one might expect. The Philistines demanded that Samson should be handed over. He was then on the land of Judah, and that unwarlike tribe preferred submission to blows. The hero mildly allowed himself to be led, but no sooner was he in the hands of his enemies than he broke his bonds "as flax that was burnt with fire," seized the jawbone of a dead ass, whose skeleton lay beside the road, killed a thousand men with this improvised weapon, and went off in high spirits singing "with the jawbone of an ass, heaps upon heaps, with the jaw of an ass have I slain a thousand men" (Judges xv:16). From this time, his boldness knew no bounds: he provoked the Philistines with repeated acts of defiance. One day he appeared mocking them, in Gaza, their remotest city. He went boldly to the house of a courtesan. They prepared to capture him. The city gates were shut, but Samson merely took the two gates, door posts and bars and all, and went off to the mountains laden with this booty.

Only a woman could undermine this holy vitality. In love once more, he came under the power of Delilah. The Philistines lay in wait for him during the visits that he made to his mistress. They promised a large sum of money to the woman if she could learn from the hero the secret of his strength. For a long time Samson, on his guard, resisted; he gave false reasons and cheated Delilah and the Philistines. But at last, weakening under her reproaches, he told the secret. "There hath not come a razor upon mine head, for I have been a Nazarite unto God from my mother's womb." Now the traitoress had only to make the poor dupe "sleep on her knees," to cut his tresses, and to call the enemy. Disarmed, the giant struggled furiously, as Rubens has shown him in one of his best-known paintings. They put out his eyes; he was now nothing more than a plaything to amuse the Philistines at their banquets.

Nevertheless Jahweh, to whom His servant made noble supplication, permitted him to take a final vengeance. One day when they had brought him to amuse a gathering with the spectacle of his weakness, he seized the columns of the great edifice in which were the Philistines who mocked him; his hair had grown again and his strength had returned. Tearing down the pillars, Samson perished under the ruins, together with his tormentors.

What a strange and pathetic destiny is that of this hero! Extreme, truculent, for a long time his existence seemed to be outside the norm of humanity, and to belong rather to a picaresque romance than to history. But at the same time, and with a strange ring of verity, it enters the subjective order, in which each of us fights combats like his. The enemy that he had to vanquish was less the Philistine than his own secret temptation, his sin. As weak as the humblest of mortals, he struggled in snares that are familiar enough. Much more than his exploits, the thing that gives him his stature is his suffering, the tragic magnificence of his last moments, and, seen through all the picturesque details of his story, the drama of the man weakened by sin but re-established through expiation.

There is something fine in the fact that these Israelites, while still so primitive and half-barbarous, should have detected behind this story of adventures the undertones of such a meaning. If only the great deeds of Samson had been retained, the range of his life's significance would have been strangely limited. But it is presented in very different terms.

He was to remain one of the most celebrated heroes of the chosen race: the elders handed on his fame from generation to generation. Whether his acts were historically decisive is to be doubted. In spite of him, and after him, the Philistines continued to gain ground until the time when the kings of Israel measured their force against them.

INTERNAL DRAMAS

The epic of the Judges takes place entirely, according to the Bible, in a providential perspective, and in order to manifest the power of God. History is forced to admit that here we have a strange fact. Everything seemed to combine in order to threaten the existence of this small race, the guardians of the Promise. Logic would lead us to expect that, dislocated by antagonisms and contaminated by local influences, they would have become absorbed into the confused mass of Canaan. This did not happen. Israel preserved its unity; as a strong minority imbued, as we have already seen, with the pride of conquerors, they were to impose their standards, their name and their God on the entire population of Palestine, and to rise above the formidable miasma exhaled by a soil peopled by idols. The victory was supernatural, but it was not, even so, won without a hard struggle.

While all these military events were taking place, three dramas were being enacted in the consciousness of the chosen people. The first arose out of the fact of the installation in the promised land itself. The nomads had become settled, the shepherds had become labourers. The result was a profound crisis that had many results. The life of cities, which the nomads of the steppes had held in such suspicion, was adopted by their sons, and with it the civilization of the Canaanites. No doubt it seems very modest to us, and the richest of men in the days of the Judges had no more than modest comfort; a few jewels, a woven saddle-cloth on his ass, a Phoenician robe dyed in purple, or an Egyptian vase, would mark a man of great fortune; Gideon, the son of a sheik, threshed his own grain. But even this small degree of luxury was enough to introduce trouble into the souls of ascetic nomads.

As a matter of fact, everything was in a state of flux. These two centuries of the Judges mark a turning point between the anarchy of tribal life and despotic centralization. It was at the end of this period that precise administrative precedents were established, and when no doubt archives were first kept; in the Books of Samuel, the least attentive reader cannot fail to notice the change-over from a collection of moral anecdotes to a precise chronicle. With writing, which had been in common use in Canaan three centuries earlier when the petty kings were sending to their overlord Pharaoh those diplomatic letters that have been discovered at El Amarna but which had now no doubt become alphabetic, the official, the tax-collector and the overseer made their appearance. Deborah had put in writing a list of her soldiers' names. And many pieces of evidence seem to indicate that the biblical record of the Book of Judges incorporates portions which were very ancient and possibly contemporary.

The time of the Judges has sometimes been compared to the Middle Ages; the traces of ancient customs lingered on amongst others that point forward to future institutions. This was the cause of terrible conflicts. In her most secret heart, Israel harboured a regret for the times that were past, for the free steppes. This people, accustomed to the meditative pastoral life, discovered that the land that had been given to them required a great deal of labour. Abel the shepherd now felt himself changed into Cain the labourer. The words, "in the sweat of thy brow shalt thou eat bread," were now realized; and this land they loved with that poignant, irreplaceable love that men feel towards whatever has been gained at the price of suffering, or at the cost of some renunciation.

The second drama is political. Scattered over a whole country, the tribes were in danger of dislocation. Their habits were nomadic, and a migration is quickly decided upon. A clan of Dan, driven out by the Philistines, moved to the extreme north of the country.[4] The "sons of Joseph," in the time of Joshua, emigrated towards "the forest"; Naomi, with her husband and her sons, left for Moab. And above all one must bear in mind the terrible exclusiveness of the tribal spirit. Separatist incidents are too numerous to count. The Transjordanians, from the time of the victories of Joshua, raised an altar in rivalry with the religious site at Shiloh. It was the same people who, long after, refused to assist Gideon and received the chastisement due to their egoism. It was Ephraim who had a bone to pick with Jephthah and who was defeated by him.

Two episodes show how violent these clashes could be. One is comic. A certain Micah, of Ephraim, had stolen from his mother.

[4] The town of Laish, where Abraham had rescued his nephew Lot (*See* p. 20) afterwards bore the name of this tribe.

The latter cursed the thief, and, fearing the curse, Micah returned the money. Part of it was used to erect a statue to Jahweh (which in itself was scarcely orthodox), and, as a good business man, Micah organized a very profitable local cult. A wandering Levite having come that way, our man proposed to him that he should become the custodian of this idol; a house, salary, food and clothing were all provided. And the alms poured in. The clan of Dan, on their way north, happened to pass. They found the Jahweh of Micah entirely to their taste, and explained to the priest how much better it would be to serve a whole tribe than a single man and carried off the idol, altar, sacred furniture, and the Levite into bargain, leaving Micah only his anger, to waste in vain lamentations.

The other incident is thoroughly disreputable. Another Levite of Ephraim was on his way to his own country, bringing with him one of his concubines, with whom he had just been reconciled. As he had to spend the night on the territory of Benjamin, he was received by an Ephraimite who lived there. During the night the Benjaminites besieged the house of this hospitable man and demanded that he should hand over the traveller. Their intentions, of which the Bible leaves no doubt, cannot be stated in plain English. The Ephraimite refused to betray the laws of hospitality and offered, in place of the guest, his wife and daughter! Finally the concubine was handed over. The next morning she was found dead, her hands clutching the door. The Levite cut the corpse into morsels and sent one to each of the tribes, demanding vengeance. Israel rose as one man. The Benjaminites were massacred, all except six hundred warriors, who fled. Later, having asked for mercy, they were given permission to take the virgins of a city of Gilead, in order to have wives and reconstitute the tribe.

We see, therefore, what forces of disintegration had to be resolved in order to maintain the unity of the chosen people. Nevertheless, unity was imposed. In the first place the very nature of sedentary life tended to weaken the individuality of the tribes and to substitute the new unit of the city. The countless intermarriages with the people of the country contributed also to softening this exclusiveness. The time was approaching when the union that Moses had imposed in the name of a high ideal, Israel was to reconstitute for very practical reasons.

Not only were political rivalries a threat to unity. The third crisis, and the gravest, was religious. The installation in Canaan was accompanied by an unmistakeable spiritual decline. For this there were several reasons. How refined these Canaanites were! the Israelites thought. How beautiful their cities, and how desirable their women! Must not their gods also be so? Would they not guard the crops better than the redoubtable Jahweh of the desert? Certainly they would not betray the Almighty, the God of Moses; they would merely arrange to confer upon Him certain attributes of the local gods and, to begin with, they would give Him a visible, tangible character that should speak to the minds of mortals. This religious evolution was not brought about all at once, but slowly, surely, it introduced into the soul of Israel elements of decadence, that were to come to a head in the time of the Kings.

Thus there grew up a popular religion of Jahweh, very different from the pure doctrines of Moses. Antique usages of Canaan, cults of high places, sacred trees, upright stones, were from now on adopted by the Israelites; and no doubt it was well not to abolish these rites all at once; Pope Gregory the Great, sending missionaries to England, was to recommend them to "sprinkle the altars of idols with holy water," but not to destroy them. But many centres of ancient Canaan had taken on a highly equivocal character. Round the *Achera*, the sacred grove, or the raised *massebah*, ritual repasts easily became orgies. The priestesses drew men by other seductions than those of mysticism. In these things lay grave danger.

This contamination even made inroads into Mosaic theology. Jahweh was no longer conceived of as the redoubtable master whose will men perform, but as a benefactor acting upon whims, whose favours could be gained by presents. Sacrifices were lavishly bestowed—and of these the priests took their share. Baal

was becoming merged with Jahweh. Idolatry pure and simple
made progress also. Images were made, in formal violation of the
Decalogue. The worst practices of the Canaanites seem to have
become acceptable. Jephthah's sacrifice of his daughter aroused
less horror than admiring stupefaction. And the practices of
sorcery, magic and necromancy, whose aid Saul sought in secret,
were gaining ground.

Nevertheless, Israel resisted these ubiquitous temptations. Side
by side with this debased religion of Jahweh, there was another.
Even in their hours of betrayal, the chosen people remembered
their divine mission. They might sin; there were, nevertheless,
extremes of infidelity and shame to which they would not go. National pride sustained their faith, and whenever they called upon
Jahweh it was with a unanimous heart once more made worthy.
National fervour and religious enthusiasm went hand in hand.
The Judges were the personification of both of these.

Resistance to infidelity has its bastions in Israel itself. In the
first place there were the Levites, whose importance steadily increased. We find them, now assembled in colleges on some religious site, now wandering from one city to another, divine mendi-
cants, always passionately devoted to their priestly functions, to
the text of the Torah, to the meticulous rites whose secrets they
transmitted. This highly ritualistic priesthood defended the integrity of its dogma with fierce vigour.

Not all the Levites, to be sure, were above reproach. We find
some who cynically selected the best morsels before the burnt
offerings were made, or who extracted excessive payments. On
the whole the priests of Levi must bear the very heavy responsibility, for which the Prophets were to denounce them, of reducing religion to a formalism, which was to be the ultimate
drama of Israel and the thing that was to blind them. But without
them and their obstinate resistance, would the cult of the One
God have survived its testing-time?

The greatness of Israel at this time is that it did, in spite of
crises and decadence, save what had to be saved. Behind para-
graphs of the Bible one glimpses holy figures, burning with the

same fire that devoured the soul of the great Moses and that shone from those of the Patriarchs. Neither Deborah nor Gideon nor Jephthah is beyond reproach. But as soon as they act in the light of God, what stature is theirs! Even Samson, in whose violence there is little virtue, bears witness to God, to whom his birth was dedicated. Only when he was driven to break his vow did he fall, and afterwards, how eloquent was his repentance!

It was the saints of Israel, of whom many are barely mentioned in the Book, who constituted the strength of the nation. There is more than one reference to men *consecrated* to Jahweh, who must not shave their hair or drink fermented liquor. Samson was one such. These Nazarites thus maintained in the very heart of a sedentary society the ascetic customs of the nomads. They preserved, even when their behaviour only too fully expressed the violence of the period, the ancient ideal. Samuel, the last of the Judges, was one of these; a fact that has great significance.

SAMUEL

Samuel is a wonderful figure—the austere heart, the soul filled with God, the noble character. His was the thankless task of being the intermediary between the men who represented the time that was coming to an end and those of the new order. He assumed this role with the simple nobility of one who sets no store on his life when a holy cause is in question.

In the mountain town of Remah, Elkanah lived with his two wives. One of these, Peninnah, had had children. The other, Hannah, was desperate because she feared that she was sterile. But this household was rich in faith. One day when her husband went to sacrifice at Shiloh, Hannah went into the sanctuary and prayed to Jahweh with her whole heart. The high priest of the Ark, Eli, an old, tired man, was sitting by a pillar. He watched this woman, whose tears ran down her cheeks, and whose whole appearance spoke of deep trouble. Meanwhile Hannah prayed in silence: "O Lord of Hosts, if thou wilt indeed look on the affliction of thine handmaid, and remember me, and not forget thine handmaid, but wilt give unto thine handmaid a man child, then I will give him unto the Lord all the days of his life, and there shall no razor come upon his head." But the priest was suspicious of that exaltation and those lips speaking silently. "How long wilt thou be drunken? put away thy wine from thee," he said. But the poor soul replied: "No, my Lord . . . I have drunk neither wine nor strong drink, but have poured out my soul before the Lord." Then Eli answered, "Go in peace, and the God of Israel grant thee thy petition." This hope was fulfilled. Hannah bore a son, whom she named Samuel, "asked of the Lord" (1 Samuel 1:20).

When the child was weaned, Hannah kept her word and took him to the temple. She told the high priest of the vow she had made, and of her happiness. Prostrating herself, she sang a canticle in praise of Jahweh: "The Lord killeth, and maketh alive: he bringeth down to the grave, and bringeth up. The Lord maketh poor and maketh rich; he bringeth low, and lifteth up. He raiseth up the poor out of the dust, and lifteth up the beggar from the dunghill . . . and the wicked shall be silent in darkness" (1 Samuel II:6–9). Then she went away, leaving the child. We see him again, older, clothed in white linen, wearing during the temple ceremonies the coat which his mother made for him each year, his little nazarite curls hanging down his back, the little servant of the temple, a young smiling presence beside the old Eli, every year more and more hoary with age. His purity is the more striking in that the sons of the high priest were two of those cynical Levites who stole the best portions of the food offered in sacrifice before Jahweh had been served.

One night when Samuel was watching before the Ark—Eli, now almost blind with age, was asleep—a voice spoke. Thinking that it was the priest calling him, the child ran three times to his room. Eli realized that God was calling the boy. And Jahweh said to Samuel that he would judge Eli's house, and that no sacrifice nor offering could atone. The high priest hastened to ask the young disciple what words God had spoken. He received the blow with perfect humility: "It is the Lord; let him do what seemeth him good." But the punishment was to descend on more than his house alone.

The Philistines continued to increase in strength. They began to make inroads into the high lands. Israel wished for a decisive battle. In order to draw fortune to their side, the Hebrews carried the Ark on to the battlefield. Horror! It fell into the hands of the enemy. At Shiloh, at the city gates, Eli awaited the news of the outcome. A long lamentation was made to him—for the news was of defeat, flight, the capture of the Ark, the death of his two sons. The old priest fell fainting, overwhelmed with grief, and broke his skull. God's judgment was fulfilled.

It was the young Samuel who revived the broken courage of the people. The Philistines profited little by their victories. The Ark that they had installed at the feet of their idol disquieted them. Was it not the Ark that brought upon them a plague of rats, followed by pestilence? They returned the sacred object to Israel's keeping, in a little village. Samuel made a successful expedition against them. Returning to his father's town, he exerted over many tribes the prestige of his virtue and his justice. He was consulted with the more confidence as he possessed an astonishing gift of clairvoyance. Under this saint of God, Israel regained her confidence.

This, however, was not enough. The leader the tribes now wished for was neither an inspired brigand nor a spiritual guide, but a real sovereign who would organize their defence and complete the conquest of the country. "Now make us a king," the people cried, "to judge us like all the nations." The people's instinct was right. No final settlement with the Philistines could be reached except by a firm union of all their forces. Nevertheless, Samuel hesitated. The last of the Judges, he still stood for the particular ideal that had predominated in Israel for two centuries. To the assembled sheikhs he replied with a diatribe against royalty. "This will be the manner of the king that shall reign over you: he will take your sons and appoint them for himself, for his chariots, and to be his horsemen . . . and he will take your daughters to be confectionaries, and to be cooks, and to be bakers." This king would take their fields, extort money from them. They would regret it!

Samuel, in fact, was an old man, and out of sympathy with the younger generation. He himself was obscurely aware of this lack of understanding. A conflict was at work in the soul of the sage of Ramah, who saw his prestige threatened by the rise of forces that he neither liked nor understood. But Jahweh spoke: "Hearken unto their voice, and make them a king!" The servant bowed to the wish of his master, even though he did not understand its drift: Samuel anointed the brow of Saul. When the course of history is changing, one man's resistance becomes mere vanity.

RUTH, AND THE SOUL FILLED WITH GOD

Although the Book of Samuel has the austere beauty of a drama in which an ephemeral fragility is measured against the power that directs the course of the centuries, there is another story that is even more moving—it is that of Ruth, the young Moabite, in whom God accomplished these simple and noble virtues that we venerate in her descendant, Mary, the mother of Jesus. The four brief passages in which she is described to us are perhaps the most perfect in the Bible. After the streams of blood that have flooded so many of its pages, the story of Ruth is a pearl of purest orient. Many painters have attempted to capture its charm, and Victor Hugo, in evoking this pastoral, captures in his verses the breath of the night, the straying perfumes, all that Palestinian enchantment whose least image so readily becomes charged with spiritual meaning.

At a time when the Judges governed the country, a famine occurred. A man of Bethlehem in Judah left with his wife and went into the country of Moab. His name was Elimelech, hers Naomi. Their two sons married women of Moab. Years passed, and Elimelech died, and his sons also died soon after him. Naomi decided to return to Judea, where she had heard that bread was again plentiful. But her two daughters-in-law were so devoted to her that they refused to leave her. They set out with her in spite of her attempts to dissuade them. "Go, return each to her mother's house," she said, embracing them. One of them, Orpah, yielded to her reasonings; the prospect of a hazardous existence in an unknown country no doubt frightened her; the other, Ruth, persisted in her determination: "Whither thou goest, I will go: where thou lodgest, I will lodge; thy people shall be my people, thy God my God." United by this deep affection, the two women set off again on the road to Bethlehem; they reached Judea at the time when the barley harvest was about to begin.

In the fields where the harvesters were busy with scythes, the law decreed that not all the ears should be harvested. Some were always left for the poor, the portion of God that the gleaners carefully gathered. Ruth, therefore, in the heat of the day stooped to gather the ears, to have food for the mother she had adopted. She went into the fields of a rich man, Boaz; he noticed her and made enquiries about her. The young woman's story touched him; he spoke to her, gave her food, and through all the time of the harvest the Moabite gleaned in the fields of this kindly man.

When Naomi learned the name of this honest farmer, a project formed in her mind. Was not Boaz her relation on her husband's side? Could he not be asked, in conformity with the custom of *levirat*, to replenish the family that death had left without posterity? He should marry Ruth and then all would be well. She dressed the young woman, anointed her with perfume, and sent her to the threshing-floor where, in the cool of the night, Boaz was surveying his workmen as they threshed the corn. The work done, he lay down on a pile of straw. And Ruth quietly approached and lay down at his feet.

In the middle of the night Boaz awoke and turned over; a woman was lying beside him: "Who art thou?" and she answered: "I am Ruth thy handmaid; spread therefore thy skirt over thy handmaid; for thou art a near kinsman." And he said: "Blessed be thou of the Lord, my daughter; for thou hast shewed more kindness at the latter end than at the beginning, inasmuch as thou followest not young men, whether poor or rich . . . I will do to thee all that thou requirest; for all the city of my people doth know that thou art a virtuous woman." And the next day, amid the acclamations of the people, Ruth was betrothed to Boaz; all that she had expended in love and self-sacrifice was recompensed. She was, indeed, as her name signifies, "she who is fulfilled," who overflows with love.

This exquisite story was written many centuries later, no doubt after the return from exile. And it is moreover worth noticing that the narrator has placed this story, so full of nobility, in those troubled times of violence and passion. In our Middle Ages also, violence sometimes gave place to the delicacy of the story of Tristram, or the ballad of Griselda. But it may well be that we should see more in these brief pages than an interlude in a savage period of history.

From the marriage of Ruth descended the "root of Jesse" of which Israel speaks, from which was to spring such glorious fruit, that genealogical tree from which the sculptors of our cathedrals have drawn so many decorative themes. The grandson of Boaz was Jesse or Isai, the father of David the great king; the Moabite, the foreigner, whose filial love brought her to Bethlehem, was to be the ancestor of Mary and the distant grandmother of Christ. This in itself is sufficient reason for leading us to see in this story another meaning besides that of history or morality.

It would be beyond the scope of this book to derive from the biblical events whose course we are following one of those symbolic interpretations that the Fathers of the Church have devoted so much time to elaborating, and of which present-day Christians, whose rationalism is too extreme, have very little conception. A tradition as ancient as Christianity has seen in the events of the Holy Scriptures not merely facts but symbols, by means of which the inspired writers announced the Christian revelation or analyzed the hidden operations of the soul. The breviary preserves to a very large extent this mode of interpretation whose symbolism is so very fascinating.[5] Manna is not only the food of

[5] I recommend the reader to study the Abbé Tardif de Moidrey's admirable essay, *Le Livre de Ruth,* to the new edition of which Paul Claudel has added a long and excellent preface on "the symbolic reading of the Scriptures" (Desclée de Brouwer).

the Israelites in the desert; the lamb sacrificed is not only the ram substituted for Isaac, or the animal whose blood saved the chosen people on the night of the passing of the Angel. The symbolism is so clear that it is impossible to mistake it.

Is not the Book of Ruth charged with mystical symbols? The names that figure in it are rich in significance. Elimelech means "my God and my King." His two sons who died young are called "Infirmity" and "Failure"; Naomi means "Consolation"; Orpah, who, called to a higher existence, fails because of her weakness, is the "Crowned One," and Ruth, who goes on to the end of her spiritual adventure, is the "Fulfilled," the one on whom the master Boaz bestows his love. Beyond this story, fragrant with the scent of the fields as it is told to us, lies, perhaps, the story of the adventure of the soul called to the contemplative life who must strip herself of the attractions of the world, and devote herself to love and charity, but whose ineffable reward fills her with a far greater joy. This interpretation goes beyond the limits of history; but among so many events in which man's wishes are less plainly at work than the providence of God, who can say where the field of criticism ends and that of faith begins?

PART THREE

FROM GLORY TO EXILE

I

THE ROYAL MAJESTY

"WHO IS THIS that cometh out of the wilderness like pillars of smoke, perfumed with myrrh and frankincense, with all powders of the merchant?

"Behold his bed, which is Solomon's; threescore valiant men are about it, of the valiant of Israel.

"They all hold swords, being expert in war: every man hath his sword upon his thigh because of fear in the night.

"King Solomon made himself a chariot of the wood of Lebanon.

"He made the pillars thereof of silver, the bottom thereof of gold, the covering of it of purple, the midst thereof being paved with love, for the daughters of Jerusalem.

"Go forth, O ye daughters of Zion, and behold king Solomon with the crown wherewith his mother crowned him in the day of his espousals, and in the day of the gladness of his heart" (Song of Solomon III:6–11).

This picture drawn in the Song of Solomon in verses that are themselves radiant like gold is not wholly the work of oriental hyperbole that magnifies people and things like a desert mirage. In Jerusalem, about 950 B.C., there did indeed reign a great king whose riches, great works, beneficence and the justice of his rule over his people assured his reputation. When Christ spoke of Solomon "in all his glory," in order to describe the height of human greatness (Matthew VI:29), He was evoking an historical reality. Never did the people of the Promise know a period of such temporal felicity as under the magnificent sceptre of the third of their kings.

It was a thousand years since Abraham, the founder of this entire edifice, had died on the same earth as was now ruled over by his distant descendant. What vicissitudes lay between the nomadic clan in its tents and the kingdom and the palace! Preserving throughout many trials the self-consciousness that their monotheistic faith rendered the more assured, Israel had accomplished the double adventure of crossing lands and centuries without losing its coherence or its identity; the nomadic shepherds had become farmers and citizens without renouncing their faith. A man does not really know himself until he has passed through all the vicissitudes of his life, sorrow as well as joy, both power and poverty. The chosen people had still to undergo the test of prosperity, perhaps in order that they might measure its fragility.

Three kings occupied the scene during the brief period—from 1040 to 935 B.C. approximately—when the Kingdom of Israel counted in the politics of history: Saul, David and Solomon. Each with his particular gifts and virtues laboured to carry out the work that circumstances made indispensable—the organization of the chosen people into a state. But in rediscovering as a human necessity that unity whose real foundation was for them supernatural, the Hebrews were only the more tempted to see in this feat above all a means of power and an occasion for self-congratulation. In proportion as their state became more glorious in the eyes of the world, the germs of death multiplied in them.

The circumstances that drove Israel towards royalty were also to favour its expanding into its fine flower. The enemy whose pressure obliged Israel to unite her strength, the Philistines, even while remaining a danger and continuing to make progress, were no longer the threat that they had been in the days when Israel had perforce to bow to the superior strength of the giants in plumed helmets. Equilibrium had been reached for the time being. In the north, the Aramaean danger [1] did not seem to be very serious; the kingdoms established between Hermon and Damascus were still sufficiently limited for the young monarchy of Israel to be able to contemplate opposing them without alarm. On the coast, the Phoenicians were entirely taken up with commerce; Byblos, the most ancient of their ports, still exported cedar

[1] On the Aramaeans, see above, pp. 16, 136.

and imported papyrus.[2] Sidon, that had for four centuries grown rich on copper from Cyprus, Parian marble, and iron and slaves from the Caucasus, had just suffered a severe blow at the hands of the Peoples of the Sea at the time of their great invasion.[3] Tyre, taking advantage of this, rose to the status of the metropolis, likewise benefiting from the absence of powerful empires in Syria and Palestine.

For this interlude in history continued.[4] No threat came from the East; Babylon was passing through a period of crises, ruin, sufferings, floods and Aramaean invasions; while Assyria, following the victories of Tiglath-Pileser I, had had to withdraw her armies to the eastern end of the Fertile Crescent, and likewise make a stand against the Aramaean bands, and was not to recover her strength until the end of the tenth century.

Egypt remained dormant. The Twenty-first Dynasty was composed of mere shadows of kings; those whose faces are known to us are remarkable for the insignificance and vulgarity of their features, their gross lips and enormous noses. At Thebes the priests of Ammon were independent, but their authority did not extend beyond the Delta; and furthermore, in about 950 B.C. Shishak, the chief of these sturdy Libyans that they employed as soldiers and labourers, was to seize their throne, and to found the Twenty-second Dynasty. There was no Egyptian political influence, therefore, in Canaan. We can judge of the weakness into which the power of the Pharaohs had fallen from a story of the period that tells of the insolence with which the merchants of Byblos treated one of his envoys; they made him wait for the wood that he had asked for, haggled over the price, and even went to the length of keeping his ship; they would not have dared to treat an ambassador of Rameses II in such a way.[5]

The world of that time seemed to pay no attention to the little

[2] On the Phoenicians, see above pp. 9, 30, 31 and the MAP OF THE FERTILE CRESCENT, p. 7.

[3] *See* p. 133.

[4] See pp. 131–2.

[5] "The Voyage of Unamun," one of the oldest seafaring stories of humanity. *See* Moret, *Rois et Dieux d'Egypte,* p. 228.

Asiatic district in which the people of God were following out
their destiny. The great events of the times were taking place
elsewhere, in Greece, where a new Aryan wave was pouring in,
the most destructive of all. Formidably armed, the Dorians advanced into the midst of the societies produced by the Achaeo-
Aegean blend of races.[6] Corinth, Megara and Epidaurus were
captured; Mycenae went up in flames; the old town of Tiryns
became a cemetery. Hesiod's "age of iron" loosed upon Hellas
its dark power for at least two hundred years, despite which the
Achaians, fleeing from these massacres to the coast of Asia Minor,
built up, in a civilization saved from the ruins, that sublime poetry
that Homer was to sing two centuries later. One might suppose
that Providence had isolated these Kings of Israel in order to
allow their greatness to flower.

SAUL, THE TRAGIC KING

At Gibeah great sorrow reigned in the tribe of Benjamin. The
Philistine menace oppressed the district; steady infiltration had
given place to conquest and occupation; an enemy governor was
making his power felt in the town. Samuel was too old to lead
Israel into battle; and besides, the Philistine had with shrewd foresight forbidden all work in iron to Hebrew smiths, even the
sharpening of an axe or a scythe. Without arms, what could they
do? Rome, in her early days, found herself similarly handicapped
by her enemy, Etruscan Porsenna.

But the oppression was to be most strongly opposed in the very
district in which it was most heavy. There they knew better than
elsewhere the weak points of the Philistines: their shortage of
troops, their unreliable allies. National sentiment was strong at
Gibeah and found its expression in Saul.

Saul was a man tall in stature, who had never been known
otherwise than as a capable peasant farmer. But Samuel was told
by God that he was the destined king. One day when Saul was
out on the mountain looking for some lost she-asses, he had the

[6] *See* above p. 132.

impulse to go and consult the old seer of Ramah; gifted seers in those days did not hesitate to put their powers to quite humble uses. In this visitor Samuel recognized the one "asked of God." Did not his very name mark him as predestined? He anointed Saul with oil, gave him proofs of his faith in his mission, and then showed him to the people. At Mizpeh, a gathering of the tribes was taking place according to custom; by the same method as Athens was to employ for electing her annual magistrates, they appealed to God to express His will by means of casting lots. The name of Saul was proclaimed. Israel now had a king, created by the twofold will of Jahweh and the people. This event took place in about the year 1040 B.C.

Saul was to reign for thirty years. Victories were expected of him, and he quickly justified his position. The Ammonites had once more crossed the Jabbok, and Saul attacked and dispersed them. His son Jonathan, a young hero, assassinated the Philistine governor of Gibeah, thereby giving the signal of a national rising. But in view of the formidable arms of the enemy, Saul wisely relied on deadly guerrilla warfare and on bold surprise attacks. The situation took a turn favourable to Israel, who raised her head again. Afterwards Saul carried on a long and successful struggle against Moab, against Edom, and against the Aramaeans in the north.

The kingdom of Israel was indebted to Saul for laying the foundations of a regular army. Gathering brave men about him, the new king founded a permanent force which the tribes had not hitherto possessed. He was the Charles VII of the chosen people, and created a system of regular companies with their ranks, chiefs of hundreds and thousands, their fighting-men, their couriers, their scouts and messengers, and young "sword-bearers." For this alone, his name deserves to be remembered.

Nevertheless, victorious as he was, Saul clearly came up against strong opposition. There was a party which did not favour the monarchy. Samuel himself never let it be forgotten that he had only named a king under pressure of necessity. And presently there was open conflict between the last of the Judges and the first of the Kings. Samuel on one occasion reproached Saul for having usurped the priestly function by himself offering a sacrifice, and on another with having violated the *herem* by taking booty. Saul was returning, covered with glory, from a raid across the Negeb; the old Judge rose up before him: "Behold to obey is better than sacrifice, and to hearken than the fat of rams. For rebellion is as the sin of witchcraft, and stubbornness is as iniquity and idolatry. Because thou hast rejected the word of the Lord, he hath also rejected thee from being king" (1 Samuel xv:22–23).

This division has a historical meaning that it is easy enough to understand. In the eyes of Samuel and of all pious Israelites the monarchy was to be theocratic. Jahweh was the master, whose will Samuel expressed; that the king should pursue a personal policy was inadmissible. The king was a man of God, and must remain so. And Saul clearly was so only in part. The crown that he had once merited he was to lose; another was to wear it.

The destiny of Saul is a tragic one and deeply puzzling. Chosen by Jahweh and discarded by Him; a man of courage, tenacity and virtue in his private life, and yet shaken by unconfessed passions; confident of a high destiny, and yet in the end leading his people to bankruptcy; one is tempted to say that God made a wrong choice. But the contradictions themselves explain him. His very ardour impelled him to break the law, his energy laid him open to sudden prostrations; this friend of the Levites, who murdered so many of them, was a man torn by conflict, carrying his destiny in his own character.

There are in spiritual history some very strange examples of souls in which the powers of light and darkness are thus in conflict. A certain Father Surin, a great French mystic of the seventeenth century,[7] showed a strange blend of outstanding spirituality and phenomena that suggested possession. In this case, the psychiatrists speak of "concomitance." Was not the same true of Saul? These natures through which God expresses Himself—Saul was sometimes seized by prophetic inspiration—have a flaw in them that easily becomes exaggerated. Poetry itself is in a high

[7] *See* Daniel-Rops, *Mystiques de France*, p. 154.

degree exposed to similar dangers. An "evil spirit from God" entered his soul and made him its victim. This drama was so strange that no one in all Israel thought of taking advantage of the occasion for overthrowing the monarchy, or even the afflicted king.

With amazement, with pain, they watched this monomaniac of persecution, who saw traitors on all sides, this violent soul whose frenzy only music could calm. But they said nothing; this, too, was the will of Jahweh, who was to carry out His designs by means of another man.

A RUDDY YOUNG SHEPHERD

The man whom Jahweh was to make His instrument was a youth of fair skin and auburn hair. Verrocchio has painted him, with his agile young body and his face in which are expressed courage and frankness; such must have been the eighth son of Jesse. "There are sometimes born," writes Renan, "in the Semitic Orient, generally hard and forbidding, prodigies of grace, elegance and intelligence." And that charm that so greatly facilitates success causes faults and even crimes to be overlooked in those who are so fortunate as to possess it! For the first time in the history of Israel a child of Judah was to come to the fore; was it of him that Jacob, in blessing his sons, had said, "Judah, thou art he whom thy brethren shall praise: thy hand shall be in the neck of thine enemies; thy father's children shall bow down before thee. Judah is a lion's whelp: from the prey, my son, thou art gone up. . . . The sceptre shall not depart from Judah, nor a lawgiver from between his feet" (Gen. xlix:8–10)?

While he guarded his father's flocks, David composed poems, accompanying himself on a harp. But another destiny was in store for him. Did not his name signify "the beloved of Jahweh"? Samuel, who in the retirement of his village lamented the infidelities of Saul, was told by God that the new representative of His will was living at Bethlehem and that he must go there and anoint him. At the house of Jesse, the seven eldest sons were presented to the prophet by turn, but God's voice did not name any of them. Was there no other? Surely not the young poet, the rhymester? But it was certainly on him that Samuel saw the sign. He looked at him, for "he was ruddy, and withal of a beautiful countenance, and goodly to look to. And the Lord said: Arise, anoint him, for this is he." From that time the shepherd boy was the true master of the destinies of Israel; but this was to remain a secret for the time being.

Here two traditions, derived no doubt from different sources, tell us how Saul summoned David to him. One says that the king, whose depression was only allayed by the music of the harp, summoned the pastoral musician. The other says that David having won a sensational victory, the king attached him to his person.

This victory is the celebrated episode that we see painted on the ceiling of the Sistine Chapel where Michelangelo has immortalized it: a slender David, mounting the monstrous corpse of a fallen enemy, raises his sword to cut off the head. The Philistines, as in the time of Samson, were making more and more frequent raids into the lands of Judah. Coming up from the Sephelah, they were driving the Hebrews farther and farther back towards the high lands. One of their leaders in particular, Goliath, a giant armed in bronze, came out every day to threaten Israel. David asked the king for permission to take up the challenge. He took neither lance nor armour, only the shepherd's common weapon, the sling; stunned, Goliath fell, and David leaped on him, took his victim's own sword and returned to the king's presence bearing the heavy head of his enemy.

All the peoples of antiquity adored strange combats of this kind. And do our wars with their great massacres amount to anything better? Rome staked her destiny on the heroism of the three Horatii, and in the Egyptian story of Senouhit, an officer of Pharaoh challenged in the same way a man of Palestine. David's glory was dazzling. And as he entered Gibeah the women ran out to meet him, improvising to their tambourines that refrain, possibly true but far from diplomatic, "Saul has slain his thousands, but David his tens of thousands."

From this time a strange series of episodes between the king and his young officer were to commence. Was it merely a question of jealousy? Was it, as some have thought, the hatred of one who fears that he may love too much? In a soul as dark as that of Saul such feelings quickly cause ravages. One day when David was playing the harp before him, he suddenly seized a javelin and threw it at the young hero; David, being agile, avoided it. While advancing him in the army, he also gave him dangerous missions in which all the chances were against him. But David with the help of Jahweh triumphed over all obstacles. Saul tried to humiliate him by promising, and at the last minute refusing, his eldest daughter in marriage; but the younger, in love with the young conqueror, married him and a little later helped him to escape from another attack made by the king.

After a number of these painful episodes, David fled. Jonathan, the son of Saul, who had entered with David into one of those wonderful friendships that one can only make at the age of twenty, warned him and helped him to escape. In this period of wandering, exiled from the court and from the towns, David was to meditate in the desert, and in sublime Psalms, he called upon God in faith: "My soul in among lions; and I lie even among them that are set on fire, even the sons of men. . . . My heart is fixed, O God, my heart is fixed" (Psalm LVII). "Thou tellest my wanderings: put thou my tears into thy bottle: are they not in thy book? When I cry unto thee, then shall mine enemies turn back: this I know; for God is for me" (Psalm LVI).

Saul, exasperated by David's flight, pursued him with demented rage. The Levites of the sanctuary of Nob having sheltered the fugitive, he gave the order to put them to death, but his soldiers refused out of pity. The king sent for Edomite mercenaries who massacred eighty-five priests. David was on his guard, in hiding at Adullam, a high, isolated hill full of spacious caves. When he learned that Saul was approaching, he fled even farther away, to the shores of the Dead Sea, into the desert of Judah. Here there occurred twice over an incident of great significance. In this guerrilla warfare, it happened that the enemies, unawares, were very near to one another, and David came upon Saul, sleeping. He did not kill him, or do him any harm; on one occasion he cut a piece out of the royal mantle, on another he took the spear and the cruse of water. He respected in his enemy the Lord's anointed. In the desert to this day it is an infamous action to kill a sleeping enemy. In Shakespeare, in the same way, the unpardonable crime—the crime of Cardinal Beaufort, of Macbeth, of Hamlet's uncle—is to murder a sleeping man.

But these wanderings had not been altogether to David's disadvantage. His prestige as a leader was so great that he had been able to make two marriages with rich and well-connected women. His guerrilla band now numbered six hundred men of proved courage. A Philistine king placed himself at his service and gave him Ziklag, near Gaza, as a place of residence. David made a number of victorious raids on the Amalekites. But it was, for all that, an exile; his country was closed to him.

Samuel was dead, "all Israel had lamented him, and buried him in Ramah, even in his own city." But Saul never forgot what the old Judge had predicted for him; perhaps he knew that David was to be his successor. In any case he had to abandon the pursuit, for a grave danger arose in the north. The Philistines were invading the plain of Esdrelon in considerable force. Saul watched them from the heights of Gilboa: "he was afraid, and his heart greatly trembled." Would Jahweh be with His people in this encounter? He hastened to cast lots; but they gave no indication. And so, desperate, and not knowing where to turn for help, the king took a strange and terrible course. At En-dor, at the foot of the Little Hermon, there lived a witch. To her he went. He himself had issued terrible decrees against those who summon up spirits. Without giving his name, he consulted the woman. She went into a trance, and, enlightened, she cried: "Why hast thou deceived me? For thou art Saul." The unhappy king told her to fear nothing, but to do as he wished and call up the spirit for whom he asked. "What sawest thou?" "And she said, An old man cometh up; covered with a mantle." Samuel! The old antagonist from whose word none ever escaped. And Samuel spoke: "The

Lord hath rent the kingdom out of thine hand, and given it to thy neighbour, even to David . . . Moreover the Lord will also deliver Israel with thee into the hand of the Philistines: and to-morrow shalt thou and thy sons be with me." Saul fell full length upon the ground, senseless.

A few days later, David, at Ziklag, was returning from an expedition into Negeb when a man greeted him. He held in his hand the royal crown and the bracelet of Saul. The battle had ended disastrously. The army of Israel had fled before the chariots of the Philistines. The slopes of Gilboa were strewn with corpses. The king's sons were dead and Saul, wounded, had flung himself upon his sword rather than fall alive into the hands of the enemy. A great emotion overcame David. These defeated men were his brothers, the people that God had confided to him. Jonathan, his friend, was dead, and Saul, that adversary that inspired his pity more than his hate. So, having had the contemptible traitor who had dared to rob the body of the dead king put to death, David took up his harp and composed an elegy. This was the "Song of the Bow," the old hymn that the Bible derives from an ancient record, the *Book of the Just.*

"The beauty of Israel is slain upon thy high places: how are the mighty fallen! . . . Ye mountains of Gilboa, let there be no dew, neither let there be rain, upon you, nor fields of offerings: for there the shield of the mighty is vilely cast away. . . . Saul and Jonathan were lovely and pleasant in their lives, and in their death they were not divided: they were swifter than eagles, they were stronger than lions. . . . I am distressed for thee, my brother Jonathan: very pleasant hast thou been unto me: thy love to me was wonderful, passing the love of women" (2 Sam. 1:19–26).

THE THRONE OF DAVID

The way was now clear that was to lead David to the throne. He was barely thirty, and confident in his own strength. Must he regard the last of Saul's sons, Ish-bosheth, as an obstacle? Abner, the king's old general, was the power behind this weak

prince. The people's approval had still to be gained. This was
done in two steps. David went first to his own tribe of Judah, at
Hebron, the ancient capital dignified by its great religious past.
And there the people acclaimed him as king. And it is an important fact that the house of David rests upon the solid foundation of these southern clans, still close to the nomadic life, and
where traditions remained, and were to remain, alive. For seven
years (probably from 1012–1005), David reigned at Hebron. The
Philistines, whose vassal he remained through his fief of Ziklag,
looked kindly upon this little king who cheated the son of Saul.
But presently the Prince of Judah grew stronger. Conflicts arose
between the north and the south; in one of these, Abner killed
one of David's nephews, Asahel, brother of Joab. David's repute
had spread abroad, so that Abner himself, astute as a Talleyrand,
negotiated in secret the fusion of the two kingdoms. He did not,
for all that, gain what he had hoped to gain, for Joab, his
brother's avenger, ran his sword into his body. Soon after this,
two of Ish-bosheth's officers brought David the head of their
master; as a king, David punished the regicides by death. Not
long after, by God's command, the last descendants of Saul were
handed over to their enemies and crucified. David was not responsible for these murderous but necessary acts, but he benefited
by them.

The second stage was accomplished. The sheikhs of all the
tribes recognized David as the Lord's anointed. It was on this occasion that the new king demonstrated the magnitude of his political ideas. If the kingdom was to have a stable throne, it must have
a capital more central than Hebron and that should be a syno-
nym for victory. Where the routes from Gaza, Jaffa, Shechem,
Jericho and Bethlehem crossed, remote enough for security, in
the heart of those high lands that are the physical and moral
bastion of Palestine, it was a notable site, worthy of the destiny
to which David was to dedicate it. The people of Canaan who
occupied it, the Jebusites, had made it a citadel. Built on three
hills, its bastion was on the hill of Ophel; a redoubt, Zion, dominated the steepest slope. The Jebusites thought their city so
strong that there was a proverb current among them: "The blind

and the lame are well able to defend our walls!" David led the attack. He had promised great rewards to whoever first entered the city. It was Joab. They found a very ancient underground channel that was the aqueduct of the citadel; Joab climbed into it, ran up the lower portion, and then climbed up the well and took the garrison by surprise. A few years ago, in the course of excavations at Jerusalem, an English lieutenant repeated this bold adventure without great difficulty.

Having become, in 1005 B.C., the master of his capital, the king applied himself at once to the task of giving it a new appearance. "The city of David" witnessed the arrival of an army of workmen and tons of material. The Phoenicians, great experts in the art of building, sent architects, skilled workmen, and wood. The royal palace arose for the admiration of the crowds. David's harem grew in size and, a sign of power to which the East attaches great importance, many sons and daughters were born to him. He was able to sing in thanksgiving: "He sent from above, he took me; he drew me out of many waters; He delivered me from my strong enemy, and from them that hated me: . . . he delivered me, because he delighted in me. The Lord rewarded me according to my righteousness: according to the cleanness of my hands hath he recompensed me. For I have kept the ways of the Lord, and have not wickedly departed from my God. . . . Therefore, I will give thanks unto Thee, O Lord, among the heathen, and I will sing praises unto Thy name" (2 Samuel xxii:17–50).

Success did not lead him to neglect difficult tasks. He had barely completed the unification of his kingdom before he had taken up arms against the Philistines who were greatly deceived if they expected David to remain a docile vassal. Sometimes in guerrilla warfare, sometimes in pitched battles, he gave them a bad time. We see him scouring the country, with such boldness that his soldiers begged him not to run the risk of putting out, by his own death, the Lamp of Israel. He led his troops right into the Philistine plain. Gath was threatened, possibly captured. Several ports came under his control, that Solomon later used as bases for his new fleet. In the north, the plain of Esdrelon was recaptured. The ancient promise was completely realized. "Remember the Covenant always," sang the king. "Obey only in the name of Jahweh! For it was He who promised to Abraham and to Jacob: I will give you the land of Canaan for your heritage." The soldier did not forget God's share.

He was to express this in a significant gesture. The Ark, since the time of Eli, had remained in semi-exile, hidden in a little town. David had it brought to Jerusalem, which was an able political move. For the capital thus also became the religious metropolis. When the Levites brought the Ark to the gates of Jerusalem, one might have seen the king, like a simple priest, taking part in the procession, and "dancing with all his might." He himself performed the rites of the sacrifice, which is the proof that the position of the monarchy in relation to the priesthood was now notably stronger than under Saul.

Thus, by David's resolution and good fortune, a stage in the history of Israel was completed. Countless expeditions against the Moabites, the Ammonites, and even against the Aramaic princes of Damascus, nearly all led by the valourous Joab, extended David's authority to the frontiers of Canaan and beyond, from the Euphrates to Sinai. Certainly we ought not to exaggerate the importance of his kingdom, which was not to be compared with the vast empires of Egypt or Babylon. But this was the first time that Israel had reached a position of such power or such a degree of organization. The basis of an administration was formed, with a chancellor, secretaries, a minister of public works, and archives. A decisive advance had been made.

The army had developed considerably since Saul's day. Round a permanent core, recruits from the various tribes gathered in time of war. A solid bodyguard of Philistine mercenaries was established, "Phleti" or "Kreti," as faithful as Louis XVI's Swiss guards were later to be; Rameses II had already drawn his "Sherdanes" from the People of the Sea, just as Napoleon raised his Mamelukes in Moslem Egypt. A picked command assured the high efficiency of that army; its heart was "the thirty" and among these, "the three," David's *gibborim* whose exploits anticipate those of Charlemagne's valiant knights.

Such was David's achievement; from many points of view it is clearly considerable. Without a hitch or a setback, as brave as Saul but, unlike him, politically able, he accomplished the unification of the people, liberated the country, and thus gave to his people that sense of glory with which success cements unity. His work was strictly national: David stood for his race and avoided all contamination. Only, possibly, the Philistines, whose military organization he admired, had a certain influence on his new kingdom; we find among the Hebrews certain traces of a Greek character, which no doubt come from them. He established a capital and a dynasty. We can understand why, in times of deep distress, Israel could never forget that glorious image or imagine the Saviour, the King of Glory, otherwise than in the likeness of David.

For posterity, which sees him through the candid record of the Bible, his humanity is no less remarkable than his greatness. We admire him as a hero, and we cannot refrain from loving him. Certainly his character is not perfect, and although he has some of the characteristics of a saint—his boundless love for the One God, his trust in Providence, his faith—we cannot overlook the fact that he is a figure of a barbarous age in which neither violence nor treachery was judged by the standards of our own laws and literature, if not of our behaviour. But what ability, what power, and what grace! As a soldier full of valour, a poet whose work has come down to us, decisive in politics, and chivalrous in war, determined in his undertakings, feeling deeply in his personal relationships, he has every quality that makes a man lovable, even those which make him like ourselves and for which we love him the more—those weaknesses through which a man is prone to fall, and which, in a noble mind, are themselves the occasion of sorrow, repentance and forgiveness.

CRISES

One evening when David was walking on his terrace, he saw a woman bathing. He made enquiries about her and was told that she was Bathsheba, the wife of Uriah the Hittite. The king's soul was not proof against his passion; he sent for the woman and took her. Uriah was an officer of the foreign legions; he was at this time engaged against the Ammonites. Soon, Bathsheba was with child. David sent Joab an order to send him Uriah. The husband returned, the king cajoled him, made him half tipsy, and told him in a friendly manner to go to his own house. But the captain, suspicious, remained at the palace among the king's guards. "Why then didst thou not go down unto thine house?" David asked the next day. "The servants of my Lord are encamped in the open fields, shall I then go into mine house, to eat and drink, and to lie with my wife?" the officer replied. Passion had made the Lord's anointed an adulterer; fear of scandal now made him a criminal.

He wrote a message to Joab, and carried felony to the point of making Uriah himself the bearer of it: "Set ye Uriah in the forefront of the hottest battle, and retire ye from him, that he may be smitten, and die." Soon afterwards an officer came to David from Joab with the news that all had been carried out according to his wish. Bathsheba shed tears for the dead man but entered the royal harem, where she was to play a prominent part.

Then Jahweh inspired a prophet, one of those wandering seers that were to be found among all the tribes, to go and denounce the king for his sin. Nathan went to the palace and said: "There were two men in one city; the one was rich, and the other poor. The rich man had exceeding many flocks and herds; but the poor man had nothing, save one little ewe lamb, which he had bought and nourished up: and it grew up together with him, and with his children; and it did eat of his own meat, and drank of his own cup, and lay in his bosom, and was unto him as a daughter. And there came a traveller unto the rich man, and he spared to take of his flock and of his own herd, to dress for the wayfaring man that was come unto him; but took the poor man's lamb." David's anger rose: "The man that hath done this thing shall surely die: and he shall restore the lamb fourfold!" And Nathan said, "Thou art the man . . . thou hast killed Uriah the Hittite with the sword, and hast taken his wife to be thy wife."

God would punish. But a great man does not continue in his sin: "I have sinned against the Lord," said David, humbling himself.

The punishment prophesied by Nathan was not slow in coming. The later events of David's reign revealed flaws in the edifice. Unity was threatened, and was to continue in danger. In great Oriental harems there are perpetual intrigues. The young rival half-brothers were for ever at odds with one another. Amnon, the eldest, had seduced one of his half-sisters; Absalom, a brother of the injured girl, killed him. This was the occasion of a breach between David and this son that quickly took a political turn. Absalom went to Hebron, gathered adherents, and led a revolt. Taken by surprise, David was forced to fly, while the rebel led a rising in Jerusalem, and underlined his victory by taking his father's concubines. This was the undoing of the ambitious youth —he wasted too much time. The old king, seeking refuge in the desert, as in the days of his youth, became once more the matchless soldier. His Philistine mercenaries remained faithful to him. The hymn that he composed on this occasion (Psalm III) speaks his confidence in Jahweh. Absalom, when he attacked, was defeated. He fled on his mule, pursued by David's champions, and his thick hair caught in the branches of a terebinth tree; his mount galloped on and he remained hanging there. Disobeying the orders of David, who would have pardoned him, Joab slew the rebel; more grieved by this sorrow than exultant in his victory, the king returned to Jerusalem, broken-hearted.

Other incidents show that, as his royal power was weakened by age, the unity of the kingdom was endangered. A party was already forming about the heir presumptive. David forestalled it; his favourite son was Solomon, son of Bathsheba; about him, besides his mother, who was extremely circumspect, were grouped the prophet Nathan, the Levites, and the *gibborim*. David consecrated Solomon; the succession was assured.

His death was now approaching. In vain, to warm his body that was growing cold, a ravishing young girl was brought— Abishag the Shulamite. She served him, but he did not even know her. For a last time, the king-poet praised his God in a hymn that seemed to tremble like his aged body. Then he died, at the age of seventy (975). He was buried under the hill of Jerusalem, not far from the place where the Ark of Jahweh rested.

SOLOMON "THE WISE"

David had been the power of Israel; Solomon was to be its glory. The one, a soldier, had conquered his throne, waged war all his life and undergone hardship and labour in order to consolidate his work; the other, to whom everything came by the privilege of birth, pursued, by way of outer manifestation, the increase of his own glory. Solomon's was a great reign to be sure, prefiguring in many respects that of Louis XIV, but the man himself is hidden behind that glitter of gold and precious stones that for forty years (975–935 B.C. approximately) glowed over Canaan: we cannot approach him. David's struggles, impulses, even his passions and weaknesses, we can measure; Solomon, as he is seen by posterity, is a remote figure, sumptuously attired. There was something of the parvenu in him in his haste to want for himself everything that he admired: Egypt had chariots, so he must buy chariots; Tyre had ships, why should not he? The masters of the Nile and the Euphrates numbered their wives and concubines by hundreds; he took a thousand. It was the same in everything, and this taste for luxury, this impulsiveness, were to prove injurious to his kingdom; no sooner was he dead than it collapsed.

Nevertheless, Israel has given him a place of honour in its tradition. His gorgeous splendour has survived in our Western memories as it has also in Moslem folk-lore. For it was his lot to be the figure in whom the sense of glory of that small nation, nomads for so long, who had known oppression once and were soon to undergo that terrible experience again, found expression. Nations, in the perspectives of history, almost always retain a sentiment of admiration and gratitude towards men who bring them misfortune but through whom they are raised above their normal level. Frenchmen, who treasure the memory of Louis XIV and Napoleon, and who even hold in high regard the murderous gangs of the Revolution, can easily understand this sentiment.

The name of Solomon signifies the idea of well-being, peace and perfection. He is the "fortunate" king, the "accomplished." If we doubt whether his reign was a time of calm and order, we have but to consider, in order to convince ourselves, that in a dream he asked Jahweh for *wisdom* rather than for any other good. In the Oriental sense of the word this means a great deal; thus it is said of the king that he knew animals and plants, "from the cedar of Lebanon even unto the hyssop that springeth out of the wall; he spake also of beasts, and of fowl, and of creeping things, and of fishes." To be wise is to possess the gift "to understand a proverb, and the interpretation; the words of the wise, and their dark sayings" (Proverbs 1:6). There is even an esoteric implication in this power, and the wise king is held also to possess the gift of divination. To be wise, is, furthermore, to acquire "justice, equity, and righteousness." These virtues come from God, for "the fear of the Lord is the beginning of wisdom"; it is therefore quite definitely to possess the knowledge of God.

All these moral and intellectual gifts are to be found in this greatest of monarchs. His name is attributed to works that express them in various ways: the Book of Proverbs, the Book of Wisdom, Ecclesiastes. His wisdom, says the Book of Kings, surpassed that of all the East and of Egypt. On the Nile similar collections of moral sentences flourished; some of them are very fine, for example, those of Amen-Enopi, dating from the Eighteenth Dynasty, and it is today admitted that the author of Proverbs must have been familiar with the latter.

The historian takes delight in giving instances of the royal wisdom in the form of significant anecdotes. Two women came before the king's tribunal. They lived together, and had both given birth at the same time. One, in her sleep, had smothered her baby, stolen that of her companion and put the tiny corpse in its place. But there was no witness. How could it be proved? We know the psychological ruse that the sage employed. "Cut the living infant in half," he said, "and give half to one, half to the other." At these words the true mother trembled inwardly. "Give the child to the other," she cried, "but do not kill it!" Apologues of this kind are popular in the East. Similar ones are to be found in Arabia, India, China and even in a fresco in Pompeii. Moslem tradition preserves another. Three brothers came before Solomon: "Our father told us, on his deathbed, that only one of us was his true son; the others are bastards; which of us is to inherit his goods?" "Bring the father's body," said the king. "Let each shoot an arrow at the dead man's heart, and the best shot shall be the heir." Only one, when his turn came to shoot the arrow, threw his bow on the ground. "No, I cannot profane the body of my father!" "The goods are yours," said the king, "for blood has spoken."

History, less poetic, attributes to Solomon many traits of wisdom—of political wisdom. He showed it from the moment of his coming to the throne in the way in which he dealt with all his potential adversaries. His father's eldest son, who threatened to become a rival, was condemned to death: the reason being he had had the audacity to wish to marry Abishag, the lovely Shulamite, which was, according to Oriental custom, in itself a pretence to power. Joab, David's general, likewise perished, killed by the mercenaries of the royal guard. The reason? Long ago he had assassinated Abner, and others since then. The truth of the matter was that the commander of the army, with his independent character, was disquieting.

Wise as he was as a politician, Solomon showed himself no less so in preserving peace among his people. During his whole reign we hear only of one minor expedition. Israel was able to eat and drink in the shade of her vines and fig-trees, and for that reason also has preserved a grateful memory of the king. His reign was in fact a period of organization and administrative progress. Government was brought to perfection and there were from that time a real vizier, a greater number of ministers, counsellors, and secretaries. The palace had its majordomo. And the country, centralized, was ruled by twelve prefects on the Egyptian model, who were inspected by a king's delegate.

One of the greatest proofs of the wisdom of Solomon was in making show of his power so that he never needed to exert it. He placed the army of Israel on a new footing by giving it chariots. Up to this time, partly from poverty, partly out of a fanatical hostility to all foreign innovations, the Hebrews had not possessed that redoubtable weapon on which depended the power of the Pharaohs, the Hittite kings, and the Philistines. Overriding opposition (for a long time to come the Prophets Isaiah, Hosea, Micah and Zachariah were to be hostile towards the new army), he had chariots built—fourteen hundred at least!—bought horses in Egypt and Silesia, created studs in Canaan, and instituted, perhaps in order to feed his eight thousand animals, the imposition of the king's tithes, which reserved for his stables the first and best of the hay crop. Hebrew youth furnished enthusiastic volunteers for this select corps.

Solomon was certainly a great administrator; like all those who have the art of ruling men, he used for political ends decisions that were imposed by necessity. The great works that he planned required considerable man-power; we know from the bas-reliefs of Egypt and Babylon what these giant buildings cost in terms of labour. Solomon used the opportunity to destroy, finally, the Canaanites, who were reduced to the status of serfs subject to forced labour. Later, when this man-power proved insufficient, he even requisitioned Israelite labour; for thoroughly organized governments, strong governments, have no doubt their advantages, but they have another side that their subjects are less ready to appreciate.

THE KING OF DIPLOMACY AND COMMERCE

David had been a soldier-king. His son had other methods; he was a diplomat and a trader. In the full sense of the word, he negotiated. In his relations with his equals, or as a demi-vassal, or as the master, with Tyre, the Aramaeans, Egypt or the princes of Edom, he always preferred the soft approach. It is questionable whether, in allowing certain threats to grow, that of Damascus in particular—he always acted in the best possible way for the future.

Egypt had only left Canaan alone because her kings had been too weak. But the policy of the Pharaohs had not ceased to envisage, for all that, the possibility of reconquering their bastion. It was during the reign of Solomon that the Libyan Shishak seized the crown and founded the Twenty-second Dynasty; the Egyptian danger suddenly reappeared on the southern horizon. Solomon employed all his talent for diplomacy, and in the twenty-fourth year of his reign the king led to a palace specially built for her an Egyptian princess who was henceforth his queen of the first rank. As a wedding-gift his father-in-law, the Pharaoh, had conquered Gezer for him, the last stronghold of the Canaanites. A semi-vassalage was hidden beneath the splendours of a nuptial cortege, but appearances were saved and peace assured.

Such diplomacy was well calculated to surmount difficulties. It is shown again in two delicate affairs. In the south, in Edom, the old king whom David had defeated had returned; all the more dangerous in that Egypt was using him as a pawn in her game. Solomon negotiated so well that this prince raised no obstacle when he wished to develop his trade by way of the Red Sea. In the north, at Damascus, a bandit chief had established an Aramean kingdom; the relations between the two young kingdoms were not of a friendly kind; but animosity did not develop beyond a few blows.

But the great matters to which Solomon gave his most careful attention were Israel's relations with the Phoenicians of Tyre. This proceeded according to a plan, carefully thought out, which envisaged the making of Palestine, a small and poor country but an ideal trading-route, into a centre of international commerce. This is an important point—it was Solomon who initiated Israel into the ways of negotiation, a career in which she was to succeed so well. And surprising as this may seem to us, he encountered many difficulties in his attempt to do so. Just as Richelieu, in attempting to develop France's sea trade, strove against indifference, and as Colbert himself had to overcome much resistance in order to induce his people to interest themselves in affairs, so Solomon found that he had his set-backs and economic crises, sometimes disturbing, to overcome.

In what could Canaan trade? Not very much: corn, oil, and wine in small quantities. Solomon's idea was to buy in order to re-sell. Horses, for example, whose import he had just organized; why not export the surplus? An example close at hand showed him how much could be gained by selling what one had not produced—that of the Phoenicians. He imitated them.

Since in about 2800 B.C.[8] a group of Semites had installed themselves on the coast of Syria, and little by little merged with many other races, as happens easily in great seaports. Sea trade had never ceased to prosper. The configuration of a country without plains, where the Lebanon drops abruptly to the sea, had forced its inhabitants to take to the water. The fine cedars, with which the mountains were then covered, provided the shipyards with wood of fine quality. Fir trees for the shipboards, cedar for the masts, oars of oak, benches of wood inlaid with ivory, fine linen of Egypt for sails, and everywhere, within the vessel, the rich stuffs of the Peloponnese—so does Ezekiel describe the Phoenician ships (Ezekiel xxvii). As archaeology reveals them, they seem to have been magnificent in their appearance, with their curved keels, rising high at the prow and the poop, with their great two-yarded masts bearing a rectangular sail, and their two long oars for steering. The largest of them were the so-called "ships of Tarshish," because they were used for the longest voyages, towards that mysterious country that may have been Spain or perhaps the Caucasus.

Admirable seamen that they were, the Phoenicians, without compass or sextant, had acquired an astonishing knowledge of the sea. They had studied every feature of the coasts that they followed; they certainly possessed the equivalent of our guides for pilots and nautical instructions, which they kept secret. One Phoenician captain, realizing that he was being followed by a

---

[8] *See* above, pp. 10, 30–1, and 179. The word "Phoenician" in Greek means "red-complexioned men." This makes one think of the Hamites of Africa whom they closely resembled in physique.

foreign craft, preferred to run his ship aground rather than let the stranger know the channel; the senate of his town congratulated him and made good his loss. And Victor Bérard, in books in which intelligence is equalled by learning,[9] has shown that the Phoenicians taught the Greeks, that Homer had access, in writing the *Odyssey,* to their manuals of navigation, and that many of the stories that enchant us—the Cyclop Polyphemus and the magician Circe, for example—are nothing more than transcriptions, deliberately made mythical, of precise geographical instructions elaborated by the mariners of Tyre and Sidon.

These navigators used to carry out their voyages with an audacity that amazes us. To sail about the Mediterranean in barques of sixty-five or ninety-five feet is in itself no mean achievement. But they sailed as far as England, and traded for tin in the Scilly Isles (the "Cassiterides"), in the Baltic for amber, and in Africa as far as the Gulf of Guinea! Jewels of Irish origin have been found in Phoenicia; and at Stonehenge, in England, blue Egyptian glass beads, undoubtedly transported by the Phoenicians. In many parts of the world, they settled permanently; they possessed trading-houses, concessions and even veritable colonies from at least twelve centuries before our era. Their "Kadesh" in Spain has become Cadiz; opposite, on the Mauretanian coast, Lixos was the port of Africa. Malta, Sicily, and the Balearic Islands had their Phoenician ports of call; at the time when Saul reigned over Israel, Utica was arising on its Tunisian creek. Two centuries later, in about 825, Dido, Queen of Tyre, intending not far from there to found Carthage, succeeded in being given "as much land as can be covered with an ox-hide." She was astute enough to cut the ox-hide into strips so fine that she enclosed a whole district.

They were truly able people, these Phoenicians, and Israel set herself to learn from them. Their ships sailed in the ports of the Mediterranean, floating bazaars offering temptation to women. In them they sold cosmopolitan gewgaws, bronze arms and glass from the Nile, perfumes of Arabia and Egyptian papyrus, Cretan

[9] *Les Phéniciens et l'Odyssée.*

and Mycenean vases, Lydian and Hittite gold plate, precious stones, and those Asian stuffs to which the purple dye of Murex gave so noble a colour. It sometimes happened that drawing up his anchor without warning, the captain would sail away and sell his beautiful clients as slaves, for the traders were not above being pirates. All this was spread abroad, and Ezekiel, anathematizing the riches of Tyre, draws us up an accurate list: "Tarshish was thy merchant by reason of the multitude of all kind of riches; with silver, iron, tin, and lead they traded in thy fairs. Ionia and the Caucasus traded the persons of men and vessels of brass in thy market. Armenia traded in thy fairs with horses and horsemen and mules. Arabia, in exchange for trash, traded ivory and ebony: Syria traded emeralds, purple and broidered work, and fine linen, and coral, and agate . . . ; Judah, the land of Israel, were thy merchants: they traded in thy market wheat of Minnith and Pannag and honey, and oil, and balm." The Phoenicians were, in fact, the English of their day: sailors and traders, colonisers for reasons of commerce; by a curious coincidence, the "nannies" of the period were Phoenician women, like the one who in Homer sold her little charge, Emmaeus. The simplified alphabet that they had adopted spread throughout the world with such success that we use it to this day, and it is on account of the great paper trade of Byblos that we still give the name of "Bible" to the Book of Books. We can readily imagine how a king, ambitious for glory, would naturally set himself to imitate such prestige.

At the time when Solomon reigned in Israel, the great power of Phoenicia was situated at Tyre. Built on islets near the coast, she had escaped the Nordic invasion. Very rich, bold in colonizing, she had her shipyards, her workshops, her docks, her banks. Her king was Hiram, who reigned approximately from 979 to 946 B.C., an opulent prince, taken up with large enterprises, an able trader. David had already had recourse to his good offices when he wished to found Jerusalem. Solomon established closer relationships with him. Scarcely had he come to the throne before Hiram had sent him an ambassador bearing his felicitations. Following this, they exchanged riddles (a common game in the East with stakes laid on the solution, naturally) of the kind we find mentioned in the Book of Proverbs: "There are three things that are never satisfied, yea, four things say not, It is enough: The grave; and the barren womb; the earth that is not filled with water; and the fire that saith not, It is enough" (Proverbs xxx). Finally, to seal the friendship, a daughter of Hiram entered Solomon's harem, and when she arrived at Zion, the people sang her epithalamion: "The king's daughter is all glorious within: her clothing is of wrought gold. She shall be brought unto the king in raiment of needlework: the virgins her companions that follow her shall be brought unto thee" (Psalm xlv).

Hiram and his Tyrians taught Israel the art of seafaring. Solomon purchased Phoenician ships and later had others built. Thanks to David's victories he had seaports—Jaffa, Dor, and perhaps Acre. In imitation of their teachers, the Hebrews cruised in the Mediterranean, and Jerusalem was diverted by the spectacle of the arrival of gold, ivory and all sorts of exotic products, including monkeys and peacocks. Boldness increasing with success, Solomon had the idea of freeing himself from Arab control in order to trade with the countries of the East, where perfumes and precious stones were to be had. At the end of the Gulf of Akaba, the port of Asion-gaber [10] was equipped with a shipbuilding yard and docks, under the direction of Phoenician sailors. Finally came the great adventure, the voyage to the land of Ophir.

A fleet of "ships of Tarshish" set out for that mysterious country. Was it India, Arabia, or Madagascar? In the names of various articles of merchandise, some authorities have thought that they could detect Sanskrit etymologies. These long voyages appealed to the imagination of ancient peoples; the Queen of Egypt, Hatshepsut,[11] had greatly added to her glory by sending five ships to the land of Punt, to the "Ladders of Incense," whither "no one knows the way, excepting the gods." From Ophir, Solomon's ships brought back chiefly sandalwood and precious stones. A red wood, of exquisite perfume, was used for the Temple of Jahweh

[10] *See* MAP: SINAI, p. 83.
[11] *See* p. 90.

and for the king's house. But, no doubt (for the Phoenicians no longer acted as guides), the expedition was never repeated after Solomon's time; for "there came no such almug trees, nor were seen unto this day" (1 Kings x:12).

So this diplomatic king, in addition to the riches that his trade brought him, gained for himself, in the eyes of his people, that mysterious prestige that belongs to the East, whose attraction Alexander, Caesar and Napoleon felt in their turn. A glorious image was impressed upon human memory. On one occasion, a foreign queen came to Jerusalem, drawn thither by the fame of Solomon. She came from Sheba, in farthest Arabia, with a brilliant suite and a great array. Her camels carried gold, perfumes and precious stones. She exchanged riddles with the king, which allowed him to admire her wisdom, and she left loaded with "all that she could desire." Sumptuous scene, worthy of the gorgeous imagination of the Italian Renaissance. So one may see it at Arezzo, painted by Piero della Francesca.

THE BUILDER

So by his commercial ability the third king of Israel became the most opulent of princes. In his time, "the king made silver to be in Jerusalem as stones, and cedars made he to be as the sycomore trees that are in the vale, for abundance" (1 Kings x:27). This magnificence was a political necessity; from the time that Israel became a monarchy it was necessary that her sovereign should take his place among the other princes of the time. But how many dangers there were! This king who, little by little, modeled himself on the autocrats of the Euphrates and the Nile, who was addressed as "My Lord" or "Angel of Jahweh," before whom the courtesans murmured, "The wrath of a king is as messengers of death: . . . In the light of the king's countenance is life" (Proverbs xvi:14–15), would not such a man, exalted by power, be tempted to rebellion against God?

Infidel sovereigns were soon to arise. If a populous harem was a necessary mark of power, the author of Ecclesiasticus very clearly stated its perils in the vengeful verses that he addressed to Solomon: "Thou didst bow thy loins unto women, and by thy body thou wast brought into subjection. Thou didst stain thy honour, and pollute they seed: so that thou broughtest wrath

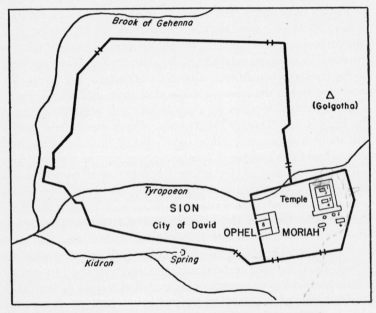

JERUSALEM IN THE TIME OF KING SOLOMON

1. Ark of the Covenant. 2. Holy of Holies. 3. Altar of Perfumes.
4. The Holy Place. 5. Columns. 6. Altar of Holocausts.
7. The Brazen Sea. 8. Royal Palace.

upon thy children, and wast grieved for thy folly" (Ecclesiasticus XLVII:19–20). And great as the king's wealth was, he had, for all that, to cede twenty towns of his kingdom to Hiram in order to pay his debts, which Hiram accepted moreover with no good grace.

The cause of these financial difficulties was the same that Louis XIV blamed himself for as he lay dying: "I was too fond of building," Solomon might have said, like the *Roi-Soleil*. But to build, greatly and sumptuously, was likewise a necessity for the new State of Israel. The glorification of God, the monarch, and the people was one and the same. Even though he half ruined himself in the process, Solomon had reached a position in which he had to construct a house worthy of Jahweh and of his own power. To David, who already intended to do so, the prophet Nathan had said that the time had not yet come. In sacred history, the name of Solomon must always be associated with the building of the Temple, which even after its destruction was to be, for mourning Israel, the focus of love and of hope—and which Christian symbolism identifies by a mysterious link with the body of the living God: "Destroy this temple," Christ was to say, "and I will build it up again in three days." Razed to the ground, and later rebuilt, the Temple of Solomon prefigures the Resurrection.

The present site of Jerusalem [12] consists of a plateau from which extend towards the south two hills, the western of which is occupied by the modern city, and the eastern divided into three gardens, the Bezetha, the Morrah, and the Ophel. This latter, which extends in a triangle between the Kidron and the little moat, now ruined, of Tyropoeon, was the only area occupied by David. Zion, the city of Solomon, was built on the Moriah, to which great religious memories cling.[13] Had not his father there received Jahweh's command to consecrate him as the Lord's anointed? The rocky hill was hewn, levelled and squared with enormous labour. A supporting wall half way up the slope made it possible to have a much larger platform on the summit. Josephus, the Jewish historian, says that the stones were cemented together with lead. And it is before these hewn blocks (or the little of them that remains at the base of Herod's constructions) that the children of Israel still come to give vent to those lamentations that have given to that ruin its name of the "Wailing Wall." Today the Moriah is a long esplanade, some 535 yards long and 351 wide, upon which rises a masterpiece of Moslem

[12] *See* Diagram: JERUSALEM IN THE TIME OF KING SOLOMON.
[13] *See* the Sacrifice of Israel, p. 26.

art, the Cupola of the Rock, called, inaccurately, the Mosque of Omar.

The temple which was to stand on the ground-plan thus prepared was to do honour to Jahweh; it must be worthy of the Most High. Besides, Solomon had the sense of glory. In describing to him the majestic temples of Egypt his Egyptian wife may well have suggested that he should build one on a similar model, and in Phoenicia he could see for himself examples of a sober and rich art. It was to his friend Hiram that he went for help. A treaty was made: in exchange for corn, barley, wine and oil, particularly the latter—the oil of olives gathered, not fallen, was specified—Hiram was to furnish gold, wood, and skilled workmen. The stone was to be found on the spot, where it was plentiful.

Jerusalem forthwith became a hive of industry; a hundred and fifty thousand workers, under the direction of thirty-six hundred overseers, set to work. The Phoenician architect who planned this edifice certainly drew his inspiration from Semitic architecture as it is to be found in the Fertile Crescent. Completed in rather more than seven years, the Temple of Solomon was of noble appearance. The first court, approached by a ramp, was an enclosure where the people were to gather. A second wall divided off the precincts of the priests, whose numbers the Levites were to supply. There was the altar of burnt offerings, with its perpetual fire and, resting on four groups each of three bronze oxen, the Sea of Brass, an immense reservoir of water for the sacrifices, symbolizing, perhaps, as in the temples of Babylon "the abyss," the primeval ocean. Before the high pylon that marked the entrance into the sanctuary, stood two columns of bronze, about twelve yards high, each of which had a name: the one signified "He will establish," the other "in strength."

The Temple proper was not very large. Compared with a cathedral, it would seem like a modest village church. It was not more than thirteen yards wide, and its total length was less than fifty yards. But its splendour compensated for its smallness. The finest woods in the world, sandalwood, cedar and cypress panelled the walls and covered the floor. Wooden grilles and deeply recessed windows admitted subdued light that lit up with fire the gold of the walls, the altar and the candelabra. There were two distinct areas: in one which was holy, the priests offered the shewbread, tended the lights of the ten seven-branched candlesticks, and burned incense over the Altar of Perfumes. A precious curtain, embroidered with purple, violet and gold on an immaculate background of white Egyptian linen, concealed a door that opened upon the Holy of Holies, where, in silence and total darkness, rested the Ark of the Covenant, guarded by two cherubim of olive-wood overlaid with gold, whose wings, outstretched over the whole breadth of the stone, were to shelter God if it should please Him to enter that place. Once a year, the High Priest, alone, entered this august tabernacle.

How far did a people who so recently had known no temple but a tent find this sumptuous edifice acceptable? There seems reason to believe that there was resistance in some quarters. But the king who laboured for its glory was thinking primarily of posterity: future generations would invest the Temple with venerable associations, and David's significant gesture of bringing the Ark to Jerusalem would be fully confirmed; henceforth it should be the one religious capital where the very soul of the people would dwell.

Solomon raised many other buildings. His palace consisted of a large number of edifices, surrounded by the same wall that also enclosed the first court of the Temple. Its chief buildings were: "The House of the forest of Lebanon," built of cedar trunks, and adorned with circles of gold, a great hall for gatherings and ceremonies; the "Porch of Pillars," smaller, evidently an ante-room adjoining the "Porch of Judgment," where, raised on six steps guarded by twelve lions, stood the king's ivory throne; the royal residence itself, divided into two buildings, one for the royal harem, the other for the Egyptian queen who was entitled to special honours. Finally it would be wrong to suppose that the only building operations of this reign were inspired by religion or luxury. Many highly practical undertakings were carried out. The city of Gezer, destroyed at the time when it was captured from the Pharaohs, was rebuilt, together with other cities that had suffered the same fate. Solomon built fortresses on his frontiers like that of Megiddo where archaeology has brought to light his stables. Warehouses were built on the roads as far afield as the vicinity of Petra.

These were remarkable works, prodigious undertakings, especially when we consider the smallness of that kingdom and the numerical weakness of the population. But we cannot attempt to estimate the suffering and labour involved in these superb achievements: Cheops and Kephren, the Pharaohs who built the Pyramids, were long held in execration. And certain symptoms reveal that towards the end of Solomon's reign an immense weariness weighed upon the shoulders of his people. Were not the last years of the reign of Louis XIV darkened by the same sentiment? But, just as we forget the heavy taxes, and now see only the beauty of Versailles, so Israel forgot the severe requisitions and the blows of the taskmasters of the labour gangs, and remembered only the day of glory when, dedicating the Temple to the Most High, Solomon, speaking for his whole people, cried, "O Lord God of Israel, there is no God like thee in the heaven, nor in the earth" (2 Chronicles vi:14); and when, in the lightning of His thunder kindling the victims of the burnt-offering, Jahweh had answered.

THE GLORY OF THE KINGS

The halo of glory that is created about certain personages is itself a fact of history. Charlemagne, the wise emperor, with his "flowery beard" of the *Chanson de Roland* lives in our memories rather than the terrible soldier with long moustaches who caused the massacre of ten thousand Saxons; and Napoleon who, moreover, helped to build up his own image, is now inseparable from the great images that he suggested to Victor Hugo.

The Bible gives us three pictures of David. In the Book of Samuel we see him as a young adventurer, blessed by God, but full of the passions of youth; in the Book of Kings as the pattern of sovereigns, with whom all others are compared; in Chronicles he is idealized to the point of passing over his crimes in silence, a statue rather than a living man. Above all, the pious and sacred character of the man by whose means Israel, through many battles, rose to power has been preserved. Jewish and Christian traditions affirm that he was himself the author of many Psalms; to others composed after him in the course of centuries, it was felt that no better assurance of their worth could be given than that of ascribing them to his authorship. And the prayers of the Church to this day borrow from that tradition of David some of their finest expression.

The glory of Solomon was already spread abroad during his lifetime, and was, moreover, turned to good advantage. On his death the priests who owed him the Temple—their livelihood—set to work to magnify his image to the point of making it almost featureless. Over the faults of the regime and the weaknesses of the man, they passed in silence. The whole text of Chronicles gives us nothing more than a picture in which the motive of edification is too plainly apparent. The "wisdom" is underlined. The Book of Proverbs, sometimes called the "Wisdom of Solomon," certainly contains two collections of maxims (from v to xxii:16, and from xxv to xxix) which can as a whole be attributed to the great king, or to his period; the rest has in consequence been ascribed to him. It is no longer claimed that the king wrote the Book of Ecclesiastes in which is developed the famous theme, "vanity of vanities! all is vanity!" In ascribing to him that latter homily of condensed and resigned philosophy the intention was doubtless to show where an excess of wealth, glory and pleasure must lead. As for Wisdom, that admirable essay in which is expounded such a profound doctrine of the ultimate ends of man, it is the work of an Alexandrian Jew who lived shortly before our own era, and who was familiar with Greek philosophy.

Amongst all these attributions there remains one which concerns us particularly: that of a slight poem, of ravishing imagery, which has never failed to enchant the hearts of successive generations. The Song of Songs is written in the language of a period at least three centuries later than Solomon. Is it a late transcription of an authentic work of the period, or is this only a literary attribution? It is a love romance pure and simple. The Shulamite (was she the Sunamite Abishag?), a ravishing maiden, brown and black as the "tents of Kedar," has been led to the king's apartments. But her love remains faithful to the one who in the wilderness, there where are the wild gazelles and hinds, leads his flocks among the anemones. From soul to soul, the two lovers speak a dialogue charged with poetry, in which the night breezes impart all the fragrance of the East. One night the Shulamite sleeps, but her heart wakes. She hears the voice of the Beloved, "Open to me, my sister, my love, my dove, my undefiled." She opens the lock with her fingers perfumed with myrrh. But the guards come and she is driven back into the harem: "I charge you, O daughters of Jerusalem, if ye find my beloved, that ye tell him that I am sick of love!" At last, pleading his cause before the king, the young man cries, "There are threescore queens, and fourscore concubines, and virgins without number. My dove, my undefiled, is but one. . . ." The king's generosity restores them to one another and the Shulamite departs towards the desert leaning on her beloved, leaving behind her the splendours of the palace.

Is the intention only to record a generous action of the king? As we have seen already in the case of the Book of Ruth, it is likely that mystical symbolism has been superimposed on the simple narrative.[14] The East deeply loves this profound play with

[14] I deliberately refrain from insisting further here on the spiritual and mystical interpretation of the Song of Songs. Indeed it seems to me that developments of that order are beyond the scope of an historical work of this kind. But, in order to forestall any misinterpretation, we must bear in mind once more that all the texts that are included in the biblical canon, being inspired, can have no other ultimate purpose than a spiritual one, and that to say that the Song of Songs is to be regarded as a love story and nothing more would be absurd. The great conception of the Covenant forms the background of this lovely poem, as it does of the prophet Hosea, or of Psalm xlv in spite of all differences of content, and it is in this light that all these developments must be understood. M. Robert, the learned professor of Scripture at the Catholic Institute of Paris, is engaged on an important work on the interpretation of the Song: I would like here to thank him for the advice that he has given me.

ideas. "The Shulamite" is "the perfect" as Solomon is "the accomplished." Is not the love story that of Israel, who was to abandon the splendours of the monarchy and return to the desert in order to rediscover the sense of her mission? Is it not, moreover, that of the faithful soul that renounces riches in order to be united with the one who is "altogether lovely," the "fountain of gardens, a well of living waters," love "strong as death"—God? And have not many Christian mystics like St. Bernard, in numberless superb commentaries, identified the lover who comes, full of youthful power, to set at liberty the lovely captive, with the Messiah, the Liberator? With the image of the opulent king, lover of profane magnificence, is thus associated that Other by whose means the spirit of renunciation came into the world: and with more reason than at first sight appears, if one bears in mind that the providential significance of the whole of this history, and its ultimate end, is Christ.

II

SEEDS OF DEATH, PROMISES OF LIFE

THE MYSTIC ROYALTY

"PRIDE GOETH BEFORE DESTRUCTION, and an haughty spirit before a fall," says one of the Proverbs (Proverbs XVI:18). No sooner was Solomon dead than his kingdom disintegrated. His splendour ushered in a period of disorder and decadence, which ended in a catastrophic collapse. In this immediate posthumous setback, inspired souls, like the author of Ecclesiastes, saw the legitimate sanction of the sins of the king; it was because he had sinned that Solomon drew down anger upon his children. To this fundamental explanation history adds other reasons for the decline that was inherent in the Hebrew monarchy.

The kingship was the outcome of a providential design. Jahweh Himself had established it. Desired for human reasons by the people who, besides, always exercise a certain control over their sovereigns, thanks to Samuel it was consecrated. Saul was anointed in the name of Jahweh. It was God again who substituted the young shepherd for the king who proved unworthy, and who yet again told David in his old age to consecrate Solomon in preference to all his other sons. That religious character that Bossuet ascribed by a grandiose analogy to the politics of the kings of France imposed very precise duties upon the sovereign. As the Lord's anointed, His representative on earth, he must above all set an example of flawless faith. His duty is to govern as Jahweh Himself would govern, with quasi-divine justice.

The religious role of the monarchy of Israel appears to have been considerable. Even the unhappy Saul served Jahweh well. If the dispersion of the tribes had continued, piety would in the end have been split up into local cults, which would have grouped themselves around every "high-place." By uniting, the nation escaped this danger and the great tradition of Moses was reinforced. David, in bringing the Ark of the Covenant to Jerusalem, gave to national unity its most manifest symbol. The throne of Jahweh, the place where He revealed Himself, was once more in the heart of the nation, in the place that now became its capital. Enclosed by Solomon in the darkness of the Holy of Holies, it partook of the very mystery of the Invisible God: it gradually became effaced by the Temple which, built originally to shelter it, became "The House of God"; and when, on the return from exile the august edifice was rebuilt, it was to become the centre of a cult that had developed to the point of going beyond any symbol of that kind, and the Holy of Holies was to remain empty.

Nevertheless, the kings of Israel were no more true priests than were the kings of France, whose mystical character is equally beyond doubt. The king belonged neither to the tribe of Levites nor to one of those colleges of prophets that spread the words of Jahweh throughout the country. And even when he was inspired by the spirit of God surprise is expressed. The ministers of the religion were still the Levites, whose organization is minutely described in the Book of Chronicles. There were thirty-eight thousand of them, of whom twenty-four thousand were true priests, the others clerks and lawyers, members of choirs or keepers of the Temple. Divided into twenty-four clans, each filled its appropriate cultural task. The branch descended from Aaron enjoyed one prerogative: at the head of that vast priesthood, the High Priest was the supreme officer of sacrifice, and he alone might enter the Holy of Holies. Priests had the exclusive right of consulting the "ephod-oracle" and the casting of sacred lots which expressed the will of God. They had also as a rule the task of making burnt-offerings, the burning of incense, and ablutions. Nevertheless the kings had certain specifically priestly functions; it sometimes happened that they themselves sacrificed victims, like the Patriarchs in the days of the desert; they also presided at those vast ceremonies at which the people gathered

in the outer sanctuary. Then the royal glory seemed to borrow its
light from the divine glory. Vested in embroidered purple, preceded by five hundred guards each bearing a golden shield, the
king advanced amid the *rinna* and *terua*, the liturgical acclamations described in the Psalms; while the trumpets uttered their
strident notes and the heavy odour of burning flesh ascended in
the smoke on the altar of burnt offerings.

That intimate association of royal and divine majesty carried
within itself certain dangers. In the time of Moses and the Judges,
Jahweh governed His people directly. Theocracy was absolute.
Leaders held only temporary mandates, and were submissive to
the will of God. With the kingship things took on a new character;
a mystical theocratic monarchy was established, but a monarchy
for all that. Jahweh had to some extent delegated part of His
powers to a man. As representative of God to the people, and of
the people to God, the king partook of the divine majesty, and
even, in a Psalm (xlv:6) the phrase "Thy throne, O God," is addressed to the king. And kings, even when they are consecrated,
remain men. What would happen if between their human and
their supernatural mission a conflict were to arise?

FIDELITY

To be sure, David and Solomon were both believers who lived
in love and fear of Jahweh. Their religious attitudes, however,
were very different. In David we feel a simple, almost a naïve
faith which left room for a certain amount of minor scheming,
and also for brutal lapses into the temptations of sin, but which
redeemed all his faults by the depth of his confidence in the
supreme mercy. Ecclesiasticus has described him admirably. "In
all his works he praised the Holy One most high with words of
glory: with his whole heart he sung songs, and loved him that
made him." Solomon's devotion was more aloof; there was something official about it. In him we see not so much the man who
bows his head under the weight of inner humility before divine
majesty as the powerful monarch who sacrifices ostentatiously to

another monarch, the ruler of the Heavens. But both have held an important place in the religious history of Israel.

Even if only a part of the writings that tradition attributes to them are in fact their work, it is not for nothing that the names of two great kings are associated with these monuments of human faith. Hebrew poetry has produced no more perfect masterpieces than some of the Psalms, and we are astonished by the profound insight of the Proverbs. That violent, highly coloured language that Renan compares to the sound of a brazen trumpet rending the air with its shrill notes, that intuitive psychology that goes straight to the heart of any matter, to the significant detail, that expression at once concise and rich that invests abstractions with images—all combine to give to these works a literary beauty which we can still appreciate. And the ideas expressed in them are those that the human heart understands at all times: "O Lord our Lord, how excellent is thy name in all the earth! who hast set thy glory above the heavens. Out of the mouth of babes and sucklings hast thou ordained strength because of thine enemies, that thou mightest still the enemy and the avenger. When I consider thy heavens, the work of thy fingers, the moon and the stars, which thou hast ordained; What is man that thou art mindful of him? and the son of man, that thou visitest him? For thou hast made him a little lower than the angels, and hast crowned him with glory and honour. Thou madest him to have dominion over the works of thy hands; thou hast put all things under his feet" (Ps. VIII).

Wretchedness and greatness of man in the presence of God! Pascal himself found no better words in which to express it.

It would be unjust to belittle the widening and deepening of religious thought that must be ascribed to the kings. They did not bring about, certainly, an advance comparable with that achieved by Moses, but they helped to turn it in a direction that was to lead to the universalism of Christianity. Jahweh is still the supreme ruler, the creator, the God of the powers of nature. He is still the national God, jealously claimed by the chosen people, so closely attached to the very soil of the Promised Land that sacrifices could not be offered to Him outside that little country in which Israel was realizing His purpose. It is this God, so near and so living, spoken of as a person, that fills the mind of the psalmists with overwhelming love. But if we still chant the Psalms in praise of the Eternal,, it is because, beyond the particularized and partial divinity that led Israel towards her destiny, the nature of God was already revealed in them in its authentic character.

The idea of divine justice also made progress at this time. While protecting His people, Jahweh also manifests toward them a rigorous equity. One might suppose that He too applied the Mosaic *lex Talionis:* David caused the death of Uriah? Three of his sons should be slain. Israel bowed its head beneath the heavy weight of that justice, but knew also that man may repent, and that then the divine justice becomes mercy.

Another idea also made progress and its destiny was to be a fruitful one. Jahweh increasingly was seen as infinitely superior to all the other national gods worshipped by neighbouring peoples— more than superior, *He exists,* while the others do not. In classical antiquity, a chief who is about to attack an enemy people attempts to conciliate their gods; makes petition to them; he is anxious not to have them against him. There is not a trace of this idea in Israel. Other gods are idols, to be despised, that can be despoiled without fear of their wrath. David's victories and the magnificence of Solomon must have further convinced the chosen people of the almighty power of Jahweh. And it is not too much to imagine that in that enlarged conception the great minds of David and Solomon prepared the way for the sublime developments that led to a Saint Paul, who wrote, commenting on the Gospel, that the national religion was a first step towards the universal religion in which "there is no longer Greek nor Jew, circumcised or uncircumcised." In many texts of the time of the kings, the Messianic intention is clear, and the spiritual descent is unbroken between David and his descendant, Jesus.

There is yet another respect in which progress was clearly made, that is in the relationship between the moral and the religious order. We have seen how in associating faith with morality Hebrew thought made a decisive advance in human thought. This was to be the favourite theme of the Prophets, but the Kings already had begun to see this link with increasing clarity. "To do justice and judgment is more acceptable to the Lord than sacrifice" (Proverbs xxi:3). In this again the Messianic gospel is foreshadowed, and the conception of the monarchy on this matter, that of punishment incurred by sin, all go to prove that such notions had gone deep in the minds of the people of Israel.

Let us not lose sight of these profound loyalties that the Hebrew royalty preserved in the time of its greatest kings. If there were faults that cried out for punishment, it was the keeping of these trusts that merited the mitigation of the divine anger. When the times of disorder and ruin had come, we shall see that the crown remained for four centuries without interruption in the descent of David, whereas in the other kingdom, in two hundred and thirty years, nine dynasties had succeeded one another. And in that we may see the proof of the divine blessing; in memory of David who had kept faith, because God "promised to give a lamp to him and to his sons forever."

BETRAYALS

A curious passage in Deuteronomy (xvii:15–20), the code in which the better part of Moses' thought is expressed, had stated the conditions that the king whom God was later to establish over Israel must fulfil: "one from among thy brethren shalt thou set king over thee: thou mayest not set a stranger over thee, which is not thy brother. But he shall not multiply horses to himself, . . . Neither shall he multiply wives to himself, that his heart turn not away: neither shall he greatly multiply to himself silver and gold. . . . That his heart be not lifted up above his brethren." This ideal of a simple ascetic fraternal monarchy was still that of the time of Saul who between two campaigns went to till his fields, and whose sceptre was the lance of a soldier. It was still David's ideal although the distance gradually widens between the austere tradition and the king of Jerusalem. With Solomon the distance becomes a great gulf. The family ties that were so powerful, and of which national ties were but an extension, extended beyond all bounds with the custom of the harem with its hundreds of inmates. The king was divided from his people by the full extent of his opulence and his pride. His heart was "lifted up above his brethren." Abundance of gold and increase of power brought their inevitable demoralizing consequences. For the fraternal and national ideal soon was substituted a rigid society in which the rich exploited the poor, where venality progressed and in which the spiritual purity of the race was compromised by all sorts of contaminations.

David's faults were those of a man, a man carried away by impulses to which he yielded. But we see that he loved Bathsheba, and the criminal passion that drove him towards her has something moving in it. With Solomon, in whom we never see such impulses of sentiment, it is a very different matter. The love of wealth, magnificence and pride are perpetually present in his life, perverting even his most authentic grandeur. We sense around him a world of intrigues and violence, masked by etiquette. And we see himself yielding to those temptations that the representative of Jahweh ought to have resisted most strongly.

David had seven wives; Solomon numbered his by dozens, perhaps by hundreds. He collected exotic beauties; the Phoenician with her heavy robes, her great gold earrings and her dusky hue; the Egyptian, daughter of the greatest of kings, followed by innumerable servants, with all the trappings of boxes of jewels, rare dishes, vials of perfumes; and many others, Hittites, Moabites, Edomites, ruddy and brown, even daughters of the enemies of Israel like the Ammonite whose son Rehoboam was to be the great king's successor.

The worst of this was that each one brought with her her customs, her faith, her gods; Solomon's policy of conciliation could not offer any serious opposition to these importations of heresies. As most of these marriages were for political reasons, it was all but impossible to forbid each new wife to build a temple for her national idols. Solomon, Jahweh's delegate on earth, builder of the Temple, unifier of Canaan, provided victims and entertainment for the priests of all the Molochs, Kamoshes and Ammon-Ras of his wives. This was worse than paradoxical. In Jerusalem, not far from the Mount of Olives, a "Mount of Corruption," is still pointed out, where, according to the Book of Kings, stood the altars built by Solomon for "Ashtoreth the abomination of the Zidonians, and for Chemosh the abomination of the Moabites, and for Milcom the abomination of the children of Ammon" (2 Kings xxiii:13).

Such was the terrible danger that royal luxury introduced into the heart of Israel. All the efforts from the time of Moses to stamp out the idolatrous tendencies of the people were now in danger of being undone. It was no longer even a matter of the local "Baals" of the Canaanites, whose benevolent aspect and restricted powers limited their prestige, but of foreign deities carried in by every tide of fashion. As the inevitable consequence of this initial betrayal grew, we see Israel passing through crises of increasing gravity. The invasion of Phoenician deities in the time of Jezebel provoked terrible happenings. And the great voice of Elijah denouncing Ahab for his infamy justly stated the drama that was to take place among the people infected with this evil: "How long halt ye between two opinions? If the Lord be God, follow him: but if Baal, then follow him."

Posterity, that was to attribute the formula of *vanitas vanitatum* to Solomon, expressed a profound truth. That reign of luxury had laboured less for the progress of righteousness and truth than for the satisfaction of royal vanities. They would turn to dust and ashes, for such is the law of reality.

LINES OF LEAST RESISTANCE

The mortal infection introduced into Israel by that apostate tolerance was the more dangerous in that there were disquieting tendencies in the body of the kingdom. History finds out the lines of least resistance in the edifice.

The kingship had not been accepted without regretful after-thoughts; even those who held it to be a necessity often regarded it with distaste. One has only to remember Samuel's strictures. Absolute though it was, the monarchy, as we have seen, was also in accordance with the popular wish and as, under an autocracy, revolt is almost the sole means of bringing about a reform, it was held to be legitimate. Against the Lord's Anointed, some of God's prophets were to encourage rebellion.

We shall see even worse things. As the prophetic movement grew up, an idea became widespread whose germ was in the moral conception of religion: that Jahweh concerned Himself with Israel only in so far as her people kept the law. The greatness and even the existence of a nation, however privileged that nation might be, meant little to Him; what He desired was righteousness and equity. If they were to break faith, the people of the Promise must inevitably perish. Therefore, what meaning had royalty? Royalty worked for national greatness—dramatic paradox, of which the writings of Solomon themselves bear the marks, and which was to find voice in the cry of Hosea, "I give thee a king in mine anger," said Jahweh (Hosea xiii:11).

Even the most brilliant things that the kings could do for Jahweh were turned against them in the eyes of the strict observers of the Law. A Temple? Was there any temple in the days of Moses? Was not religion purer in the poverty of tents than among the gold of the sacred precincts? The old nomadic ideal that lived always in the heart of Israel rebelled against the imported luxury, the pagan splendour of these ceremonies. And history, confirming this judgment, was to show us the spectacle of the riches of the Temple drawing upon Jerusalem Egyptian, Philistine and Chaldean raids; even a king of Israel scandalously pillaged them. These pious treasures were indeed rather seeds of death than signs of life.

To these fundamental causes of dissolution were added others more immediate. In the first place, discontent against taxation and labour conscription continued to increase. A social crisis threatened. For what were the gangs of woodcutters, mountain quarry-men and the oarsmen in the galleys of Azion-Gaber working? To enable a king and his wives and favourites to live in luxury, to support the great! The great advance in civilization in the time of Solomon had increased the gulf between the rich and the poor out of all measure. Great proprietors grew up at the expense of small ones. "Woe," cried Isaiah (v:8), "unto them that join house to house, that lay field to field." And, pointing an avenging finger at luxurious women favoured by fortune, he foretold for them the days of distress and corruption to come, when, "the Lord will take away the bravery of their tinkling ornaments about their feet, and their cauls, and their round tires like the moon, the chains and the bracelets, and the mufflers, the bonnets, and the ornaments of the legs, and the headbands, and the tablets, and the earrings, the rings, and nose jewels, the changeable suits of apparel, and the mantles, and the wimples and the crisping pins"—all the appurte-nances of elegance and sin.

These rancours were ready to crystallize in rebellion. In the time of Solomon, a revealing incident foretold grave crises to come. A certain Jeroboam, of the tribe of Ephraim, had been appointed by the king as superintendent of works in his district. The son of a poor widow who had risen to this high position by his own efforts, he yielded to ambition and prepared a revolt whose social character cannot be doubted. This rebel was a Spar-tacus of Israel. But he found significant support. A visionary named Ahiah, who was an anti-royalist agitator in the region of Shiloh, encouraged the revolutionaries. He even declared to Jero-boam that the sons of the oppressive king, unfaithful to Jahweh, should not govern the chosen people, and tearing his garments into twelve pieces, gave ten of them to the rebel, in that way fore-telling the schism of the tribes. Jeroboam, however, did not suc-ceed in his attempt, and his rising was suppressed by King Solo-mon's police. But he took refuge in Egypt where he bided his time —that is to say, the death of the king.

This episode reveals still another rift, the gravest of all, and the one which was to bring down the whole edifice. Jeroboam was a man of Ephraim, that is to say, one of the tribes to the north of Judah. The north was jealous of the south. The proud "house of Joseph," Ephraim and Manasseh, had not seen without bitterness the mediocre tribe of Judah attain to supreme power. The royal centralization went against the ancient anarchistic tendencies of the tribes. The Benjaminites were indignant that after Saul the king was no longer of their number. And David had had to put down separatist revolts—that of his son Absalom, another led by one Seba, of Benjamin. In fact, it was as if Israel and Judah had been two allied but separate ethnic groups temporarily united by the resolution and the power of the kings, but whose deepest desires tended towards separation. All these causes of disintegration were to come into play simultaneously when, in the disillusionment of an opulent but gloomy old age, the king who had thought to make Israel powerful by adorning her with gold and sandalwood died in 935 B.C.

THE SECESSION

Rehoboam succeeded his father. The succession was legitimate, but he was half a foreigner, the son of an Ammonite mother; worse, he was weak-minded and surrounded himself with young fools. The southern tribes accepted him without demur, but those of the north took advantage of the circumstances to make conditions. When the new sovereign visited Shechem, the ancient patriarchal sanctuary, in order to discover the sentiments of the people towards him, he was met by delegations charged with complaints. And, which presaged no good, the mouthpiece of the malcontents was none other than Jeroboam, who had returned from Egypt on learning the news of the king's death.

With a little tact, the young king could have dealt with the situation. But he behaved with utter stupidity. What they asked was, after all, not unreasonable. "Thy father made our yoke grievous; now therefore make thou the grievous service of thy father, and his heavy yoke which he put upon us, lighter, and we will serve thee" (1 Kings XII:4). Rehoboam had not even the excuse of having yielded to an impulse of the moment. He took three days. He consulted the old men who had been the counsellors of his father; they told him that with fair words the situation could be settled. But he also asked the opinion of boys of his own age, who, needless to say, were for taking a strong line. Adopting their opinion, Rehoboam presented the people with the following answer, "My father made your yoke heavy, and I will add to your yoke: my father also chastised you with whips, but I will chastise you with scorpions" (1 Kings xii:14).

The result of this tactful policy soon became apparent. The old revolutionary slogan current among the tribes of the north ever since the time of the second of the kings was heard again among the hills. "What portion have we with David? Neither have we inheritance in the son of Jesse: to your tents, O Israel. Now see to thine own house, David." All might not yet have been lost, but Rehoboam made the same mistakes as Louis-Philippe who, when he wished to quell the Parisians, entrusted his troops to Bugeaud who was held to be responsible (falsely as it happened) for the massacres of the Rue Transnonain. He sent the chief of public works, the slave-driver in chief, the man responsible for the raising of taxes. He was stoned to death and the riot became a revolution. Rehoboam lost no time in mounting his war-chariot and returning to Jerusalem. For a few days he entertained the idea of reconquering the north by force of arms, but he gave up the notion. The secession was completed in the same year as the death of Solomon, in 935 B.C.

While the south, remaining faithful to the son of the legitimate king, constituted a small state confined to the territory of Judah, together with some elements of Benjamin and Simeon, the ten tribes of the north proclaimed as king Jeroboam, the rebel and anti-royalist. History has its ironies. The new sovereign made haste to affirm his independence of the other by establishing a cult of Jahweh on his own territory. "It is too much for you to go up to Jerusalem," he said to his people. "Behold thy gods, O Israel, which brought thee up out of the land of Israel." And he had two golden calves made, one of which he placed at Dan, the other at Bethel. Then, fearing perhaps that the Levites, servers of the Temple of Solomon, might cause trouble, he instituted as priests men who were not of their tribe.

Certainly he had no intention in so doing of establishing a schism. The "calves" were supposed to represent Jahweh by a simple compliance with the popular taste for images. Moreover, in the north the people of the south were blamed for destroying the national unity. "Hear, Lord, the voice of Judah and cause them to return to their people"—but from the very beginning of the northern kingdom the symptoms of the evils that were to ravage it were apparent: the germs of foreign heresy, of syncretist contamination. Jezebel and her cortege of idols were not far off.

We cannot refrain from a sense of sorrow when we contemplate the violent overthrow of the work of the kings which from disaster to disaster, from one crisis to another was to proceed to total disintegration. Nevertheless this decadence itself has perhaps a supernatural significance that Renan, who cannot be suspected of any bias in favour of a providential interpretation of sacred history, has pointed out in a notable passage: [1]

"The religious future of Israel depended upon the liberty of the prophets. Now such liberty was absolutely incompatible with the existence of a stable government; this liberty that would undoubtedly have perished in a strong state, the Josephite Kingdom, in spite of terrible conflicts, always defended. Jerusalem, on the other hand, the capital of a very restricted territory, found itself reduced to the condition of a head without a body. Powerless in the political and military spheres, it became a religious city purely. David, whose one thought was to build a strong city, had in fact built a holy city. Solomon, who had thought to build a city of tolerance, had raised a citadel of fanaticism. The enclosure was prepared for one of the most remarkable conflicts of history. All winds conspired to fill the sails of those who carried out a divine mandate. All that was done against them turned to their good, because what was done against them in suppressing the egotistic element in them forced them to fall back upon their sacred mis-

[1] *Histoire du peuple d'Israel.* II, 188.

sion. If Solomon's work had succeeded, the strength of Israel would have been dissipated in the orgies of the young fools who surrounded Rehoboam; Israel and Judah would have been in no way different from the little ephemeral kingdoms that arose and perished in neighbouring countries. The vigorous secession of the Josephites destroyed the mundane future but assured the transcendental destiny of Israel."

"Unless a corn of wheat fall into the ground and die . . ." Jesus was to say.

THE ASSYRIAN TERROR

Humanly speaking, there could have been no worse folly than this split under the circumstances in which Canaan was shortly to find herself. Nothing could have more directly impeded the current of history.

There are moments in the course of centuries and civilizations when a fatal phenomenon of expansion seems to take place. Through wars, conquests or revolutions, the narrow circle is broken, a great aggregate is formed which remains until it is broken up again by internal forces, crumbles, and a new cycle begins. Thus Greece developed from the city-state to federations, and finally to the Macedonian Empire; Rome, herself growing up out of a grouping of small cities, grouped about her hundreds of nations and became synonymous with the Mediterranean world. In France a like development took place from fief to kingdom, the same that today is, willy-nilly, bringing about among the countries of Europe an internationalism that has already been imposed in the sphere of economics.

In the Near East towards the middle of the tenth century B.C., after the pause in history that had enabled the kings of Israel to build their small but beautiful house, the time of great empires began to dawn. After several centuries of disorder, the Fertile Crescent wanted peace at all costs. The new masters who arose established it, but at what a price! The ancient empires had had something patriarchal, something of the family, in their structure.

Hammurabi in his attempt at unification remained a kind of Charlemagne; with the Assyrians and the Persians we enter an era of rigid tyranny, of highly organized societies that anticipate our modern states. What could the two little kingdoms of Canaan do against this process of history that threatened them with destruction?

The great danger was to come from the north. Egypt, who was rising again and was once more a threat, intervened in her traditional buffer state; the Pharaohs once more appeared on the Jordan. But they no longer had the power of Rameses II or the Sesostris dynasty. They represented a somewhat uncertain factor in the resistance to redoubtable armies, and by reason of their vacillating policy were more a hindrance than a help to the kingdoms of the chosen people.

Meanwhile a power was growing up, against which no help could prevail. Assyria was beginning to recover from the confused troubles that had followed on the death of Tiglath-Pileser,[2] just at the time when Solomon's kingdom was breaking up. In the ninth century, under Assur-nazir-pal II, of whom we have many monuments and inscriptions, she resumed her policy of expansion: the Mediterranean once more saw soldiers with coats of mail, gauntlets and conical helmets, whose appearance anticipated in an extraordinary manner the Normans of William the Conquerer as they are depicted in the Bayeux tapestry. The eighth and seventh centuries mark the apogee of Assyrian power under these Sargons who, proudly reviving the name of the great conquerer of three thousand B.C.,[3] subjected Babylon and extended their empire over the whole Fertile Crescent and beyond, from Iran to Ethiopia—Sargon II, Sennacherib and Assur-bani-pal, whose power and splendour became legendary among the Greeks as Sardanapalus. The ruins of their palace at Khorsabad bear witness to their glory. The petty kings of Canaan might think themselves

---

[2] *See* above, pp. 135, 179.

[3] *See* above, p. 10. The choice of name is significant. In the same way Napoleon borrowed from the Roman emperors much of their symbolism and spoke of "Charlemagne, our glorious predecessor."

masters in their own houses. But the real lord, the real power was the man with the curled beard and the high tiara in the shape of a helmet who, coming down from the mountains of the Upper Tigris, imposed his terrible yoke on the whole of Mesopotamia.

The Assyrians had always been brave soldiers. In the ninth century their army became the best of their period. It included specialized corps for all kinds of operations—heavy infantry for shock troops with helmets and armour, light troops for speed, corps of sappers trained in bringing down the walls of cities, by rolling up their mobile towers against the fortifications. Rivers were no obstacle to these conquerors; each soldier carried on his back a skin bladder which when blown up served as a pneumatic raft. Their chariots, above all, were redoubtable, for they were heavy, well designed to resist blows and missiles, and each carried three men, two of whom were heavily armed.

A justly sinister reputation went before the advance of these soldiers, and the terror spread abroad often rendered fighting unnecessary. No nation has ever left a name coupled with so many terrors. Mutilation, blinding and impalement were the least of the evils that the Assyrian kings imposed upon the vanquished; often they flayed them alive and covered the walls of their cities with their skins. They even boasted of it. "I took the enemy king by the hand," writes Assur-nazir-pal, "and I flayed him. I stretched out his skin on the wall. Three thousand of his soldiers were slain in battle. Of the many prisoners, some I consigned to the flames, others blinded; I cut off the hands, ears and noses of many more. I made a pile of severed heads, and others I hung upon the vine-stems."

The glory of Assyria was to be transient. Nothing solid can arise on a basis of power and terror alone. The empire of the Sargons, a colossus with feet of clay, quickly collapsed. But before it disappeared, its sword of wrath was to strike across the history of Israel. An instrument in the hands of God, Asshur was to be powerful only "until the Lord had accomplished his work," as Isaiah had foretold.

THE SPIRITUAL DRAMA

Torn in two, and soon afterwards caught up in the Assyrian cyclone, and at the same time at the mercy of the violent spiritual torment to which a religious people is peculiarly subject, Canaan was to live through centuries of suffering. It is the third of these three dramas that the biblical texts bring most clearly into prominence as the one that explains the other two: If the kingdom divided against itself were to perish, if the soldiers of Asshur ravaged the valleys of Israel, it was because the people of Israel deserved to be punished by reason of their infidelity. The supernatural perspective is introduced into this picture with poignant clarity. The sufferings, the crises, the defeats are as nothing, for they are only consequences; the essential matter is the spiritual drama that marks that decadence with sublime grandeur and makes of it one of the highest moments of human history.

The people of the Promise were for many centuries the prey of temptation. It assailed them on every side. Idolatry grew out of the very soil where nature sprouted *achera*, sacred groves, and *masseboths*, the menhirs. It spread from the royal palace where the pagan influences of the harem sometimes became so powerful that the cult of Jahweh became absolutely extinct. It poured in with the Assyrian hordes, for the religion of the conqueror has prestige in the eyes of the vanquished. How could a people, who had always had to struggle against their own tendencies in order to remain pure, escape from this multiple contamination? It is natural that they should have succumbed, "prostituted themselves" as the prophets say.

At this time the pagan "high-places" drew crowds to their orgiastic ceremonies. About the temples of Baal and Astarte, the impure perfumes of the temple prostitutes drew men. The golden calves of Jeroboam throve. Jezebel and Athaliah had all too many followers for their Tyrian idols. Any god might become an object of adoration; even the cult of Jahweh became infected with doubtful practices; the bronze serpent, the relic of Moses, was adored in certain quarters as the equal of God, as if it were itself the supreme power.

But Israel's greatness was that she did not succumb to these temptations altogether. The national existence of the chosen people kept to the faith, to that fierce monotheism that it had managed to preserve. If that faith had disappeared, all would have been lost with it, and we should not remember Israel today more than the Amalekites or the Kingdom of Edom. The faith was saved because there were men who, in different spheres of life and by various means, stubbornly resisted the invasion of heresy.

The resistance had two main aspects which can be defined approximately as that of the Levites and that of the Prophets. In the priestly circles, fidelity to Jahweh was largely a professional matter, which is not, however, to say that it was not sincere. As servants of the Temple, they resisted the waves of idolatry and stood firm within their precincts, multiplying their holocausts and burning incense over the Altar of Perfumes. It is a normal reaction of threatened doctrines to stiffen into rigid ritualism. There was dignity in this attitude, and the Levites did Israel good service in preserving the memory of her glory even in the days of her deepest distress. But it also produced a formalism whose tragic consequences were to be experienced all too soon.

Other elements' resisted by attempting to break with those things that seemed to be the roots of the evil—excessive luxury and the increasing wealth of the landowners. A certain Jonadab, son of Rechab, founded in the ninth century an ascetic sect on which he imposed a strict rule: "Ye shall drink no wine. . . . Neither shall ye build house, nor sow seed, nor plant vineyard, nor have any: but all your days ye shall dwell in tents; that ye may live many days in the land where ye be strangers" (Jeremiah xxxv:6–7). This experiment of the Rechabites is a strange one. It still exists. But this return to nomad habits, this rigid Nazarite cult, went against the current of history that had established the chosen people on the land. Moreover, had not Jahweh given them the "land flowing with milk and honey"? It was the spirit of the

nomad life that had to be rediscovered, the spirit of renunciation
and poverty. This was understood by certain men who were
opposed alike to the ritualism of the Levites and the errant puri-
tanism of the Rechabites, but in whom the purest religious aspiration was manifest—the Prophets.

THE PROPHETS

Here we enter upon the most magnificent chapter of the history
of Israel. The whole of the Old Testament rests finally upon three
foundations: Abraham to whom the promise was given and from
whom the whole development unfolds; Moses who gave the
chosen people the means to survive; the Prophets who, uncover-
ing the true vein of the providential message, formulated the
veritable mission of Israel.

For a long time certain individuals had stood out among the
Hebrews as being gifted with special powers. In ancient times
they were known as "seers." They knew truths hidden from the
common run of men. Deborah had been of that line, and also
Samuel, who was consulted on every kind of problem, even when
a man had lost his she-asses. Clairvoyance was to some extent professional, and there were even colleges of divination. Certain
among them went further and, refusing to be confined within the
limits of a special study, penetrated to fundamental principles.
They wrestled, defended, attacked. God, they said, spoke through
them. Sometimes, possessed by the divine spirit, they uttered
mysterious words, warnings, presages, threats. In certain gatherings of these visionaries, collective enthusiasms would sometimes
break out and, accompanied by music and perhaps under the
influence of certain drugs, these mouthpieces of the spirit uttered
their discourses. It is unnecessary to point out how easily impos-
ture and corruption could be insinuated into such an institution.
These professional prophets were often false prophets, and Christ
Himself was to say of them that it was often hard to distinguish
the false from the true.

Nevertheless, in this not always very pure tradition, in these questionable circles, arose the most powerful and admirable religious personalities of the period, those who are referred to as the Prophets, who truly did speak in the name of God. They themselves disowned their connection with the others, the more or less dervish confraternities that throve in such numbers. "I was no prophet, neither was I a prophet's son," Amos exclaimed (Amos vii:14), by which he meant that he was not a prophet by profession.

The prophetic era began under the kings, that is to say during the period when the cult of Jahweh was undergoing the dangers already described; although sometimes, by extension of the term, the name of "prophet" is given to those men of earlier periods who spoke in the name of Jahweh, like Moses and Samuel. It was in the reign of David that the Prophet Nathan told the king of the punishment that would overtake his adultery; in the reign of Solomon, Ahiah, tearing his mantle, foretold the division of the kingdom. In the ninth century, the spirit of prophecy found expression in the great personalities of Elijah and Elisha, the passionate enemies of idolatry. From the year 800 B.C. onwards for three centuries, this spirit was to animate a whole series of extraordinary men, among whom was one of the greatest figures of human history, Isaiah; these Prophets are known as *writers*, for as a rule, in the Bible, we possess records written by themselves of the four *major* Prophets—Isaiah, Jeremiah, Ezekiel and Daniel—and of the twelve *minor* Prophets. These men were solitary and non-conformist, guided only by their passion for the absolute. They came from all classes, and their psychology is extremely varied. Amos was a drover, a working man who had educated himself but who still preserved his revolutionary tone. Hosea was a rich peasant with a gentle heart. Isaiah belonged to the ruling class and knew politics from the inside. Zephaniah was even a member of the royal family, and Jeremiah the son of a priest. But there is much in common among them, for they all saw their mission in the same light. Israel saw them come and go, clad in a terrible picturesqueness, dressed in the skins of animals or mantles of goat's hair, living in the most extreme simplicity. They respected no worldly convention. The ladies of the court, painted and perfumed, Amos called "cows of Bashan," as a beggar might have called them "bitches." Ezekiel prophesied to them that they would before long be raped. Jeremiah, predicting the Chaldean domination, walked in the streets harnessed like an ass. And Isaiah went naked to show what the condition of Israel was to be in the days of wrath. Nevertheless, they were regarded by the people with troubled respect. Foreign kings—the Assyrians themselves—felt their prestige. They did not like to hear what they had to say, but felt that a redoubtable power spoke through them.

One word accurately describes the essential thing about them, the very word by which they are known: prophets, according to the Greek derivation, are those who "speak on behalf of someone." They are the mouthpieces of God. They begin all their prophecies with the words, "Thus saith the Lord," or "Hear the word of the Lord!" Their mouths speak terrible things in spite of themselves. "The Lord hath spoken, who can but prophesy?" says Amos. And Jeremiah, "O Lord, thou hast deceived me, and I was deceived: thou art stronger than I, and hast prevailed: I am in derision daily, every one mocketh me. For since I spake, I cried out, I cried violence and spoil; because the word of the LORD was made a reproach unto me, and a derision daily. Then I said, I will not make mention of him, nor speak any more in his name. But his word was in mine heart as a burning fire shut up in my bones, and I was weary with forbearing, and I could not stay" (Jeremiah xx:7–9).

Their style, of which the above is an example, is elevated by the incomprehensible power that animates them. As with all inspired men, be they Arabs, Greeks or Romans, it falls into the rhythm of poetry.

Not that they ever wrote for the sake of writing. They were men of action and what they said was the means of extending their influence. Their doctrine is never expressed in abstract terms; they reacted to the impact of events as ardent polemicists. But from these phrases, dictated by necessity, arises a sublime poetry.

Therein lies the mystery. These men were inspired directly by God. No one any longer pretends, like certain materialist critics of the past, that there is any question of psychological disorder. M. Lods well says, "It would be to misunderstand the evidence of history, let alone Paul, Mahomet, Luther and Pascal, to maintain that the ecstatic state is incompatible with a sane and vigorous intelligence." [4] As with the great mystics, the secret of the Prophets does not reside in the more or less strange guise under which they are presented to us. Visions and ecstasies are but signs. God is manifest in them according to laws that we do not know; they too have their "dark night," like St. John of the Cross. We can state the results of the fact of prophecy without understanding its mechanism. In this universe that normal men do not penetrate, we sense a grandeur, as of something deeply mysterious and immensely potent.

THE SPIRIT OF PROPHECY

Into that Israelite society of the time of the Kings, menaced by the worst spiritual maladies, the Prophets were to cut like scalpels into a diseased body. Of all the elements of resistance to disintegration offered by the chosen people, they were by far the most efficacious. Nothing stopped them; they never shrank. Consequently they provoked against themselves the most fierce resistance. Jesus in a celebrated utterance was to say to a Hebrew of His day, "Ye are the children of them which killed the prophets" (Matthew xxiii: 31). A passage in the Epistle to the Hebrews (xi:36) also speaks of the sufferings endured by the Prophets—stonings, mockings and scourgings, beheading with the sword—the least of them was imprisonment. Their witness is comparable to that of the martyrs, and for similar reasons. Speaking in God's name, they openly broke with society and convention. When they

---

[4] *The Prophets of Israel*, p. 62. In quoting here M. Lods' remark, well-founded as this may be on facts of psychology and on observation, I do not intend to place those mystical experiences attributed to Luther and to Mahomet on the same incontestable level as those of St. Paul.

affirmed that ritual is nothing in comparison with moral and spiritual effort, they seemed to attack the privileges of a religion in which ritualism played a large part. The authorities of priesthood and state alike mete out hard treatment to spiritual rebels; they have good reason to fear them.

If we consider the religion of the Prophets as a whole (taking into account the variations resulting from individual differences and from an evolution taking place over several centuries), we cannot fail to be filled with admiration for the extension that they brought about in the old Hebraic monotheism. It is true that many elements that they were to develop already existed in embryo, and they no more broke with the spiritual tradition than did Jesus Himself. "Think not I am come to destroy the law, or the prophets: I am not come to destroy but to fulfil," might equally have been said by the Prophets. But they brought into the light of day that moral monotheism whose slow progress we have followed down the course of the centuries and that is, in fact, their fundamental role in history.

For them, Jahweh is not only the One God, the ruler and creator of all things; He is, above all, the God within, whose veritable temple is the heart of man and whose justice is absolute. This affirmation was enough to cause a rupture with their contemporaries. What? The God of Israel, who led His people out of Egypt, who had shown an uninterrupted preference for them, could Jahweh abandon and repudiate His children? Yes, the Prophets replied, because Israel had been unfaithful, not only in the letter, but in spirit, and had violated justice and love. This idea of the punishment and destruction of the chosen people constituted an intolerable offence to public opinion; but even at the price of their lives, the Prophets maintained their position; was not Israel's ruin the best possible proof of the universality of the Almighty?

As they saw it, Israel did indeed continue to be a privileged people, and they even repeated again and again that God had multiplied benefits in their favour. But while the usual conclusion was that Jahweh was bound to give tokens of outstanding favour, the Prophets dared to say that divine election imposes more duties than it confers privileges. Amos, speaking in the name of God, said, "You only have I known of all the families of the earth: therefore I will punish you for all your iniquities" (Amos iii:2). The terrible misfortunes that they foresaw would be punishments: Assyria was to be "the scourge of God"; righteous, his hand was raised against all the nations who merited punishment, and who all must undergo it in their turn.

God orders the entire universe. Nothing escapes Him. He is above all, superior to all creatures, indescribable unless by way of such stupefying images as those of the vision of Ezekiel, transcendent. But He is also the holy God, "Thrice Holy," of Isaiah. Justice is His will, equity His nature. All that menaces justice is an outrage to God. Amos, Isaiah, Micah and many more, say again and again that the true worship of God is righteousness. "I hate, I despise your feast days, and I will not smell in your solemn assemblies. Though ye offer me burnt offerings and your meat offerings, I will not accept them: neither will I regard the peace offerings of your fat beasts. Take thou away from me the noise of thy songs; for I will not hear the melody of thy viols. But let judgment run down as waters, and righteousness as a mighty stream" (Amos v:21–24).

In the divine justice, however, we already find the highest trait of equity, which is to be merciful. The charity of Jesus is latent in the prophetic message. Even in His just anger, God restrains Himself in pity: "Mine heart is turned within me, my repentings are kindled together. I will not execute the fierceness of mine anger, I will not return to destroy Ephraim: for I am God, and not man" (Hosea xi:8–9). And Jahweh, speaking with the voice of Jeremiah, cries, "Return, thou backsliding Israel, . . . and I will not cause mine anger to fall upon you: for I am merciful . . . and I will not keep anger for ever" (Jeremiah iii:12).

There is an immense hope in this conception. No, declare Jeremiah and Ezekiel, the saying that "the fathers have eaten a sour grape, and the children's teeth are set on edge," is not true. Every man is responsible for himself, and shall be judged by his own actions. If the expiation is sufficient, God will pardon. When the Israelites shall have reached the depths of their sorrow, God says, "Then will I sprinkle clean water upon you, and ye shall be clean: from all your filthiness, and from all your idols, will I cleanse you" (Ezekiel xxxvi:25). God also promises that "a new heart also will I give you . . . I will take away the stony heart out of your flesh, and I will give you an heart of flesh" (*ibid:* 26); and He will put His own spirit within them!

Whence did the Prophets derive this wonderful conception? Resemblances of detail can be found, for example, with the wisdom of Amen-Enopi, the Egyptian, in which it is said that "man is the clay and straw, but the mason is God"; or with the papyrus on which this fine formulation is written: "Who harbours sorrow, God will recompense." Themes of the highest morality are to be found almost everywhere in the history of humanity. But what constitutes the greatness of the Prophets of Israel is that several centuries before Confucius and Buddha, and in a way that we may fairly describe as unique, they fully realized the synthesis, already indicated in Moses, between morality and religion. For all their intelligence, the Greeks arrived only very imperfectly at this idea. Therein lies the inspiration of the prophetic message.

Another thing that the Greeks did not discover, and that the Prophets of Israel affirmed in grandiose language, is the necessity of attributing to the world itself, as it exists, a moral significance. Before injustice, violence triumphant, all those violations that make up the stuff of history, the Prophets are those who never are resigned. While classical antiquity on the whole despises misfortune, the Prophets regard it with respect. In speaking of the "poor of God," the "humble ones of the earth," the "oppressed," they use words of infinite mercy. The spirit of poverty speaks through them. Christ praising in the Beatitudes the "poor in spirit," is in line with the perspective opened up by these generous souls.

How did this message penetrate the society to which it was addressed? In the course of years the Prophets adopted three successive attitudes. The first to appear were charged only with admonitions, with the uttering of warnings against manifest temptations; if Israel sins, punishment will come. By way of example, they announced specific misfortunes like those that overtook David in order to bring him to repentance.

But infidelity grew and became general; the entire nation sinned, and the entire nation must therefore be punished. Henceforth the terrible voice prophesied catastrophe. Do what they would, Israel should not escape. A lamentable, outrageous attitude from a human point of view; we can almost excuse the violences that were done to the Prophets when we consider the indignation that they must have provoked. When Canaan, struggling with the worst of dangers, looked for some way of escape, it must have been terrible indeed to hear an Isaiah or a Jeremiah sneering, "What is the use? The Assyrian and the Babylonian are merely the instruments of the divine anger. You cannot escape your fate. You must expiate! You must suffer! Capitulate as soon as possible, for that is the wisest course!" Some historians have gone so far as to say that the Prophets were paid by the enemy to use this language of demoralization. Such an attitude can only be understood if we cease to interpret the history of the chosen people according to ordinary human standards, and see in it the purpose that it expresses. It was through the expiation of her suffering that Israel, in fact, recovered herself, and if these catastrophes had never occurred, it is more than likely that her unique character would have been lost.

Moreover, when brute force, carrying out the divine decree, had plunged the chosen people into misery, it was that very election of which the Prophets were to remind them. They were to reaffirm the favor of Jahweh whose very chastisements were the expression of His love. Moving towards the national cult of Jahweh which adversity had spiritualized, they were to appear as champions of the true religion. "The Law and the Prophets" were no longer distinguishable. Meanwhile, in their message of hope an image emerged which had already begun to take form in the time of David—that of the Messiah, the saviour of Israel.

The time of the Prophets is strictly circumscribed. They appeared and disappeared. The day came, lamented by the Psalm

(LXXIV) in which "There is no more any prophet: neither is there among us any that knoweth how long." Doubtless they had spoken their message. And that greater light that they had foretold was approaching. But they had provided for the soul of Israel, hot after sin, "sources of living water" at which humanity has never ceased to quench its thirst.

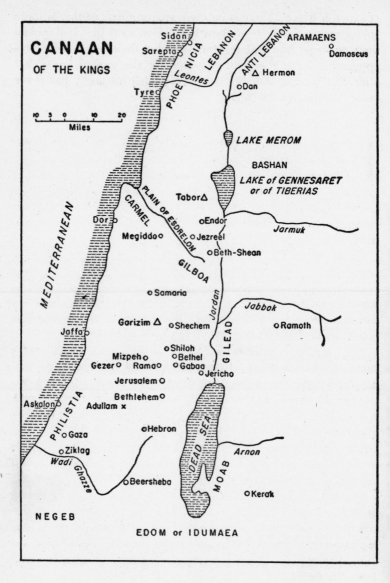

CANAAN

OF THE KINGS

Miles
10 5 0 10 20

MEDITERRANEAN

Sidon
Sarepta
Tyre

PHOENICIA
LEONTES
LEBANON
ANTI LEBANON
ARAMAENS
Damascus
Hermon
Dan

LAKE MEROM

BASHAN
LAKE of GENNESARET
or of TIBERIAS

PLAIN OF ESDRELON
CARMEL
Dor
Tabor
Megiddo
Endor
Jezreel
Jarmuk
Beth-Shean
GILBOA

Samaria
Jabbok
Garizim
Shechem
GILEAD
Ramoth
Jordan

Jaffa

Shiloh
Mizpeh
Bethel
Gezer
Ramo
Gabaa
Jerusalem
Jericho
Bethlehem
Askalon
Adullam x

Gaza
Hebron
Ziklag
DEAD SEA
MOAB
Arnon
Wadi Ghazze
Beersheba
Kerak

PHILISTIA

NEGEB

EDOM or IDUMAEA

III

THE KINGDOM DIVIDED AGAINST ITSELF[1]

THE DECLINE

FROM THIS TIME ON there were two kingdoms. In the north, Jeroboam ruled two thirds of Solomon's kingdom. He controlled a larger population and greater riches than David's grandson, restricted to infertile Judah, and so legitimate did the usurper appear that his kingdom was called Israel. But an ardent heart in a fragile body is better than a great amorphous organism.

Judah was small, and scattered with arid mountains. But her population constituted a solid block, under an illustrious dynasty, centred about a venerated capital. The plains of Israel, plains exposed to the menace of Aram and Asshur, having neither a natural centre nor unquestioned leaders, went through graver crises, and Israel was the first to fall.

This split ushered in a decadence. If the kingdom had had a succession of Solomons, who can say to what power it might not have risen. But the dislocation, the troubles that it created, the dangers to which that weakness exposed Canaan, brought with it a decline. The material progress of the tenth century disintegrated. The influence of the chosen people on their neighbours faded. For centuries—two and a half in the north, just under four in the south—a series of disorders, civil wars, and foreign invasions ushered in an inevitable movement towards extinction.

This was, in fact, one of those unhappy periods when it seems as if the stream of history is lost in the sands and wastes. A narrative of noble simplicity is succeeded by an appalling complication, increased by the identity of names in the two kingdoms. We would

[1] "Every kingdom divided against itself is brought to desolation," said Jesus (Matthew XII).

gladly leave all those Jorams and Joashes and Ahaziahs of Israel and Judah to their bloody conflicts. But among them a few remarkable personalities stand out, sometimes on account of the magnitude of their crimes, sometimes by the greatness of their almost hopeless efforts. And moreover, against this background riddled with corruption, the Prophets stand out in their full greatness, witnesses of the undying spirit.

Herein lies one of the clearest signs in which we can perceive the realization of the divine Promise. The chosen people made of that decadence an occasion of greatness. It was not their destiny to become one of those great powers that conquer vast territories. Solomon, in his luxury, certainly went against the deepest purposes of divine Providence. As Israel saw the decline of her temporal power, her spiritual supremacy affirmed itself and looked towards the future. Under the threat of extinction that weighed upon it, the kingdom divided against itself was to preserve its sense of identity, and an immense effort was made to collect, edit, publish, and distribute the texts that expressed its spirit. We certainly owe a great part of the Bible to the zeal of men of that troubled period.

The very worst times have their supernatural witnesses, those pure souls who, perhaps, restrain the divine anger from irrevocable punishment. When the great religious wars broke out, Ignatius Loyola was to found his militia, and St. Vincent de Paul discovered his Way of Charity during the violences of the Fronde. The period of dislocation of the two fragments of ancient Israel is also one of those during which piety found expression in deeply moving terms. The tradition of David was continued in the writing of Psalms. Perhaps temporal suffering only helped to refine the sense of confidence in God expressed in them. In a petition of moving beauty, the soul seeks for consolation; she "seeks for God," she knows that He is found only in the prostration of humility, at those times when we speak silently within ourselves: "As the hart panteth after the water brooks, so panteth my soul after thee, O God" (Ps. xlii:1).—"Yea, though I walk through the valley of the shadow of death, I will fear no evil: for thou art with me" (Ps.

xxiii).—Because it has sown seed that has ripened even in our own times, this period of decline deserves to be thought of as one of the most significant periods of human history.

This appears all the more remarkable if we look at it within the framework of history as a whole. At the time when the genius of an Isaiah was to find utterance there was nothing comparable in the world of the period. In order to find anything worthy of comparison with the great Prophets, we should have to go as far afield as India at the time when Buddha taught the people his admirable morality and his philosophy of negation (about 600 B.C.), or the plateau of Iran at the time when Zoroaster, reforming the ancient Aryan religion, propounded his dramatic dualism. For the rest, what do we find? The giant growth of Assyria? But what has that kingdom of brutal mercenaries, rising too rapidly to power and as quickly declining, left to humanity? Greece was still concerned with the body; in Sparta, under the legendary Lycurgus (ninth century) was developing that regime of the barracks for which it was to be known in classical times; in Athens the ethnological fusion that was to produce the triumph of its great century was already in process, passing, by way of a series of crises, through many regimes, from kings to Eupatrides, from archonship to Strategus, from Cylon to Draco (seventh century) and to Solon (sixth century), towards the democracy that was to be the basis of its greatness. But we find nothing spiritually comparable to the message of the little chosen people, and if Hellenic colonization was already (from the eighth to the sixth centuries) preparing the framework in which human thought was to develop, it was at this time still only concerned with making money and sea-trading. As for Rome, lost in the mist of fables since the hypothetical date of 753 B.C. when Romulus had traced with his plowshare the sacred furrow, she was still very humble, at war with dangerous enemies, making her way, already stubborn. Who could have discerned, in the little city of Numa Pompilius, Tullus Hostilius, Aneus Marcus and the Tarquinus, the future queen of the world, the field in which the spiritual seed sown by the Prophets should be sown, to ripen for Christ?

THE IDOLATROUS QUEENS

Divided by mortal enmities, the dynasties of Israel and Judah were unable to realize the danger to which they exposed themselves by conflict. A war broke out that lasted for fifty years. A grim experience ought to have opened their eyes to the peril. In about 930 B.C. Shiskak, the Libyan Pharaoh who had recently founded the Twenty-second Dynasty, re-appeared in Canaan, partly in order to consolidate his northern frontier, partly to avenge himself on the Hebrew kinglets who were related to his hated predecessors by the marriage of Solomon. But not content with capturing Jerusalem and pillaging, besides the Temple, the famous golden shields of the "house of the forest of Lebanon," he advanced without scruple into the territory of Jeroboam, his late protégé. In due course the two protagonists of the schism died, but the war continued. In the northern kingdom, crises occurred in the palace. Nadab, son of Jeroboam, was murdered by the usurper Baasha, whose son Elah was assassinated in his turn. Zimri, his murderer, lasted for just seven days: he was left no other alternative than the supreme resource of death by burning himself (886 B.C.) in his palace where he was besieged by one of his generals.

This rebel was Omri, a man of intelligence and energy. His dynasty (the fourth in fifty years!) [2] was one of the best in the history of the northern kingdom. He decided to make peace with Judah. This was wise. For if the threat of Egypt had grown less, the power of the kingdom of Damascus, in the north, was growing alarmingly. The Aramaeans [3] were in process of expansion, and groups of them were founding principalities as far afield as the Persian Gulf; on the north-east frontier of Israel, Ramoth, the stronghold of Gilead, had recently fallen into their hands. Omri must have acquired prestige by making a stand against them, for in Assyrian records his kingdom is always referred to as "the land of Omri." He did even better in giving his state a capital. Hitherto the capital had changed continually. He bought a hill, excellently

---

[2] See the CHRONOLOGICAL TABLE at the end of this volume.
[3] See pp. 16, 137 and 178.

chosen from the point of view of resisting sieges, and built there his city, Samaria. His walls, carved in relief, still remain, enclosing round a central court an impressive suite of rooms. Omri, in fact, resumed the policy of Solomon; his influence was to be felt throughout the whole region around Palestine; near the Arnon a stele has been found in which a Moabite kinglet, Mesa, has recorded the great events of his reign; he admits that at that time "Omri held Moab in subjection."

Was he imitating Solomon also in another respect, or was he acting from reasons similar to those of his predecessor? He established the most friendly relations with the Phoenicians, and his son Ahab married Jezebel, the daughter of the King of Tyre. A legend records that on the day the Tyrian princess arrived at the palace, a raven flew away, carrying a reed. It alighted in Italy and, planting the reed in the ground, foretold that there the enemy should arise by whom the whole of Israel should fall into servitude —Rome. With Jezebel an element of disintegration was in fact introduced into Samaria. She was a woman of great force of character, remarkable in many ways. She had complete power over her husband. With her came a taste for luxury, industry, and trade; great building operations were undertaken. Houses became those palaces of ivory, where "string music bewitched the heart," described in the Psalms, filled, no doubt, with those objects of fine workmanship, vials of perfume in the form of women, pots of rouge, combs, and ivories that were sold throughout the Fertile Crescent. But above all the Phoenician brought with her her gods, the detested Baal and Melkart of Tyre, Astarte and her priests— nearly nine hundred of them, according to the Bible—who ate at her table, and whose frenzied rites, bloodthirsty cutting of their living flesh, whirlings and ecstasies outraged the worshippers of Jahweh. Worse still, not content with demanding only a place for her idols, Jezebel set about to establish them as supreme, and began to persecute.

It is not surprising that the husband of this heretic wins scant praise from the Bible—"the impious Ahab" (875–853), however, was better than his reputation. Continuing his father's policy, he held the Aramaeans of Damascus in two furious battles. Later, reconciled with them for the time being in an anti-Assyrian alliance, he led ten thousand men and two thousand chariots in the battle of Karkar, in 853, where the all-powerful king of Syria, invading from Karkemish, failed to win a decisive victory and had to retire. Finally, in attempting to recapture Ramoth Gilead from the Syrians of Damascus, he was wounded by an arrow and having refused to leave the field of battle, died standing, his blood making a pool in his chariot. But Hebrew tradition sets little store by his victories. The flame of life was not kindled in this luxury-loving and sceptical king; it burned on the lips of his enemy, the Prophet Elijah.

He was a kind of savage hermit, dressed in goatskins, inured to the most severe asceticism. He came from the wilderness of Gilead, he arose out of the desert where the birds of the air supplied his food. His very name was a mission—"Jahweh is God!" This witness of the Eternal appeared before the idolatrous royal pair and announced their punishment. And then followed the "days of Elias" of which St. Luke speaks (Luke iv:25), "when the heaven was shut up three years and six months." The country wilted with thirst; Elijah, taking refuge at Zarephath near Sidon, bided his time; he lived in the house of a poor widow who took him in out of charity, and whose oil and corn he miraculously multiplied, and whose son he recovered from death. When he judged that the trial had been enough, the Prophet reappeared before the king.

Ahab, impressed, accepted a contest between the priests of Baal and the prophet of Jahweh. On Mount Carmel two altars were raised and victims prepared; let each of the gods make his power known! The idolators danced, shouted, and tore their cheeks. Nothing happened. "Cry aloud," Elijah mocked them, "for he is a god; either he is talking, or he is pursuing, or he is in a journey, or peradventure he sleepeth!" (1 Kings xviii). He in his turn approached the altars, prayed to Jahweh, and "the fire of the Lord fell and consumed the burnt sacrifice, and the wood, and the stores, and the dust." The prophets of Baal were thrown into prison; and in the evening "a little cloud like a man's hand" appeared over the sea, announcing the divine blessing.

Jezebel, furious, tried to put Elijah to death. But he escaped to the desert of Negeb, and afterwards went to Damascus, where his prestige was such that the king of Syria allowed himself to be anointed by him. At the same time he anointed Jehu as future king of Israel, and elected his own successor in the person of Elisha.

Thus did that intrepid figure stand firm in the face of idolatry. His purpose was not only to defend monotheism, but also the justice of which Jahweh is the guarantor. Ahab and Jezebel coveted the vineyard of Naboth; as the latter was unwilling to sell it to them, they fabricated a false charge against him and had him condemned to death. Then the spirit of God moved Elijah and he appeared once more as the accuser. Just when Ahab had entered into possession of the stolen vineyard, the terrible prophet denounced him, confronted him with his iniquity, and foretold his doom: his dynasty would come to ruin, himself be slain. As for Jezebel, the dogs of the streets should make a meal of her body!

Such was Elijah, who seemed to live by the flame of God. Could such a man die? One day as he walked with him on the way to Jericho, his disciple Elisha saw suddenly between them a chariot of fire and fiery horses; and "Elijah went up by a whirlwind into heaven" (2 Kings ɪɪ:11). At the time of the Transfiguration, it was he who was to appear with Moses speaking with Christ, the living symbol of a fearless faith.

The divine sentence was not long in being realized. Ahab died, and his successors were mediocre. The Syrians of Damascus besieged Samaria and an attempt to recapture Ramoth failed. The Moabite kinglet Mesha revolted, and an expedition had to be made against Kir-haraseth, his capital. Grave discontent disturbed Israel; Jehu took advantage of this, and seized power (842 B.C.). He was supported by those who were faithful to God, all those who saw in the misfortunes of the nation a sign of divine anger. With him was Elisha, on whom the spirit of Elijah had descended, and who, like his master, possessed miraculous gifts, who had raised a man from the dead and had healed of leprosy a soldier with a sincere heart. This revolution took on an openly religious character. The new dynasty was that of Jahweh's avengers.

Jehu, without warning, left the army and arrived at Jezreel just as the king of Israel was receiving the king of Judah. Taken by surprise, the kings went to meet him. "Is it peace, Jehu?" "What peace, so long as the whoredoms of thy mother Jezebel and her witchcraft are so many?" A terrible massacre followed. Elisha, in the name of God, had ordered the slaying of the whole of the house of Omri; and that order was carried out all too well. Ahaziah, king of Judah, was slain in the bargain. Soon after, numbers of Baal's votaries were wiped out.

As for Jezebel, she met the death foretold by Elijah, but she met it with nobility. Hearing the news of the conqueror's arrival, this woman no longer young painted her face and attired her head, *"pour réparer des ans l'irréparable outrage,"* as Racine wrote of her. She went to a window and greeted Jehu as a murderer.— "Throw her down," ordered the new king. She was killed on the pavement and her blood bespattered the walls. The horses trampled on her corpse, and when they came to bury her, there remained only *"l'horrible mélange"* of *Athalie*, *"d'os et de chair meurtris, et, traînés dans la fange, des lambeaux pleins de sang et des membres affreux que les chiens dévorants se disputaient entre eux."* Elijah's word had been fulfilled. Jahweh had gained a dazzling victory in Israel.

Soon after the party of the true God carried out a similar vengeance on another idolatrous queen, in Jerusalem. What had been happening in the little kingdom of the south during these events? Since peace had been concluded between north and south, Judah had appeared mainly as a satellite of its more powerful neighbour, associated with the wars undertaken by Samaria, and in constant touch with the dynasties of Israel. At the same time, the cult of Jahweh remained more intact there; under Jehoshaphat, the fourth king (873–849 B.C.) an attempt towards strict observance had even been made. But in Jerusalem, as in Samaria, the virus of idolatry had made inroads. Jehoshaphat had married his son Joram to Athaliah, daughter of Ahab and Jezebel. Athaliah, and with her Baal and Astarte, came in triumph to Zion.

Athaliah was indeed an astonishing woman, and Racine had good reason to describe her, in the words of one of her adherents, as *"reine éclairée, intrépide, élevée au-dessus de son sexe timide."* She dominated her husband; when he died, she made her son Ahaziah regent. On the day when she heard the news of the tragedy of the north, the revolt of Jehu, and her son's death, fearing that one of the royal children would be used against her, she ordered the massacre of all of them. Thus in possession of the throne, she ruled, and ruled well in a certain sense; the policy of her frontiers was firm and successful. But idolatry, no longer merely tolerated as in Solomon's day, tended to become official, and *"l'amour pour la religion, traité de révolte et de sédition"* (Racine).

The party of the faithful was still too strong for her. A revolt broke out, engineered by the Levites. A little child, Joash, had been saved from the massacre. When he was seven years old, the conspiracy of Jahweh's supporters felt that the time was ripe. The army itself, apparently, supported the rebels. Courageously, Athaliah made for the Temple; she was driven out with violence. Scarcely outside its precincts, she was surrounded by armed partisans, and a moment later, *"le fer a, de sa vie, expié les horreurs."* In the south, as in the north, Jahweh had triumphed.

AMOS, HOSEA AND JONAH

Nevertheless, He does not appear to have given any sign of satisfaction. Jehu, to get even with Damascus, came to terms with Assyria and paid tribute to her; this diplomacy was a failure, for Assyria having turned its attention towards the east, Israel had to stand alone against the Syrians of Damascus. Jehu was thoroughly beaten and Joash only managed to avoid the sacking of Jerusalem by offering the victor all the treasures of the Temple. This Joash, in whom so much hope had been invested, was a poor specimen. Not satisfied with having inflicted this humiliation on Judah, he returned to idolatry, no doubt from weakness rather than malice, for he also took an interest in the sect of Jahweh, whose finances he organized and whose sacred buildings he repaired. Hated and despised, he was at last killed by his own entourage. Soon after this a war broke out between Israel and Judah, in which Jerusalem was captured.

The eighth century opened with a more peaceful and fruitful period. It was remarkable in both kingdoms for the reign of two excellent kings. In Judah, Uzziah ruled for fifty years (789–738 B.C.); Edom having been conquered, trade was resumed in the Red Sea; many developments in agriculture took place, for the king "loved husbandry" (2 Chronicles xxvi:10). The cult of Jahweh had a place of honour, even though the pagan "high places" were still frequented by the common people.

Meanwhile Israel, under the strong rule of Jeroboam II (784–744), enjoyed a happy period. Damascus, troubled by palace intrigues, was no longer a threat; Assyria, for the time being, was not interested in the Mediterranean. All the lost territory was reconquered. Trade with the coast revived.

The flow of gold brought its usual results. License increased among the wealthy bourgeoisie of Samaria; faith declined, and society became again what she always is in times when, in Péguy's words, we see *"l'argent devenu roi à la place de Dieu"*—hard, unjust and inhuman. Prophets now arose (the first of those whose actual words are preserved for us), formidable opponents.

Amos was a man of the people, living by breeding cattle and collecting seeds of the sycamore—not a prophet by profession, as he is careful to tell us. But Jahweh had spoken with the voice of a lion, and the Prophet set out to declaim his message. In Israel all seemed to be well; crowds even went on pilgrimage to the holy places of Bethel, Gilgal, and Beer-sheba. The voice of the Prophet thundered. In the grandiose style of a funeral oration, he mourned the approaching ruin of Israel. Terrible threats fell from his lips; earthquakes, pestilence, droughts, the invasion of enemies who would pillage and deport the people, everything would be obliterated in unimaginable horror during which time the oracle of God would be silent.

The earliest in date of the writer-prophets, Amos anticipates them all in other respects also. The very style of his thought is the same as the others were to adopt. Sin and punishment, the Assyrian attack, all are to be found in him, and even the future glory of Judah—a great destiny is foretold for that "hovel of David."

The things that Amos most strongly condemns in his contemporaries is their appalling hardness, social injustice, and the oppression of the poor by the rich. Jahweh, God of justice, mocks at their sacrifices; what He desires is righteousness and brotherly love. And what do the chosen people do? "Lie upon beds of ivory, and stretch themselves upon their couches, and eat the lambs out of the flock, and the calves out of the midst of the stall; . . . chant to the sound of the viol, and invent to themselves instruments of music . . . drink wine in bowls, and anoint themselves with the chief ointments: but they are not grieved for the affliction of Joseph" (Amos vi: 4–6). They may run to their sanctuaries, but their sins will find them out, because of their shamelessness; "a man and his father will go in unto the same maid"; but above all because of their inhumanity, "because they sold the righteous for silver, and the poor for a pair of shoes; that pant after the dust of the earth on the head of the poor, and turn aside the way of the meek" (Amos ii:6–7).

A society built on such foundations is condemned to death; "Shall horses run upon the rock? Will one plow there with oxen?" Neither can the unjust prosper! There is but one conclusion, one moral lesson: "Hate the evil, and love the good, and establish judgment in the gate: it may be that the LORD GOD of hosts will be gracious unto the remnant of Joseph" (Amos v:15).

We may well wonder what effect the apparition of such men can have produced. No doubt they were at first regarded as fanatics. But what when circumstances seemed to prove them right? Jeroboam II had not long been dead when crises began again, revolts, assassinations; and the Assyrian menace rapidly grew on the horizon. Hosea was now the foreteller of wrath. What he most strongly denounced in the Israelites was their religious infidelity, their "prostitution" to false gods. He himself, in one of these symbolic gestures that the seers loved, had married a "wife of whoredoms" and had given to the children borne to him by her the significant names of "unloved" and "not my people." Like Amos, he reiterated that sacrifices have no value in themselves; what matters is "the knowledge of God" (Hosea vi:6). This mystic speaks of God in terms worthy of a Lydwinne or a Gertrude. Like many mystics, he uses the language of human and even carnal love in order to speak of the love of God; the people of Israel is the bride of Jahweh, her betrothed; God loves her tenderly; and therefore the infidelity of Israel violates that heart so full of love. It is to be found everywhere. You prefer politics to prayer, you build forts, you rear war-horses? Fools! The terrible Assyrians will conquer you, unless God intervenes. You trust in kings? Power, greatness? What does that amount to? Only faith in God matters. What can be expected of a nation in which idolatry flourishes, where Baal is worshipped, and crowds gather at the pagan high places? The "calf made by a workman," adored in Samaria, disgusts the Prophet. And always he draws the same logical conclusion: "O Israel, return unto the Lord thy God; for thou hast fallen by thine iniquity" (xiv:1).

Nevertheless, a hope dawns across his threatening words. Israel in her distress will rediscover Jahweh. God will "speak to her heart" (ii:16), and divine compassion will be moved (xi:8). After their misfortunes, the faithful will return from Egypt and Assyria and dwell again in their houses. To that promise of survival and redemption, the faithful of Jahweh, those who listened to the threats of the Prophets, clung for consolation.

It was for this reason that in pious circles they liked to tell the astonishing and rather comic story of Jonah, the Prophet who was swallowed by a fish. One day this man was told by God to go to Nineveh, capital of the Assyrians, and declare to that ferocious people that they too would be punished. Little wishing to undertake such an adventure, Jonah embarked on a ship bound for

Tarshish, fleeing from "the presence of the Lord." But a fearful tempest struck the ship, the visible mark of the divine anger. The crew, terrified, blamed Jonah and threw him into the sea, whereupon the waves instantly subsided.

But God "desireth not the death of a sinner," but that he "turn from his wickedness and live." An enormous fish appeared, who swallowed Jonah and sheltered him for three days in its belly. There the Prophet began to pray to Jahweh. He sang all the psalms that he knew. God was mollified, and the fish "vomited out Jonah on dry land." Now, full of courage, he proceeded to Nineveh, and in its streets prophesied approaching destruction. He imagined that divine anger would forthwith smite the city, but God recalled him to a more just understanding of His designs. In bloody Nineveh were there no innocent children and animals who had done no wrong? In this curious story, written down at a much later date but no doubt a traditional story of Israel, is there not a message of hope? The God who rescued Jonah from certain death, who even had pity on the Assyrians, would He not in the end extend His compassionate hand over His people? Israel, in her adversity, clung to that hope.

THE END OF SAMARIA

In the year 745 an adventurous king came to the throne of Assyria, Tiglath-Pileser III. Having made himself master of Babylon, where he had himself crowned by the name of Pul used in the Bible, he began to take a new interest in the Mediterranean countries. There was never any lack of opportunity for intervening in Syria and Palestine; the growth of the power of Nineveh involved the small neighbouring states in a political crisis singularly favourable to the designs of a conquerer. In Samaria and also in Jerusalem there were two parties; the pro-Assyrians admired the power of the Mesopotamian kings, and saw no alternative to a policy of total submission to their will; but they were opposed by an anti-Assyrian party who were in favour of an alliance with the Pharaohs against Nineveh; but this party had not sufficiently taken into account the weakness of an Egypt that was divided into three rival and decadent kingdoms. The choice was between the Nile and the Euphrates, just as at the time of the League, France had to choose between England and Spain.

After three revolutions and three royal assassinations within a year, Menahem, who was finally reigning over Samaria, opted for submission to Assyria, and Tiglath-Pileser III numbered him among his tributaries. His son followed suit; but the tribute claimed by Nineveh was heavy; a soldier, Pekah, led the discontented party and overthrew, together with the king, the Seventh Dynasty of Samaria. Reversing the policy, he gathered forces for a rising against Assyria. The king of Judah, invited to join in a revolution, refused: Pekah thereupon decided to settle accounts with him. Besieged in Jerusalem in despair, the king sacrificed to the Phoenician Baal Moloch, but in vain, his little eldest son; he was attacked at the same time by Edom, which rose in revolt and captured the ports of the Elanitic Gulf, and by the Philistines, stirred from their sleep. In desperation, Ahaz, the heir of David, committed the unpardonable act which was to bring down destruction upon Canaan: he asked help from the Assyrians.

This help came without delay. Tiglath-Pileser descended on the frail coalition, broke it up, sacked Damascus, and swept Palestine. The Assyrians cost Ahaz of Jerusalem dear, for he had to pay tribute. They "distressed him, but strengthened him not" (2 Chron. xxviii:20). But they cost his enemy still dearer. The northern kingdom lost the whole of Galilee and Transjordania, and found itself reduced to the mountainous country of Samaria. In its very capital, Nineveh placed a man with Assyrian sympathies, a certain Hoshea, whom his subjects naturally regarded as a traitor. But on the death of Tiglath-Pileser III, this Hoshea, yielding to pressure, reversed his policy overnight, and an alliance was patched up with Tyre and Egypt against Assyria.

Once more the savage warriors in coats of mail reappeared. Shalmaneser blockaded Tyre on its islet, and then turned against Samaria. Egypt did not send so much as a single chariot. Hoshea tried to come to terms, but was captured and put in chains. The anti-Assyrians shut themselves in the city, which resisted heroically for three years. In the course of the struggle, Shalmaneser died and was succeeded by one of his generals, Sargon II, the great Sargon who built the palace of Khorsabad. Its strength exhausted, Samaria capitulated.

In his annals, Sargon recounts the following: "In the first year of my reign, I conquered Samaria. I deported twenty-seven thousand people, I took their chariots for my army, I laid tribute upon them. The people of the country, prey in my hands, I made to live elsewhere, and I set my major-domos to govern them, and they paid taxes as people under my rule." The kings of Assyria, did, in fact, practise this policy of deportation on a large scale, and it may be said that the terrible churning up and levelling down perpetrated by them made the establishment of later Babylonian, Greek and Roman Empires in the Fertile Crescent a simple matter. Of the deported people of Samaria, some were settled near Harran (cruel irony, in the land of Abraham), others on the middle Euphrates and at the foot of the Zagros range.[4] In their place, a mixture of peoples from all corners of the Empire were brought into Samaria; a score of different idolatries were thus blended with the cult of Jahweh in Galilee and Samaria. From these people sprang those "Samaritans" that the Jews in the time of Jesus hated so bitterly.

The little kingdom of Judah had witnessed with horror the destruction of Israel. Saved for the time being from catastrophe, Judah was from now on to assume a role whose importance was out of all proportion to the small size of its territory. In Judah, henceforth, and in Judah alone, the torch of faith was still to burn. It was towards Judah that the populations oppressed by the Assyrians were to turn. Its name was, henceforth, to stand, by a sort of abridgement of history, for the whole of the chosen people, the people of Judah, the Jews. And there, in clear realization of the supernatural significance of the tragedy of Israel, a remarkable effort was to be made to place that faith on an un-

[4] *See* MAP OF THE FERTILE CRESCENT, p. 7.

shakeable foundation: this was to be the work of Hezekiah and of Isaiah.

ISAIAH AND HIS TIMES

In the year of Uzziah's death, prosperity reigned in Judah. A man of Jerusalem named Isaiah was meditating in the Temple (Isaiah VI). In a vision God appeared to him. Seraphim, six-winged angels, those burning ones whose task it is to consume away sin, stood before him crying one to another, "Holy, holy, holy is the Lord of hosts: the whole earth is full of his glory!" Trembling before the face of the Most High, Isaiah uttered a prayer, "Woe is me! for I am undone; because I am a man of unclean lips, and I dwell in the midst of a people of unclean lips." But one of the seraphim, flying towards him, carried a burning coal that he had taken from the altar with the tongs, laid it on his lips, and said to him, "Thine iniquity is taken away, and thy sin purged." And the voice of the Lord said, "Whom shall I send?" "Here am I, send me," Isaiah replied, without hesitation. "And he said, Go and tell this people, Hear ye indeed, but understand not; and see ye indeed, but perceive not. Make the heart of this people fat, and make their ears heavy, and shut their eyes; lest they see with their eyes, and hear with their ears, and understand with their heart, and convert, and be healed!" "Lord, how long?" asked the Prophet. "And he answered, Until the cities be wasted without inhabitant, and the houses without man, and the land be utterly desolate, . . . But yet . . . as a teil tree, and as an oak, whose substance is in them, when they cast their leaves: so the holy seed shall be the substance thereof." Thus began the vocation of the Prophet who, during those years of reversal in their history, embodied the conscience of the chosen people, and worked more than any other man for their future.

The personality of Isaiah is indeed magnificent. He undoubtedly belonged to the ruling classes, and was clearly familiar with political problems, a man of action with remarkable insight. But he was at the same time a man inspired, a mystic, the living proof that it is possible at the same time to be filled with the Spirit

and extremely effective on the material plane—as were also
Joan of Arc or Saint Teresa of Avila. He was an ecstatic, a
visionary; on occasion he performed eccentric actions in order
to impress the popular imagination; he had the gift of healing,
and cured the king (with figs—an odd remedy of which, however,
mention is made on the Syrian tablets of Ras-Shamra, and which
the Arabs use to this day); as a seer, he foretold the future with
astounding exactness; as a divine magician, he dared to ask for
a sign. His style is of such magnificence that even in translation
it moves us as only the words of an unparalleled master of language can do. It achieves a classical perfection in the Hebrew
language. "Thought and language," says Renan, "in him reach
a point beyond which one feels that either language would break
down or thought be impaired."

The books that bear his name form a group that, beginning
with his own times, anticipate the future in wild visions, announce the destruction of Jerusalem, the exile and the return.
Their authenticity has been much discussed. Non-Catholic critics
ascribe to him only the first part, which is concerned with his
own times, and attribute the later sections to another prophet,
"the second Isaiah," living at the end of the Exile. Some critics
even subdivide the books into the work of several "third Isaiahs."
But the Biblical Commission of the Catholic Church still maintains the attribution of the whole to the great Prophet.

Amos has stressed the divine justice that punishes rich egoists;
Hosea, divine love that is injured by betrayal. Isaiah dwells upon
the divine power. "The Lord shall be exalted in Judgment." He
is the Holy, the glorious, the transcendent. If the people deny
Him, His anger breaks forth. Man's virtue lies in faith, in obedience. "If ye will not believe, surely ye shall not be established"
(vii:9); "in quietness and in confidence shall be your strength"
(xxx:15). To accept, to place ourselves in His hands, to trust
in God, is the one admonition of the great Prophet; its echo is
still heard in the very heart of the Christian world.

What, then, can those who have rebelled hope for? "The ox
knoweth his owner, and the ass his master's crib: but Israel doth

not know, my people doth not consider. Ah, sinful nation, a people laden with iniquity, a seed of evildoers . . . Why should ye be stricken any more? Ye will revolt more and more! The whole head is sick, and the whole heart faint. From the sole of the foot even unto the head there is no soundness in it" (Isaiah 1). Punishment will descend upon the faithless nation. The vine that yields only sour fruit will be uprooted. Samaria will be stricken, and in its solitudes a man will devour the flesh of his own arm. Assyria, God's instrument of vengeance, shall in turn be destroyed by reason of its fierce pride. The other sinful nations too shall perish, Moab, Edom, Egypt, and Tyre, "whose merchants are princes, whose traffickers are the honourable of the earth" (XXIII). But let not Jerusalem exult in their downfall; even if it is not Assyria who shall punish her—for her sword shall be diverted from Zion—sin still cries out for vengeance. Another power will arise to execute justice.

Can nothing avert this fatality? Yes, "Cease to do evil; learn to do well; seek judgment, relieve the oppressed, judge the father-less, plead for the widow . . . though your sins be as scarlet, they shall be as white as snow" (1). But Israel will neither hear nor understand. She will fall into the extremes of misery pre-ordained, and only then, repenting, will her soul find pardon. A servant of God will arise among the people; he will come out of the East, the one whom God has "called . . . to his foot" (XLI). The oppressor of the people will be destroyed by a power "from the north"; Babylon shall fall. God's alliance with His chosen nation will be re-established. Jahweh will call the captives from their captivity, and those who live in shadow shall return to the light of day (XLIX), and the voice of the Prophets shall cry, "Awake, awake, stand up, O Jerusalem. . . . Shake thyself from the dust . . . loose thyself from the bands of thy neck . . . thou has drunken the dregs of the cup of trembling" (LI–LII).

These words shook Israel like the voice of thunder. And at the same time, in the lands of the south, another Prophet, Micah, de-claimed like threats, denouncing the powerful who think only of plunder, who devour the flesh of the people and grind their bones, so that the sins of Judah cry for vengeance. "Therefore shall Zion for your sake be plowed as a field, and Jerusalem shall become heaps, and the mountains of the house as the high places of the forest" (Micah III:12).

There can be no doubt that it was under the influence of these prophetic movements that King Hezekiah, grandson of Uzziah and son of that Ahaz who sacrificed his first-born to Baal, did "that which was good in the eyes of Jahweh." He was undoubtedly intelligent, devout and active. Issuing an appeal to Hebrew patriotism, he gathered about him many elements surviving from the debris of the northern kingdom; often, from this time, he is in fact called "the King of Israel." He instituted a commission to which was entrusted the task of establishing the traditions that in the overthrow of Samaria were threatened with extinction. (There is a reference to this in the Book of Proverbs, xxv.) Above all, he attacked the idolatry that continued to pollute the cult of Jahweh. The Assyrian altar that Ahaz had constructed in the Temple was removed. He instituted a campaign against sacred stones and *massebahs* that recalled the ancient paganism. High-places were destroyed and their dubious cult suppressed. Even the bronze serpent, memorial of Moses, that had become an object of worship, was smashed to pieces.

Hezekiah, then, appeared as a champion of the most authentic cult of Jahweh; he was, besides, an energetic ruler who, fore-seeing that Assyria would one day threaten Judah with the same destruction as had overtaken Samaria, took steps to prepare for the possible eventuality. He prepared a store of weapons and piled up arms. The walls of the citadel were repaired, and a new tunnel was dug to assure a better water-supply in case of siege; this is the underground piscina of Siloam that still exists and on which a curious inscription has been discovered, the work of the engineers who bored it.

Circumstances seemed to be very favourable. Assyria was occupied by an Aramaean prince, Merodach-Baladan, who, from near the Persian Gulf, was threatening Babylon. This newcomer had made friendly overtures to Hezekiah and sent an ambassador to him. Negotiations with Egypt, where the power had recently fallen into the hands of an Ethiopian Dynasty, the Twenty-fifth, were also in progress. Isaiah, alone, or almost so, preached disaster. He had no faith in these alliances, nor in any other diplomacy; Israel's only strength lay in her faith in God. He was all too right. Sennacherib, the new king of Assyria, drove out Merodach-Baladan, pressed on to the west, and overthrew the little Mediterranean states one after the other, Sidon, Ascalon, Lachish (he has fully described and illustrated his victories in his bas-reliefs), and finally he attacked Jerusalem. Hezekiah, intimidated, sent tribute to the conqueror; but Sennacherib demanded complete surrender; Jerusalem prepared to make a final stand.

There happened at this time, in the year 701, a singular event in which Israel saw the hand of God. "Taken like a bird in a cage," as the Assyrian phrase goes, Hezekiah had a very slender chance of escaping his destiny. Now Tirhaka, the Ethiopian Pharaoh, a brave man whose powerful features reflected a calm courage, advanced from the south. Isaiah, who had said all along that the catastrophe would be averted for this time, proved to be right. The Assyrian "shall not come into this city, nor shoot an arrow there. . . . By the way that he came, by the same shall he return" (2 Kings xix:32). One night "the angel of the Lord went out, and smote in the camp of the Assyrians an hundred fourscore and five thousand: and when they arose in the morning, behold, they were all dead corpses" (2 Kings xix:35–36). Herodotus, writing two centuries later, tells this story in such way as to confirm the biblical text. He speaks of an invasion of rats that attacked Sennacherib when he reached the Delta. The sudden disaster with which the Angel of God smote the Assyrians was the plague, the scourge of God.

But Isaiah, in the midst of the rejoicings occasioned by that unlooked-for victory, wore a face of mourning. Lamenting the sorrows of Israel that he foresaw in the near future, he proclaimed to his compatriots that they were no better than dead men already. "Eat and drink, for tomorrow we die!" he mocked.

Hezekiah, a devout man, believed his words, for he feared God; but, after his death, Manasseh reversed his policy. A Jewish tradition relates that this impious king martyred the greatest Prophet of Israel, by having him hewn into two pieces. Isaiah left behind him not only the burning record of his words, but a group of faithful disciples, of converts, who, when the divine vengeance was accomplished, were to be the promised healers. Thus did this man of genius, who distinguishing for the first time the individual from his group, foreshadowing individual salvation, sow the seed of the future greatness of the chosen people; for a national religion, he substituted what was to be a community of the faithful, later to become the Church.

THE APOGEE OF NINEVEH

The pious king was succeeded by an impious king. Manasseh reversed his father's policy; immediately after the miracle of 701, the infidelity of Judah reached an extreme. For this there were perhaps several reasons. In the first place, the young king ascended to the throne at the age of twelve, and it is possible that his accession coincided with a seizing of power by a party hostile to the Levites and to the supporters of Hezekiah. Besides, time was already effacing the memory of Jahweh's extraordinary mercy. The miracle, however, was incomplete, for Assyria had not been destroyed and was, on the contrary, more powerful than ever.

The long reign of Manasseh (689–641) coincided in fact with the apogee of Assyria, of which the little kingdom of Judah was a vassal state. The affair of 701 had not involved the loss of Palestine, of which the kings of Nineveh remained suzerains. Until his death Sennacherib continued to exert his control over Jerusalem; having nothing to fear from this quarter, he turned his attention to Babylon, constantly in revolt, and in about 689 he demolished it. After his murder, the result of a palace intrigue plotted by his sons, which the Bible exultantly records, his successor, Esarhaddon, whose mother was a Babylonian, rebuilt the city. On the northern frontiers, fifty years later, hordes of Cim-

merians and Scythians began to pour into the Fertile Crescent;
Esarhaddon held them, for the time being, in check; in the west,
the little kings, among them Manasseh, were giving no trouble,
that is to say, were paying tribute. But in Egypt the Ethiopian
Pharaohs were once more gaining prestige for the crown. The
powerful Assyrians advanced against them, and ascended the
Nile as far as Memphis; this was only a temporary victory, for
Tirhaka, taking refuge in his mountains, bided his time in order
to take his revenge.

It was now that the greatest of the kings of Assyria, one of the
most famous conquerors of all history, made his appearance,
Assur-bani-pal (668–626). On the death of their father, his elder
brother had inherited the throne of Babylon, leaving him Nineveh.
A tireless soldier, great organizer, relentless conqueror whom one
would admire were it not for the train of bloodshed and terror
that he left behind him, Assur-bani-pal fought continually in
every corner of his empire. He resumed the Egyptian campaign,
took Thebes, the ancient capital, which never completely recovered from the cruelties that he inflicted upon it. His elder brother
having raised against him a vast league of Elamites, Egyptians,
Syrians and Aramaeans (in which Manasseh was imprudent
enough to participate), Assur-bani-pal advanced on Babylon,
and, knowing what lay in store for him, the conquered king
burned himself and all his household in his palace. All the allies
were defeated in turn; Manasseh was fortunate enough to escape
with a few months of captivity, with chains on his hands and
rings in his lips. Towards the south-east, the kings of Elam, in
spite of that legendary valour that we can still see on the faces of
statues of the period, had to submit, and Suza, their capital, was
shamefully pillaged. Assur-bani-pal was master of the Fertile
Crescent and the surrounding countries.

He was resolved to add to the glory of his conquests those of
civilization. For the Assyrian nation, whose very name suggests
bloodshed, has left an art that is often magnificent, and of which
innumerable examples have been excavated. The dynasty of the
Sargonides, and the reign of Assur-bani-pal in particular, was a

time of prolific flowering. Khorsabad, their palace city, is a masterpiece in the colossal style, with its terrace of twenty acres, its innumerable courts, its walls three yards thick, its six thousand square yards of bas-reliefs. Its enamelled bricks, on which the blue powder of lapis-lazuli shines with incomparable brilliance, are ornamented with countless stylized flowers and animals. Over the gates of the palace, genies, winged bulls, and crouching lions kept ferocious guard. Their animals are truly remarkable; whether the artist be representing the head of a horse, hunting mastiffs, the famous wounded lioness, or the lion with his jaws dripping blood seen in the British Museum, the Assyrian sculptors always achieve a realism and simplicity of expression that our own Rude and Barye have never surpassed.

We can well understand how such prestige dazzled the petty kings of Canaan. According to the ideas of antiquity, the success of any nation reflected the power of its gods. To all the other reasons that impelled the Israelites, continually torn between the true God and idolatry, towards polytheism, was added the desire to placate a victor by propitiating his gods. Thus Ahaz, fifty years earlier, impressed by the sight of an Assyrian altar, had hastened to construct one in the Temple of Zion. Things were much worse in Manasseh's reign. Not only did Baal and Astarte reappear, but the astral cults of Mesopotamia also received a new impetus. Shamash, the sun, Ashur, the king of the gods, the idol of the arrow and the winged disk, and Ishtar, the great Assyrian goddess, were worshipped; the votaries of "the queen of the skies" multiplied. Even in the Temple of Solomon, altars were dedicated to these false gods; the sanctuaries gave official shelter to the same sacred prostitution that flourished in Babylon. The people of Jahweh had fallen low indeed! The Phoenician practice of throwing young infants into the fire in honour of Baal-Moloch had taken on a terrible importance. Manasseh himself offered one of his sons and the place set aside for "the burning of their sons and their daughters "in the fire" was named "the valley of slaughter." Never before in its history had Israel sunk to such depths of ignominy.

THE REFORM OF JOSIAH, THE FALL OF ASSYRIA

Some resistance, however, did exist. One divines rather than clearly sees a prophetic opposition in the reign of Manasseh. When after two years of impious reign the son of the infidel king was assassinated, his grandson Josiah succeeded him (639–609). Josiah was a boy of eight. Jahweh's party came into power, no doubt by a popular revolution. During the thirty years of his reign Josiah "did that which was right in the sight of the Lord, and walked in the ways of David his father, and declined neither to the right hand, nor to the left" (2 Chronicles xxxiv).

The new reign, then, saw a return to the observances of the cult of Jahweh, and at the same time, since idolatry was to a large extent a product of vassaldom to Nineveh, a national revival of faith. The Temple of Solomon was purged of the idolatry that defiled it. A campaign of destruction was waged against the old Canaanite fetishes, sacred groves, menhirs and high-places. Even the provincial cults of Jahweh were suppressed in favour of the single Temple of Jerusalem, and the priests of these little altars came to swell the numbers of those serving the only holy place that was to remain in Canaan. Josiah even had the courage to go among the northern tribes that were, in principle, under Assyrian domination, to pursue his task of the destruction of idols.

During the overhauling of the Temple, a surprising discovery was made. According to the account given in the Book of Kings, the High Priest Hilkiah found the Book of the Law that had been lost. He gave it to Josiah to read, and he, pious soul, was shocked to discover that his father had not obeyed the words of this book. Following this, he carried out a fundamental religious reform. According to tradition, the scroll discovered in some hidden corner of the Temple was Deuteronomy. Does the Bible wish to indicate in symbolic terms that in the time of Josiah it was decided that the Mosaic principles should be strictly applied? Or does it refer to one of the copies made by Hezekiah that had been overlooked during the troubled times of Manasseh? Undoubtedly a legislative reform was imposed. Isaiah had denounced "unrighteous decrees . . . to take away the right from the poor of my people" (Isaiah x); at almost the same time, the plebeians of Rome were to repair to the Sacred Hill to obtain a formulation of the laws in order to rescue justice from the arbitrary control of those in power, and the reforms of Solon in Athens also turned on the writing down of the laws of the community.

The purpose of the reform, at all events, is clear. Relying on the principles that their inspired ancestor Moses had laid down, but which a people not far removed from primitive violence did not always put into practise, Hezekiah and the priests who surrounded him spiritualized the old conceptions, the ancient rites; they extracted from them their human content. They tried to make man's social life less hard; the obligation to leave in the field the ears for the gleaners was revived, with its delicate charity; the rest on the seventh day, commemoration of the Mosaic observance, was related to the worker's need for rest. A great part of the teaching of the Prophets thus became law. It is about this kernel of texts henceforth known to all, that traditional elements were gathered; the whole was to become the Bible.

Josiah's reform is therefore of considerable importance. It was to make it possible for the chosen people to pass through the worst hours of their history without the loss of any of their essential traditions. Were there not dangers attendant upon this opposing of the rigid letter to the spirit ever renewed? "Ye shall not add unto the word which I command you, neither shall ye diminish ought from it" (Deut. iv:2)—did not this prepare the way for the conflict which was to arise later, in which the people of the Book were to be deaf to all living teaching, and to the Gospel?

This return to strict orthodoxy had also a political significance; we may even go so far as to admit that it was made possible by political conditions in the first place. Assyria was marching towards decline as rapidly as she had attained the height of her power. Many dangers threatened her.

In the incoherent aggregate of her vast empire, many elements
were merely biding their time in order to revolt; Babylon in
particular, who remembered her ancient splendour, and where
a powerful core of non-Assyrian resistance existed, was ready, at
any moment, to become the base for new attacks. In the remote
protectorate of Egypt, national forces had revived and regrouped
themselves. The brief incursion of Assur-bani-pal had merely
served to rid the country of the Nile of its provisional masters of
the Twenty-fifth Dynasty; the Ethiopians had withdrawn to their
mountains and henceforth were to look towards the south; one
still finds the descendants of these exotic Pharaohs in the Ruanda,
a district near the Belgian Congo, where the cult of the cow still
survives as in the days of Isis-Hathor. The princes of Saïs had
succeeded them; although described as viceroys by their distant
overlords, they had made themselves independent. This Twenty-
sixth Dynasty deserves to be well remembered. These Psammeti-
chuses and Nechos were to revive, for the last time, the ancient
grandeur of the Pharaohs. Although they were not particularly
powerful, they ventured to undertake great things in their politics.
One of them, Necho II, sent Phoenician ships at his own expense
to explore the coasts of Africa. Their art, the flower of decadence,
full of subtle combinations, at once realistic and poetic, prepares
the way for that efflorescence that was to cover the precious
masterpieces of the Isle of Philae. Egypt was ready to play her
new role in the Fertile Crescent.

But there were graver dangers for Assyria. Once more great
waves of Aryan invasion were in motion. This was the time when,
at the other end of the Mediterranean world, France was occupied by those tribes which were to become the Gauls. On the
plateaux of Iran and Elam, two Aryan peoples, the Persians and
the Medes, had been settled for the past three hundred years.
They had recently been awakened to full self-consciousness by
the religious reform of Zoroaster. For the moment the Medes
were dominant, and their city of Ecbatana was rising to the status
of a capital. And what was worse, these were only the advance
guard of inexhaustible bands of barbarians: Cimmerians, Treres,

Bithynians, and above all the terrible *Achkanaz* of the Bible, the Scythians. Assur-bani-pal, as Rome did later, at first made use of the barbarians in his service; attacked by Phraortes, king of the Medes, the first time he defeated him unaided; the second time, threatened by Cyaxares, son of Phraortes, he sought aid from those terrible horsemen, ancestors of the Kurds. This was merely to open the route for them.

The innumerable hordes of whom Herodotus already spoke with fear poured from the Caucasus and swept over Media, Assyria and the Fertile Crescent. In Palestine they placed garrisons, like that of Beisan, afterwards called Scythopolis. They reached the Delta, where Psammetichus took them seriously, then they retired as suddenly as they had come, just at the time when the great Assur-bani-pal died, in 625.

These events had demonstrated the weakness of the Assyrian domination. The ruin of Nineveh, foretold by the Prophets of Israel, was to become a fact with astonishing rapidity. Assur-bani-pal's successors were undistinguished. One of their generals, Nabopolassar, set up in Babylon an insubordinate feudal regime. When he was sent against Cyaxares and his armies, who once again were advancing from Zagros, he came to terms with the enemy, and together they marched against Nineveh. After shattering assaults, the great capital fell. It was wiped out so completely that for twenty-five centuries no one knew even where it had stood. The last king of Assyria took his own life by leaping into the flames (612). Thus disappeared a terrible people, the scourge of God. "When thou shalt cease to spoil, thou shalt be spoiled; and when thou shalt make an end to deal treacherously, they shall deal treacherously with thee," Isaiah had proclaimed (Isaiah xxxiii).

The fall of Nineveh was, in the most exact sense of the word, providential for Jerusalem. A sudden access of joy kindled the heart of Josiah. This descendant of David was to prove himself worthy of his ancestor in his courage if not in his ability. He drew himself up in his tiny province as proudly as Solomon in his glory. What would happen? Did the end of the Assyrian mean security?

Two tendencies now showed themselves in Judah. They are clearly to be found in the prophets whose voices were heard at this time. One is that of an exalted nationalism that believed that the good days had returned. Nahum represents this opinion. Jahweh in destroying Nineveh has shown His people that He has pardoned them. "The Lord is good, . . . and he knoweth them that trust in him" (Nahum 1:7). Reconverted, pardoned, Israel was able to take courage again. But the other tendency, that of Jeremiah and Zephaniah, was pessimistic. Jahweh had destroyed Assyria; did that mean that there were no other enemies to be feared? And had Judah indeed expiated her sins? The text of the law is all very well, but it is nothing unless the heart of man is reformed. Treacherous Judah "hath not turned unto me with her whole heart, but feignedly" (Jeremiah III:10). Another calamity would come from the north, a destroyer of nations like a lion; she would be punished, "Zion, the comely and delicate" (VI). The day of Jahweh was at hand, "a day of wrath, a day of trouble and distress, a day of wasteness and desolation, a day of darkness and of gloominess, a day of clouds and thick darkness, a day of the trumpet and alarm against the fenced cities, and against the high towers. And I will bring distress upon men . . . and their blood shall be poured out as dust, and their flesh as the dung" (Zephaniah 1).

Puffed up in his foolish optimism, Josiah waited for God to reward him. But it was not in temporal success that his work was to bear its fruit. An Assyrian remnant had taken refuge in the region of Harran. Necho II, with an exact sense of political balance, decided to aid them and prevent Babylon from wiping them out altogether. He advanced northwards across Canaan. "You cannot pass," said the kinglet of Jerusalem. The Pharaoh gently insisted. Josiah refused categorically. At Megiddo a battle was engaged: the Hebrew king could do no more than get himself killed with honour. Soon afterwards, at Karkemish, the Babylonians drove back Necho, who returned to Egypt. The sacrifice of the last nationalist leader of Israel had been in vain. The name of the royal prince who commanded the Babylonian army was Nebuchadnezzar.

BABYLON AND JEREMIAH

The new master of the world was no less formidable than the old. Babylon had once more become the political centre of the Fertile Crescent. But if that neo-Babylonian dynasty, the last of the Mesopotamian race that history was to know, blazed with the extreme brilliance often possessed by civilizations about to fall forever, nothing was changed in the satellite states that gravitated in the orbit of that sun. Nebuchadnezzar II (604–562) was no less heavy a burden to them than Assur-bani-pal. His methods of war were no less cruel than those of his predecessor. Danger still threatened Judah.

The collapse of the nationalist dreams of the ill-fated Josiah brought about a grave crisis in the little kingdom. His sons disputed the throne, and one of them, Jehoiakim, possessed himself of it with the help of Egypt. Four years later, Nebuchadnezzar arrived in Canaan and entered Jerusalem. Between these two powers the wretched fragments of Israel were tossed like a wreckage. Political unrest was succeeded by religious troubles. What could be more natural? They had just seen the most pious of the kings lead the nation to disaster: what had Jahweh done, where was his power? Ah, the people said, in the days of Manasseh and the idols we were happy! And now, with a return to the faith, comes famine and the sword. And they turned to the foreign gods again. In the streets of Jerusalem one might have seen men, women, and children offering cakes to the "Queen of the Skies," Mesopotamian Ishtar. "Solar columns" appeared at the crossroads. According to the account given by the Prophet Ezekiel, in the very precincts of the Temple the votaries of the Phoenician god of vegetation, Thammuz, the Adonis of the Greeks, made their ritual lamentations in commemoration of his death and called for his resurrection, while inside the Temple itself other sects offered incense to animal idols after the manner of Egypt. And if one had met men carrying branches in their hands, one would have known that these were the proselytes of the rising sun.

This constant spectacle of a people returning to its vomit is wearisome. But the drama of Israel over the course of centuries is the drama of the soul: illuminated by grace, clearly perceiving the law by which it must live, but troubled in turn by the excitement of power or by despair, it approaches the narrow door by a way that we know all too well. Overcome once, sin must always be resisted anew; in the spiritual war triumph is never more than provisional, and the most ecstatic happiness is the worst of dangers even in the souls of the greatest saints.

The man to whom fell the superhuman task of warning Israel in these last days was Jeremiah. The son of a priest, he had less of the political leader about him than had Amos or Isaiah, but his denunciations and lamentations have a majesty all their own, at once human and religious. He was a kindly man with a tender heart, a mind profound in every way. He had no wish to assume the terrible mission that God forced upon him. In order to obey the Most High, he sacrificed everything; he did not marry, he had no family. Never did he appear at public rejoicings; he might have been thought as "insensitive as a wall." Yet all the while a drama was playing itself out in him, whose record in all its overwhelming sincerity he has left to us. He who loved his country above all, was accused of being a traitor. He who would gladly have loved and been loved, was covered with contempt! But such was the will of Jahweh; it must be obeyed! His task it was to speak, and speak he did.

As a writer, to be sure, he is not Isaiah's equal; his metaphors are flatter, his inspiration less sublime, but when he voices the sorrows of his people, those sorrows that he felt in advance in his very flesh—"My bowels! my bowels! I am pained at my very heart; my heart maketh a noise in me; I cannot hold my peace, because thou hast heard, O my soul, the sound of the trumpet, the alarm of war. Destruction upon destruction is cried; for the whole land is spoiled; suddenly are my tents spoiled, and my curtains in a moment. How long shall I see the standard, and hear the sound of the trumpet?" (IV:19–21). The God of Isaiah was the master of that power that no man can offend with impunity; the religion of Jeremiah is more subjective, better adapted to our common distress; his God is the God that men discover in their sorrow, and who is never more near than when we touch the depths of misfortune.

The eminent service that Jeremiah rendered to Israel was not well received; that would scarcely have been possible; God's will must be accomplished and expiation must follow. And he knew, besides, that the Ethiopian cannot "change his skin, nor the leopard his spots. Then may ye also do good, that are accustomed to do evil?" (xiii:23). But by speaking as he did, he made it possible for his people, in their low of disaster, to recognize the just hand of God, and in repentance to find healing.

With what did he reproach Jerusalem? Simply those things with which all the other Prophets had reproached her—infidelity; "they have set their abominations in the house which is called by my name, to pollute it" (vii:30); of having worshipped these idols of wood, "silver spread into plates . . . brought from Tarshish, and gold from Uphaz"; of wearing "blue and purple . . . clothing" (x:9); of immorality—of being a nation of adulterers (xxiii:10); of persisting in social injustices, of cynical violation of the Mosaic laws, those, for example, that forbid that any Israelite should be kept as a slave for his whole life. In these many faults the chosen people must be made to see the cause of their misfortunes.

Moreover, in the midst of the political complications in which Judah was struggling, Jeremiah's attitude was one of extreme simplicity. The strongest power was that of Nebuchadnezzar, therefore it was he in whom the will of God was manifest; from which it followed that the wisest course was submission. Humanly speaking, he was a defeatist; spiritually, he preserved the future. A certain Hananiah having foretold the imminent ruin of Babylon and the deliverance of Israel, Jeremiah fought against him fiercely and treated him as a false prophet. He sarcastically reminded the pro-Egyptian party, strong in numbers, of Necho's collapse after Karkemish: "Egypt is like a very fair heifer, but destruction cometh; it cometh out of the north" (xliv). The spectacle of this honest man who could only, and without intermission, announce defeat, because he could see beyond the immediate situation, is truly terrifying. Babylon is to be the sword of divine vengeance. Samaria has been given her "bill of divorce." Jahweh will even repudiate hypocritical Judah. "I will make Jerusalem heaps, and a den of dragons; and I will make the cities of Judah desolate, without an inhabitant" (IX:11). Not, to be sure, because He favours Babylon, who will in her turn see her pride chastised, and to whom God says, "Thou art my battle ax and weapons of war: for with thee will I break in pieces the nations," but, "I will render unto Babylon and to all the inhabitants of Chaldea all their evil that they have done in Zion" (LI)—not for the glory of any nation on earth, but only in the name of the Most High. Only when the punishment shall have been meted out and Israel have understood its full extent will mercy be shown again; and, as a symbol of his hope, there, in the country for which he foretold so many disasters, in the very midst of Judah, Jeremiah bought a field!

It goes without saying that such an attitude could not fail to bring down furious anger on the head of the man of God. He had written down his oracles and sent his secretary Baruch to read them to Jehoiakim, the king, who, mad with rage, tore up the manuscript and threw the pieces into a brazier where they burned. At the same time another prophet called Uriah was martyred for having said similar things. Jeremiah himself was thrown into an empty cistern; but they did not dare to leave him there to die, for he was after all a famous man in Israel. Nevertheless, he had to go into exile for a time.

History goes to show that the inspired man was right in his political prognostications. Once Nebuchadnezzar was out of the way, Jehoiakim and his party made advances to Egypt. Once more an alliance against Mesopotamia was established. Jeremiah had warned Jehoiakim of his own fate. He would be killed and not even receive honourable burial; he would be buried like an ass. Nebuchadnezzar knew, needless to say, of these intrigues against him. First he sent an advance column that ravaged the country. Then, in 597, he came in person. Jehoiakim met his death exactly as the prophet had foretold; his son Jehoiachin surrendered. He was sent into exile in Babylon, with his mother, his court, and all the eminent men of Israel, officers, and artisans; this was the first deportation of Judah. Nebuchadnezzar, thinking that the lesson was sufficient, placed a man of his own choosing on the throne—Zedekiah, a son of Josiah—and returned to the Euphrates.

THE FALL OF JERUSALEM

"Quos vult perdere . . ." The spirit of nationalism became more violent than ever in Judah. There were rumours of a revolt of Elam against Babylon; voluble optimists abounded; they waited for a miracle. The tiny states of Syria and Palestine formed an alliance of mice against the terrible wild-cat of Babylon. Necho, who had learned his lesson at Karkemish, had refused to support a league of this kind; his successor, Psammetichus II, after hesitating for a while, followed the same policy; but a new Pharaoh, Hophra, in 588 allowed himself to be won over by this contagious folly, and sent troops to Tyre in order to make the Phoenician city a base of operations against Nebuchadnezzar. In Jerusalem, the last descendant of David played his part of mountebank with all the gravity of a clown; this wretched Zedekiah was a man of small intelligence and indifferent character, whose fate would be comic if we did not know in what tragedy his slender hopes were to founder.

Nebuchadnezzar was not a man to be flouted. His reply was immediate. In the very year in which the coalition was founded, he arrived on the Orontes (588). Some divisions were sent to blockade Tyre, which, in its island, resisted for thirteen years before it fell; then he advanced on Judah to smash the league by destroying its central bastion. Jerusalem was surrounded, and the siege began.

The resistance offered by little Judah was worthy of its great history. Perched on its hill, the citadel of David was not easy of access. Although swelled by thousands of men who had taken refuge there from the surrounding country, the garrison lacked neither arms nor food supply. Nobody, to be sure, could have imagined that it would be possible to defeat the Chaldean army, but by holding out for a time they might give Pharaoh time to come to the rescue, or, who knows? God might repeat the miracle of 701! Persecuted and threatened, Jeremiah alone continued to preach his superhuman defeatism. For a moment, hope revived: an Egyptian army was reported to be in the plains of Idumea, and Nebuchadnezzar left his positions and advanced to meet it. It was at this time, perhaps, that Habakkuk, in a fine hymn, praised God, the vanquisher: "God came from Teman (Idumea) and the Holy One from Mount Paran, scattering death before Him."

Vain hope! Jeremiah alone was not deceived. "Behold, Pharaoh's army, which is come forth to help you, shall return to Egypt into their own land. And the Chaldeans shall come again, and fight against this city, and take it, and burn it with fire" (xxxvii:7–8). Defeated or bought off, the Egyptians did in fact retire; the siege of Jerusalem was resumed, more severe than ever. Famine broke out, bringing with it epidemics: the *Lamentations* of Jeremiah give us a terrible picture of those days of horror. "Their skin cleaveth to their bones; it is withered, it is become like a stick; the tongue of the sucking child cleaveth to the roof of his mouth for thirst; the young children ask bread. . . . The hands of the pitiful women have sodden their own children; they were their meat." So terrible was the plague that men in the streets cried the warning cry, "Unclean! Depart, depart! Touch not!" At last the Chaldeans succeeded in making a breach, and the final assault began.

This was terrible indeed. It is easy to imagine the violence of these fierce hordes who had been held in check for eighteen months. Women and virgins were dishonoured, leaders hanged, and no mercy was shown to the old. The Temple and the palace were looted, and the city fired so that nothing remained of the holy city but smoking ruins. As for Zedekiah, who had fled with his family, he was overtaken and captured. Nebuchadnezzar sent for this rebel; and before his eyes, he had his three sons eviscerated, and afterwards, so that that terrible sight should be his last, he had his eyes put out. This was a custom of the Assyrian kings; Sargon had himself represented in stone putting out with his lance the eyes of a vanquished king. A mass deportation was ordered. The flower of the nation was sent to Mesopotamia. This was in 586, three centuries after the death of Solomon.

Jeremiah, who was at first flung in with a batch of captives, was released by special order from Nebuchadnezzar, who regarded him with respect. But soon afterwards, caught up with a party fleeing to Egypt, he was martyred by them, doubtless because he continued to speak distasteful truths and refused to become involved with those who were saying that the exile would not be of long duration. In Jerusalem, an honest man called Gedaliah, whom the Babylonians tolerated as governor of the conquered country, did, meanwhile, all that he could to lighten the sufferings of the people. A fanatic assassinated him. Various sporadic disturbances broke out, which a Chaldean official suppressed by means of a new deportation.

And so the people of the Promise travelled once more, as in the days of Abraham, along the routes of the Fertile Crescent, not in faith and hope but in misery and dereliction. Many Assyrian and Babylonian bas-reliefs give a clear picture of these mournful caravans. Some travelled, bound together in groups, under the guard of soldiers in conical helmets; while others, their hands tied behind their backs, or their lips pierced by a ring, were led like cattle. And others again in the pitiable cohort that is a feature of every exodus, having flung into hand-carts their few household treasures, their children, their old people, trailed endlessly on under the blazing heat of the sun.

It was not in power and glory that Israel was to see the divine promise fulfilled, but the terrible ordeal was rich in meaning. The people of Canaan in losing their land were to become that spiritual leaven that, mixed into the dough of the nations, was to raise them to such great heights, but at the same time to inject them with so much bitterness. The history of Israel was beginning a new chapter—that of the Jews. And in sorrow the stiff-necked race, obstinate in sin, was to return to its faith, as it poured forth its lamentations in the unforgettable Psalm to which we still turn for consolation in our griefs (cxxx—*De profundis*):

"Out of the depths have I cried unto thee, O Lord. Lord, hear my voice: let thine ears be attentive to the voice of my supplications.

"If thou, Lord, shouldest mark iniquities, O Lord, who shall stand? But there is forgiveness with thee, that thou mayest be feared. I wait for the Lord, my soul doth wait, and in his word do I hope. My soul waiteth for the Lord more than they that watch for the morning. . . . Let Israel hope in the Lord: for with the Lord there is mercy, and with him is plenteous redemption. And he shall redeem Israel from all his iniquities!"

PART FOUR

JUDAISM AND MESSIANISM

I

THE EXILE AND THE RETURN

BABYLON, "THE LADY OF KINGDOMS"

D URING THE FIRST HALF of the sixth century B.C. Babylon
was the capital of the East. The break-up of the Ninevite
Empire in 612 had been the signal for a rapid rise of all
the states that the Assyrian collossus had overshadowed. The
Mediterranean and the neighbouring parts of Asia prospered.

This was the time when, "under the fairest skies that men have
ever known" (Herodotus), the cities of Ionia, Ephesus, Miletus,
and Samos, growing rich by selling carpets, textiles and wine,
rose to a life of luxury and pleasure, and recited, instead of the
virile epics of Homer, the elegies of Alcaeus and Sappho. On
the neighbouring plateau, the descendants of the Sherden,[1] the
Lydians, under the rule of a vigorous dynasty, slowly but surely
extended their empire. The Hellenic cities were to become their
vassals. Their capital, Sardis, was a great trading centre, one of
whose districts was distinguished by the name of the "Good
Quarter"; and their king, Croesus, who covered the Greek shrine
of Delphi with gold, acquired in addition to political influence a
renown which has made his name famous to this day. Even in
Egypt, the revival noted under the Twenty-sixth Dynasty continued under Amasis, an able and subtle man, Hellenic in spirit
(569–526), whose reign was not without charm, to judge by the
records. These state that he governed each day only until noon,
for what bow can remain stretched all the time? Did he not, besides, dismiss certain judges who had in his youth acquitted him
upon his protesting his innocence, because, by so doing, they
had proved their stupidity? On the borders of the Iranian quadri-
lateral, in those lovely valleys where roses, orchards, and pasture

[1] The Sherden had constituted the guard of Rameses II. See p. 134.

for horses flourished, the Medes of Cyaxares (625–585) and Astyages (585–553) waxed strong; after the fall of Nineveh all the north of the Fertile Crescent had passed into their control; the river Halys had divided them from the Lydians, ever since, during a battle fought on its banks on May 28, 585, an eclipse of the sun (predicted, moreover, by Thales of Miletus) had struck terror into the adversaries; and in their obscure southern vassal, Cyrus of Persia, the Kings of Ecbatana did not yet perceive the man of destiny.[2] Ever far towards the west, great states were rising to dazzling heights: Carthage, heir to the glories of Phoenicia, extended its trade from Bizerta to Sardinia, from Tripoli to the Balearic Islands. Marseilles was rising, and had colonized Corsica. The mysterious Etruscan nation—the Tyrrhenes of that time—dominated Italy and the Tyrrhenean Sea that preserves their name; Syracuse, under the rule of its tyrants, was beginning to rival those maritime powers. But none of them knew anything of a little Italian township then under Etruscan control that was later to conquer them all.

Among these flourishing states one stood out above them all— Babylon, the "Lady of Kingdoms" (Isaiah xlvii:5). From the Persian Gulf to the hills of Harran, and across Syria as far as Egypt, extended her influence, with various shades of authority ranging from protectorate to domestication. Nebuchadnezzar enjoyed a prestige as great as that of Assur-bani-pal or Sargon. As notorious as they for blood-thirsty violence, he earned more admiration than they did, for this magnificent ruffian loved the arts.

We know of great Babylon not only because of the thorough excavations carried out, since 1899, by German archaeologists, but also from ancient records. Herodotus, Diodorus, Strabo, Quintus Certius have left a marvellous record of it; and yet they knew it only as we know Versailles as a city fallen from its status of capital, a mere shadow of its former splendour. What, then, must it have been in the days when Nebuchadnezzar at the height of his power was amassing its treasures?

[2] Map: The Empires, p. 314.

The city was built in a square, divided diagonally by the Euphrates. A surrounding wall, twenty-seven yards in width, with a cavalry fort every twenty yards, surrounded it like impenetrable armour; the fortifications of Constantinople that so much impressed our Crusaders and Villehardouin, or the Great Wall of China, must have resembled that gigantic military structure. It would have taken a man fifteen hours to walk all over it. Where the Sacred Way, reserved for processions and triumphs, entered the city, the "Gate of Ishtar" raised its massive portals, decorated with nearly six hundred fantastic animal figures. The river was spanned by a bridge of five arches. The seven piles are still visible, great brick structures encased in stone, whose angles cleave the current. In the colossal temples, the *Zikkurats,* towers built in stages, proudly carried once more the ancient names [3] of "house of the lofty brow" and "house that upholds heaven and earth." On terraces faced with sandstone, limestone and basalt, the palaces covered acres with their buildings and courtyards. And descending by terraces to the banks of the Euphrates were the "hanging gardens" with their avenues of rare trees acclimatized from distant countries, their flights of steps, and their cascades, while in the shelter of the arches that supported them cool rooms gave shelter from the summer heat.

It was to this world of dazzling splendour that the pitiful cohort of the remnant of Israel came. The contrast is moving; but of the powerful empire and the little conquered nation only one was to survive, and that not the one whose greatness was visible to the eye. There is little trace now of Babylon, pillaged by many conquerors; a few enamelled bricks, cylinders, and little objects. But with Israel it is far otherwise. When Nebuchadnezzar imprinted in the clay his finely carved seal of two fighting ibexes, rampant, to sign the order of deportation for an insignificant people in Canaan, how should he have known that if his name were to survive in human history it was only because he was the conqueror of Jerusalem, its providential executioner?

[3] *See* pp. 71-2

THE FRAGMENTS OF ISRAEL

Israel was divided into three fragments. We will not consider here the remnants of Samaria which either disintegrated in exile in the melting-pot of Mesopotamia or decayed on the spot under all the adulterating influences of the immigrations. We are concerned only with Judah.

One section of its inhabitants remained in Canaan, humble people, peasants and shepherds, and a very small minority of the wealthier classes, whom Babylon had reason to trust. Life was hard. "We gat our bread with the peril of our lives" (Lamentations v:9). Nationalist bands and Chaldean troops fought over the country; the towns, and especially Jerusalem, had been sacked, and presented a grievous spectacle; and Edom too "shed the blood of the children of Israel by the force of the sword in the time of their calamity" (Ezekiel xxxv:5). In this distress some forsook Jahweh, saying that He was powerless; others bowed their heads and murmured, "The crown is fallen from our head: woe unto us, that we have sinned!" (Lamentations v:16). The burning of the Temple was commemorated by an annual fast; the Lamentations of Jeremiah were chanted with weeping; and to the sacred rock where stood the altar of God the faithful came with their offerings. History will rediscover these people who remained in the land of their fathers; after the return they were to be reunited with the exiles.

Other elements were lost forever, like those whom we have seen setting out towards Egypt, taking with them, by force, Jeremiah. Others went to Syria and Asia Minor. This was the first manifestation of that great, mysterious and disturbing phenomenon, the Jewish dispersal, the *diaspora*. They departed to find a more peaceful life under other skies; as people of means, they bought land, and, a detail worth noting, did not yet show any preference for trade and banking. In the Isle of Elephantine, in the middle of the Nile, just downstream below its first falls, and opposite Assuan (Syene, in Greek), six rolls of papyrus were found in 1904 which proved to be the archives of a Jewish colony established by Psammetichus II. These men were soldiers, mercenaries of Pharaoh, employed to guard besides the frontier of Egypt the route to Ethiopia and the quarries of that same fine "syenite" used in the obelisk in the Place de la Concorde. It appears that in these places of voluntary exile, where there was no question of suffering, spiritual life was soon degraded. We find the usual argument that Jahweh is not all-powerful, that misfortune has overtaken us; let us turn to the Queen of Heaven. At Elephantine, the mercenaries did build a temple to Jahweh, which was in itself exceptional, but they also worshipped Ammon-Ra, and the One God of Moses was scandalously associated with a female divinity.

The germ of life, which would one day take root in Canaan, resided in the groups of exiles. How many of these unfortunate people were there? Here we touch upon the very mystery of this history. Of the hundred thousand inhabitants of Judah, a few thousands were led away; between four thousand six hundred and ten thousand, the Bible says, presumably referring to men of an age to carry arms; with their wives, old people and children, the number would still not have exceeded twenty-five or thirty thousand. The spiritual destiny of humanity, the future of monotheism, rested on that small number of people—or even fewer indeed; only upon those among them who were faithful, and who understood the significance of the drama, and who did not despair.

Their condition was at first pitiful. Like all great buildings, those of Nebuchadnezzar required enormous man-power, and Israel, as in Egypt long ago, was forced to align bricks under the scourge of taskmasters. But the vitality of these people soon manifested itself in an astonishing way. Jeremiah, in a wise letter (Jer. xxix), had counselled them to be prepared for a long exile, seventy years, he said, and, therefore, to build houses, to found families, and to work. This was done. If we look at the Jewish colony fifty years after the catastrophe, what do we find? On the Middle Euphrates, in the district of Nippur, Israelite villages were prospering beyond belief. The poor exiles had thousands of slaves. Many of them had made enormous fortunes, like the bankers

Murashu whose account books have been preserved, who had
clients even as far away as Persia. With money they had acquired
political influence, and Nebuchadnezzar's successor Evil Merodach was well disposed towards them and even freed their old
king, Jehoiachin; from the story of Daniel we know that they even
penetrated the court. From a terrible lot, they had, in fact,
wrested a very acceptable destiny.

This amassing of wealth was to have, besides, a great importance when the time came to return. These Babylonian magnates
financed the restoration of Canaan, just as the Greek bankers of
Constantinople financed the rising of the Klephts and Palikares,
or the Rothschilds have supported contemporary Zionism.

It would therefore be wrong to picture a slow destruction of
the chosen people in wealthy Mesopotamia. They made money,
and they no longer suffered materially; but they experienced none
the less for that the grief of exile, and despair for their lost country. It is these feelings that inspire the loveliest of the Psalms
(cxxxvii), "By the rivers of Babylon, there we sat down, yea, we
wept, when we remembered Zion. We hanged our harps upon the
willows in the midst thereof. For there they that carried us away
captive required of us a song; and they that wasted us required
of us mirth, saying, Sing us one of the songs of Zion. How shall
we sing the Lord's song in a strange land? If I forget thee, O Jerusalem, let my right hand forget her cunning. If I do not remember
thee, let my tongue cleave to the roof of my mouth; if I prefer not
Jerusalem above my chief joy!"

Well knowing that their religion was their strongest weapon,
the chosen people accomplished during the exile a remarkable
effort of fidelity. The rites belonging to Jahweh's worship were
strictly observed; circumcision, rest on the Sabbath, commemoration of the Pasch. The priests, who had no longer a temple, as
their cult could only be practised on holy ground, were held in
high respect. The faithful grouped themselves about them, and
their places of meeting became synagogues. A veritable caste of
jurists and scribes was constituted for the purpose of tending the
law—ardent upholders of the more rigorous observance.

But above all, the lesson whose seed the Prophets had sown with such difficulty bore fruit. In their exile, the chosen people had recognized the punishment of their faults, and resolved to expiate them. The "return" so greatly desired was in the first place a return to God: in Hebrew, as in English, the same significant verbal ambiguity exists. While the debris of Samaria was absorbed into Mesopotamia, the remnant of Judah held firm. Jeremiah had foretold this repentance, and do we not find in Isaiah the decisive explication of the whole drama? In His supreme power, Jahweh had chosen to reserve for His people a special destiny. He has made them the "light of the Gentiles." Israel was to be His witness, His servant; a divine mission was conferred upon them. The desolate and torn nation suffered in a cause greater than their own. They might not perish, the little band of people deported from Judah, because in them alone was deposited the doctrine of the true God; one day, astonished, the kings and the nations should see it exalted; they should learn from the Jews that of which they were still ignorant, from them should come the salvation of the world. Thus did Israel in her distress come to conceive her mission; her providential role took on a new significance.

EZEKIEL

Most remarkable of the guides who directed Israel during the exile was Ezekiel, the third of the major prophets. He had been taken in one of the first convoys of deportees, in 597, at the same time as King Jehoiachin. The son of a priest, and inspired with the prophetic spirit, he united in himself the two currents which were to keep alive the soul of Israel. He was a strange man, austere, fanatical: the vision of the horrors that were to overwhelm the enemies of Israel filled him with frenzied joy. He it is, nevertheless, who formulated, in the name of Jahweh, the phrase of supreme mercy, "Have I any pleasure at all that the wicked should die? said the Lord GOD: and not that he should return from his ways, and live? (XVIII: 23). He was a great poet in the fantastic and tragic genre, of the order of Edgar Poe, William Blake, or

Hölderlin. His visions are described in bewildering terms of hallucination, and even in his life he abounded in symbolic acts, as when he took hair, burning a third, cutting up a second third with the sword, and dispersing the rest, as an image of the destiny of Israel.

One day when he was beside a river, the air came towards him like a cloth of flame. A dazzling mass as of molten metal gave forth lightning. The Prophet knew that Jahweh was present. A strange chariot with whirling wheels, mysterious figures in which images of man mingled with those of bulls, eagles, and lions, appeared to him during the ecstasy. In the depths of the sky crystal gleamed, and a throne of sapphire appeared and the wings of angels beat with the sound of great waters. "Son of man, stand upon thy feet, and I will speak to thee," said a voice. "I send thee to the children of Israel, to a rebellious nation . . . be not afraid of their words. . . . Be not thou rebellious like that rebellious house: open thy mouth, and eat that I give thee." The scroll that a heavenly hand offered to him, Ezekiel swallowed, and it was as sweet as honey. Then, filled with the divine message, he slowly tore himself from his ecstasy, and went to announce to the people the message with which he was charged (Ezekiel II).

His prophetic task was in the first place to lead his compatriots back to right thinking. At that time Jerusalem had not yet fallen, and the most foolish hopes animated the exiles. False prophets abounded, and only succeeded in drawing down upon themselves and on their brethren Chaldean reprisals. Ezekiel set to work to destroy these mirages; Jerusalem would be destroyed; everything went to prove it: her sins that had not been redeemed, and the fatal course of history. Until the necessary degree of punishment had been meted out, the disintegration would continue. Therefore let the exiles rely on no one but themselves, for in them resided the future of Israel.

While Zedekiah was staging his vain and final revolt, Ezekiel, who had just lost his wife, the "delight of his eyes," did not even put on mourning, reserving himself for a very different sorrow, one filled with the image of imminent catastrophe. Now, "in the twelfth year of our captivity, in the tenth month, in the fifth day of the month, that one that had escaped out of Jerusalem came unto me saying, The city is smitten" (xxxiii:21). The Prophet, emerging from his silence, his "dark night," arose and, commenting on the event, showed to the people its supernatural significance.

From this moment, humanly speaking, all hope was lost. Cohorts of those newly deported arrived, and to these masses overwhelmed with grief Ezekiel began to preach a new lesson. Overnight the stiff-necked people had become pliable. They were ready to listen to the prophetic message. For twenty years the preacher of consolation obstinately continued to speak to them of their past greatness, and of the divine promises made to Israel that still held good. He kept alive the national consciousness; he directed towards the future forces that in sterile nostalgia for the past would have turned to weakness and waste.

He did not belittle past faults, but called them to mind continually. Yet it was not sin, but redemption, that he stressed. Fully aware of the drama of the fall and the redemption, the Jewish mind henceforth was to place it at the centre of its religious conception; the whole of spiritual life was to be illuminated by it, and the theology of St. Paul is in direct line with the teaching of Ezekiel.

The admirable conception of individual responsibility, already indicated by Isaiah and Jeremiah, took on for him an essential importance. He devoted a whole chapter (xviii) to it, and reverted to it constantly. The exact justice of God, if it chastises all nations, as all the Prophets had said, also takes note of the effort of every individual. Like Jeremiah he protested against the teaching that "the fathers have eaten sour grapes, and the children's teeth are set on edge." He went further; no, the son of the impious should not be punished for the father's faults. No, the virtues of their ancestors would not prove any defence for their faithless descendants. Everyone is responsible for himself, to himself. To each, God gives His love and offers the opportunity of salvation. This salvation is still, no doubt, envisaged in the limited terms of this world, but it is a personal salvation; individual religion has made progress. And if he insists less than Jeremiah on the inner sorrow of man and his need for consolation, Ezekiel brings into light the conception of divine grace and the gift which it makes to every individual.

Under the influence of all these fruitful ideas, the soul of Israel in exile returned to life. The ancient law, the Torah, of which they had, probably, brought only a few written fragments with them, but which they preserved in their memories, was revived; they again studied its texts. Ezekiel added new interpretations. Besides being a prophet, that is to say, the mouthpiece of the spirit of God Himself, he knew as a priest the importance of rites and liturgy; he specified its modalities. This was the third aspect of this rich personality; he became a legislator and jurist. He built up for the future the constitution of the community of the faithful.

Thus, at the moment when all seemed to be lost, a man was found who told Israel not to despair. The supernatural flame that burned in his soul kept alive the sacred fire of the mission of the nation. Not for a moment did the nation in exile doubt that the grace of God would wipe away their sins, that they would return to their devastated land, and there rebuild a paradise (xxxvi). The astonishing visions that the great mystic described were in the nature of promises. Once, in a vision, he saw a plain covered with dry bones; at the word of Jahweh, the spirit had returned to these poor skeletons; their flesh burgeoned, the skin was stretched anew, and at an immense gust of wind the dead returned to life (xxxvii). Rescued from death itself, the chosen people would rebuild their Temple. On another occasion, Ezekiel described the future sanctuary: remote from human defilement, on a holy hill, surrounded by the dwellings of the just, admirable, all but inaccessible, but with a stream of living water flowing from its heights to appease the thirst of the desolated lands where the Dead Sea stretches its leaden waters (xl *et seq.*). On yet another occasion, he evoked the supreme ordeals of the hour when, returned to the Promised Land, pardoned, Israel would have to support the demoniacal forces of Gog and Magog, who, like the Scythians, advanced into battle on galloping horses. But by the hand of God the defeated enemy would perish on the ground, and, redeemed, Israel would see the face of God (xxxviii, xxxix). The face of God, that was what must be contemplated in the future. The Kingdom of God was approaching. The community of the redeemed must await the coming of the Messiah, of Him in whom the glory would be consummated; and Jerusalem, changing her name, could thereafter say of herself "the Lord is here" (xlvii).

THE EXEMPLARY STORY OF JUDITH

Nations in distress have need of symbolic figures in which they can see themselves, magnified. Thus in her trials Israel clung not only to the grandiose images of an Ezekiel but to illustrative stories which perhaps belonged to an ancient tradition, or may possibly have originated in the international traditions that were common to the whole of the Fertile Crescent, but which were given by the chosen people an altogether special significance, and which they charged with high spiritual meaning.

They told, for example, the story of Judith, the woman who when men were in despair, their courage gone, had alone embodied resistance, and whose force of spirit had, by the grace of God, destroyed the power of enemies. Nebuchadnezzar, in his anger, had sent an army to Palestine to punish his vassals who had refused to pay tribute; but the high priest Joacim inspired them with courage, persuading them to multiply their fasts and prayers and to leave the rest in the hands of God. The town of Bethulia was besieged and seemed doomed to certain destruction; the enemy had cut the aqueduct. There was talk of surrender, when a woman went to the chiefs of the city and proposed to them that she should make a last attempt: she was a widow, rich, beautiful, but of great holiness. They accepted, praying that God would aid her; "she washed her body all over with water, and anointed herself with precious ointment, and braided the hair of her head, and put on a tire upon it, and put on her garments of gladness, . . . her bracelets and her chains and her rings and her earrings, and all her ornaments," and went to the camp of the enemy general. The barbarian received her with a civility inspired by the most agreeable unspoken anticipation. After making him wait for several days, the lovely visitor agreed to dine with him. The pleasure of the feast, the rich wines, the tempting presence, fuddled the rough soldier; later, alone with Judith, he slept. The daughter of Israel did not waver: taking the sword that hung on a pillar, she approached the bed, took the drunken man by the hair, and beheaded him.

The next day, from the city walls, they showed the enemy soldiers the head of their general, and the army fled in terror, pursued by all the tribes of Israel. "Sing unto my Lord with cymbals," Judith sang. "Assur came out of the mountains from the north, he bragged that he would burn up my borders. But the Almighty Lord hath disappointed them by the hand of a woman!" When, probably in about 350 B.C., this glorious episode was written down, the facts of history had already become a little blurred. Nebuchadnezzar, "King of Assyria," is always the symbol of brute force, but Holofernes, the general killed by Judith, bore the name of a Persian soldier, mentioned by Diodorus of Sicily, who lived at least a hundred years later.

THE FABLE OF TOBIAS

Weakness can, to be sure, with the aid of God, triumph over force. Is anything impossible with God? In the story of Tobias also, the popular mind heard the assurance of providential promises. An atmosphere of profound charity permeates with sweetness this romantic story; Claudel, drawing from it a moral,[4] observes that it might be an illustration of the Gospel text, "Where two or three are gathered together in my name, there am I in the midst of them," and that the conclusion to which it points is that "God is love." This story in which the living and the dead, men

[4] *L'Histoire de Tobie et de Sara.*

and angels, live together in simple fraternity had a message of comfort for this unhappy people whose need to experience a like turn of fortune was so great.

Among the captives taken to Nineveh at the time of the fall of Samaria was a just man called Tobit. He was married, and had a son bearing the name Tobias. This perfect servant of God had never worshipped the golden calves; every year, going up to Jerusalem, he had offered to the Unseen his first fruits and his tithes. In exile, unlike so many of his compatriots, he kept his faith. Having obtained an appointment near the king's person, he used his influence to help the exiles. With exceptional courage, he buried the bodies of his brothers, butchered by the Assyrians.

God, however, put his faithful servant to the test. One day while he slept, a swallow dropped dung in his eye. Blinded and ruined, he heard those about him saying, "Where is thy hope?" And he answered them, "Speak not so, for we are the children of saints, and will look for that life which God will give to those that never change their faith from him." His wife, embittered, mocked him. But resolute in the love of God, he taught his son to honour his family, living and dead; to have God ever in his thoughts; never to do evil, to obey the Lord; to give alms and never turn a deaf ear to the poor; if he became rich, to give much in charity, for that is to amass true riches; to be pure and humble; to pay his servants well; to do nothing to others that he would not like others to do to him; and to bless God always.

Holiness was to have its reward. Tobit had, long ago, lent a large sum of money to a distant relation who lived up in the plateau of Media at Rages. Could not his son be sent to collect that money? But the journey was long and dangerous. However, just at that time, a stranger of pleasing aspect appeared, who offered to lead the young man to his destination; this was the Archangel Raphael, one of the seven angels before the face of God, in human form. Delighted, young Tobias whistled for his dog, and went with this companion. When they came to the Tigris, a monstrous fish attacked him, and his travelling companion showed Tobias how to seize it by the gills and land it; this fish provided good food for the journey; the liver and the entrails the angel told him to keep, for these were magical objects with the power of driving away demons and healing the sick.

At Ecbatana, through which the two travellers must pass, there lived a young Israelite woman called Sara, who was in deep distress. Seven times she had been married, and seven times her husband had died, slain by the demon Asmodeus, jealous of her human lovers. She prayed to God to come to her aid. Led to her by his angel, the young Tobias, who was found to be Sara's cousin, asked for her hand. The father of the young girl, unwilling to go into mourning for an eighth son-in-law, hesitated. And Asmodeus was already on the prowl. . . . But, by burning the liver of the fish, Raphael drove away the demon. Sara and Tobias were married, while the obliging angel went to collect the debt at Rages.

The three returned to Nineveh. Old Tobit, distressed by his son's long absence, came to meet them. And the dog, who had been on the journey, ran ahead as though to give the news, joyfully wagging his tail in greeting. This was a happy reunion, softened with tears of joy. Instructed by his companion, the young Tobias rubbed his father's eyes with the gall of the fish, whereupon they opened again to the light of the sun. It remained only to repay the kindly travelling companion. But when the old man broached the subject, the mysterious guide made himself known. God had sent him to aid a faithful soul in distress. Fading into the air, the tutelary spirit vanished, as in Rembrandt's famous painting.

Interpretations and commentaries on this romantic story have abounded. Theologians and scholars have wondered whether we are asked to take in a literal sense the magical elements which it contains. There are inexplicable facts, but these the biblical narrator attributes to the will of God. Many critics, including some Catholics, have freely admitted that the story is a popular romance without any historical basis. Others, favouring a symbolical interpretation, see Sara as symbolizing the human soul, continually tormented by the demon, freed by the young saviour associated with the image of the fish.

History reveals, with a smile, that the narrator, writing, to be sure, long after the times described, has been guilty of many inexactitudes: mentioning Rages as existing in the eighth century, whereas it was built in the third; confusing Salmanasar with Sargon, besides a number of geographical blunders. Not that these things have any great importance. But the facts of real historical interest, as revealing the popular sentiments of piety, are the noble morals of old Tobit, his deep respect for the dead, and strictness in observances. The story also reveals some curious foreign influences: demonology was highly developed in Assyria and Persia, and exorcism was held in honour. Liver in these countries had many elements of magic, and there have even been found bronze or clay livers which were used by apprentice diviners for learning their trade. The demon Asmodeus, Sara's terrible lover, is the Persian Aeshma Daeva, the demon of luxury; Rages was an important religious centre of Iranian Mazdeism; we find in Mesopotamia, Iran and India the theme of a dead man who shows gratitude to whoever has given him burial; and even in the sympathetic character of the dog we have a reminder that in Persia that animal was sacred, and that infernal torments were the punishment of those who ill-treated dogs. The story of Tobias, therefore, owes much to foreign influences, but it bears the imprint of Israel and her hopes. In the same way Wagner borrowed from the French cycle of the Grail and the Round Table many of the themes of his dramas; was his work any the less fresh or Germanic for that reason?

THE EXEMPLARY STORY OF JOB

The same applies to the finest of all the exemplary stories of the Old Testament, that of Job, the righteous man, which had certainly been traditional for a very long time. This man would seem to have lived in the time of the Patriarchs, when Joseph was taken into Egypt as the captive of wandering bandits. Ezekiel couples him with Noah, and his name is mentioned in the Book of Tobias. His dramatic adventure certainly belongs to a tradition of folklore that was not exclusively Hebraic; there is in Babylonian literature a story of a just man suffering; the dialogue with his soul of a man weary of life occurs in the literature of Egypt; and in India the Markandeya Purana tells the story of the noble conduct of King Harischandra who, afflicted with the most terrible disgraces, supported his trials with heroism, and finally recovered all that he had lost. It is not certain, however, from what source the theme found its way into Israel; the Bible speaks of Job and his people as "orientals," and in the Hauran district, east of Gilead,[5] where the rich volcanic lands support large herds of cattle, one finds outside the villages heaps of dung from the stables which are burned for manure, and where, in the evenings, beggars gather about the glowing embers for warmth. Perhaps, however, the story of Job is no less an expression of the high Jewish spirituality for being of international origin; the poetic genius who, after the return from exile in about 550, created from it the thoughts and the rhythms which move us to this day, clearly understood this. If the story of the righteous man was called to mind in the villages of the Euphrates, it must have been easy to draw from it the most inspiring lessons of hope. It is likely that many of the metaphysical and moral themes that it also contains are later additions, the product of the great genius of the author; in particular that of the retribution of good and evil in a sphere beyond this life.[6] But, in its simple outline, it exalts the faith of a nation which, however tolerable its dunghill may have been, felt itself to be in misery and placed its faith in God.

One day when the angels had assembled in the presence of the Most High, the fallen angel, Satan, "the adversary," to whom all human happiness is hateful, came into their midst. God said to Satan, "Whence comest thou?" and Satan replied, "From going to and fro in the earth, and from walking up and down in it." "Hast thou considered my servant Job; that there is none like him

[5] *See* MAP: PALESTINE AFTER THE EXILE, p. 240.
[6] We will return to this question later. *See* the last chapter.

in the earth, a perfect and an upright man, one that feareth God and escheweth evil?" "Doth Job fear God for nought?" Satan mocks. "Hast not thou made a hedge about him? . . . Thou hast blessed the work of his hands, and his substance is increased in the land. But put forth thine hand now, and touch all that he hath, and he will curse thee to thy face." And God gave Satan permission to put Job's faith to the test.

A series of catastrophes then descended upon Job. His great herds were taken by robbers, his farms were destroyed by lightning. The wind of the desert destroyed his house in a hurricane, burying all his children in its ruins. But Job did not rebel. "Naked came I out of my mother's womb, and naked shall I return thither: the Lord gave, and the Lord hath taken away; blessed be the name of the Lord!" Enraged, Satan went further. Stricken with terrible boils, Job prostrated himself in the village dunghill, scraping his sores with a potsherd. And his wife, the scold whom Dürer has represented emptying a bucket of ordure over the holy man, bade him "curse God and die." His friends told him that to deserve such punishment he must have been guilty of great sins. And he, despairing, calling for death, confessed that in the eyes of God no man is righteous. But throughout their derision and mockery he remained faithful. At times a cry of woe was wrung from him: why should sinners live happy, and he suffer to these extremes? But immediately he would return to his prayer, believing that if his conduct had not been free from blame, God would consider his sufferings and accept them in expiation of his sins. He cried to his Lord, "I know that thou canst do everything, and that no thought can be withholden from thee. . . . Wherefore I abhor myself, and repent in dust and ashes." He continued to hope.

Then, restoring to Job his former state, God gave back to him fourteen thousand sheep, six thousand camels, a thousand yoke of oxen, and a thousand she-asses; and he had seven sons and three daughters whose names signified the Dove, Perfume and Fard— all of them of great beauty. "So Job died, being old and full of days." And so repentant, striving to earn new chances, the remnant of Israel was able to nourish its soul with the same hope.

THE MIRACLES OF DANIEL

When this hope had become something more than a mere dream, the exiles were able to tell one another of the last and strangest of the prophets, observed in a cloud of fire. Daniel is not known to us, as are Isaiah, Jeremiah and Ezekiel, by his own writings. We read of his life in a narrative told in the third person, in a difficult text, part of which was written in Hebrew, part in Aramaean during the third and second centuries, and part in Greek. His very name raises problems; in Ezekiel (xiv:14, 20; xxviii:3) one has the impression that there had been in antiquity a man of the same name, perhaps the "Danel" whose wise deeds are recounted on the Phoenician tablets of Ras-Shamra. Historically the Book of Daniel raises difficult questions; Belshazzar did not succeed Nebuchadnezzar, who, moreover, never was mad; but one of his successors, Nabonidos, was mad for seven years. "Darius the Mede," conquerer of Babylon, is unknown, and could not have been the great Darius, who was a Persian and reigned from 522 to 485 (whereas Babylon fell in 539). Non-Catholic critics maintain that Daniel was a mythical personage, invented during the third or second century B.C.; most Catholic critics admit that we are here dealing with facts whose veracity is certainly open to question.

All the same, through the singular episodes of which he is the hero, Daniel stands out clearly enough. His character, as a literary critic would say, is convincing. The Bible presents him to us young, fervent and grave, as Michelangelo has depicted him.

He was one of a group of pages whom Nebuchadnezzar (?) had brought up in his palace; he studied the "literature of the Chaldeans." But, as a devout young Jew, he refused to eat the flesh of animals that had not been slaughtered according to the Mosaic rites, which, however, did not prevent him from thriving on vegetables, for God protected him. The first occasion on which he manifested his prophetic mission was in the episode of the chaste Suzanna and the lecherous "elders." A young woman, whose name means "anemone," was indeed the flower of Israel, beautiful, virtuous, and respected by all. Two old rogues having seen her in her garden made shameful proposals to her, and then, because she repulsed them, publicly accused her of adultery. They had seen her with her lover with their own eyes; more agile than they, the youth had fled, but the woman was taken and deserved death. Just as the innocent victim was being led to her execution, the young Daniel, inspired by the spirit of God, cried out, "I am clear from the blood of this woman. . . . Return again to the place of judgment, for they have borne false witness against her!" Ordered to conduct the appeal himself, he separated the two accusers. "Under what tree," he asked them, "did they commit adultery?" One of them said, under a mastic tree; the other opted for an evergreen oak. Whereupon, both were stoned to death.

With wisdom beyond his years Daniel combined occult gifts. The wise Prophet expounded dreams as Joseph had done for Pharaoh. Nebuchadnezzar summoned him to interpret a dream which had troubled him extremely. A colossal statue with a head of gold, arms of silver, thighs of brass, and feet part iron, part clay, which had fallen at the blow of a stone from the mountains, symbolized the successive kingdoms of Mesopotamia. Daniel foretold beforehand of Cyrus and Alexander and Rome, and the ultimate ruin of them all. In admiration, the king loaded the Prophet with honours, but many enemies attacked him. On one occasion one of his closest friends accused him of treason because he had refused to worship the image of the king, and he was condemned to be burned to death. On another occasion his enemies had him flung into a lion's den. But God preserved his intrepid servant; at the command of the Prophet, the fire abated its heat, and the young man, unharmed in the furnace, sang the glory of the Creator; while the lions, as gentle as domestic pets, lay down at Daniel's feet. As for the king, stricken with a mysterious affliction, and out of his mind, he lived for seven years in the fields, eating grass.

It was not only from these miracles that the people of Israel derived hope. Daniel, in visions like those of Ezekiel, prophesied the end of their sufferings, the return to the land of their heart's desire, divine forgiveness, and prosperity. In seventy weeks of years, the great liberator of Israel would be born; an "anointed," a "messiah," who was to redeem sins, expiate iniquity, and bring in a rule of eternal justice, but whose life would be cut short. He saw grandiose visions in which the Son of Man arose in glory, after the four winds of heaven had blown a tempest and the four symbolic beasts had come out of the sea. He would come, the great Judge, He whose throne is surrounded by flames; a river of fire would flow before Him; thousands of servants would obey His orders, and the books should be unsealed.

Under these magnificent symbols, compilers were to discern those promises that we still read into them, and to find in them the sublime metaphysic of judgment from beyond life, and of salvation through the passion of Christ. We shall return to this conception. But Israel in exile awaited, above all, its immediate liberation.

One night, when Belshazzar, who succeeded Nebuchadnezzar on the throne of Babylon, was feasting with his wives and concubines, drinking wine from the sacred vessels of the Temple of Zion, "in the same hour came forth fingers of a man's hand, and wrote over against the candlestick upon the plaister of the wall of the king's palace: and the king saw the part of the hand that wrote. Then the king's countenance was changed, and his thoughts troubled him, so that the joints of his loins were loosed, and his knees smote one against another" (Daniel v). He sent for his diviners and astrologers. But none could, or none dared, read the writing. A queen suggested sending for Daniel, to whose knowledge Nebuchadnezzar had formerly recourse. The Prophet of God appeared and spoke.

The three words traced on the white plaster were, *Mene, Tekel, Upharsin:* counted, weighed, divided. "God hath numbered thy kingdom and finished it. . . . Thou art weighed in the balances, and art found wanting. . . . Thy kingdom is divided, and given to the Medes and Persians." That same night, Babylon, besieged, fell, and Belshazzar was slain.

THE FALL OF BABYLON AND THE GLORY OF CYRUS

At the time of the exile the very idea of a collapse of Babylon must have seemed an absurd chimaera. Fifty years later history had made it a probability. The disintegration of the Chaldean empire was as rapid as that of Nineveh: no rule can with impunity impose by force alone a domination that brings with it no benefits, nor arouse without danger twenty nations to see a potential liberator in every enemy of the state. Nebuchadnezzar's successor saw many crises and revolutions. His son Evil Merodach reigned for two years, and then was killed by a brother-in-law. He left a situation so troubled that his son only managed to hold the throne for four months. A revolt, inspired by the priestly class, put in his place a son of a priestess, Nabonidos, who was to dig the grave of the great kingdom of Babylon (556). He was a strange character: scholar, artist, mystic, and crowned priest. Taking no interest in political matters, Nabonidos was wholly preoccupied with cults and rites. On one occasion he departed for years together to meditate in a distant oasis, in a state of religious mania, making it impossible in his absence to celebrate the national festival of the New Year. On another, in order to group all the great gods of Mesopotamia in Babylon, he stripped all the temples of their idols, exasperating the populations concerned. At Harran, his birthplace, the old lunar god Sin enjoyed a revival; but the stars in which he believed did not favour this lunatic king, and his son Belshazzar was unable to save the situation.

This was not the moment to abandon the sword for the censer! A danger had arisen in the south-east of Mesopotamia: the Persians had just completed the unification of Iran under their domination. In a remote district of the empire of the Medes, Achaemenes, a feudal vassal, had made himself more or less independent in about 570; his grandson Cyrus, an adventurer of genius, dared to defy the suzerain. Detested for his cruelty, betrayed by his troops, Astyages fell in 552. Media passed under Persian control. A new capital was founded, Pasargadae. Thirty years later Achaemenes' empire was to weld the Fertile Crescent, Asia Minor and Egypt, into the greatest empire that there had yet been, to stand until the day when, encountering an unforeseen obstacle, this giant was brought low at Marathon, Salamis and Plataea.

The year 522 marks a great moment of history. The Aryans had at that time leaders who were sturdy peasants, young and inventive, ambitious but humane. The two kindred nations, the Medes and Persians, had already reached a high level of civilization. They possessed a religion whose moral beauty cannot be denied. Still in its early stages was that doctrine which through many transformations was to touch so many souls throughout the centuries—that the Roman army was to find in the cult of Mithra; that the great Persian kings of the Sassanid Dynasty practised until the time of the Arab invasions; from which the Manichean heresies, and even later to some extent those of the Albigensian Catharists, penetrated the very heart of Christianity; and which the Parsees of Bombay follow to this day. Zoroaster, the reformer— Neitzsche's Zarathustra—had but recently carried out his religious revolution. The wars of Cyrus had undoubtedly a religious character, and his politics reflect the commandments of a profoundly humane doctrine.

During the epoch of the Achaemenidae the Persian religion, which was already no longer pure Zoroastrianism (the reformer was unquestionably a monotheist), was essentially dualistic. Life is the stage of the incessant warfare between god and evil. When Ormazd created the world, Ahriman entered it as a fly and infected it. The vermin of evil has since then swarmed on the earth, and in the human heart, and until the last day, when in a great combustion the whole of creation will vanish away, the battle between the forces of light and those of darkness must continue. Certainly there were dangers in a metaphysic that tended to condemn all creation as irreparably damaged, and the cult of the "pure" Albigensians, who later practised sacred suicide, was its logical outcome. But beside the mythological polytheism of the Greeks and the Babylonian cults of magic, it was high. Ormazd was conceived as an invisible god that no image could represent, "the god of life, purity and truth." The rites were very simple, as they are to-day in Bombay or on the borders of the Caspian. The immaterial flame that rose from faggots of odoriferous wood was venerated. Priests or Magi, clothed in linen and crowned with tiaras, presided at the sacrifices and libations of *homa*, the sacred liquid. All that was impure was taboo, and the dead, lest their corrupt bodies should defile earth, water, or fire, were neither buried nor thrown into rivers, nor burned, but abandoned in those "towers of silence" where birds of prey devoured them.

As it is formulated in the *Avesta*, the sacred book of the Persians which was compiled only at the beginning of our era, the morality of this nation appears to be very high. It was so certainly in the times of the Achaemenidae, for the Greek Herodotus, who can scarcely be suspected of partiality for his enemies, speaks of it with respect. What did Ormazd demand? That we should help to conquer Ahriman, by upholding all that is good on the earth and by combatting that which is evil. Inner purity, benevolence and loyalty were so many conquests gained for the perfect god against the evil one; it was because they obeyed these principles that the Persians were just and clement toward Israel.

In the hour of Babylon's downfall something more than political power was changing; so also was the whole conception of life. All was to be changed in the immense domain over which the Achaemenidae extended their power. Even art bears the marks of these transformations. To those massive constructions in the colossal style that had always been built since the days of Sumer and Akkad, the Persians added an element new in these countries —pillars. Pasargadae and Persepolis have left to archaeology grandiose but harmonious ruins. Slender columns, with finely carved bases and capitals formed of two fore-quarters of bulls welded together, surrounded with orderly rows the great halls; only the great hypostyles of Egypt can be compared with them. Less realistic than that of the Assyrian animal-carvers, Persian sculpture has in the highest degree the decorative sense. Decoration is combined with architecture with a facility that we only find elsewhere in the great temples of India and Indo-China. Exchanging the poor material, clay, for a composition of lime, quartz, and powdered flint, Persian workers in ceramics produced glazed bricks and pictures as iridescent as enamel—mysterious plants with stylized stems, strange beasts, griffons, winged bisons—decoration that covers with shining colours the immense walls of their palaces.

The "Frieze of the Archers" at the Louvre gives a good idea of this dazzling and intricate art: in green turbans, tan boots, and long cream robes with girdles of ochre or green or yellow and trimmed with emerald, carrying on their shoulders a white bow and in their hands silver-hilted lances of the royal guard, they are the very types of an irresistible power, sure of itself. Even in the phrases of an enemy, Aeschylus, the greatness of Persia appears, much as it already was essentially when Cyrus realized his coup d'état: that of a nation through whom civilization was to progress.

No sooner was he master of Iran than Cyrus embarked upon his conquests. The destiny which compels the kings of Asia "to wage struggles in which ramparts crumble" and "in which the son adds to the glory of the father" (Aeschylus) caught up the Achaemenidae, and never were they to be freed from it. Croesus, king of Lydia, alarmed by the progress of Persia, attempted to form an alliance against Cyrus with Amasis of Egypt, and with Sparta; had not the Delphic oracle said that he would "destroy an empire"? It referred to his own. Twice defeated, blockaded in Sardis, the wealthy king only escaped with his life thanks to the benevolence of the Persian morality, and not, as the Greek legend relates, through the intervention of Apollo. Cyrus pressed on to the coast and threatened the Greek cities; Miletus surrendered, and the rest were defeated in battle; Asia Minor was subjected by the Aryan king. Would he turn towards Babylon, the only adversary worthy of him? "This hero, favoured by fate, was a wise man," says Aeschylus. He made a great detour, and subjected the lands of the Caspian as far as the borders of the Indus. Then, in

540, he decided that the time was ripe. Nabonidos was at the height of his follies. Cyrus came down from Zagros.

Belshazzar, who was ruling as regent for the mad king, had his work cut out to keep order. In that mosaic of completely subjected peoples treachery was common. A Babylonian governor of the region of the Persian Gulf, Gobryas, went over to the enemy. Defeated on the Tigris, the Babylonians took refuge in their capital. It was believed to be impregnable; yet it fell in fifteen days (539). That credulous historian Herodotus tells how the Persians diverted the course of the Euphrates to enter the city by means of its dry bed. It is more likely that Cyrus had a fifth column in the city; one of his inscriptions says in plain words, "All the people of Babylon, Sumer and Akkad, including the great and the rulers, bow before me, kissing my feet, and rejoicing in my domination." Babylon, which had ruled by the whip, fell; the master of the world was now the Aryan from the mountains, in a white turban and an embroidered robe, who believed in a God of justice and goodness.

It was of him that Isaiah had prophesied, "Thus saith the Lord to his anointed, to Cyrus, whose right hand I have holden to subdue nations before him; . . . to open before him the two leaved gates; and the gates shall shut" (xliv). And he also said, "He is my shepherd, and shall perform all my pleasure: even saying to Jerusalem, thou shalt be built; and to the temple, Thy foundation shall be laid" (xliv). While they anxiously awaited the realization of that promise, Israel acclaimed the king of Persia as their liberator.

THE DECREE OF CYRUS

The thing for which they had scarcely dared to hope came about. Cyrus gave permission for the remnant of Israel to leave and return to their country. Some have wondered whether, in this gesture of good will, we are not justified in seeing the particular consideration of a worshipper of one transcendent and moral God towards a monotheistic people. But it is unnecessary to adduce this argument. Cyrus was inclined to clemency on principle, and also out of interest. The Persian domination was not that of a preying power shamelessly exploiting the vanquished. Strict, meticulous, and administrative to a degree, it nevertheless allowed to subjected nations as much liberty as was consistent with the order and security of the state. Besides, that Persian nation of whom Herodotus said that they were "strongly inclined to adopt other people's ideas" probably hoped to conciliate the gods of the vanquished by respecting them.

Cyrus himself had told how he spared the Babylonian temples, how, indeed, he had the idols of Marduk and other gods whom Nabonidos in his zeal had carried off "restored to their places, in their eternal dwellings." He behaved in exactly the same way to the Jews; perhaps, if we are to believe Josephus, he had heard of their prophecies concerning him, and endeavoured to play, in history, that honourable and providential role. At all events, the man whom Isaiah did not hesitate to call "the Lord's anointed" and the "Messiah" did not deceive the hopes of Israel.

In 538, a decree was signed by the great king, and sent out with an administrative directive. The Bible has preserved these two documents for us in the Book of Esdras, under this form: "Thus saith Cyrus king of the Persians; The Lord of Israel, the most high Lord, hath made me king of the whole world, and commanded me to build him an house at Jerusalem in Jewry. . . . Whosoever then dwell in the places about, let them help him, whose, I say, that are his neighbours, with gold, and with silver. With gifts, with horses, and with cattle, and other things, which have been set forth by vow, for the temple of the Lord at Jerusalem" (1:3–4, 6–7).

A shout of exultation echoed through the villages of the exiles. Everything, then, was happening according to the Promise! The Prophets had spoken the truth. O happy day! This wretched people had, after all, a future. Everything seemed radiant to them, even the hard road that lay before them. "The wilderness and the solitary place shall be glad for them; and the desert shall rejoice, and blossom as the rose. It shall blossom abundantly, and rejoice even with joy and singing: the glory of Lebanon shall be given unto it, the excellency of Carmel and Sharon, they shall see the glory of the Lord, and the excellency of our God!" (Isaiah xxxv:1–2).

And later, recalling their hour of rejoicing, they repeated a psalm of joy (cxxvi), "When the Lord turned again the captivity of Zion, we were like them that dream. Then was our mouth filled with laughter, and our tongue with singing."

ESTHER

The departure was organized, but not all the Israelites could bring themselves to leave Babylon. This is too natural a fact to call for any explanation. To leave meant to abandon, or to sell at a low price, land and business concerns, to give up situations, break ties of affection. Josephus does not hesitate to admit that if many Jews remained in Babylon, "it was chiefly in order not to lose their property" There therefore remained in Mesopotamia Jewish colonies that extended all over the Persian empire; they anticipated exactly those with which we are familiar in modern Europe and America. Some exploited the land, others became bankers (like those Murashu whose wealth was so great at the end of the fifth century) or traded. Documents of the period prove, besides, that some reached high administrative posts: inspectors of canal rents, receivers of taxes, a keeper of the treasury of Susa. And the Bible contains a touching and dramatic little book which suggests that already there existed an anti-Semitism very much like that known in European history.

The story relates to the fifth century: Xerxes was king of Persia, the grandson of the great Cyrus, the same whose great fleet was lost at Salamis, defeated by the triremes of Themistocles. Racine wrote of him by the name of Ahasuerus, the Latin form of the Hebrew Achashwerosh, which is itself a transliteration of the Persian Akshayarsha from which the Greeks derived Xerxes. This indifferent strategist had more success with women than with warfare, and was given to spending much of his time on affairs

of the harem. In order to replenish his store of wives, he sent out
on one occasion a search for "beautiful young virgins." Among
these was a ravishingly beautiful Jewess, Esther, ward and niece
of a learned and holy man, Mordecai. Finding favour with the
king, she became queen. She gained influence over the king, and
surrounded herself with young compatriots. Racine pictures these
amiable attendants as at Saint-Cyr dominated by Esther as a de
Maintenon—and Mordecai, being clever, planned to take advantage of the situation. He had advised his niece not to disclose
her origin. And he, little by little, insinuated himself into a high
position near the throne, "at the gate of the palace." On one
occasion in particular, he rendered the king a signal service; hearing by chance of a plot, he warned the monarch through Esther,
and saved him.

But among Ahasuerus' entourage, a powerful vizier, Haman,
harboured a violent hatred against the Jews. He was presumably
a descendant of an Amalekite king whom Saul had hewn in
pieces (1 Samuel v:32–33), and he had also more personal reasons
for his jealousy of Mordecai. He persuaded the king to order a
great "pogrom" against a people who lived apart, followed their
own principles, and rebelled against the royal laws; all the Jews
of the empire were to be put to death on a single day. A decree
was issued announcing the extermination, and Haman cast lots
to decide upon the day on which this decree should be put into
effect.

Mordecai took action. He told his niece that the fate of her
people was in her hands. Her rise to eminence had a providential
significance. "Bethink you, God has not chosen you only to be
a vain spectacle for the people of Asia; for a nobler purpose he
reserves his saints" (Racine). She went to the king, confessed
to him her race, and begged him to spare Israel.

At the same time Ahasuerus, chancing to read in the daily
chronicle of his reign the account of the service that Mordecai
had rendered him, was surprised to see that he had received no
recompense. He sent for Haman, and said, "What shall be done
unto the man whom the king delighteth to honour?" Believing

that this peroration boded good to himself, the vizier replied, "Let the royal apparel be brought that the king useth to wear, and the horse that the king rideth upon, and the crown royal which is set upon his head: . . . and bring him on horseback through the street of the city." Whereupon the king commanded Haman: "Do even so to Mordecai the Jew."

Saved from massacre by Esther's intervention, the Jews took, — it must be admitted, cruel revenge. "The Jews smote all their enemies with the stroke of the sword, and slaughter, and destruction, and did what they would unto those that hated them." And the gentle Esther even persuaded the king to allow this counter-pogrom to continue for another day! Haman and all his sons were slain.

This narrative, illustrating the divine protection of Israel, is certainly of historic interest, and gives a first-hand picture of the reaction of other nations to the presence of those Jewish colonies that were determined to live apart from the nation as a whole. It proves that there was contact between these Hebrew colonies and the Jews who had returned to their own country, for this message of reassurance from distant Persia was included in the tradition of Israel; and to the commemoration of this victory the feast of the "Purim" is attributed—the celebration of delivery from those "lots" that Haman drew, and that brought disaster upon him.

THE RETURN

Meanwhile the returning pilgrims, the people of great faith, who, upheld by a supernatural hope, had risked all and left everything in order to return to Zion, had set out. How many were there? According to various figures given in the Bible, we can assume that there were thirty thousand, a large figure when we consider that this was the maximum number that we can give to the exiles when they left their own country. It proves, moreover, that Israel in captivity had indeed prospered. They went in successive convoys, under the guidance of religious or political leaders. The high priest Joshua led one party; Zerubbabel, of the family of king Jechoniah, another; this was the Jewish prince whom the Persians appointed governor, for, says Herodotus, "it was their custom to respect the sons of kings, and to restore to them the crown, even if their father had fought against them." Between 537 and 522 there must have been a series of Jewish migrations, and the Promised Land was repopulated.

The exiles did not re-establish themselves in the society of Palestine without difficulties. During seventy years of absence fields and houses had often been occupied by some Israelite living in the neighbourhood, or by one of those foreigners, Edomite or Moabite, who had taken advantage of the wars to infiltrate into the country. Those who found their lands lying fallow, and who had only to expend labour in recovering them, were among the fortunate! As if to impress His people that, even in His mercy, He still expected a great effort on their part, Jahweh did not make matters easy for them. The prophet Haggai said, "Ye looked for much, and, lo, it came to little" (1: 9); rust, mildew, and hail attacked the harvests. The passage of the Persian armies under Cambyses, on their way to attack Egypt, brought the usual unpleasantness of corvees and requisitioning. But they did not allow these things to discourage them. Before personal comfort came the glory of God. They had brought from Babylon the holy vessels, given back to them by the Great King. The Temple must be rebuilt Until the day when the foundation of the Temple was laid, Haggai afterwards recorded, the corn did not fill the barns, the fig-trees, the olives, the pomegranates, and the vines produced nothing. But from that day God blessed them.

THE REBUILDING OF THE TEMPLE

To rebuild the Temple—what did this mean? In the religious conception that the Prophets had introduced, the real Temple of God is interior; its sanctuary is situated in the hearts of the saints. Ought they, then, to say, with Isaiah, "The heaven is my throne,

and the earth is my footstool: where is the house that you build unto me? and where is the place of my rest? For all those things hath mine hand made, and all those things have been, saith the Lord: but to this man will I look, even to him that is poor and of a contrite spirit" (LXVI:1–2). It would have been too much to ask of this nation to renounce all tangible sign of their hope; nations need their legends, they live by myths no less than by realities. The very sight of the ruins of the Temple was grievous to their eyes, and had not Isaiah himself mourned to see that "our holy and our beautiful house, where our fathers praised thee, is burned up with fire" (LXIV:11)? Public opinion demanded this reconstruction, difficult through it might be.

It was singularly so indeed. Seven months after the return, in a mood of enthusiasm, the work was begun. "They gave money also unto the masons, and to the carpenters; and meat, and drink, and oil, unto them of Zidon, and to them of Tyre, to bring cedar trees from Lebanon to the sea of Joppa" (Ezra III:7). Joshua and Zerubbabel laid the first stone, in a ceremony in which the grave joy of the young was mingled with the tears of the old who remembered the past. But very soon difficulties arose. The money that they had brought from Babylon was soon exhausted. Busy with their personal tasks of putting fields and houses in order, the Jews found it hard to provide the labour for the building. Relations with neighbouring states deteriorated. The Samaritans, who regarded themselves as the brothers of the returned Jews, offered their assistance. But proud Judah, scorning the aid of these tainted people,[8] these semi-idolators, quarrelled with them, and sporadic fighting broke out. This combination of circumstances resulted in a bitter decision: to break off the work. Disappointment was keen. Some doubted whether Jahweh was still the guide of Israel. The fervour of the early days of the return little by little gave way to practical materialism: they built houses, and slipped into the old ways of grasping egoism. For fifteen years—535 to 520—it seemed as if the Promise was in vain. But God watched over them, and His prophets were to speak again.

[8] *See* above, p. 255

Meanwhile Cyrus had died. In 529, ten years after his triumphal entry into Babylon, while fighting against some Scythian tribes on the northern frontier of his state, he disappeared. How? The death of this great adventurer is one of the mysteries of history. Herodotus, always fertile in anecdotes, says that he fell by the hand of Tomyris, queen of the Massagetae, for whose son's death he had been responsible. She, having cut off his head, flung it into a vase full of blood, crying, "Since you love blood so much, drink it!" But according to Xenophon he died of an illness, and to Ctesias, of a wound.

His son Cambyses (529–522) performed the feat of conquering Egypt He was a grave man, given to violent resolves. Disturbed by rumours of intrigues by his brother Smerdis, he had him assassinated, and afterwards, filled with remorse, kept always with him the portrait of the murdered man. He was a good general, and lost no time over the Nile expedition; he subdued the Delta, succeeded in bribing the Greek mercenaries in the service of Pharaoh, and blockaded the unfortunate Psammetichus III in Memphis, which fell after a desperate struggle. Egypt from this time was under Persian dynasties. But Cambyses' later days were bitter; a campaign in Libya, at that time Carthage, failed and so did another in Ethiopia An adventurer, pretending to be the returned Smerdis, troubled the empire. Cambyses' mind was darkened. He had executed, on impulse, many of his court, including his sister Roxana; in Egypt he was guilty of sacrilege in striking down with his sword the bull Apis, incarnation of Ammon-Ra; and his death was undoubtedly the result of his neurasthenia.

Darius I, a distant cousin, succeeded him (522–485). But this election, engineered by one political party, displeased others, and revolts ensued. In Babylon, a pretender claiming to be the son of Nabonidos proclaimed himself king. At Susa, a feudal lord did the same. Darius had to fight nineteen battles before he quelled these agitations: from the Caucasus to the Indus "his armies had no stain on their glory," Aeschylus later wrote, and the famous inscription of Behistun on an immense rock-face bears the record of his expeditions to this day. After this, he organized the empire in great detail and, from the height of his formidable throne, observed with growing anger the Greek cities, these miserable little townships that dared to aspire to an influence in his maritime fief, the Aegean.

These remote happenings, in the immense empire of which Judah was only an insignificant district, had their repercussions at Jerusalem. These troubles that shook the powerful edifice gave rise to the reflection that human political constructions are fragile and that, in their future ruin, Israel might recover her independence. They also decided further parties of Jews to leave Babylon and return to their country: a useful influx of wealth. Haggai and Zachariah, the two Prophets of this period, voiced ideas that were just then at work in the minds of the faithful.

In eight strange visions Zachariah contrasted with the great empires that proceeded inevitably to their ruin, the growing glory of Israel; at one time he spoke of horsemen on red, speckled, and white horses, riding over the whole earth; at another, of celestial blacksmiths who hammered the nations in all four quarters; at another, of the Book of Judgment, flying above the earth and scattering curses upon the pagan peoples. But Jerusalem, meanwhile, was to grow. Jahweh would be as a wall of fire; a messenger would come who would measure out her fields, and prepare her works; two olive trees would grow, the priest and the king, and when they had done penance, and their fervour had revived, their soiled garments would be taken from them and white robes given to them in their stead.

At the same time Haggai spoke. He reproached his compatriots vehemently for their indolence. The Temple had not yet risen above the ground. "Is it time for you, O ye, to dwell in your cieled houses, and this house lie waste? Go up to the mountain, and bring wood, and build the house; and I will take pleasure in it, and I will be glorified, saith the Lord" (1:4, 8). As in the great days of Jeremiah or Ezekiel, the prophetic utterance had an immediate effect. Zerubbabel and Joshua and all the people heard the word of Jahweh, and the work was recommenced.

A significant incident happened at this time that shows that this resumption of the building was partially inspired by political considerations. The Persian empire was disturbed. The governor, the "satrap" in control of Judah, asked for explanations, no doubt put on his guard by the jealous vigilance of Samaria. They replied by invoking Cyrus' decree. The archives of Achaemenidae were carefully kept; Darius unearthed the relict of his great predecessor and confirmed it, even giving subsidies to Israel and warning the Samarians to keep their mouths shut if they did not want to be "hanged from their roof beams" and see their houses "converted into rubbish heaps."

In four years and a half the Temple was completed. Solomon had taken seven years. But the new sanctuary, compared with the old, was insignificant indeed. "Who is left among you that saw this house in her first glory," says Haggai (II:3), "and how do you see it now? is it not in your eyes in comparison of it as nothing?" They had retained the general appearance, the two courts, and the Holy of Holies. But they had had to make do with limited means: instead of the ten seven-branched candlesticks, there was one only; precious sandalwood no longer perfumed the sacred rooms. It was no longer the place where with all their might a proud people glorified themselves in glorifying their God. But, simple as it was, it served as a centre of worship where a community of the faithful might feel themselves in communion with a purer divinity, whose true worship rested upon an interior gesture of the soul and who extended His love over broken hearts.

The kingdom of Israel was never to revive. The Jewish community was to take its place. And, as if with symbolic intention, this Temple that was now rebuilt was to remain empty. That of Solomon had sheltered the Ark; the Ark was no more, burned in the days of the catastrophe or, according to legend, hidden by the Prophet Jeremiah in an unknown cave on Mount Nebo. A temple without any symbol was fitting for Jahweh, the invisible God. It was no longer on memory, however precious, of the past that Israel was to expend her strength, but upon that future of which

Isaiah, Jeremiah, Ezekiel and Daniel—and at that very time, Zachariah—had spoken to them; a future in which was the growing image of the King who should come, "just and having salvation" (Zachariah ix:9), and who should enter Jerusalem amid shouts of joy.

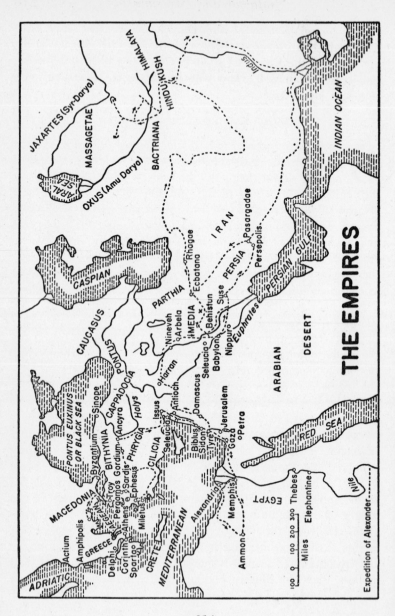

THE EMPIRES

II

THE TIME OF THE GREAT EMPIRES

WHILE EMPIRES RISE AND FALL

ETWEEN THE COMPLETION of the Temple and the birth of
Christ five centuries elapsed, but the Bible tells us almost
nothing about them. We are told of only a few events at
the beginning of that long period, and then of the much later feats
of arms of the Maccabees. It is as if, in the history of modern
France, we possessed only a chronicle of the reign of Charles VII
and an account of the 1870 war. One might suppose that the
editors of the Bible wished to indicate, by that silence, that during
these years of waiting we ought to consider not so much events
as the inner life of the chosen people.

Nevertheless, all round the canton in which the exiles lived, a
succession of dazzling historic episodes were once more taking
place. These five centuries were those during which Greece, at the
plenitude of her unique success, made her imperishable contributions to human thought, then again decayed, undermined by
the very excess of her intellectualism, her exclusiveness, and her
vain love of words. During these centuries, the monumental Persian empire, already humiliated by the city-states of Hellas, was
to see the rise, to her ruin, of the Hellenic empire, the work of an
invincible conqueror whose youthful triumphs so marvellously
prepared the ground for later civilization. During these same
years, the legions, conquering provinces as a peasant extends his
fields, appeared with their helmets and their javelins on all the
shores of the Mediterranean, and, from many overthrown kingdoms, built up the Roman unity. The impact of these great
events must have been felt in the little Palestinian state; but its
only response was to guard against them, something far more important than any illusory political liberty, namely, the faith by
which it lived.

Therein lies the true drama of these five centuries, in the fierce opposition that Israel offered to all these forces of state control, unification, and syncretism that threatened it with extinction. To give way would have been to perish; Israel knew this, and in spite of occasional moments of weakening, all too natural, she held firm. This seems a small part to play in history, but in fact Israel's history is that of her faith. A little religious state, obscure among immense empires, she saw them rise and fall each in turn, and she, whose only arms were those of prayer, survived. In Greco-Roman society, with its extremes of luxury and misery, whose external order went with such shattering crises, Israel is like a little island of certitude. But, at the same time, the necessary exclusiveness with which she surrounded herself narrowed the field of her spiritual development itself and obliterated her future.

For, at the end of that period it is no longer the temporal destiny of the Jewish nation that matters; it is in the sublime image of the Son of Man that all the events and experiences of the long history of Israel were to be realized; He was to complete that revelation of which the chosen people had only accomplished the first stages. And it was, moreover, during these five centuries that the decision was reached by which, in refusing the new message, the people of the Promise were to refuse to give that history its decisive meaning, and during which they prepared their own downfall at the tree of the Cross.

Charles Péguy in some well-known passages of his *Eve*, has depicted Christ as the heir of an immense past—the conquests of Alexandria, the dreams of Plato, the laws of Aristotle, the "shipwrecks of Rome," "of a world already old." Let us grant to the little Jewish community these five last centuries of that witness, for, without her, and without her stubborn fanatical resistance, the essence of the heritage would never have been transmitted.

THE PERSIAN EMPIRE

The Persian empire, of which Palestine at this time formed a part, was a highly organized state. From the shores of the Aegean to the Himalayas, from the Sahara to the sea of Aral, over an area six or seven times the size of France, a single master ruled, the Great King. Twenty nations, one-time enemies, had peace imposed upon them: monarch by divine right, deriving his power from Ormazd himself, the King of Kings ruled the whole empire from one of his capitals—Persepolis, Susa, or Pasargadae. Great splendour emphasized the princely majesty: a golden throne and sceptre, a Median robe with wide sleeves, a high tiara glittering with precious stones. His reign was despotic, but that despotism was benevolent after so many centuries of carnage.

Zoroastrianism was a religion far from oppressive, and highly tolerant if not uniquely so The official language was that of the majority of the inhabitants of the Fertile Crescent, Aramaean. Strict state control imposed a disciplined existence on all his subjects for the king's greater profit. An administrative hierarchy assigned his exact place to each of its members, from the youths of noble birth trained at court for public service to the highest of the nobility, the "equals" and "kinsmen" of the king. Such was the system that imposed on everyone the necessary duty of being a unit in a giant mechanism.

The empire was divided into provinces—between twenty-three and thirty—each under a satrap, often a member of the royal house, practically a king in the country under his charge, having even the right to declare war, but who was kept under control by a multitude of detailed precautions. Assisting the satrap, and keeping careful watch on him, were a secretary-chancellor and a general, who could only be replaced by the central power, and all three were, besides, under the control of supreme inspectors, "the eyes and ears of the king." Splendid roads crossed the immense territory with postal relays, forts at all strategic points, and regular couriers; the three hundred and fifty leagues that divided Susa and Sardis could be travelled in ten days. Everywhere there were garrisons ready to go into action. But there were also everywhere collectors of taxes who were responsible for raising 120,000 measures of corn in Egypt, 364 thoroughbred horses in Cilicia, 180,000 sheep and 400 mules from Media, and for diverting the equivalent of a million francs in gold into the imperial funds! In imitation of the kings of Lydia, the Persian sovereign had had money struck, "darics" on which he was represented bending a bow: they were current everywhere.

We are bound to admire that pacific labour. The East under Darius I enjoyed a time of prosperity. Agriculture was improved, trees were planted, canals dug, hunting reserves were enclosed. And we know from his correspondence that the king was watchful, above all, to prevent the abuse of power, and that he was attentive to all appeals to his justice.

It was in the reign of Darius I (522–485) that this empire reached its apogee. But already the germs of decay were at work. It is not good for nations to become accustomed to avoiding all risk, all initiative. The Persian state was not inhuman like that of the fierce Assyrian tyranny, but it was so in another way, in that it reduced the human individual to a mere cog in a machine. All power, beyond all question, was vested in the king. What would happen if that king were mediocre? The great adventure of the Median wars, in which on two occasions formidable monarchs were defeated by a few thousand resolute men, was to reveal two truths of history: that the strictest state discipline is of no avail on the battlefield, against the force of a free people fighting for its rights; and that great empires born of war, committed to a policy of continued expansion, vacillate dangerously when they can no longer expand. In 490, at Marathon, and in 480, at Salamis, Athens arrested the advance of the Persian colossus. A hundred and fifty years later, invading the soil of Asia, Alexander, the Greek leader, was to challenge the already weakened descendant of the great Cyrus, the good Darius II, and, at Granicus, the empire of the King of Kings was to fall.

NEHEMIAH AND THE WALLS

For two centuries, then, from the return from exile until the victories of Alexander, Palestine was under Persian domination. A district within a satrapy, she had a governor nominated at Susa, chosen from among the Jewish people according to a system still

practised today in European protectorates. But she had also a true
national leader, who was recognized as the real authority among
the people, the High Priest (this title was always employed from
this time on). He it was who represented the Jewish community
before the state authorities; the elders of the people, the priestly
aristocracy, gradually built up around him a senate that was later
to become the *sanhedrin.* However little may be known of the
events of this period, we have the impression that Israel was not
unhappy under these remote despots, but that, nevertheless, troubles not infrequently arose between them. The chosen people,
unable to forget their ancient greatness, were not so much grateful
for the restoration of their country as bitter on account of their
lost liberty.

Two incidents demonstrate the effort of the Jewish community
to strengthen itself materially and morally, and with both are
associated two great figures—Nehemiah and Esdras.[1] It is likely
that both are authentic autobiographies.

The walls of Jerusalem remained in ruins as they were left after
the sack of 586. Were they to be left in that condition, at the
mercy of all the bandits of the desert? When Persia appeared to
be weakened after the defeats of Xerxes, some Jewish nationalists
began to think of rebuilding the fortifications of the city. Artaxerxes began his reign among troubles of the kind that regularly
accompanied the Persian successions. The work was begun. All
went well when, once again, Samarian jealousy threatened to put
an end to everything. Warned by his officials, who represented
Jerusalem to him as a city against which he must be on his guard,
Artaxerxes gave the order to stop the work. The local satrap was
over-conscientious, and, soon afterwards, the news reached the
Jewish colonies in Mesopotamia that misfortune had again descended on the holy city· "the wall of Jerusalem also is broken

---

[1] A difficult question of chronology arises here, which we will merely
indicate. According to the biblical texts, comprising the Books of Esdras
and Nehemiah, which are no doubt fragments of a large collection containing the Chronicles, it is difficult to follow the order of events in the time
of these two personages. It is admitted today that the events of Nehemiah
preceded those of Esdras. In any case the two were contemporary.

down, and the gates thereof are burned with fire" (Nehemiah r:3).

This took place in about 446. As a matter of fact, the crisis that Israel went through at that time was even more serious than was suggested by the rumour of the broken walls. There was something corrupt at work among the People of God. High Priests were making fortunes by collecting taxes for the Persian king, or by installing their relations as bankers in the precincts of the Temple. These immediate successors of fervent men like Ezekiel married foreign women. The cult itself was debased. Old, worn-out beasts were led to the altar, piety was purveyed at cut prices.

Now, at the court of the King of Kings there was a practising Jew serving as a cup-bearer. When this news reached him, Nehemiah was overwhelmed. The master observed his favourite's sadness, and asked him the cause. Taking advantage of the opportunity, Nehemiah begged to be allowed to return to Jerusalem, the place of his fathers' supulchres, with full powers to set things to rights. Artaxerxes consented. He gave to the faithful cup-bearer a document investing him with the government of Judah, orders for requisitioning building materials, and a guard of escort. Nehemiah arrived in Jerusalem in the spring of 445.

This man—who there is reason to suppose was a eunuch—gave proof of remarkable courage and energy. From the first, he took rapid action. During the night, with a few companions, he went to inspect the ruined walls. Then, at once, and with astonishing rapidity, he set the people to work. Every family, every trade guild, was assigned its place in the labour-corps. Everything proceeded with such speed that the enemy was disconcerted; by the time they had reorganized themselves, Nehemiah was on his guard; his men "with one of his hands wrought in the work, and with the other hand held a weapon." Trumpets were ready to give the alarm on the approach of the enemy. And in fifty-two days the work was completed. Jerusalem henceforth could look upon her neighbours undismayed.

And with the same energy Nehemiah built other walls than those of stone; he also built up the moral fortress that was equally threatened. He summoned to him all those who aimed at the prophetic ideal. He chose them among those of pure Israelite race, without any foreign contamination. He took measures to prevent mixed marriages, a constant source of pagan infiltrations. He drove out of the Temple the bankers who profaned it. And he even carried out a social reform, bravely attacking that old abuse of the societies of antiquity the problem of debts, compelling the rich to relax their rapacity Having thus purified his country and revised its ancient principles, Nehemiah's work was done. "Remember me, O my God, for good!" he exclaims, in the concluding words of his autobiography. He had, besides, helped to bring to the notice of the people the man whose work was to complete his own, Esdras.

ESDRAS AND THE LAW

This man was a scribe, also belonging to one of the Jewish colonies that had remained in Mesopotamia. He was very different from Nehemiah, who was given to holy and terrible violence and who did not hesitate to strike heavy blows at the enemies of Jahweh. Esdras was gentle and calm, a jurist and theologian. Throughout his long life—he died at the age of seventy-five—he was dominated by one concern—for the Law. The Torah! This was to be the moral defence, the paragon of Israel. And the Jewish tradition that reveres Esdras as the equal of the great prophets, associates his name with an essential stage in its spiritual destiny: that in which the text of the Law became for the chosen people the basis of their whole existence. It is said that he dictated, miraculously, ninety-four holy books, of which twenty-four were public, "to be read by the worthy and the unworthy," and the other seventy secret, "reserved for the wise alone." And if this story belongs to the domain of fable, history reveals to us the scribe reading the Law to the people, commenting on it with indefatigable zeal, and, together with Nehemiah, obliging all the rulers, elders, priests, and later the mass of the people, to swear solemn fidelity to the holy precepts; founding, in short, that dictatorship of the Book that was to be so characteristic of the regime of the Jewish community.

What is the real significance of this episode of the Babylonian scribe going to Jerusalem to establish there the reign of the Law? Certain critics explain it as follows: in theological circles at that time ancient texts were being edited, different versions being collected, and this new edition being read in the Holy City seems to have provoked great enthusiasm. This is a possible explanation. Pisistratus, in Athens, a century earlier, sought to acquire fame by editing Homer. We must also take into account the fact that the Aramaean vernacular rendered the old Hebrew text inaccessible to the mass of the people. Translations and commentaries were necessary. In any case, the plain fact is that, as a result of the apostleship of Esdras, the Book assumed an importance that it had not hitherto enjoyed. It has been suggested that this was the result of a subtle manoeuvre by the priestly caste, and some critics have claimed to detect, in the very editing of the Bible, the traces of priestly bias. But the matter must be looked at from a higher standpoint. At the moment when the great voices of the prophets ceased to sound in Israel, the holy text preserved their heritage and integrated their message in a definitive form, whose authority was established once and for all.

It was not only to the abstract rules of the Law that Esdras devoted himself; this learned man was also a man of action. He gave his mind to the solution of very concrete problems. For example, he went further than Nehemiah, who had for the future condemned marriages with foreigners; he anathematized even those already existing. A commission was appointed that examined such cases and ordered that foreign wives and their children should be sent away. If Nehemiah had raised walls of stone around Israel, to keep her intact, Esdras established that "barrier of the Law," in whose shelter Jewish exclusiveness was to grow.

These stern reforms produced crises. There must have been in Jerusalem, as in all human communities, the lukewarm and the cunning and those given to compromise, who found that it paid to modify in certain respects the strict application of the Law.

We have evidence of such sentiments in a serious episode, the schism of the Samaritans. Until now the bastard race, although envying Jerusalem, had felt themselves still bound to her by ties of religious fidelity. To be sure there were any number of deviations in that fidelity, but in worshipping Jahweh under the aspect of a golden calf, Samaria thought no harm, and its monotheism included a certain tolerance towards neighbouring gods. After the reform, the situation deteriorated. A group of priests of Judah, in disagreement with the tendency of the reforms of Nehemiah and Esdras, left, taking with them a copy of the Law. They arrived in Samaria, and were welcomed there. Presently, on Mount Garizim, from whose heights one can see the magnificent panorama of Hermon and the ranges of Gilead, while in the west the sea sparkles between reddish hills, a temple arose; Shechem set up in rivalry with Zion. This was the beginning of an unreasonable hatred; Ecclesiasticus was to speak of the shameful nation that dwells in Sichem, and Jesus was to shock His listeners by giving, as an example of charity, the act of a Samaritan. A few hundred of these schismatics remain to this day; they live near the site of the Sichem of antiquity, where Vespasian later constructed his "Flavia Neopolis," Nauplius.

THE BIBLE

Henceforth the Jewish community is the people of the Bible, the "guardian of promises" as St. Paul calls them; and it is from the time of Esdras that the collected texts took their final form, that under which we read them.

Josephus, the Jewish historian of the first century, claimed for his people the glory of possessing "not a multitude of works, full of contradictions," but an unique ensemble to which one can refer continually. That ensemble "which one approached with reverence" is the book of books, the book par excellence; in Greek *Biblos,* the Bible. And, by a curious circuit, this Greek word itself leads us back to the countries of the Levant, for *biblos* comes from *Byblos,* the Phoenician city of remote antiquity, the great market for papyrus. If we call our holy book the "Bible" it is because five thousand years ago a Syrian port was already selling to the world Egyptian paper!

The Old Testament, that is to say the portion that belongs to the years before the birth of Christ, was gradually built up over the course of centuries. We have followed its successive contributions; Moses made the first contribution in the form of the essential of the Law; about that central kernel were grouped the stories of historical events intimately connected with this Law, based on ancient documents. Then the Prophets added their contribution; we have seen Jeremiah compiling his oracles into a volume. Finally, other texts were to be included on account of their spiritual value, works of poets and sages like the Book of Job, or the Song of Songs, while a great current of mystical fervour over many centuries contributed the Psalms. This formation, therefore, extends over a considerable length of time, approximately a thousand years.

But here three problems present themselves. First, that of transmission. How were such ancient traditions preserved? We have seen [2] that the use of writing is attested among the Hebrews from their earliest history; Moses, Joshua, and Samuel are described as writing; in the times of the Kings a veritable chancellory existed. We must also bear in mind the role played by memory among primitive peoples.[3] We can therefore conclude that the traditions of Israel were preserved at once by oral recitation and by texts that embodied at least the most essential things. It goes without saying that these two modes of transmission explain certain errors and imprecisions in the text. Repetition from memory leaves the door open for many modifications. Hebrew writing itself, having no vowels, permits confusions. (For example, the root *dbr*, according to the vowels assigned to it, can mean: *discourse, pest, to speak, pasture,* and *sanctuary*.) And finally, in times in which there was less respect for texts than there is today, there must have been some deliberate alterations made by this or that editor.

[2] *See p. 103.*
[3] *See p. 77.*

A second question is: at what moment did that collection of traditions, which grew with the very flow of life, become fixed? This happened precisely at the period that we have reached in our history In Babylon and Alexandria as well as at Jerusalem, from the fifth to the first century B.C., great editorial work was done. The best historians of the times worked in turn on the Law, the Prophets, and on the other traditions. Ancient texts were used; sometimes, indeed, they were assembled rather clumsily, without trouble being taken to harmonize them. The essential Mosaic meaning was also transmitted, but the versions must have varied. Thus we find in the Pentateuch at least three sources; the most recent, indicated by the letter *P*, seems to have been edited in the spirit of the Priests; another is referred to as "source *J*" or *Y*, because in it God is called Jahweh; and the most ancient seems to be that in which He is called Elohim, "source *E*." This work of synthesis once completed, the text was to be much more stable and to resist much better all tendency to transformation.

Finally, the third problem: at what moment were these texts presented as sacred, binding on the people to carry out their teachings? We have seen with how much difficulty Moses succeeded in inducing respect for a few simple precepts, and how frequent, throughout history, were Israel's infidelities to his Law. The memory of the Mosaic revelation was revered; the old texts were preserved in the archives, but this did not yet constitute what the Greek word *canon* implies, a rule, a measure, a model. It is from the seventh century through the efforts of Josias, and later through the famous "discovery" that the Law began to assume this role. In the fifth century, after two centuries of work and meditation through the years of distress, Esdras imposed the holy Book on the entire nation, to be its safeguard. In the course of the centuries that followed, the "canon" was defined—that is, the collection of those books that are regarded as fundamental and inspired by God. By about 150 B.C., the list was very largely established in its main outline.

The biblical canon, as the Catholic Church defined it in 1546 at the Council of Trent, comprises forty-five books in the Old Testament. The first five constitute the Pentateuch, the five foundations of the Law: Genesis, Exodus, Leviticus, Numbers, and Deuteronomy. Then came the historical books: Joshua, Judges, Ruth, the two books of Samuel, the two of Kings, the two of Chronicles, Esdras, Nehemiah, Tobias, Judith, Esther, and the two books of Maccabees. The books of poetry and wisdom comprise Job, Psalms, Proverbs, Ecclesiastes, the Canticle of Canticles, Wisdom and Ecclesiasticus. In the fourth section are the Prophets, the four "major": Isaiah, Jeremiah (with Baruch), Ezekiel and Daniel; and the twelve minor. The Jewish canon, followed likewise by the Protestants, includes only thirty-nine books, omitting Tobit, Judith, Wisdom, Ecclesiasticus, Baruch and the second book of Maccabees; and the grouping is a little different: the Law (the Pentateuch only), the Prophets (including Joshua, Judges, Samuel and Kings, considered as earlier Prophets), and finally the other writings.

But these differences leave intact an agreement on the essential fact that the Bible is an "inspired book." What is meant by that? "Inspiration," Pope Leo XIII wrote in the encyclical *Providentissimus Deus*, "is a supernatural impulse by which the Holy Spirit has inspired and directed the sacred authors, and assisted them in their writing, so that they should preserve accurately, and wish to report faithfully, and express with an infallible verity all that God directs them to write, and that only." This wise and penetrating definition—"an impulse"—allots to human intelligence, human wish, and to divine power their due places in the work. It certainly corresponds to the conception of the orthodox Jews, for whom, as St. Paul said, "all the Scripture is divinely inspired."

It is clearly beyond our subject to ask in what measure divine inspiration corresponds with historical exactitude. If the critic, who sees the Bible as a historical document, reduces the facts in the crucible of his analysis, their dogmatic verity is not thereby destroyed. The test that we read is expressly declared to be the work of God, but by the intermediary of man: this accounts for certain fabulous details, or the many different styles, which are inevitable enough. On the other hand, the pseudo-scientific theories of concordism that during the last half-century have attempted to classify the facts of the Bible like facts of modern geology, astronomy, or biology, have produced only superficial criticisms.

In order to understand the true sense and scope of the biblical text, we must take into account the men who formulated the divine word. Our modern conception of history comes from the Greeks. Thucydides is in no essential respect different in outlook from our contemporaries. But the Eastern attitude is different. The differences between past, present, and future seem less important. A prophet announcing the future because he was a prophet, was believed just as though he had spoken of actual events. The *midrasch*, or instructive apologia, makes very free with history (Tobias or Judith are examples). But that is not to say that their religious lesson is not a real one.

We must also bear in mind the progressive nature of the divine revelation in the Bible. It progresses as though God had wished to educate, little by little, the chosen people, and, through them, humanity. The conception of the Almighty and of the moral law developed continually. The centuries of Israel reveal to us a regular progress in religious history, a progressive spiritual ascent. The Bible, then, is the record of a *revelation*; it is not merely, as so many free critics claim, a sort of theological legend of Israel; its content lies in history, it is historical; but it is only fully understandable in its supernatural perspective, arising out of a mystical event, the vocation of Abraham, and proceeding towards a complete elucidation of the human mystery by the Man of whom St. Paul says, *finis enim Legis, Christus* (Romans x:4), the end of the Law, Christ. We may find dross in the Old Testament, but in the Gospels we look for it in vain.

The fundamental work of that Jewish community that we see as so obscure among the giant empires, that entitles it to imperishable glory, is that it has perpetuated and made available for all humanity the religious tradition and the religious values of which its race was the depositary. It is likely, indeed certain, that in so doing, the Jews embodied these values in rigid forms, hardened and narrowed by a dangerous exclusiveness. But suppose, for a moment, that that little community had never existed, or that it had allowed itself to be absorbed into the pagan mass; what a treasure of beauty of spirituality, of wisdom, humanity would then have lost!

FROM ATHENS TO ALEXANDRIA

This literary, historical and theological work to which the tribes of Israel devoted themselves, let us therefore consider in this perspective: it certainly appears as one of the great moments of the human spirit, even apart from its supernatural significance. And this, besides, is a better way of approaching the question of historical parallels. The fifth century B.C. is dominated by the radiant image of Athens. Victorious over the Persians, heart and soul in that maritime league of Delos that made the Aegean Sea a Hellenic lake, she was the brilliant city, "the school of Greece," as Pericles says, one of the supreme realizations of all those possibilities that human intelligence offers to man. But although she was the spot whence we received from Aeschylus, Sophocles, Euripides, Aristophanes, Socrates and Thucydides our great common heritage of their immortal works, although she was the supreme city of genius, which, on her high hill, built to the vigilant goddess of reason her marvellous wild beast's cage, the Parthenon, all this must not make us forget that at the same moment, in a little district of Judea, a text was being prepared that in richness of spirit is at least equal to those of the tragedians and the philosophers, and that Phidias and Pericles are the exact contemporaries of Nehemiah and Esdras.[4]

Moreover, dazzling as is the "Greek miracle," it cannot disguise the fact that the splendour that so enchants us is only one side of a human reality that had another, sorrowful and tragic; that the forced labour of thousands of workers in the mines of Laurium and the quarries of Pentelicus paid dearly for that beauty, that a

[4] Esdras went to Jerusalem at the time when Socrates, in Athens, drank the hemlock (399–398 B.C.).

contempt for human life was taken for granted in a "democracy" that was built up on slavery and that a religious thought of that intelligent nation—with the exception of a small spiritual elite—that mythology without either metaphysics or morality, was far inferior to the faith of Jahweh's most humble worshipper.

As a matter of fact, Athens and Jerusalem perfectly embody the two opposite poles of the human mind—that which seeks for the explanation of the world, life, and man in terms only of the intelligence and that which, for that supreme elucidation, relies only upon faith. During the fifth century these two experiences were being pursued apart and in total and mutual ignorance; a day was to arrive when they would come face to face in the drama of the Maccabees; history was to prepare for this confrontation by means of a long detour.

We know how quickly the Greek success of the fifth century went to ruin. Glorious Hellas carried in herself the seeds of death: the rivalries of cities, their insurmountable jealousy. Scarcely had they come to terms among themselves when Asia attacked them; peace was hardly made, when sterile conflicts broke out again. Athens, that represented at once a great power and a great idea, thought only of turning her victory to her own advantage. Her allies hated her; Corinth and Sparta envied her. Twenty-eight years after Salamis, a new war broke out; the most civilized race in the world was to perish in civil war. This was the Peloponnesian War (431–404), frightful, inexcusable. Athens, in the power of demagogues, threw herself into adventures of supreme folly. Complicated by internal strife between authoritarians and democrats, the conflict became barbarous. But who can understand the real significance of that drama, the progressive exhaustion of the dying Greek race, Athenians in the lists of Syracuse, Spartans in the Island of Pylos, on fruitless expeditions? After seventy years of carnage, the death of Epaminondas on the battle field of Mantinca (362) is symbolic; the best blood of Greece was poured out in vain.

Meanwhile in a distant province, towards the north, a nation had grown up, the Macedonians. With the ancient virtues that he drew from his own soil, Philip combined others that he had derived from the Greeks themselves. He learned from them the methods that he used to defeat them. The moment had arrived when unity was indispensable; the patriotism of Demosthenes was noble but archaic and obsolete. The real heir of the whole of Greece was the leader of the redoubtable phalanx, the father of the greatest conqueror that history has ever produced, Philip, father of Alexander.

And then began the amazing adventure, the most remarkable, beyond doubt, that any human being has ever achieved. A young man, endowed with all the gifts that beauty, strength, genius and intelligence can bestow, seized a whole world between his hands. Surrounded with a glory that seemed almost supernatural, he bent nations and distances, destinies and events, to his will. If any existence has ever illustrated the eternal verity that history is neither the unrolling of blind automatisms, nor the result of obscure chance, that it is made by men, and bears the mark that they imprint upon her, it is that of the youth to whom the inevitable violence was never seen as the end or the measure of an action, and whose finest victories were alike the fruit and the promise of thought.

Alexander was Greek, profoundly Greek, product of the greater Greece that he envisaged, and possessed in a greater degree than any other man the prodigious power of magnetism. A pupil of Aristotle, initiated by him into the idea of greatness, trained by him in a strict moral discipline, he achieved at once what their exclusiveness had never allowed the little city states to accomplish. United in their common wish to avenge on Asia the outrages of Darius and Xerxes, the Greeks were, through him, to sow over an immense field a grain which, but for him, would have withered on the stony ground of their hills.

When Alexander, at the age of twenty, succeeded his father (336), deep-seated causes of weakness that the Persian empire contained within itself had reached a point at which palliatives and good will were no longer effective. Under Artaxerxes II (405–358), the extreme feebleness of the throne of the Achaemenidae was made clearly apparent when Xenophon's ten thousand Greek mercenaries, who left with Cyrus the Younger to attack the King of Kings, had been able after their defeat to withdraw right across the empire, from Mesopotamia to the Aegean, without being molested—that glorious retreat described in the *Anabasis*. Alexander's contemporary was Darius III (335–330), a handsome, serious, and chivalrous man, a model son and husband, but whose high sense of royal dignity was not matched by energy.

Into that amorphous mass, Alexander penetrated like a swordblade. Thirty-five thousand men were all that he required. Having sacrificed to his model, Achilles, on the altars of Troy, the young hero marched from victory to victory; and every combat was a stage in conquest. At Granicus, Asia Minor was opened to him; at Issus, all the routes of the Fertile Crescent. Invulnerable Tyre fell after seven months. On the borders of the Nile, hailed as a liberator, he assumed the pschent of the Pharaohs, and founded, on a generous impulse, Alexandria; he had himself saluted as the son of God and master of the world by the priests of Ammon. At a single battle, Arbela, the whole of Mesopotamia fell to him. Successor of the Great King, master of the whole empire, thanks to an astonishing series of raids across mountain snows and the fires of the desert, he even went beyond its boundaries on the banks of the Indus, where furious charges of the elephants of Porus could not prevail against his calm courage.

But these military undertakings he saw only as a means. What he wanted, what he envisaged in the future, was a united world, a universe in which the Hellenic vitality, fertilizing the inert Asiatic masses, would realize something much greater than the domination of a single man, the reign of an immense human idea. "Thus," said Plutarch, "knowing himself used by the gods to be the lawgiver to all, and to reconcile humanity, he desired that all men should regard the entire world as a single fatherland." And, adding to his image the tragic shadow of an unachieved destiny, he died in the prime of his youth, at the age of thirty-two, without having known anything of life except those things by which a man becomes great (323).

This epic barely touched Jewish history. In the course of the summer of 332, on his way to Egypt, Alexander went through Canaan. He probably went by the coast route, and at Gaza he encountered some difficulties. Flavius Josephus, quoting a Jewish tradition, claims that he penetrated Judea, and that outside Jerusalem the High Priest, vested in his robes, went to meet him and hailed him as the destroyer of the Persian power whom the Prophets had foretold. The young master was most benevolent; he promised Israel the freedom of her laws, and even offered a sacrifice in the Temple of Jahweh. It is thought today that this is a fable, invented by the Jews at a later date to confer titles of respect upon their kings as having received their power from the Macedonian.

Much more important than this anecdote is historical fact. From this time, Hellenic domination succeeded the Persian empire. And in the new world, born from these great conquests, the Jewish community had to play a different role, to defend her soul against new perils.

THE HELLENIC EMPIRE

Having at first intended to maintain the imperial unity under the fiction of a regency, Alexander's generals very soon fell into savage conflict. Seventeen years after the death of the great conqueror, in 306, his state had been dismembered forever.

Antigone, in Macedonia, claimed to have the sole right to the royal title, but he dominated only the Greek peninsula where the last revolt of Athens had failed; his successors, the Antigonides, with slender resources but as national leaders of a small nation, were to be the guardians of the Greek world against the barbarians of the north, and to safeguard the development of a remarkable civilization to which belonged the victory of Samothrace and the Venus of Milo.

In Egypt, the Lagides (the Ptolemies), who pretended to the succession of the Pharaohs, concerned themselves less with glory and high politics than with commerce, money, and the pleasures procured by these, from the noblest to the basest. Established on a state system that has never been surpassed, even by the Incas, expert in diverting into their treasuries the wealth of the Nile, they were to enjoy for three centuries a luxury in which morality counted for little among philosophers and hetaerae. Living in an atmosphere of domestic assassinations, they nevertheless gave to the world the Museum of Alexandria, Pharos, the translation of the Septuagint and the Platonic tradition. Cleopatra was the fine flower of that decadent civilization, irresistible and deadly.

Finally, the descendants of Seleucus, bravest of Alexander's lieutenants, were to reign, in principle, over all the countries of Asia. In actual fact, the area under their domination quickly shrank to the Fertile Crescent, where their capitals were Seleucis in Mesopotamia and Antioch on the Orontes. They alone, of the three dynasties, had a wide political sense. One of them was even a great man—Antiochus III. But they could not prevent whole provinces from making themselves independent: Bactria, in northern Asia (now Russian Turkestan), Pontus, and Pergamos in Asia Minor. And, besides, they had the misfortune to stand in the way of the future masters of the world, the implacable Romans. Their mark, however, remains in Asia to this day, where the Syrian communities still count their years from the date when the Seleucids inaugurated their reign, in 312 B.C.

But these political divisions are of secondary importance, as are also the incessant troubles of which the Orient was the scene until the day when, thirty-one years before our era, Augustus imposed the Pax Romana. More significant than these events is the history of a society which, in many respects, is reminiscent of our own. It is no longer that of small cities, states of modest dimensions; it is a larger world, in which Europe, Asia, and Africa feel themselves to be associated, in which man's vision is enlarged, in which commerce is international, in which operates the synthesis of complex elements, of the debris of all the ruined civilizations of Nineveh, Babylon, Egypt, Lydia, and Persia; heterogeneous material that Hellenism, whose thought and language were universal, was to cement. Greek was spoken at that time from the Indus to Marseilles, from the Caucasus to the oases of the Sahara. Even in remote Bactria, that unifying influence was felt, whose range extended, beyond, as far as China. It was not an empire in the political sense, but the empire of a form of civilization, of Hellenism.

In order to understand the violent hatred that Israel opposed to the seductions of this Hellenic world, we must take into account its enormous charm. Never has any epoch, with the exception of our own, known such activity, such interchange of goods, people, and ideas. The great cities of the time rivalled our own: Alexandria, numbering a million inhabitants, was a giant agglomeration, with wide avenues, a port swarming with the ships of all nations, whose public gardens contained exhibits of wild animals, and whose museum with her library of seven hundred thousand volumes, her show cases of natural history exhibits, her observatory, her faculties and academies, was the unchallenged intellectual centre of the world. Antioch, on the Orontes, then a port, was a market that drew the caravans of the whole of Asia. Greek and Phoenician fleets brought to the roads of Pierian Seleucis and Latakia the products of the Mediterranean. Pergamos, capital of a tiny kingdom, was a brilliant centre of Greek traditions, with a gymnasium dominating, on the slope of its hill, three stages of terraces, one for children, one for older students, and the third for scholars, and whose librarians, in order to be independent of the Egyptian papyrus supply, invented the "paper of Pergamos," parchment. This developing world surrounded the rock of Israel with its feverish activity. Against all these temptations of luxury, immorality, cosmopolitanism, and also against the Platonic philosophy, the poetry of Theocritus, the mathematics of Euclid, the Jewish spirit must defend itself. Civilizations of extreme refinement and superior intelligence blend inextricably the best and the worst, those things that exalt man with those that degrade him. It is very difficult to draw the line between admissible and inadmissible elements.

This Hellenic world played a great role in history. Like our own, one feels it to have been transitional. It was punctuated with crises. Society was shaken to its foundations; social conflicts, with strikes and revolutions, are added to political conflicts. A many-sided moral drama was played out whose symptoms were superstition, love of pleasure, a falling birth rate, birth-control propaganda, an excessive domination by women, who, freed from child-bearing, assumed men's tasks and under whose influence society disintegrated. Art itself disintegrated, and if, at Pergamos in the Gigantomachia, or at Alexandria Lagidus, it still showed fine technical qualities, it too often replaced creative vigour by mere activity and striving for effect. Nevertheless that brilliant and corrupt universe, in mingling peoples and nations, prepared the way for future unification. Rome, thinking to dominate it, was in its turn to be absorbed by it, but was also to give it a political stability. And the field was then to be ready for another sowing.

RESISTANCE TO HELLENISM AND THE MACCABEES

Between this Hellenistic world and the community of Israel there was total opposition. It was a question of different conceptions of life. The same words, for a Greek and for a Jew, meant totally different things. Liberty, for the one, was that of a city, rather anarchic, in which men made their own laws and were free to worship whatever gods they chose; for the other, it was the right to obey an infinitely strict Law, the work of a single God, who had no equals. Wisdom, for the Greeks, was the science that increases knowledge through the intelligence; for a Jew, it was the veneration of faith and the fear of God. The two peoples who were at that time doing the most for the future of humanity mistrusted each other profoundly. There is not a trace of Greek influence in the Bible, except in the very late Book of Wisdom, and the ignorance of the ancient historians concerning the Jews is astonishing. Manetho, the Egyptian, only repeats fables like that according to which the Israelites were descended from a lepers' colony.[5] Polyhistor even thought that Moses was a woman;

[5] *See* above, p. 87.

Eupolis described Abraham as a giant who built Babylon, and Posidonius declared that the Holy of Holies housed an ass! Nevertheless, however much the Jewish community kept itself apart from Hellenic influences, it felt itself besieged. The ancient cities of the Philistines were Greek; Greek also was neighbouring Syria; and in Jerusalem itself a whole party advocated learning in the school of those who, at that time, represented the flower of civilization.

After the death of Alexander, Palestine fell to Ptolemy, and remained under Egyptian domination for twenty-three years. Under the first three Lagidae, she was prosperous and peaceful as of old. The only political incidents were those caused by the conflict between a family of priests, the Oniades, who were the religious sovereigns, and a feudal family, the Tobiades, who, from their fief in Ammon (the ruins of their fortresses have been discovered) constantly interfered in the affairs of the Holy City. Under Ptolemy IV (221–203) things went less well; passionately interested in theology, this Greek Pharaoh took it into his head to unite his various states by means of religion. In an audacious synthesis, combining features of the cults of Osiris and Dionysus, the Lagidae had created a Greco-Egyptian god, Serapis, whose legend of death and resurrection had considerable beauty. Under the pretext that another name for Dionysus, Sabazios, closely resembled the word Sabaoth, Ptolemy IV tried to identify the god also with Jahweh. But he encountered a vigorous resistance and seems not to have insisted.

It was not by force, to be sure, that Hellenism threatened to penetrate into Judah, but rather by all kinds of infiltrations. If the people as a whole, with their sure instinct, remained rebellious against the contamination of Greek thought, the rich and powerful, even among the priestly class, felt its prestige. Meanwhile the Hellenism of the Lagidae was nonchalant enough; but when Palestine passed under the Seleucid domination, the problem was to arise in a more urgent form.

In 223 a sovereign of the highest order came to the throne of Syria, Antiochus III. His energy earned for him the epithet of

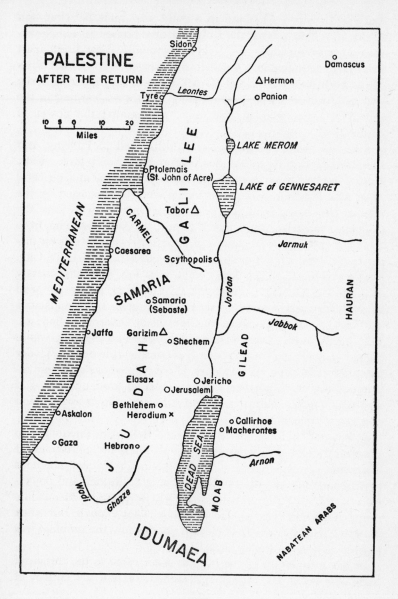

PALESTINE
AFTER THE RETURN

Miles
10 5 0   10   20

MEDITERRANEAN

Sidon

Leontes

Damascus

△Hermon
○Panion

Tyre○

LAKE MEROM

GALILEE

Ptolemais
(St. John of Acre)

LAKE of GENNESARET

CARMEL

Tabor △

○Caesarea

Scythopolis○

Jarmuk

Jordan

SAMARIA

○Samaria
(Sebaste)

HAURAN

○Jaffa

Garizim△

Jabbok

○Shechem

GILEAD

J U D A H

Elasa×

○Jericho

○Jerusalem

Bethlehem○

○Callirhoe
○Macherontes

○Askalon

Herodium ×

DEAD SEA

○Gaza

Hebron○

Arnon

MOAB

Wadi

Ghazze

IDUMAEA

NABATEAN ARABS

337

Great which the antique world bestowed upon him, and, if he
had the misfortune to find himself in the way of Rome, he did
what he could to avert disaster. Under him history was again to
take on the grandeur of the times of Alexander. Resuming the old
policy of all the masters of the Fertile Crescent, he decided to
take Palestine from Egypt. In 200, near the sources of the Jordan,
in a place named Panion because the mountains there were hollowed in grots and niches sacred to the god Pan, he destroyed
the army of the Lagidae. Ten years later he was to suffer the
terrible defeat of Magnesia (190), in which Rome wrested from
him the whole of Asia Minor. But Palestine remained under the
rule of his descendants.

Under the domination of that ambitious dynasty, Greek propaganda at Jerusalem took on new force. Using every possible
means to insinuate themselves, the Greeks presently had a Greco-
phile party working for them—or rather, two parties, one of
Egyptian tendency, the other Syrian, but both admiring the
methods, the thought, and the elegance of the Greeks. The orthodox Jews attacked the Hellenized Jews with ferocious violence:
they violated the Law! They ignored circumcision! They encouraged athletic sports in which nudities were revealed! Already,
under Seleucus IV (187–175), a great outrage had occurred.
Seleucus, incited by the clan of the Tobiades, sent his minister
Heliodorus to pillage the treasures of the Temple of Jerusalem;
but three angels of God, one of them on horseback, rushed on
him and prevented him from committing the sacrilege. Delacroix
has illustrated this angelic dressing-down magnificently on one
of his great murals at Saint-Sulpice.

But things were much worse in the times of Antiochus IV
(175–163). This extravagant prince—whose proud majesty earned
for him, by a popular cynicism, a change in this royal title of
Epiphanes ("the god manifest") to the more accurate one of
the Epimanus ("the crazy")—on the pretext of unifying his states
ran his head right into the Palestinian hornets' nest. Pious Jews
saw him as "the devourer, the unjust one in purple, the cruel, the
rejector of the light." Coming to Jerusalem to settle one of those

innumerable quarrels with the Hellenized Jews, he sacked the
High Priest Onias III and put in his place his brother Jesus, who
immediately adopted the name of Jason Antiochenes, rebaptized
Jerusalem with the name of Antioch, and began building a
gymnasium. This only led to a violent crisis which demonstrated to Antiochus IV the necessity for employing other
methods.

But at that moment a sharp misfortune overtook him. Just
when he was preparing to seize Egypt, the Romans, his friends
the Romans, forbade him bluntly to advance any farther. The
scene has been preserved. Popilius Lenas, the envoy of the Senate,
brought the message to Epiphanes to clear out of the land of the
Nile. "Let me think," said the king. With the end of his stick the
Roman traced a circle round Greece. "Think there!" Antiochus IV
gave way. But he came to the conclusion that he must, henceforth, at all costs, reinforce his states with a solid Greek armature
with which to resist the Roman menace. He arrived in Jerusalem
still angry and violated the Temple. Entering the Holy of Holies,
he took all the treasures that it contained, candelabra, the altar of
gold. Pious Jews were killed in thousands. A military governor
was installed in Zion. The walls, the beloved walls built by
Nehemiah, were destroyed. A Greek citadel, the Akra, was built
beside the Temple and occupied by a strong garrison. And finally,
on December 15, 167, in the Temple itself was erected that
"abomination of desolation" prophesied by Daniel, the idol of
Olympian Zeus, doubtless by order of Antiochus himself. Henceforth, it was forbidden to read the Torah, to keep the Sabbath,
or to circumcise infants. It was a typical religious persecution,
the first known to history. But against this impious tyranny the
people of Israel arose.

At first there were individual acts of resistance. Some, rather
than violate the Law, rediscovered for themselves the old patriarchal ideal, and fled into the wilderness with their flocks and
herds; these were called "the pious," the *Hassidim*. Others carried heroism further. Israel told with admiration of the martyrdom
of the saintly old man, Eleazar, who being compelled, by having

his mouth forced open, to eat pork forbidden by the Law, spat it out, and not even pretending to swallow it, chose death rather than set a bad example (2 Maccabees VI). And also of the sacrifice of a mother whose seven sons, rather than violate the Law, allowed themselves to be tortured, from the eldest to the youngest, a mere child; the mother herself encouraged them to endure death rather than to apostasize (2 Macc. VIII).

Then, suddenly, these passive and sporadic acts of resistance were united into a redoubtable movement. Men arose, an entire family, the Maccabees, in whom the anti-Hellenist party found their leaders. Antiochus IV was occupied on the Euphrates where the terrible Parthians, Scythians from the shores of the Caspian (the same whose shooting of arrows over their shoulders as they retreated has remained proverbial), were causing him grave anxiety, and was not able to oppose the insurrection with all his forces. And it was the last glorious page in the history of Israel.

We see, as in the days of David, courage blossoming and heroism becoming contagious. In Judas Maccabeus, "Judas the hammer," who gave his name to the family, the Hebrew epic was to find one of its most splendid figures; the enthusiastic Jews chanted his praise. "In his acts he was like a lion, and like a lion's whelp roaring for his prey" (1 Maccabees III:4). One of his brothers, Eleazar Avaran, "gained an immortal name" by a far from commonplace feat of arms. Seeing, in the mêlée, the elephant in royal harness, he slipped under the animal, thrust his sword into it, and died, crushed by the fallen beast.

The revolt began with that of the father, Mattathias, who, in the town of Modin, killed an apostate Jew and the Greek official who tried to make him sacrifice to idols. About him gathered many of the faithful, and the pursuit of the Greeks and the renegades began. From the year 166, under the command of the third son of Mattathias, Judas Maccabeus, this became an implacable guerrilla warfare. The Greek governor was overcome and put to death; four relief expeditions were treated in the same way. Within two years the Syrian sovereign had been compelled to change his policy. He restored to the Jews their reli-

the temple of Mount Gari
as the champion of the Je
with silver stolen from the
to follow the observances
powerful king, as of Solon
poral glory lacked those s
things are ephemeral and

Such was the situation i
rivalries of petty princes,
sion of the activity of ants
them. To an embassy sen
against the Seleucids, Rome
in her own good time. This
community was to know its
the thick eyebrows, with th
Mediterranean world was, y

ROME AND T

The events that gave the
tion of the Mediterranean
description. I shall only poin
which have some special sigr

When the Jews returned
principality under the Etrus
aristocratic revolution of 509
their yoke—an event that wa
by the rape of the virtuous L
rebuilding of the Temple of J
was to enter the scene with as
during the fifth century, the R
extended its domination over t
Volscians, and the Etruscans
Tables (450) was promulgate
Nehemiah was rebuilding the
the Etruscan citadel of Veii (40

gious liberty. Judas returned to Jerusalem, purified the Temple by throwing down the idolatrous altar, reformed the priesthood, and reassembled the holy books dispersed during the persecution (164).

This success did not satisfy the enthusiasts of Judas' bands. The Akra still defied the Holy City. They must fight on for political independence! The situation became yet more intense. Judas Maccabeus continued to win victories, but he in his turn met with defeats; on the first occasion, he was saved only by the death of Antiochus Epiphanes and the ensuing dissensions. Taking up arms again, he won a last triumph over Nicanor, the leader of elephants, but at last being surrounded on the hills near Jerusalem with few troops, he fought a last battle for honour, in which he was killed.

Two of the hero's brothers succeeded him in the command, Jonathan and Simon. The people, marvelling at the achievements of this family, no longer even considered having a leader who was not a member of it. Obviously a strong Hellenophile party still remained, but the bulk of the nation formed a solid bloc behind the Maccabees. Jonathan and Simon were in turn elected as high priests. The war against the Greeks continued; but the new leaders were not merely soldiers, like Judas. They also employed diplomacy. We even find them appealing to Rome, whose shadow at that time was beginning to stretch over the East, although in fact they were given only verbal sympathy. But chiefly they took advantage, very cleverly, of the incessant quarrels that divided the Seleucid kingdom. Appointed military governor of Judea, and in actual fact an almost independent prince, Jonathan even captured Jaffa in 147, thus gaining access to the sea. After his death, as a result of one of those intrigues in which the court of Antioch was so expert, Simon actually achieved the goal of their long struggle. In 142 King Demetrius II abandoned the citadel of Akra, which was destroyed, and recognized Jewish independence. The community once more became an independent state. The first Jewish coins were struck. And Simon, who held the title of "hereditary High Priest," the acknowledged leader of

Judea, if he did
respect for the p
was, in effect, a ne
as the Asmoneans,
as we call the firs
mythical Merovius

It seemed, inde
been triumphantly
to deviate from hei
the return from ex
freedom could be
the only kind that n
on the temporal pl
posed themselves to
to combat. They b
elegant princes, in
deviation, the enteri
result was a reversal
of the resistance, be
suspect leaders; they
it was at this time th
separatists. And it wa
rigid form of religion,
of exigency rather tha
erned the chosen peop

This new problem
Hyrcanus (134–104) s
a traitor (134–104). H
to the Seleucid Antioc
tage of his death to
embarked upon a polic
was larger than David';
Idumea to Scythopolis.
policy of systematic Ju
on several occasions to
Galilee, and, paying off

of the religious reform of Esdras. In a second stage, Rome conquered Italy: she escaped, with difficulty, sporadic threats from the Gauls, and the tenacious incursions of the Samnites from the mountains. She conquered the great Greek city of Tarentum and drove back into the Epirus mountains the brigand Pyrrhus, in spite of his elephants and his courage. Then, caught up in the momentum of her own conquests, she gradually began to transform the Mediterranean into a Roman lake, "Mare nostrum," and to be drawn into a policy of intervention in the East.

These events of history, which we have been too much inclined to consider in isolation, were in fact continually acting and reacting upon each other. The diplomatic map was as complicated in the third century B.C. as in our own day. Already in the fifth century, Carthage, allied with the Persians, had suffered a decline when the Greek victories had weakened Darius and Xerxes. If, in the fourth, Rome was able to pursue her patient effort, this was in a great part owing to the fact that the whole world had been drawn towards the East by Alexander. In the third, when the war to the death broke out in which Rome ruined Carthage, the conflict caused innumerable repercussions in the East. During the first Punic War (264–241), it was the Spartan Xanthippus who commanded the Carthaginian army. During the second (218–201) the Antigonid Philip V of Macedonia helped Hannibal in his struggle against Rome, and when the Punic leader, defeated, was compelled to leave his country, it was with the Hellenic kings that he sought exile. Antiochus III was inspired by him to make war against the menacing power, and it was Prusias, King of Bithynia, who by his betrayal constrained the great Carthaginian to poison himself.

Thus Rome found herself involved in the affairs of the East almost involuntarily. And could she, besides, resist the mirages of those gorgeous lands, those civilizations of such supreme intelligence? She threw herself against them with her accustomed vigour. Four compaigns sufficed to gain her a foothold. At Cynoscephalae (197), the strategy of the legion overcame the celebrated tactics of the phalanx; the Macedonian was defeated. At Magnesia, near Smyrna (190), the Seleucid Antiochus III, was conquered in his turn. Rallying under Perses, Macedonia made a bid for freedom; her defeat at Pydna (168) possessed Paulus-Emilius of the whole kingdom, which he dismembered; of Greece, which became his vassal; and even, by a repercussion, of a great part of the kingdom of Pergamos. This was the time when, in Judea, the great anti-Greek rising of the Maccabees was beginning. Finally, in 146, the last Hellenic effort failed. The East was to pass inexorably into the control of the sons of *Lua Mater*, while Carthage, for a third time defeated, suffered under the pitiless blows of Scipio Aemilianus (146).

In 100 B.C., then, the Eastern Empire was in the hands of Rome. What remained of the heirs of Alexander, the remnants of the Seleucids and the Ptolemies, were compelled to gravitate in her orbit. This fact in relation to Sacred History is of considerable importance. Not, indeed, because of the changes of master that were to take place in Judea—the Persians, the Lagides, the Seleucids and the Romans—the name of the distant overlord changed, but the tutelage remained onerous; but the contact of the Romans with the East was to have great consequences. Even from the point of view of Rome it was undoubtedly calamitous: in turning towards the east without having Romanized the west, whose new countries of Africa, Gaul, and Spain would have brought prosperity to her peasants, Rome, dazzled by these brilliant civilizations, was to succumb to their malefic charm. Her antique virtues were not to be proof against them. "They took ample revenge by giving us their vices!" says Juvenal. Her hard-working race was to be exhausted, ruined by the competition of eastern corn and unlimited slavery. Rome was to perish, finally, of the oriental virus. But, by imposing on the whole Mediterranean and on Asia in particular the unity of her discipline, she was without knowing it to prepare a magnificent field of expansion for those spiritual themes that the little nation of Israel pursued in pious meditation. This world, extended by Rome, was to be the future Christendom.

RELIGIOUS UNREST IN THE ROMAN WORLD

In one sphere in particular this influence of the East on Rome was to be felt profoundly: that of the soul and of the spirit. A realistic and practical nation, the Romans lacked that curiosity in secret matters and eternal verities, that interior awareness, without which nothing great is ever accomplished. They derived their interest in science, the germ of their art, their first literature, and to an even greater degree a religious stirring that was to have far-reaching results in them, from Greece and the East.

Neither in Greece nor in Rome could the official religion satisfy the aspirations of a pious soul. Athenian polytheism, with its subtle fables and civic deities could only appeal to the intelligence and reinforce patriotism. The Roman cult, cold and prosaic, subordinate to politics, attempted nothing more than to assure to the State the divine protection by a strict performance of rites. The multitudes of temples, the proliferation of monuments at crossroads, deceived nobody. In Greece atheism had its beginnings in the sixth century. Xenophon and Colophon did not hesitate to say that they did not believe in gods who behaved no better than men; in the fifth century the sophists openly declared their scepticism, and, in spite of violent reactions of official dogmatism like that which, in 395, caused Socrates to drink the hemlock, religious disintegration was in full swing. In Rome resistance lasted a little longer, but by the end of the Punic wars its influence was weakening. Claudius Pulcher threw the sacred hens into the water because they had not given him any notice of his misfortune. Marcellus, so as to be sure of not seeing any omens, drew, half in joke, the curtains of his litter. And we have the word of Juvenal that even "the children no longer believe that there are *manes*, or a subterranean kingdom, black frogs in the Styx, and a pilot armed with a boat-hook who, in a single boat, ferries over all those thousands of human souls!"

But nothing would be more wrong than to suppose that such a religion appeared adequate to everyone. There were certainly souls who sought with spiritual anguish for some solution to the

great problems. Part of that spiritual aspiration went into philosophy. Plato had led his disciples to the supreme Good, Aristotle
had discovered the *primum mobile*, but neither postulated a god
in the religious sense of the term. When, in the fourth century,
Pyrrhus counselled the abstention from all desire and all will,
when Epicurus taught submission to the laws of Nature, when
the Stoics exalted the tension of the soul that makes man equal
to the gods, these were rather means of eluding the religious
problem than of solving it. It was by the influence of the eastern
mysteries that, transformed and thrown into confusion, the old
paganism was to be imbued with fervour.

The eastern world had always been a melting-pot for all kinds
of cults. Rome, coming into contact with this world, found,
adopted and spread these throughout the immense empire conquered by her legions. These oriental religions appealed to men
in a number of ways, to the worst and to the best in them.
The disturbing attraction of the mysteries, the splendour of
ceremonies, the ecstasies that originate from extreme inner tension, or, more prosaically, from the consumption of intoxicating
potations, the equivocal ceremonies of a sensual character, all
were to be found there; but they were also to see the growing
hope of a humane god that man could love, teaching an ethic of
penitence, capable of restoring to the soul its lost purity, and
affirming besides the hope of a life beyond death, and eternal
beatitude.

This invasion of oriental cults began as soon as Rome had
established relations with the East. It took many forms. Sometimes there were attempts to revitalize the old gods of the Roman
Pantheon by infusions of oriental mysticism. Bacchus, becoming
Dionysus, borrowed from the strange Thracian god his legends
and his promises; but that irruption of mystery was so violent that
it produced terrible scandals like those which, in the second
century, were implied by the word "bacchanalia," the sense in
which we still use it. The old Roman Hercules was transformed
under the influence of Pythagorean thought, and took on, more
or less, the role of a liberator and savior. Later the exotic gods

themselves took their places side by side with the old divinities of the Capitol.

In 204, under the threat of Hannibal, the black goddess of Phrygia, henceforth called Cybele, was brought to Rome; her arrival was even the occasion, it is said, of a miracle, for the vessel that brought her statue ran aground and it was enough for a vestal to tie her girdle to the prow to float it again. We see spreading and becoming extremely popular this violent form of mysticism that sometimes demanded of its adepts the sacrifice of their virility, those colleges of priests (or *galles*) whose Phrygian cap still remains the symbol of liberation, those ecstatic ceremonies in which, amid shouts, the beautiful Attis, under the appearance of a tree, was invoked to be reborn to eternal life. Then there were the Egyptian divinities, that "Serapis" invented by the Ptolemies, who had borrowed from the ancient myth of Osiris the image of the just god dying to overcome death and associating men with his immortality, and Isis, his wife, who in spite of many contradictions was seen as the moral initiator venerated in stern asceticism, and who promised healing; "Serapeion" and "Temples of Isis" arose all over the Roman world, and everywhere in autumn was celebrated "the discovery of Osiris," with funereal chants and supplications. Later Asia sent new waves: the Phoenician Astarte, the Syrian Aphrodite, "the lady of the wild beasts" of Anatolia, the mermaid goddess of Ascalon, the dying and resurrected god Adonis of Byblos. And all those Baals who had, as we know, so long assailed the faith of Israel, stampeded across the Roman world, and with them the worst elements of mass religiosity, superstition, immorality, fetishism, and bloodthirsty ritual, together with the highest that the metaphysical aspiration of man could attain. Of these Asiatic gods, the one whose career was most spectacular was Mithra, the young heroic divinity of the Persians, whom the great mixing of peoples wrought by Alexander had first begun to popularize, and whose cult the Roman army propagated with fervour. His personal drama was that of a victim, his metaphysic and morality were of a high order, products of the Iranian doctrine, and his

was studied, where children went to school, where legal causes were pleaded and decisions made; built in the style of whatever country they might be living in, the synagogue included all sorts of annexes which, from meeting halls to piscina, made it the centre of Jewish life. The elected chief was its *rabbi,* and under him were various priests, a lector of the Torah, a translator, and a sacristan.

These communities regarded themselves as integral parts of the nation of Judah. The Roman state even acquiesced in their theoretical allegiance to the ruler of Palestine. Jerusalem remained the object of unanimous veneration, and thousands of pilgrims—even millions, according to Josephus—went there for the feast of the Pasch. From the age of twenty, every Jew, wherever he might live, paid an annual tribute to the Temple: holy money," carried there by a mission in solemn state and protected by the Roman law. It was in the direction of distant Zion that they turned when they prayed.

Two of these Jewish colonies have a particular importance in history—those of Alexandria and of Rome. When the great Macedonian founded his city, he attracted Jews to it by guaranteeing to them the same rights as to Greeks. They prospered there, and contributed very greatly to the rapid success of the great commercial centre. They became more or less Hellenized, and it was in that Alexandrian community that the first translation of the Bible into a foreign language was made. According to an apocryphal tradition Ptolemy II (285–247), in order to enrich his library, asked the High Priest of Jerusalem to send him scholars to carry out, in his country, the translation of the sacred book. Shut up in their cells, the seventy-two old men had completed in seventy-two days seventy-two translations that miraculously coincided! From which, by rounding the number, the name of the Septuagint is given to this version. This is only a story: the work took a hundred and fifty years, and is very unequal, varying with the translator. But, in allowing non-Jews access to the sacred text, the Septuagint must have had a profound effect and contributed very greatly to spreading the thought of Israel.

In Rome also, where they established themselves later, the Jews were soon numerous. Cicero speaks of their cohesion, their communal sense and their spirit of enterprise, but deplores the fact that so much good Roman money was exported by them to Jerusalem. Caesar protected them so well that on his death they mourned him with wailing; and Augustus was well disposed towards them. Later they were to have their catacombs where they buried their dead; on the walls Jewish symbols can still be seen, seven-branched candelabra, cupboards for the Torah. Situated at the very heart of Roman power, they spread with it, and we find synagogues everywhere that the legions went.

Between these Jewish groups and the populations that sheltered them, what were the relations? Were they influential? The Hellenization or Romanization of the Israelites seems to have been negligible. Externally, the Jews adapted themselves; they spoke Greek or Latin and lived in the style of Alexandria or of Rome. But this was purely superficial. Apostasy was rare; we hear of very few Judaeo-Greek marriages. On the intellectual plane the same phenomenon is repeated that we have noted every time the Jewish spirit has come into contact with a nation of high civilization; they take over elements in order to revitalize the old national basis. Thus Philo, a Jew of Alexandria in the first century, was to be responsible for an extremely intelligent fusion between the religion of his people and the metaphysic of the *Logos* that he took from the Platonic tradition.

If they underwent little influence from the communities among whom they lived, how, on the other hand, did these people regard the Jews? There is no simple answer to this question; for in the centuries before Christ we see Jewish proselytism developing and at the same time a growing and characteristic anti-Semitism. This race that lived apart, whose distrust of idolators was only too obvious, whose spiritual aspirations were incomprehensible to the immense majority of Greeks and Romans, were quickly to provoke irritation, distrust and hate. At Alexandria a veritable breeding-ground of anti-Semitism was created which spread throughout the world the worst rumours, the most perfidious calumnies against the people of Jahweh. Men like Apion, the Alexandrian grammarian who opposed Josephus, and Apollonius of Rhodes, are real professionals in the anti-Jewish war. And even serious people were under grave misapprehensions about Israel. Cicero speaks of their "barbarous superstition"; Tacitus covers them with inept abuses; Juvenal accuses them of the worst kind of sectarianism. One can imagine, then, what must have been the attitude of the masses! Worship a single God, without images? What an idea! Their real god was an ass, if not a pig. The proof? Their dislike of eating the flesh of that animal. They ate unleavened bread? That was because originally the bread was stolen! Very disturbing too were those secret gatherings. Perhaps they performed unspeakable rites! Perhaps they sacrificed human victims to their horrible god! Everything about them disquieted the Roman bourgeoisie; their smell, which Marcus Aurelius mentions; their perpetual activity, their astuteness, and it is easy to imagine the obscene jokes that must have been made at the expense of the "skinned ones" on the subject of circumcision.[7]

Nevertheless, the spiritual themes of which Israel was the depository began to spread. In that Greco-Roman world haunted by religious unrest there were soon found numbers of men and women who discovered the greatness of the religion of the spirit, that pure aspiration towards an invisible God in whom goodness and mercy were perfectly realized. Jewish propaganda became intense. While at Jerusalem Samaritans were repulsed, in the *diaspora* conversions were sought after. Personal proselytism of individuals was encouraged. A whole literature, designed to make the Jewish ideal known to the pagans, grew up. Josephus, the historian, provides one example, and it is also in these circumstances that, during the first century B.C. was written the Book of Wisdom which the Catholic Church includes in its canon. The synagogues became centres of meeting for all those who were

[7] A Christian reading the ignominies of Roman anti-Semitism must remember that similar calumnies were later to be the cause of the persecutions.

thrown into confusion by the profound social, moral, and spiritual crisis into which the world was plunged. In spite of the public measures which were presently taken to oppose this propaganda, it was felt in all circles, from patricians to the most humble, and above all, among women in great numbers. Had not Isaiah said that Israel would be raised above all the nations, and that the peoples would turn to her, as the servant of Jahwah?

But this very proselytism bore the marks of Jewish exclusiveness. In order to enter the community, all its precepts must be accepted, the strict legalism and circumcision. This often discouraged converts. Thus there came to be a class of semi-converts: "fearers of God," who, without becoming part of the Jewish community, had adopted the faith; the centurion of the Gospel was no doubt one such. This proselytism was noble, and certainly introduced elements of grandeur into pagan society; but it was not yet the magnificent universalism of the Apostles, for whom there was neither Greek nor Jew, circumcised nor uncircumcised.

Thus, at the very moment when Christ was born, this Jewish *diaspora* had prepared for His followers the groups among which their influence was to be spread: by the word, in these scattered communities, and also by sacrifice and martyrdom, for anti-Semitism was to prepare the way for persecutions.

HEROD

Meanwhile Rome, in her eastern advance, arrived on the borders of Judea. In 63 B.C., the legionaries thronged the Promised Land.

The descendants of the Maccabees had steadily deteriorated. All those qualities that had distinguished their ancestors had been betrayed; the national ideal had given place to shady political combinations, and the religious ideal to depravity and the most abominable kinds of violence. The conflict between the Sadducees and the Pharisees became civil war. A son of John Hyrcanus, Alexander Jannaeus (103–76), took the title of king, while keeping also that of High Priest; the pharisaic revolt against him was so violent that he renounced it again in terror; and the image that we preserve of this cruel despot is that of his banqueting among his concubines, while before him on the terrace of the palace six hundred crosses stood, each bearing its victim, while under the eyes of these dying men executioners massacred their wives and their children. Under Queen Alexandra Salome (76–67) the Pharisees triumphed in their turn, and they took advantage of this to establish their influence solidly in the *Sanhedrin*, the assembly of the elders that formed the council of the High Priest, and to introduce into it those doctors of the Law, so infatuated with minutiae, who were to be the worst enemies of Jesus.

From 67 B.C. decadence increased apace. The two sons of Alexandra, Hyrcanus II and Aristobulus II, waged a deadly civil war. Antipater the Idumean, governor of his province on behalf of Israel, intervened in the conflict; even the Arabs of distant Petra appeared before Zion where Aristobulus was besieged. The moment struck that Rome had waited for in order to intervene. Rome did not long delay.

Pompey was in the East. The man whose career was to end so disastrously, cut short by Caesar's sword, was at that time at the height of his glory. He had just concluded his campaign against pirates who had been destroying ships and threatening Rome with famine. Mithridates, king of Pont, the last Hellenist prince in whom some of Alexander's courage remained, had been pursued into the Crimea and driven to commit suicide; unable to poison himself, because he had long accustomed his body to all kinds of poisons, he ordered a soldier to eviscerate him. Syria was a Roman province. When the fratricidal kinglets of Jerusalem asked for help, Pompey took his opportunity.

Taking refuge in the Temple, the partisans of Aristobulus made a desperate resistance. The legionaries dug trenches, installed catapults, and erected mobile towers. In the autumn of 63 B.C. the son of the old dictator Sulla was the first to enter by the breach. A massacre followed which was less the work of the Romans than of the hatred between Sadducees and Pharisees. Priests were killed at the altar, and Pompey, sword in hand, moved and intensely curious, drew aside the curtain of the Holy of Holies, went into the sanctuary—and found it empty.

From this time, Palestine was under direct control from Rome. Undoubtedly this was greatly to her advantage; roads, aqueducts, baths, and fine buildings were the happy results of the *pax romana*. But the Jews were very soon less sensible of that material prosperity than anxious on account of the danger to their faith that resulted from the influence of a powerful master. A state of latent resistance, of defiance, grew up; these sentiments increased when Rome elected Herod of Edom as the governor of Israel.

This indeed was the revenge, after many centuries, of Esau over Jacob; a sign, perhaps, that the time was approaching when Israel's mission should have been completed. The Idumean was a man of the desert, a semi-barbarian, of half Jewish and half Arab blood, a ruler that Israel was bound, on principle, to detest. But from father to son, these barbarians had proved themselves excellent diplomats. They understood where the future lay, and Rome had no better friends than they were. Antipater, who governed under the rule of the feeble Hyrcanus II, pursued the Roman policy with zeal; he accompanied Caesar when, in 47 B.C., the conqueror of Gaul passed through Judea on the way to Egypt —and Cleopatra—having been given by him the title of a Roman citizen, with an appreciable remission of taxes. He aided the legionaries in suppressing a little national rising in Israel. His son Herod followed the same policy, even when in the great crisis of the Parthian invasion that threatened so terribly Rome in the East, everything seemed to combine against the sons of Lua, and the last of the Asmonean kings only kept his crown by the grace of the Caucasians. The desired result was obtained. In 40, Mark Antony and Octavius, who were still associated, feasted their friend Herod in Rome and recognized him as king. He was to reign for thirty-six years (until 4 B.C.)

The personality of the magnificent, the abominable Herod, is a strange one. Capable of the most base acts, sometimes making a gesture of nobility, and having the sense of greatness, he remains in fact the barbarian who retains only the appearances, sees only the trappings of a civilization that, with him, is only skin deep. But what intelligence! What diplomacy! At the time of his reign Rome was undergoing grave crises; Caesar fell at the stroke of Cassius, who succeeded him; Mark Antony, enemy of the assassins, governed next, soon to be supplanted by Octavius. Herod, whose whole policy was orientated on Rome, was somehow able to remain on good terms with all these successive men of ambition. Such a *tour de force* compels admiration. When the victor Octavius, after Actium, approached the eastern provinces, the reversal of allegiance that Herod, Antony's old friend, carried off was worthy of a Talleyrand or a Frederick II. If this tyrant had been no more than a diplomat and a military leader who, in spite of limited means, extended his kingdom into Transjordania and towards the north, we might have admired him. But he had many other traits, and on too many accounts arouses our horror.

One ruling passion dominated his life: the passion for the throne, the frantic desire to rule, and as the very methods that he employed to maintain his power would have made any rebellion legitimate, more and more uneasy and suspicious, he ended by living in a state of mad mistrust, in the atmosphere of Macbeth. He struck first at his own family—among his ten wives. Mariamne, the favourite, through whom he was able to claim the inheritance of the Maccabees, because she was an Asmonian, on the merest suspicion was put to death, serene and contemptuous; her children followed her to the tomb, and even when the despot had only a few days to live, he still had enough strength to execute another son. Augustus was right, when, in a Greek pun, he exclaimed, "Better Herod's pig than his son!" (*uios*—son, *us*—pig), because, as a servant of Jahweh, Herod did not eat the forbidden food!

Needless to say the same methods were freely used against anyone who was suspected of the fault of harbouring opposition. There were several attempted revolts during his reign; on each occasion blood flowed. Could it have been otherwise? Who can say? The Jews hated him; had they not been terrorized, they would certainly have rebelled. Such is the vicious circle of despotism. Herod could scarcely have followed any other maxim than that of *oderint dum metuant*. When Cleopatra subjected Mark Antony to her yoke, Herod, with great acumen, gave the Roman advice both brief and judicious: "Kill her!" And he, when Cleopatra attempted to seduce him, slipped away, and even toyed, perhaps, with the idea of ridding himself, his friends, and history, of the fascinating Egyptian.

Nevertheless, the murderous barbarian had more attractive sides to his character. On one occasion at least he was humane. When famine reigned in Palestine (25 B.C.), he excused all taxes, and sold all the golden objects in his palace in order to buy corn from Egypt to give to the people. His character was far from simple. After he had executed his beloved Mariamne, the image of her death haunted him forever after; he cried her name aloud in the palace that her death had made empty, and he ordered that she should always be spoken of as though she were still alive. Perhaps this murderer had a heart.

His love of fine architecture, for town-planning, was no less astonishing. He had a sense of construction, whether for utility or for splendour. The fortresses that he built or rebuilt were intelligently placed; Macheronti, for example, above the Dead Sea, and Herodium, near Bethlehem, which was to be his tomb. Samaria, rebuilt by him as Sebaste, still contains impressive ruins, and the port of Cesarea, which he made larger than the Pireus, remains a lovely shell. Jerusalem was transfigured under his domination. A theatre, an amphitheatre, and a hippodrome were built; games, with wild beasts and gladiators, amused the crowds. A fortress-palace to which, in the days of Antony, he had given the name of Antonia, dominated the holy city with its three great towers and its gleaming marble. And most important of all—this was to be, he thought, the definitive monument of his greatness— he set in hand the rebuilding of the Temple.

The building that had been erected in the days of the Persians was, decidedly, too insignificant. Did not Solomon owe his glory to the prestige of his Temple? The Idumean assembled the people, explained his projects, and allayed their suspicions. Ten

thousand labourers were set to work, and in less than ten years
the work was finished. The sanctuary was as like as possible to
that of Solomon, but the outer buildings far surpassed his, for
by means of supporting walls and embankments, twice the area
was obtained. Three stages, successively rising, surrounded the
sanctuary; the court of the gentiles, surrounded with porticoes;
that of the women, into which Iraelite women had the right to
enter; and finally the court of priests, where stood the altar and
the Sea of Brass. In that construction nothing was lacking that
the splendours of Hellenistic art could provide. The 162 columns
of the central, so-called "royal," portico, were so large that it took
three men to encircle one of them. The ornamentation and the
sacred vessels were all made of costly materials. A golden vine
adorned the sanctuary and the seven-branched candlestick—the
same that we see on Titus' triumphal arch—was of rarest workmanship.

The Jews, however, were not won over by these attentions and
largesses. The Idumean with blood on his hands remained hateful to them. They were indignant because he took part financially
in the building of pagan temples at Actium, Sidon, Damascus,
even in Athens! The Pharisees accused him, secretly, of wishing
to be made divine, and when he placed an immense golden eagle
on the door of the Temple, indignation was widespread; that
bird, was it not a disguised symbol of the king himself? The
whole community instinctively resisted Romanization as it had
the Hellenism of Epiphanus. About to fall into ruin, Judah, rigid,
petrified in the love of her Law, resisted everything that might
taint it.

The end of Herod, if Josephus is to be believed, was of a piece
with his life in its horror and frightful picturesqueness. A disease
of the intestines drove him beside himself; an incessant burning
and an insatiable hunger tortured him; pus and worms exuded
from his body. He was carried to the springs of Calirrhoë, in the
hope that the warm sulphurous waters might afford him relief;
in the first bath he fainted. Half mad, haunted by the phantoms
of his victims that he had no longer the strength to banish from

his nights, he died in a terrible frenzy, commanding that after his death all the most important Jews in the kingdom should be put to death, so that at least tears might be shed on his tomb.

Such was the last of the great figures of Israel; he has been called "the Great," and he merits, in a sense, that title, for his intelligence, his courage, his ability in turning to the best advantage mediocre opportunities. But it is significant that the final image of him is one of horror, a hideous caricature of Solomon. After him his kingdom was divided between his sons and quickly descended into the total ruin that was sealed, in the year 70 of our era, by the suppression of the last Jewish nationalist revolt, the taking of Jerusalem by Titus, and its destruction.[8]

For, when Herod died amid universal hate, a child already lived somewhere in Egypt who had been compelled to flee from Palestine in order to escape the threats of the despot, and that child bore a message of love. Jesus was in the world,[9] and the Gospel has psychological truth in its favor when it shows us Herod massacring the new-born infants to rid himself of an eventual rival. The events of this reign and those that follow have neither human nor historical interest; their importance lies elsewhere. When the Jews, in a supreme effort, were struggling to throw off the Roman yoke, the choice had already been made that condemned their message as sterile, and the world no longer looked towards the hill where the Temple was ruined, but to that other close to it—only a shallow ditch divides them—where, between two malefactors like a common criminal, the Messiah of Israel died on the Cross.

[8] The present volume stops with the birth of Christ. We refer readers to the second volume of this sacred history, *Jesus and His Times*, for all that concerns the succession of Herod.

[9] It is known that the dating of the birth of Jesus in the year 1 of our era (754 after the foundation of Rome) is an error. It was at least four years later than the actual date. Jesus was probably born in about the sixth year before our era.

III

THE INNER LIFE OF THE COMMUNITY

S O THE EMPIRES moved towards their destinies; but always more or less menaced by these giant powers, more or less agitated by internal crises, the little Jewish community meanwhile pursued her silent meditation and deepened her knowledge of God. It is this inner life, much more than the events of history, that must concern us. The moral and spiritual world that grew up during these five centuries was the world in which Christ was to move; the oppositions that He was to encounter have their roots in the Jewish speculations of that epoch; the men that we see on His road, those Pharisees and Sadducees that the Gospel speaks of, were what those centuries of waiting had made them.

The Bible allows us to penetrate deeply into that Jewish mind of these latter days. If, as we have seen, the historical books are very incomplete, we have, on the other hand, magnificent evidence in all those moral and spiritual writings dating from the period after the Exile. Certain of these purport to be based upon ancient themes and are even placed under the patronage of an illustrious author; but all express the sentiments of the community and of its dispersed annexes. The Book of Job, Ecclesiastes, Ecclesiasticus and Wisdom are the chief of these, together with a great number of Psalms. We also find much evidence in the so-called works called *Apocryphal* that the Church has not retained in its canon. These fall into three categories—those "on the fringe of history," like the Book of Jubilees, the Martyrdom of Isaiah, the Letter of Aristes, the third book of *Esdras,* and the third of Maccabees; moral and poetic works, like the Psalms of Solomon, the Odes of Solomon, the Prayer of Manasseh, the fourth

book of Maccabees; and lastly a class that the Jewish mind during the last period particularly relished—the apocalyptic, like
the Book of Enoch, the Ascension of Moses, the Testament of the
Twelve Patriarchs, the Sibylline Books, the fourth of Esdras, and
that Apocalypse of Baruch which La Fontaine so greatly admired.
Secular sources are of considerable importance; in particular that
Flavius Josephus who was contemporary with Christ, and whose
Jewish Antiquities, in spite of his exaggerations, performs for us
the service of filling in, as regards facts, the gaps in the Bible,
and whose *Answer to Apion* enlightens us on the psychology of
his compatriots and their adversaries. Finally, the enormous mass
of rabbinical literature gives rise to many strange comparisons.
As is well known there were two great classes of these: the *Targums* or commentated translations of the Scriptures, and the
Talmuds that are their interpretation; the two most famous talmudic collections are those of Jerusalem and of Babylon, both
of which are divided into *Michna,* or doctrical exposition, and
Gemara, or written reports of doctrinal discussions.

We cannot but admire the gravity and the fervour with which
these Jews of the last five centuries discussed ineffable matters.
That enormous literary output allows us to participate in a continual dialogue in which the great questions are raised and solutions hammered out, in which the only end pursued is patently
the search for truth and certitude.

The most varying temperaments are revealed, and theses challenge one another. When, after the return from Babylon, an
unknown poetic genius took the traditional theme of Job as the
argument of the book that bears that name, he put the whole
anguish of a soul into his work. That the just should be unfortunate, that the wicked should remain unpunished, these two
great bewildering problems of the human mind form the central
theme of his meditation. The long discussion between the righteous old man and his friends expresses the flux and reflux of all
the emotions that throng in upon us when we meditate upon these
mysteries. Can a just God permit in this world that He governs
the horrors of which we are witnesses? Job's response was to be

the most sublime that it is possible to imagine: absolute, disin-
terested confidence in the Master; the recompense that God finally
accords him is a concession to the Jewish spirit of that time,
which had to have that compensation on earth; but in truth, Job
appears to us as already recompensed by his holiness in itself, by
his love of God.

Baffled by this problem of retribution that is capable only of
a metaphysical solution in relation to the eternal life, the Jewish
mind was conscious of the whole extent of the problem. The Book
of Job speaks of it with passion, that of Ecclesiastes with lucid
pessimism: "There is one event to the righteous and to the
wicked; to the good and to the clean, and to the unclean; to him
that sacrificeth and to him that sacrificeth not: . . . This is an
evil among all things" (IX). In life, "all is vanity": wisdom and
morality, prosperity and pleasure. What then remains? In this un-
satisfactory existence, never to lose sight of the mind of God,
nor cease to refer all things to Him!

"Whoso feareth the Lord, it shall go well with him at the last,
and he shall find favour in the day of his death." Having thus
affirmed the same confidence and proclaimed that "to fear the
Lord is the beginning of wisdom," Jesus son of Sirach, who wrote
in the second century a little before the time of the Maccabees,
ceased to ask insoluble questions and wrote the concrete, practical book that we call Ecclesiasticus, a series of precepts for the
guidance of life, advocating reasonableness, mistrust of women,
the weighing of words, and sobriety of diet, for "none can escape
God."

Still later, in the first century B.C., in Alexandria, an unknown
philosopher who placed his book under the patronage of Solomon was to glorify Wisdom, that divine manifestation that not
only imposes upon man the prudence and moderation of Ecclesiasticus, but directs his whole destiny in this world and the next.
Commenting on the history of Israel in the light of this idea, he
presents its supernatural sense and resolves the problem of justice
on earth by daring to say that just souls are in the hands of God
and that if their lot on earth seems unhappy, that they are, never-

theless, at peace and certain of a dazzling recompense, whereas the impious are punished.

These differences of opinion are in themselves evidence of the richness of that spiritual universe. Its domain extends far beyond that primitive religion of Jahweh to which monotheism and a cut and dried morality seemed all-sufficient; once again—and this is the fourth stage—the history of Israel brings to us an enlargement of religious consciousness. There has been much discussion as to whether that enlargement ought not to be attributed to foreign influences, and non-Christian criticism claims to discern in the Judaism of the last centuries actual exotic importations: the figure of Satan, the concepts of Paradise and Gehennah are Persian, the doctrine of retribution in another life, Greek or Egyptian. That, being a corridor open to many influences, Palestine borrowed from other nations images of concepts seems even less open to question at this period than in the most remote times. But these acquisitions remain always within the spiritual trend which all the earlier history of the chosen people had followed. Nothing occurs to break its logical development. Such influences as were felt were most often reacted against; reacting against such pressures was one of the chief ways in which the Jewish mind was led to define specific points of its doctrine. No one would say that Catholicism borrowed elements from Luther or Calvin; but for all that, the decisions of the Council of Trent are the consequences of the Reform because it obliged the Church to define more closely her own beliefs.

Far more than foreign influences, what counts in the development of Jewish spirituality is its own powerful work upon its own ideas that was carried out in the course of these five centuries. Grand in her discoveries, if fallacious in what she refused, the spirit of the community posed for itself a number of fundamental questions. On the replies that she made depended her future attitude, and her destiny was definitely decided by them. We may judge severely the solutions that she found for her problems; we cannot underrate the greatness and the richness of the meditation in which these were set forth.

THE ORGANIZED COMMUNITY

It goes without saying that these solutions were not formulated all at once, in the abstract, and that they were the result of a long evolution, the slowly ripened fruits of a national history. It is absolutely impossible to say at what precise moment in these five centuries a particular moral attitude, a particular metaphysical conception, prevailed. In the same way, the organization of the community was not the consequence of a decision made in a single final gesture but of a perfecting of institutions according to their inherent logic and under stress of events. We must envisage the Jewish community in the flow of its life if we are to understand its religion fully.

What was Judah after the exile? What was it to remain to the end? Neither a church in the Christian sense nor a State, for it was no longer sovereign and was under foreign control. But, within successive great empires, it succeeded in preserving so much liberty as was indispensable for its faith. "Judaism," Father Lagrange has rightly said, "was a State constituted by the close alliance of race and religion, of civil and religious legislation in a single law, by the exercise of a single authority in the hands of the High Priest." This regime, the only one of its kind known in any time or place, was bound to lead to a political theocratism, and to a clericalism which, in actual fact, expanded in it. To the degree that the community, in the midst of threats, crystallized about the principle that safeguarded it, those on whom such a regime rested took on more and more importance.

These were, essentially, the Priests and the Scribes, the men of the cult, and the men of the Law.

The priestly class was limited. After the centralization of religion that commenced with David and which immediately after the Return became definitely fixed, only the descendants of Aaron were priests.[1] In order to serve Jahweh, a man must prove his membership in the sacred family, and whoever could not do so was precluded. Divided into twenty-four classes, the priests

[1] *See* above, p. 122.

were responsible for the Temple functions in turn, each for a week. As for the Levites, they were confined to the part of servants; they provided guards for the building and the treasuries, the porters whose duty it was to forbid entry to the uncircumcised, to the *goyim,* and the innumerable musicians who during ceremonies played on the harp, the trombone, or the tympanon.

There was, then, a whole little religious world whose life was connected with the Temple and centred around it. The minute, monotonous ritual, the daily public sacrifices, the great annual feasts, occupied from twenty to twenty-five thousand men. Their functions were paid for out of the enormous funds contributed by the whole of Judaism. Needless to say, their number, their functions and the sums of money that they handled made their influence considerable.

At their head, the High Priest alone had full powers; after the exile, he was in fact the chief servant of Jahweh, and there was no longer a king to dispute that title with him. He alone could penetrate into the Holy of Holies; he alone could perform the most solemn sacrifices; given the constitution of the community, based on religion, he was, at the same time the political chief, and it was by a very logical evolution that the Asmoneans, the High Priests, made themselves kings.

This clerical theocratism was so deeply rooted that the foreign masters of Israel themselves took it into account; when, from the time of Herod onwards, the High Priests, in principle appointed for life, were frequently proclaimed and deposed by the Romans, the latter did not, even so, dare to select them otherwise than from the very few families—descended, of course, from Aaron— who traditionally provided them. In the time of Christ, Annas, deposed by Rome, was replaced by Caiaphas, his own nephew. The priestly caste was in a sense the core of Judah, and its domination seems not to have been questioned.

Actually, things were not so simple. In proportion as the Law, the Torah, came to take in Israel the leading place that we have seen it to occupy, those who knew it most thoroughly grew in power. These were the *Scribes,* those Doctors of the Law whose beginnings we have seen in Babylon. They taught the text, but they also commented on it; they extended its application; they applied its affirmations with rigour. By them and by their teaching —and they all had, more or less, schools about them to which the faithful came in crowds—the Law, its reading and meditation was made the foundation of religious life; that is to say, they worked according to methods very different from those of the priests.

Their real field of action was the *synagogue,* the centre of meeting that appeared very modestly in the Exile and which afterwards took on enormous importance in Judea no less than in the *diaspora.* In principle, this institution was not in opposition to the Temple. But there was no ritual in the synagogues; they merely read the Law and the Prophets. If the priestly caste was attached to ritual, the scribes had certainly an intellectually and spiritually higher conception of religion. But both these tendencies inclined in the same direction: both attached too much importance to the letter; when it was a question of assuring the exactitude of a ceremony or that of a commentary on the Torah, both these clans were supercilious to a degree; and the danger was, as we shall see, the misconception of the very spirit of religion.

These two tendencies, at the time of the birth of Jesus, were uneasily united in the supreme counsel of the community, the *Sanhedrin.* That assembly which claimed to originate in the counsel that surrounded Moses, was, in fact, gradually evolved over the course of the five last centuries. It had at first been purely sacerdotal and aristocratic, and it still included the princes of the priesthood spoken of in the Gospel, representatives of the priestly families. But in the course of the battle of the last centuries, Doctors of the Law had made their way into it, and these, by reason of their juridical and religious knowledge, had gained great influence. The traditional number of the *Sanhedrin* was seventy members; presided over by the High Priest, it was at once a supreme court of law, a theological arena, and a counsel of government. Nothing could better illustrate the character of the

Jewish community than its composition, in which religion and
politics were combined.

This conception of the community was in itself the cause of an
inextricable mingling of political and religious antagonisms. Two
Greeks or two Romans might argue over the idea of liberty or the
rights of the electorate without any mention being made of
Athena or Jupiter; in Jerusalem all discussions were tinged with
theology, which did not, however, tend to make them any less
acrimonious!

Two large parties thus defined, at once religious and political,
held the stage, and their controversies bulk large in the history of
the last centuries before Christ: the Sadducees and the Pharisees;
but, in addition, other sects and groups multiplied; the picture
of sects in Judea is as complex as that of the parliamentary parties
under the French Third Republic!

The Sadducees were the self-satisfied and complacent lovers of
security. Good Jews, needless to say, very strict in applying the
Law, especially when it was to their own advantage. Patriots,
to be sure, but patriots so discreet as to be suspicious of any too
vigorous resistance to the ruling powers, and who, in the Seleucids or the Romans were ready to see the guarantors of the
established order, the bulwark of solid fortunes. So much for
their politics. In religious matters, as these aristocrats were in
close touch with the priesthood they favoured ritual and tradition.
The Law, and nothing but the Law! Late dogmatic developments
were to them suspect, and, still worse, speculations bearing on
the after life and the resurrection of the dead; the disillusioned
wisdom of Ecclesiastes and the pragmatism of many of the
Proverbs were in harmony with their way of thinking. There was
little fire, little enthusiasm among these self-satisfied ones; their
influence on the people was not strong; and as regards the reign
of the Messiah, it would not be true to say that they did not
believe in it, but it was certainly not one of their major pre-
occupations.

It is more difficult to judge the Pharisees impartially; Jesus' maledictions of these "hypocrites," these "whited sepulchres," still ring in our ears (Matthew xxiii:27). But, apart from the fact that such a condemnation may not have been universal, it is important to understand how the devout Jews had come to deserve it. Devout they certainly were; they were descended from the *Hassidim* [2] who had been the soul of the national resistance to the forces of dissolution; when the Asmoneans had allowed themselves to deviate, many among them had adopted an attitude of hostile reserve and had drawn apart; they were called the "Separate," *Pharisees*, and, on several occasions, they had been persecuted, for their influence on the people was great. States have never liked opponents of this kind; but, without that scorn and that righteous indignation might not a great part of the message of Israel have been absorbed into Hellenism?

In politics the Pharisees were nationalists and opposed to foreigners. They did not advocate resistance by force, but, as one of them said to a Roman governor, "they would rather die than break the Law." Their spiritual attitude is entirely explained by their devotion to the Law; not, as with the Sadducees, to the strict sense of the letter; but incessantly commented on, reflected upon and enriched with precepts; a Law that proliferated in endless observances. That Torah they knew better than anyone; they claimed also to practise it better. All the Scribes were not Pharisees, but all the Pharisees were scribes. From the Law and the Prophets they had drawn logical conclusions touching individual retribution, life after death, and the resurrection of the body. Thus, in many respects, that small party—perhaps six thousand—recruited from all classes of society, whose spiritual leaders were a butcher, a vendor of sauces, a shepherd, and a blacksmith, a true community whose members called one another "brother," played in Judaism the role of a ferment. By their grave demeanour, their incessant prayers, they introduced an element of dignity into society; undoubtedly a great deal of the spiritual evolution of the last phase was due to them.

[2] *See* above, p. 342.

What was their fundamental doctrine? After having been extremely severe with them, history and criticism, both Catholic and independent—Renan has nothing to say for them!—is tending to moderate its judgment a little. In the time of Christ, did not a certain Rabbi Hillel, a Pharisee, teach precepts like this: "All the law is—not to do to another what you would not have him do to you. . . . My soul is a guest on earth, and I have towards it the duties of charity. . . . Do not judge another before you have been in his place. . . My humility is my exultation. . . . In the places where you find no men, be a man!" This doctrine is noble and very close to that of Christ. But Pharisaism carried within itself its own dangers, as a certain wise Pharisee well knew when he distinguished among his brethren seven classes, only one of which could claim to be perfect! Religion as they conceived it was in danger of becoming purely intellectual and speculative, and tended to replace faith by science. What was more serious, it allotted to observances such importance that the spiritual element was in danger of being stifled. To judge by the multiplicity of their rites and formulae, one would think that religion consisted only of paying tithes and repeating stereotyped verses. Finally— and this above all was what Christ saw in them—human nature is such that apparent rigours serve as masks for comfortable complacencies and the Tartufe is hard to distinguish from the truly devout.

Various tendencies arose as offshoots of this strong party of Pharisees, which illustrated various religious and political nuances. The most curious was the party of the *Zealots*, Pharisees in doctrine but in politics much more violent. "They have," wrote Josephus, "a fanatical love of liberty and acknowledge no master but God." As revolutionaries, they opposed the established powers; as terrorists, they did not hesitate to kill without ado those whom they considered traitors to the Jewish cause; they were also called bandits or *assassins*. The Roman police had endless difficulties with them; and they were among those responsible for the disastrous revolts in which Israel was to perish.

The *Essenes*, on the other hand, distinguished themselves on the religious plane. Forming a veritable order, with superiors, a novitiate, vows—including those of celibacy—sharing their goods in common, wearing symbolic white clothing, they surpassed the Pharisees themselves in rigour, keeping the Sabbath in a total fashion, multiplying their ablutions. Their doctrines were considerably different from those of official Judaism; for them the soul, existing before the body, passed for the time being through the body before returning to the state in which it originally existed. They practised no animal sacrifice, the inner religion being the one thing necessary. These Essene communities were scattered throughout several townships; the chief of these was at Engadi, not far from the Dead Sea.

Without going so far as to practise these austerities, certain Jews placed themselves, temporarily or definitely, in an analogous moral situation while remaining in society; these were the *nazirs* or *nazarenes* who continued a very old institution.[3] They consecrated themselves to God—for periods of at least a month—making three vows: not to cut their hair, not to drink wine, and not to approach women. It seems that this practice of temporary vows was very widespread.

GOD

Such, then, is the framework in which Jewish thought was elaborated. There is a certain greatness in having made these purely religious problems the central interest of life. In the apocryphal text known as the Letter of Aristes, a king of Egypt exclaims, speaking of the Jews, "They derive everything from God, as the starting point of their discussions; whence their superiority." Not only of their conversation, but of their very life. Judah, during the last centuries, became fully aware of its submission to God; the community lived under His eye, and one could hear, literally, the cries of love that ascended towards the Most High: "Not unto us, O Lord, not unto us, but unto thy name give glory, for thy mercy, and for thy truth's sake" (Psalm cxv);

[3] Like Samson in the time of the Judges, *See* p. 159.

or again, "Whom have I in heaven but thee? and there is none upon earth that I desire beside thee. My flesh and my heart faileth: but God is the strength of my heart, and my portion for ever" (Psalm LXXIII).

This God was conceived as the ancestors had always conceived Him: one, needless to say. But monotheism had become so much a matter of course that it was never questioned. During earlier epochs, the "stiff-necked people" had returned often to their idols as to their vomit. But that was all over. The prayer of morning and evening, the *Schema* (Hear!) carried its full weight. "Hear, O Israel! Jahweh our God is the one God." And the rabbinical tradition tells with pride of one of its saints, Aqiba, martyred for his faith, his flesh pierced with iron spikes, repeating with love that prayer, dwelling on the last word, "One"—*Echad*—as his soul left his body.

At the same time as this unicity, all the divine attributes were more clearly conceived. That immensity of power, of majesty, of intelligence and of love that a Christian understands when he speaks the name of God, the Jewish community understood with a profound intuition. He was the Great, the Most High, the Lord of Glory, the Master of Heaven. He was conceived as pure spirit, for "with him there is neither eating nor drinking"; as eternal, the "liver of centuries"; as the holiness of all holiness, who commands man to be holy "because I am holy"! The world was erected by him out of nothing, by His will, and the Jewish liturgy develops profoundly that idea in affirming that Creation is continuous. "He renews daily, in his mercy, the work of creation." He is also the God of pity and mercy. His justice, which is perfect, does not do violence to His forbearance; for the rest, as the Psalm *De Profundis* says, if He were to take note of human iniquities, who should stand before him? All this theodicy whose stages we have followed from Abraham, through Moses, and the Prophets, had almost arrived at its complete revelation.

Nevertheless, in this respect we can already discern one of the grave contradictions of Israel in its latest phase. This God was seen as immensely high in relation to the infinite smallness of man. From the third century, they did not even dare to pronounce his name. In prayers, the priests themselves did not utter it. Even the substitute, *Adonai*, was generally unspoken. This necessitated the use of allusions and synonyms; among these were "the Place," "the Heaven," "the Presence," "the Glory," "the Majesty." It was as if God was in some way becoming more remote from man; no one any longer lived with Him in that kind of sublime familiarity that we saw, long before, in Abraham.

This attitude of mind had its good and its bad side. The deep reverence of God is a virtue. And, in regarding Him as very remote from man, the Jewish mind was led to a consideration of certain aspects of the divine power which, accessible to the intelligence or intervening more directly, were henceforth to be more generally studied and venerated. The *Word* of God, His utterance, from which all things proceed, which is at the source of the Creation; the *Holy Spirit*, which, without yet being conceived as a divine Person, was already recognized as the power that expressed itself through the Prophets, and as that which sanctified souls: here we have a considerable spiritual deepening. Man felt the need to break down a little the gulf that separated him from God.

For a similar reason Jewish thought, at that time, gave great attention to angels. These had always been present even in the most ancient history of Israel, from the days of the Patriarchs: from this time, these pure spirits, these innumerable higher creatures, partaking of the attributes of God, were to play a much larger part in religion. It is not necessary here to have recourse to a theory of direct foreign influence; this conception was in the earlier tradition of Israel. A great difference, besides, is to be noted between the Jewish conception and that of the Persians; in the Iranian doctrine, the angels and demons are emanations of the two opposite principles, the god of good, and the god of evil; in Jewish thought, the evil angels proceed, as do the good, from the one unique God, and have merely fallen into the abyss by their own fault, by virtue of their liberty as created beings.

Thus, then, on the one hand we find in the doctrine of an in-

finitely powerful and distant God progress in the understanding
of ineffable things. But on the other hand we discern certain warp-
ings and deflections which were to have serious consequences in
the future. Surely this God was decidedly too remote! The religion of the Patriarchs showed us Jahweh visiting His friends: that
of the Prophets gave us His teaching directly through the mouths
of certain men; now God expressed Himself only under the fixed,
rigid forms of the Law. In reading the rabbinical texts, we have
the impression that some minds suffered as a result of that distance, and that there were pious souls who felt the need of
drawing nearer to God in a more intimate union. But this aspiration had not yet triumphed by reason of some obscure kind of
excessive fear, and in the formula *Adonai Schebaschaïm* there
was not that infinity of love that a Christian puts into its English
equivalent, "Our Father which art in Heaven."

This remote God scarcely ever intervened within the human
soul. Prayers, rites, and observances were all-sufficient; grace
occupied a much smaller place. The poignant sense of our inner
wretchedness had not yet found its consolation in a God mysteriously near, who suffers with every human being. More an-
thropocentric than theocentric, this Jewish doctrine in the last
instance leaves man isolated, in the chaos of a distress against
which God Himself can do nothing.

And lastly, the gravest deviation of all, the one which finally
led Jewish thought into one of its impasses: since this God, so
high, so remote, had expressed Himself for, and by, Israel, was
He not the God of Israel in the most egoistic sense of the term?
The arrogance of little Judah, proud of her mission, quickly led
her to draw the logical conclusion, and to enclose the people
of the Promise in a sterile exclusivism.

THE CHOSEN PEOPLE

Here we come to one of the spiritual problems before which
Israel, cornered, flinched and drew back like a horse before an
obstacle. No one questioned the fact that they were the chosen
people. The most humble of their sons was filled with that certi-

tude. It was clear from all that history had taught; it had been proclaimed by the Prophets: during the exile, it was this certitude that had safeguarded the nation and enabled her to revive.

This election, of which there were so many signs, whence did it proceed? It was not easy to say. Was it a spontaneous grace of God? Many believed so, and some went so far as to say that the creation of the world had, as its supreme end, this election. Others thought that it was Israel's merits that had earned this destiny for her. "God said to the Israelites: Since you make me the unique object of love in the world, I will do the same towards you, and make you the unique object of my love in the world" (Talmudic text). At all events, the notion of the *Covenant* held a fundamental place in doctrine and in faith. On this doctrine depended the reciprocal affection between God and His people; whoever opposed Israel, opposed God Himself; the chosen people must be holy, because God is holy; and the very faults of the predestined nation, effaced by God, served His providential intentions.

This doctrine has had in history such extensive implications and led Israel to such a high ideal, that one cannot but admire it. Even in its most temporal aspect, it is moving. The love that devoted the sons of the Promise to the Promised Land, that exaltation of Palestine in the hyperbole of poetic vision, the despairing tenderness of the rabbinical prayer, "If I forget thee, O Jerusalem . . .," all that complex of sentiments that proceeds directly from the certitude of election, touches us with the sense of true greatness. And many centuries after the ruin of the Temple, if it can be said of the Jews scattered throughout the world that too many of them have allowed to perish, together with their faith, the very root of their spiritual life, one regards with respect, on the other hand, those handfuls of heroic Zionist bands who, determined to find a country once more, a foothold and a reality, find it inconceivable that that land should be any other than that Palestine, infertile, small, and exposed to threats, which was the place where the divine Promise manifested itself for all time.

But that fanatical attachment on the part of the chosen people brought with it almost inevitably a deviation that is all too human: those in whom self-regard and self-esteem is strong are very likely to end by despising others. "Love your neighbour," said Leviticus, but who is that neighbour? Is a pagan the neighbour of the faithful? On the reply given to that question was to depend a whole spiritual attitude: universalism or particularism—which was to triumph?

In actual fact, the two currents were both present in Judaism. There were those who attached great importance to the promise made to Abraham: "In thee shall all the families of the earth be blessed." Had not Jeremiah foreseen a time when all nations should know God? Isaiah, an era of universal peace? Malachi, well being for all the earth? Had not Jonah been astonished to hear God Himself pardon the infidel nations? And had not the Psalms sung of infinite mercy extended to all creatures, of love whose wings shelter all the sons of men? So the wisest of the Jews accepted and recognized that universalism implicit in the worship of Jahweh. No, wrote a doctor of the Law, "foreigners are not idolaters when they follow the practice of their fathers," and another said that the virtuous *goy*, even though he does not know the Law, is "like a high priest." According to this view, the chosen people are the messengers of the word; it is they who, invested by God with that mission, transmit it at the price of so many sufferings; a day would come when the just would receive it for the benefit of a reconciled world.

But one has the impression that this stream of universalism was, in Judah, much less powerful than the other, that of a particularism that was soon to become intransigent. We must not be too ready to cast the first stone: we must remember the extremely difficult conditions under which that tiny nation had had to safeguard its existence. Those complexes of inferiority and resentment, of which contemporary psychology speaks, do not at all predispose man to feel himself the brother of humanity. But if Israel has excuses, we must not forget at the same time that this nation was always full of pride and that contempt for foreigners had always been deeply rooted in them.

When the Talmud gave as its answer to this fundamental question: "No, a pagan is not your neighbour!" it certainly expressed the opinion of the majority of Jews. In the Letter of Aristes we find this revealing assertion: "The Legislator has closed us within the iron walls of the Law in order that, pure in body and soul, we should not mix with any other nation." Even at the time when, in the *diaspora*, the Jews practised proselytism for their ideas, it was not out of universalist sentiment, but, on the contrary, in a particularist spirit, by the imposition of circumcision, annexing new members for Judaism. All that in the Israelite tradition had an immense force of expansion, was paralysed by that sombre and intransigent exclusivism. These races, "accursed from the beginning," soiled with all the vices, scarcely human, deserved no consideration. The logical conclusion is the celebrated phrase of a rightly placed rabbi whom the Talmud, however, has not codified: "The best of the *goyim*—kill him!" A day was approaching when the great voice of the Sermon on the Mount was to reply to these sterile feuds: "I say unto you, Love your enemies!" (Matthew v:44); and later, St. Paul was to abolish even the external signs, those obstacles to the conversion of Gentiles. When these days came, the Jews, irritated, were to refuse to recognize their most authentic doctrine in that cry of universal love: they crucified Jesus, and fell upon Paul intending to kill him (Acts xxii:21). "The Jews," says Tacitus, "bear towards all men a hostile hatred." This was the first of the crossroads at which Judaism and Christianity were to separate.

THE LAW

To that conception of divine election the cult of the Law was closely wedded. St. Paul, listing the privileges of Israel, mentions "the Law, and the service of God, and the promises" (Romans ix:4), and that "unto them were committed the oracles of God" (iii:2). Why had Jahweh given His law to the progeny of Abraham and Jacob? Was it on account of their merits? because only that nation was capable of comprehending it? That was discussed, but what was never discussed was the imperious duty imposed upon Israel of maintaining the precious trust, of studying and putting into practise its teachings.

Historically, this is a perfectly just conception. The Law certainly constituted the invulnerable armour that prevented Israel from yielding. It protected her against herself and against others. This the nation instinctively realized when on the return from the Exile they wished the religious duties to be formulated in definitive terms. The Law was the constitution of the politico-religious community of the last centuries. It was the body of doctrine in which Jewish thought was summarized. As a time when the religions of antiquity demanded so little intelligence, it was a body of knowledge and at the same time a code and a dogmatic treatise.

The very word Law, which, following the Septuagint, Josephus and St. Paul both employed as the translation of "Torah" (*nomos* in Greek), does not render the richness of the Hebrew term. *Law*, in English, suggests something rigid and formalistic. The Torah, a religious teaching revealed by God, was as much a light for the spirit as a rule for the will. And it is difficult to convey the note of love that a pious Jew must have put into those two syllables. For the Torah was the object of a veritable cult; it was regarded almost as a living being, "the eldest daughter of God"; it was practically identified with Wisdom; the entire universe was obedient to its intentions, and Creation was made by it and for it. Jewish accounts show us Jahweh Himself as obeying its precepts and spending the Sabbath day in reading the commandments. This strange piety towards a text is expressed, for example, in Psalm LXIX in which, in twenty-two strophes each of which begins with a letter of the alphabet, the tenacious application of a pious mind lists all the benefits following submission to the Law. Pascal and Bossuet have both recorded their admiration of these austere sentences: they certainly correspond to the most fundamental genius of the Jewish soul.

What, then, is the Torah? It is essentially the Holy Scriptures, the doctrinal body that we have seen formed into the canon; the

Mosaic precepts of the Pentateuch still occupy a prominent place in it, but the teaching of the Prophets is equally venerated. This written law is supplemented by an oral law; thus throughout the course of centuries a commentary grew up, a jurisprudence, whose purpose was indeed to facilitate the application of the Law in special cases, but whose result in fact was all too often to increase to a bewildering extent definitions, observances, and taboos. The Scribes, those eminent specialists in textual matters, were the chief agents of this proliferation.

Jews of the community took a strange delight in threading their way among this wild tangle of rules. Everything was to be found in it, from the highest precepts to the most minute observances. To study the Law was the most honourable of all occupations, the only one necessary. The putting into practice, in life, of all these prescriptions was the sole object of the faithful. The Law dictated in minute detail the rules of conduct, from the age of marriage, which it fixed at eighteen, to the ornamentation of vestments. There is a whole world of commandments, "light or grave," "preceptive or interdictory," and our modern mind recoils before this infinite complexity. But to see in the Law only its tyrannous aspect would be to fail entirely to understand the spirit of the Jewish community. It was a burden, and a very heavy burden: St. Peter called it an unbearable yoke (Acts xv:10); but the Jews enjoyed bearing it. Obedience to the Law filled them with exultation and delight; the more precise it became the dearer it was to them. This joy in submitting to a very heavy commandment, a joy that is the basis of military greatness, the Jews experienced very deeply, and it would be altogether wrong to suppose that this formidable legalism led simply to a moral automatism. There were, of course, Jews mechanically applying strict precepts, who reduced their religion to a cold conformity; but the best amongst them found it possible to avoid that danger and to live, within the framework of the text, a free spiritual existence and inner life.

But here was another danger from which they were less able to escape and to which the majority succumbed; the Torah, based on a rule of conduct, placed on the same level formal precepts and spiritual aspirations. These even came to be entirely reversed. It was with this that Christ was to reproach the Scribes and Pharisees: for raising tithes on the least of things while violating the gravest commands of the Law, those concerning justice and mercy, and good faith (Matthew xxiii:23, 25); for thinking their duty to God performed when they had minutely followed all the rituals and all the observances. And what rites! What observances!

THE LETTER AND THE SPIRIT

One day when a High Priest was officiating, he poured the lustral water on the ground instead of sprinkling it on the altar: this was to take sides in a dispute between two modes of performing the rite, each of which had its fanatics. It seems that on that particular day the partisans of the "water on the altar" were more numerous than those of the "water on the ground." Now it was the custom on that feast to come to the Temple with palms and also with fruits, lemons or citrons. The High Priest soon discovered to his cost what it meant to break with such venerable traditions: a hail of projectiles descended upon him; exasperated, he called for the guard, and this affair of water ended with an abundant effusion of blood.

Such incidents were by no means rare in the Jewish community; one might even say that they happened in the ordinary course of events. Great political events had in Jerusalem only the most stifled echoes; the struggle of the Gracchi and the conquest of the Gauls by Caesar no doubt only aroused the briefest comment in the precincts of the Temple. On the other hand, when a religious Jew descended from his mule because a friend began to speak to him of holy things and he did not wish to remain in a sitting position when referring to the Divine Majesty, or when another, one day during the Feast of Tabernacles, refused to eat two figs that were offered him outside his tent, immediately the entire community was in ecstasies, and such glorious actions were immediately recorded in writing.

The rites and observances that thus surcharged the doctrine had various origins. Some preserved the memory of very ancient precepts which were applicable in circumstances since forgotten, and which were no longer understood. The Doctors of Law must have had most fertile imaginations in order to explain how water mixed with the ashes of a red cow—red, not brown, be it noted—was particularly efficacious in effacing defilements; or why the leper who touched a bird and afterwards let it fly must necessarily recover. Certain of these rites had a very obvious symbolic value: such as that of the "scapegoat," that was charged with the sins of Israel by imprecatory formulae and then driven into the desert. But others are utterly obscure, for which reason they were only applied the more rigorously.

Most of these were born of commentaries, the work of Scribes. Did they not boast of having "added hedge to hedge," and made the Law as "pointed as a nail"? This proliferation of precepts and commandments and interdictions led to a positive mania of scruples. Was it lawful to eat an egg laid on the Sabbath? Ought one to drink water from a spring into which an unclean receptacle has been dipped, or ought one not to consider that a drop from an unclean pitcher causes the impurity to spread right to the source? One might fill many pages with such precepts, taken at random: there are nine hundred on the gathering of gourds alone!

And what casuistry resulted from this entanglement! One must not eat produce set aside for the Temple tithes; but what ought a man to do, who, having dropped a basket of asparagus intended as an offering, discovers that it has sprouted? On the Sabbath day one must neither tie nor untie knots, but what kind of knots are meant? There is a whole chapter of commentary on this question. Neither must one write more than two letters, but which two letters, and taken from what alphabet? A twenty-page commentary was not considered excessive for this important enigma. And, as always happens in such cases, when laws become excessive, human wit is ingenious in eluding them. For example, on the Sabbath day, in order to carry a parcel for a distance exceeding the permitted two thousand cubits, one could fabricate a fictitious domicile and thus make the journey in a series of stages. The habit once formed, the tendency was to cheat in much more serious matters, those concerning real moral laws. For example, the old and noble commandment that laid down the obligation to leave for the poor whatever fell during the harvesting was more and more circumvented. Fall? What exactly did the word signify? Was it that which fell from the open or from the closed hand? Behind or in front?

Here we see a second stumbling-block which, in his majestic simplicity, Christ was to place under the feet of Israel. At His word, forthwith, things were to be put back in their proper order. There was to be no more question of confusing sins committed in hate, in violence, and with deceitful intent, with trifling infringements of meticulous laws. Whatever was inhuman in the law, Jesus was to refuse. He was to remove what Renan so well described as "the blight of religion." Christianity, in formulating that great precept, "The letter killeth, but the spirit giveth life," was to pass upon the absurd narrowness of Jewish legalism a judgment against which there is no appeal.

JEWISH PIETY

There undoubtedly existed, nevertheless, a Jewish piety, simple, human, and touching. Through the "hedge" bristling with precepts, entire faith in God, strong confidence, and love, often passed with admirable energy. For Christians today the vast majority of the Judaic observances are a dead letter, but our daily prayer still uses many of those psalms in which Jewish piety was able to discover such eloquent phrases with which to praise God.

One need only open at random that collection of a hundred and fifty psalms in which over so many centuries Jewish fervour expressed itself, in order to be moved by the spiritual quality that they manifest. It is doubtful whether any religion at any time has given to faith a higher and a more powerful expression. Although they were undoubtedly used in the great ceremonies, many of them have nevertheless the poignant quality of personal utterances. The most intimate piety finds expression in them. All the emotions of man are to be found in them: fear, despair, joy, gratitude. There are psalms for all occasions—mounting the steps of the Temple, leaving by the road to the desert—for life is a perpetual prayer. And what mystic has better expressed the desire for inner renewal in which the soul is filled with the love of God, than does the magnificent Psalm LI: "Behold, thou desirest truth in the inward parts: and in the hidden part thou shalt make me to know wisdom. Purge me with hyssop, and I shall be clean: wash me I shall be whiter than snow."

What, in Jewish legalism, seems to us excessive, served nevertheless to remind pious souls that the whole of life is consecrated. Prayer played a great part in everyday existence. The well known formula of the *Schema*, "Hear, O Israel . . .," to be recited every morning and every evening, was often repeated in all kinds of circumstances. Or the *Eighteen Benedictions* were recited, expressive of man's noblest emotions of adoration and hope. These fixed prayers did not exhaust the fervour of such souls; far from it. And we know that the Jews practised also that kind of prayer without formula, that spontaneous speech of the soul with God that leads to the highest spiritual states. Fasting, which many imposed on themselves voluntarily in addition to the days on which it was obligatory (the Pharisees fasted on Tuesdays and Thursdays), had also the sense of prayer. And if we have perceived in the casuistry of the Scribes devious means of eluding the Mosaic precepts of charity, it would be false to suppose that Jews as a whole despised that virtue. They piously repeated the maxim of Simeon the Just who lived in the third century B.C.: "The world has three foundations; the Law, the cult, and charity."

That cult itself seems very foreign to us, with its vast slaughter-house installed in the court of the Temple, those 1,093 kids and 113 oxen sacrificed annually for official sacrifice alone, those minute rites of legal purification, and those great rhythmic chants that punctuated the ceremonies. But it would certainly be unjust to suppose that religious souls did not perceive their profound significance even through strange or dazzling appearances. The love that the whole nation bore towards the Temple, the dwelling of the Most High, and which is expressed in so many psalms, was a deep and sincere sentiment, one of the spiritual roots of Israel, "one for a one God," says Josephus, "and common to all, as God is common to all." Sabbath observance, which, in the innumerable prohibitions that define its nature, seems to us so dry and so disconcerting, had another sense for those who saw before everything its spiritual purpose: a whole day during which, in recollection and refusal of all common duties, man had but one thought, one desire, to raise himself to God.

It was not only individual piety which in that religion found the means of exalted self-expression, but also collective, communal piety, in which everyone felt himself associated with all his brethren, and participated in a reality that, in space and in time, extended infinitely beyond himself. This is the sense of the *Church*, of the assembly, that so many Christians in our days have despairingly allowed to perish. . . . The pious Jew who came often from a great distance to the Temple of Jerusalem to take part in some ceremony or to celebrate the Passover, felt himself united with all his compatriots, living and dead. Each of the great Jewish feasts had therefore a very marked national sense. On the day of Expiation—*kippur*—the purification of the Holy of Holies with blood, and the driving into the desert of the scapegoat recalled to each the fact that he participated in the sins of all, that he had to redeem his father's faults as well as his own. The three feasts of "the pilgrimage" commemorated, in a very ancient ceremonial, great dates in the history of Israel: the Passover, on which a lamb was always sacrificed as in the time of Moses, rejoiced the soul with the memory of that providential benefit, the exodus from Egypt; the feast of the Weeks, fixed on the date of a very ancient agricultural ceremony, had become the festival of the promulgation of the Law, admirable manifestation of the Holy Spirit, of which our Pentecost, which succeeds it, retains the memory; the feast of Tabernacles, when each man must live in a tent, recalled to Israel the splendour and the purity of the days of the desert. And still other feasts marked other anniversaries—that of the "lots," the triumph of Esther; that of the "dedication," the reopening of the Temple after the triumph of Judas Maccabeus. As in our own Middle Ages, Jewish life was punctuated and attended by multiple signs of a piety that penetrated no less deeply into the soul for being official.

To these truly religious souls, St. Paul was to bear witness that they were zealous for God (Romans x:2), and if he adds, "but not according to knowledge," it is more in sorrow than in condemnation. Whatever may have been the errors in which the Jewish spirit went astray, how can we condemn a nation that was able to find phrases as simple in their sublimity as these: "As the hart panteth after the water brooks, so panteth my soul after thee, O God. My soul thirsteth for God, for the living God: when shall I come and appear before God?" (Psalm XLII).

THE DESTINY OF MAN

But, even more than in the domain of piety, it is in the moral and metaphysical orders that the Jewish community is worthy of admiration. Without deviating from the general line followed by Israel from the first, she was able to give to the ancient notions a scope and a depth of which no other people of that time furnished an example. Jewish philosophy, Jewish humanism, compared with their Greco-Roman homologues, have at once a coherence, a sense of reality, and a far greater elevation. In this domain, more than in any other, the little community of Judah prepared the way for Christ.

We have seen how, in the course of centuries the notion of responsibility acquired, little by little, the attributes by which we know it. For the primitive conception of collective guilt that brings down upon all the punishment merited by a few, and makes it impossible for the individual to run any risk other than as a member of the community, the prophetic teaching had substituted that of personal responsibility, in which each is accountable for his own destiny. The problem of sin was then posed to the Jewish consciousness in a way at once more compelling and more clear. They meditated on the teaching of Genesis; the great theme of original sin furnished for reflection its admirable symbols and its logical explanation; they felt evil as a wound, a blemish on integrity, on the purity of the soul, but a wound capable of healing in proportion as man sought to make good prevail. Thus was established the conception, spiritually so fertile, of a perpetual combat against sin, of an effort to rediscover lost innocence by penitence and expiation.

Jewish morality, as it appeared during these last centuries before our era, is the most incontestable sign of the greatness of Israel. The day, already far distant, when the nomads of Abraham and Moses had conceived it as associated with religion, when they had affirmed that their God was the God of Justice, they had laid the foundations of an immense edifice which, even to this day, supports civilization. On this construction, the Jewish community, since the Exile, had not ceased to work. In order to please God, it was necessary to be good, upright, equitable, chaste, and humble. Kindness in human relations, respect for women, pity for slaves, the practice of charity: Judaism has taught these laws of fraternal morality. At a time when the society of antiquity was slipping into a laxness that was to lead to decadence, in Judah, on the contrary, we find an effort towards purity, dignity, modesty, all the more remarkable in that the Semitic people were strongly addicted to the pleasures of the flesh. It must also be noted that in this we have not a philosophy reserved for a few intellectuals, but a rule of life professed by an entire nation.

But this morality came up against a blank wall: the problem of retribution. This had always preoccupied the mind of Israel. For a long time it had been taught that the recompense of good conduct must be meted out by God on earth. This was the unanimous opinion of the ancient Hebrews. The just man benefited by a long and happy life. From this to the conclusion that disasters and misfortunes are merely punishments, was but a step. Now the most elementary experience goes to prove that this is not so in reality; one knows too many just men who are overwhelmed with misfortunes and too many wicked men who spend their days in happiness. A solution to this enigma had therefore to be found: the dramatic dialogue of Job and his friends explored to the point of anguish the depths of this problem.

It is here that we see again the meaning of that progressive revelation of which Israel was the agent and the witness. Everything was accomplished according to a marvellous logic. "The law of Moses," Bossuet says, "gave to man only a first notion of the nature of the soul and of its felicity." But simply by following the road on which it already was, the Jewish spirit was to indicate the direction in which lay the solution. Already the sages of the Law taught that one must not serve God "like a valet expecting a tip," and that man's happiness is "in the commandments, not in the wages of the commandments." This idea of a purely spiritual recompense developed and took root. It is not in this fleshly life that God rewards the just, but in another way, and elsewhere. Where?

At this point the idea of death, as Israel had conceived it, constituted a terrible obstacle. Until the exile, the current idea of the life after death was very vague and meagre. It was thought that the soul, or a sort of double, fled towards an ill-defined place, *sheol*, "the region of shadows and the shades of death" of which Job speaks, "the enduring silence," mentioned in a psalm. What did the soul do there? What did it experience? It was not known. It was repeated in a hundred ways that in any case, it was sad to die; God Himself seemed not to be interested in the dead, and the idea of a judgment beyond the tomb, long entertained by the Egyptians, had few roots in the Jewish soul.

It was during the Babylonian distress and the efforts of the return that the metaphysics of life after death took its due place in Israel, as if the stubborn hope to which the community had in its history borne witness, found its equivalent in the supernatural order. The idea that death is not an end but a transition, that it leads to another life, that man escapes from its destruction, that he some day revives—this idea that permits the solution of

the enigma before which Jewish thought stopped short, was to
progress slowly and was in the end to illuminate the whole of
Judaism. Already Isaiah had cried: "Thy dead men shall live,
together with my dead body shall they arise. Awake and sing, ye
that dwell in dust!" (xxvi:19); and Job, in a passage of magnificent inspiration had said, "in the skeleton re-clad in skin, in my
flesh, I shall see God!" Not everyone accepted this doctrine which
revived ancient Judaism in so surprising a fashion; the Sadducees refused to do so, and Ecclesiastes is by no means clear on
the point. But this conception carried in itself too much power,
too great an attraction. Soon the immense majority were to think
with Daniel (xii), "And many of them that sleep in the dust of
the earth shall awake, some to everlasting life, and some to shame
and everlasting contempt." And Wisdom derives grandiose developments from this conception.

Thus, the conception of life after death became marvellously
renewed. It became fully satisfying for the spirit; it filled with
enthusiasm those who, in absolute confidence, awaited the coming
of God. After death, man would be judged; he would enter into
an eternity of happiness or pain; a day would come when he
should find life again, according to his desserts, and this resurrection, conceived as not only spiritual but as associating the soul
with the body in the same eternal destiny, was the seal of the
entire human greatness, of the flesh united to the spirit in a
mutual responsibility.

There is a remarkable fresco at Orvieto by Signorelli, Michelangelo's predecessor, representing that prodigious hour in which
men return to the light of day. The dead are emerging from their
tombs; some are still hideous skeletons; others have already received again their muscles, their skin, their smile. Two or three
are in an intermediate state, half corpses, returning to life. One
still sees the trace of bones, the stigmata of the tomb; but already
flesh is re-forming and learning to live again. And the effort is
visible in them, the effort towards eternity. Before this great
image one thinks of that people, lost on its barren hills, minute
among boundless empires, who, spontaneously, embodied in that

belief all the profundity that morality, metaphysics, and faith can attain.

What remained to make that religious effort complete? The fundamental fault of this Jewish doctrine was its placing of the whole responsibility on man. The Jews had possessed—Israel had always had—a very high sense of the dignity of the individual. But man alone cannot find the solution to the problem of sin. It is all very well to say how man must combat evil and to outline the virtues that he must acquire; but if man has been mutilated by original sin, if he can no longer by his own power pursue the effort towards lost purity, how can he escape from that insoluble contradiction? His spirit shows him the road to follow; his soul in its wretchedness cannot of itself follow that road. The reply Israel was able to find in another aspect of her thought; here she was strong. But to the Messianic doctrine that originated with her the Jewish community was not to give its whole implication, and this was to be the third, and decisive, stumbling block.

MESSIANISM

By *Messianism* we mean a current of thought, very ancient in Israel which took on gradually considerable force and profundity, to the point of becoming one of the characteristic aspects of Jewish spirituality; and which led to the revelation of the image of a being at once human and supernatural, whose apparition on earth should inaugurate an era of well-being.

Fundamental for the study of the community of Judah as well as for that of Jesus, the problem of Messianism is certainly the most delicate of all those raised by the thought of Israel. In speaking of it, we must avoid expounding its conceptions too much in the light of the Gospel, in hearing with Christian ears words which for the Jews had quite another sound. It is essential to preserve perspectives, to mark out with dates the spiritual current; but this is practically impossible, for the biblical editors gave little attention to this; and, when we use phrases like "Messianic hope" of a very ancient epoch, that of the Kings for example, it is necessary to observe that at that time this was only a manner of speaking, and that Israel then did not employ these terms at all in the sense in which we now use them.

Too many pious manuals and well-meaning sacred histories accustom their readers to the belief that between the "Messianic" predictions and the realization of the Gospel there exists a line of perfect evidence, of rational logic. Many honest Christians, filled from their youth with that naïve belief, find themselves disconcerted when they discover that the word *Messiah* has practically never—with perhaps one exception—in the Old Testament the sense which we now give it; that the image of the envoy of God, suffering for all men, was less common than that of a powerful king, sometimes violent and hard on his enemies, and that in fact the idea of the Saviour is rather implied than expressed. In order to form a balanced opinion on Messianism, three precautions must be taken: to replace this spiritual concept in the historical conditions in which it arose; to distinguish carefully the substance of this message from the literary terms in which it is clad, and whose oriental emphasis is inclined to be disconcerting; and to see it not as a coherent system of thought, emerging all of a piece from the brain of a philosopher, but as an immense presentiment which, over centuries, expanded in the Israelite soul, expressed itself fragmentarily in the words of some inspired writers, but which did not become entirely clear and comprehensible until such time as the Incarnation of Jesus Christ gave it its fulfilment.

Freed from all these pious traces, the Messianic idea only appears the more admirable and its incomparable grandeur is one of the most authentic signs of the mission of Israel. Together with monotheism, Messianism is an unique event in religious history; the two ideas are, moreover, inseparable, and it is in the perspective of the purest Jahwism that the idea of the Messiah is revealed. The resemblances that have been detected with the Iranian theme of *Saoshyant*, descendant of Zarathustra, who is to purify the world by fire, or with resurrected Osiris, whose consoling reign the Egyptians awaited, do not amount to more than external parallels, always so easy to find in religious matters. They do not take into account the origin of the Messianic tradition whose source is very clearly within the depths of the Jewish psyche.

Messianism was originally connected with the certitude that Israel had always had of her mission. God had chosen them as His privileged ones, His people of witness. Solemn promises, a "covenant," had established this engagement which is formulated in many texts. Could Jahweh break faith? No. The prophet Micah affirms, "Thou wilt perform the truth to Jacob, and the mercy to Abraham, which thou hast sworn unto our fathers from the days of old" (vii:20). Thus, the just and merciful God would intervene when the hour should come. He would assure at once the glory of His people and the triumph of His own cause. Israel, guardian of the Promise, should reign over a world in which the Law would be known to all.

This theme, which had contributed towards making so dazzling an image of the monarchy of Solomon, in which was to be seen the prefiguration of that glorious reign, took on a very different meaning when misfortune had broken over Canaan. National ruin, the deportation into Babylon, far from destroying hope, reinforced it. It was even that hope which, by the voice of the Prophets, encouraged the desolate people by forcing them to consider not the sad past, but the future full of hope. The return to their country, the restoration of the Temple, the stubborn resistance to the influences of Hellenism, all the events of history interpreted in this perspective, reinforced the faith in the Word; unhappy, humiliated, reduced almost to nothing, the chosen race was, nevertheless, promised universal domination. As the witness of monotheism, Israel, who knew the price of this message, doubted less than ever the triumph of God and her personal restoration.

To this first and fundamental idea, a second was added in proportion as the doctrine of retribution and judgment after death grew up within the Jewish soul. The present world flourished in its impiety; even among the chosen people themselves there was all too much infidelity. The unhappy situation in which Israel found herself was the sign of this general disorientation, but the situation had been merited by all the sins committed in violation of the Covenant. Patience! God would put all in order. A day would come which should be the day of Jahweh: "a day of darkness and not light," says Amos; "cruel, full of wrath and burning anger," according to Isaiah, on which sinners should be punished. Certainly that terrible and glorious manifestation of justice would be long in coming; Ezekiel even quotes a saying that, "Time prolongs itself; all visions remain unrealized." But it was certain; it would happen, inevitably.

Thus was established in the thought of Israel a mysterious concept in which the vision of the ultimate destiny of humanity and the certitude of the restoration of Israel were more or less confused. The judgment of souls, the reward of the just, the return of the chosen people to power, all these elements entered into those strange compositions of which the Books of Ezekiel and Daniel provide good examples, and that Jewish apocryphal literature multiplies to excess, incoherence, and absurdity. Needless to say, according to the quality of the souls that abandon themselves to such meditations, some insist rather on the spiritual joys of the glorification of the just, others on the more temporal advantages of a triumph in which Israel should recover her greatness.

The two currents of thought united, therefore, in what the evangelist St. Luke was to call "the redemption of Israel" (1:6, 8; II:38; XXIV:4). How was this phenomenon to be produced? Sometimes it was thought that Jahweh would accomplish it in person, sometimes that He would act through the intermediary of some privileged being. This second conception took on an ever increasing importance in proportion as Jewish theology, forcing into sublimity its conception of God, became more and more removed from all trace of anthropomorphism, and considered that a spirit so pure could not condescend to intervene in a world so base; the idea of an intermediary therefore arose by a logical process.

In the whole of the Old Testament, those who had received a holy unction, for example kings like David or some High Priests, bore the title of the Lord's *anointed*; in Aramaean, *Meschiah*, messiah; in Greek *Christos*. It was by that term that the mysterious mediator to come in the name of God to assure "the redemption of Israel," and the judgment was naturally designated. In consequence, this name of Messiah was not only applied to the one whom we now so designate; thirty times the Old Testament used it to designate a king whose personal name it sometimes was; in other circumstances, it qualifies a priest or a patriarch; Isaiah even uses it of Cyrus (XLV:1), and Habakkuk of the entire nation of Israel (III:13). There is not in the whole Bible any precise passage, except one in Daniel, in which the term *anointed* can be understood as absolutely predicting our Messiah: that passage in which the Prophet foretells that from the decree authorizing the rebuilding of Jerusalem to the Messianic era, sixty-nine weeks of years shall pass (IX:25).

Such, then, is the essence of the theme. But it is evident that in the course of centuries it developed. In its origins, it was no more than a distant presentiment. In Genesis (XLIX), when Jacob blessed his son before his death, he exclaimed, "The sceptre shall not depart from Judah, nor a lawgiver from between his feet, until Shiloh come; and unto him shall the gathering of the people be." And Balaam, the Prophet, constrained by God to refrain from anathematizing the chosen people, cried, "I shall see him, but not now: I shall behold him, but not nigh: there shall come a Star out of Jacob, and a Sceptre shall rise out of Israel" (Numbers XXIV:17).

When the crown was established in Israel, it was natural that the Messianic idea borrowed many of its traits. Had it not in itself a great religious significance? Was not the king the Lord's Anointed? The Messianic hope was, for a time, to be merged in admiration of the royal majesty, and this interpenetration of the two notions was to be one of the deepest causes of the refusal of the Jews to imagine the Messiah otherwise than in the guise of a majestic monarch. At that time, Messianism manifested itself through the idea and the image of the monarchy. In Psalm II, for example, the Lord's Anointed, the King of Zion who reigns on the Holy Mountain and who breaks the nations with a sceptre of iron, is called the son of God—"Thou art my son; this day have

I begotten thee." Thus these texts can be read in a double sense, as referring at once to a historical king and to a supernatural messenger; David, speaking of his sufferings, uses terms that apply perfectly to the Crucified.

Finally, with the great tragic crises of the ruin of Israel and the exile, Messianism took on a new character. It became more moral, more spiritual. The Prophets whose task, as we have seen, consisted in developing religion in the sense of the inner life, saw the Messiah much less in the aspect of the imperious ruler than as a mediator, a pastor, a peacemaker. Isaiah, consoling his brethren, spoke with tenderness of that servant of Jahweh who would teach in kindness, who would never be understood and who would give His life in expiatory sacrifice. The more the idea of a religion of the spirit, of personal responsibility, progressed, the more that image of the Messiah became sublimated. When the Messiah should come, He would judge the good and the evil, and as Isaiah so finely says, when the olive tree is shaken, only a few olives will remain, "two or three berries in the top of the uppermost bough, four or five in the outmost fruitful branches thereof" (xvii). As the allusions to the coming of the Messenger multiplied, so did his character become enriched, and thus the revelation of the Gospel was prepared. In the Old Testament as well as in the Apocryphal books, the idea of justice, closely associated with the coming of the Messiah, is continually expressed. "It is he who is to gather the holy people, and govern them with justice," says one of the noncanonical psalms, attributed to Solomon.

In the latter days of the Jewish community, the Messianic theme was formulated according to a scheme that may be reduced to its essential lines of thought—noting, by the way, that all systematization in such a sphere excludes the infinite variety of individual meditations and reflections. The apparition of the Messiah would be marked by great tribulations and terrors. Blood would flow from wood; stones speak; nations would be troubled; the sun shine at night, and the moon rise three times in one day; salt water flow among the fresh; reason and intelligence would be looked for in vain. These images from an Apocryphal book of Esdras give an idea of the reveries that imagination built up around the waiting for the Messiah. But these sufferings were to have a meaning. They were to turn humanity to repentance; it was then that, according to Jeremiah, God would say "Return, ye backsliding children, and I will heal your backsliding" (III:22). The Messiah was to be preceded by a prophet, who should be no other than the mysterious Elijah, who was not dead, according to tradition, but had been caught up into heaven. Malachi and Jesus, sons of Sirach, both announced his return: he would lead back the hearts of children towards their fathers, he would quiet anger before it broke out. Then would come the reign of God and of His messenger.

How was this reign to unfold? Would there be two periods, a Messianic era preceding God's coming in glory? Or would the two be merged? This point was discussed. In the main, all were in agreement in admiring its splendour, in being certain that this would be the time of the definitive covenant between Jahweh and humanity, that covenant of which Jeremiah said that the foundations should be established never to be removed. But of the effects of this coming they could give no clear account. Would it be merely a human domination, as widespread and as magnanimous as possible? Would it be the return to a new paradise, where men would live a life of unending delight? Would it be a purely spiritual exaltation of the souls of the just? Hypotheses were also multiplied touching the duration of the Messianic era, which according to some was to be a thousand years. But in any case, all were unanimous on one point—the theatre of this return in glory: it could be in no other place than Jerusalem, the Holy City, in a Promised Land marvellously renewed that this reign should be accomplished. Baruch, in the Apocrypha, even speaks of a manna that is to nourish men until the consummation of time.

We see, therefore, into what complex images had led this long meditation that Israel had been elaborating for centuries. Much more than the details, what must be grasped is the strength of the impulse, the intense aspiration that worked in the soul of

the chosen people. Some have asked whether this Messianic waiting was equally eager throughout the whole of society, whether
the rabbi and the scribes attached great importance to it,
whether the rich and fortunate, those prudent in politics, pinned
their hopes wholeheartedly to this coming of a Messiah who
would reduce their privileges to nothing, and—who knows?—
might provoke incidents with Rome. Must we take literally the
bitter reflection of a Pharisee, "If you are taking a cutting, and at
that moment the Messiah is announced, finish your graft. You will
have plenty of time to go and meet Him!" Most likely the difference was one of emphasis; cultured people thought chiefly of
the last judgment; the humble thought of the triumphant reign
of the one who was to bring them consolation and revenge. A
zealot and a Sadducee had different conceptions of the same hope.

But it is beyond all doubt that on the whole, during the last
centuries, the Jewish community lived on that hope. One has only
to open the Gospels to be convinced of this. "Art thou the Messiah?" they asked John the Baptist. "Art thou he that shall come,
or must we look for another?" the Precursor asked Jesus. The
Samaritan woman declared, as a fact admitted by all, "I know
that the Messiah shall come." One could cite many similar texts.
This Messiah, they had thought to recognize, more or less, in the
likeness of Cyrus, the conqueror of Babylon, or of Zerubbabel,
one of the leaders who brought back Israel from exile; or even
of Alexander; and Josephus, like the servile flatterer that he was,
declared that the prophetic verses applied very well to the Roman
Vespasian!

To recognize the Messiah—this was, therefore, for the Jewish
community the most important of all problems. Upon its solution,
the nation's destiny was to depend.

WHO WOULD THE MESSIAH BE?

As a matter of fact, the "Messianic doctrine"—if we can call
such a complex collection of notions a doctrine—contained nothing
that would enable men to discern unmistakably the expected

Messiah. Many Jews held, on this point, the view that St. John the Evangelist attributes to certain inhabitants of Jerusalem, that "when Christ cometh, no man knoweth whence he is" (vii:27).

There were, however, some certain, or at least very generally admitted, indications. The most fundamental was that the Messiah was to be a supernatural being, a "son of God." In the famous second Psalm, do we not read this revealing assertion: "The Lord hath said unto me, Thou art my Son; this day have I begotten thee. Ask of me, and I shall give thee the heathen for thine inheritance, and the uttermost parts of the earth for thy possession"? Other psalms and prophecies, like that of Daniel, confirmed this opinion. A similar conception is formulated in various ways in that apocalyptic literature in which is expressed, not without inextricable excesses of imagination, the most ardent of Jewish aspirations; the Psalms of Solomon, the Book of Enoch, the Apocryphal books of Esdras exalt this royalty of the Messiah. Without being exactly a god, he was to participate in the divine majesty; he was to partake of the grandiose and sometimes terrible attributes ascribed to Jahweh in the Scriptures; but he was also, as a psalm ascribed to Solomon says, "the just king, under whose reign there is no iniquity, the king who shall have pity on the frightened nations, the king free from all sin, the king who never grows weak, because he is strong in the fear of God."

To this idea was added another. The Messiah was also to be a "son of man." This expression, which was born in the times of the Prophets, with Ezekiel and Daniel, soon took on a very particular significance. It designated the mysterious messenger who, intervening in the name of God among men, must partake of human nature. In one of his visions, Daniel had announced His coming. "I saw in the night visions, and, behold, one like the Son of man came with the clouds of heaven, and came to the Ancient of days, and they brought him near before him. And there was given him dominion, and glory, and a kingdom, that all peoples, nations, and languages, should serve him: his dominion is an everlasting dominion, which shall not pass away, and his kingdom that which shall not be destroyed" (vii:13–14). In the Book of Enoch, the Messiah is represented as a celestial man, a being at once supernatural and human; begotten by God before time, and kept in reserve until his hour should come. It seems certain that the great majority of Jews expected the Messiah to be "a man among men," as Tryphon later described Him to St. Justin. Some insisted on this divine and transcendent side, others (above all the Doctors of the Law) rather on his human side; but the synthesis of these two elements was very generally admitted.

This, however, did not make it possible to identify in concrete terms the man who, among the "sons of men" should carry within himself the divine promise. There is indeed something moving and dramatic in that waiting and that search. What if the Messiah were already born? What if, without anyone knowing it, His reign was already begun? Pious Jews must have asked themselves such questions in the anxiety of their meditations. Who would He be? Would His name be *Emmanuel*, "God with us," as the Prophet Isaiah had foretold? (vii:14), or *Jahweh sidquenou*, "God is our justice" according to Jeremiah (xxii:5, 6; xxxiii:15, 16)? By dint of scrutinizing the texts, they thought that they had discovered this or that characteristic. He was to be, according to Psalm cx, "a priest for ever after the order of Melchizedek." Everything indicated that he was to be a descendant of David.[4] Isaiah expressly said this in that eleventh chapter in which he so well describes the future king: "And there shall come forth a rod out of the stem of Jesse, and a Branch shall grow out of his roots." And Jeremiah also confirms this prophecy. Like the dynasty of David, he was to come from Bethlehem. "And thou, Bethlehem, the fertile," the prophet Micah exclaims, "little among the thousands of Judah, yet out of thee shall he come forth unto me that is to be ruler in Israel." A son of David, He should yet be greater than His great ancestor, because David calls Him his Lord, and the Psalms show Him sitting at the right hand of God. These very precisions only increased the mystery. All that concerned Him

[4] The Roman Emperors Vespasian, Domitian and Trajan had the descendants of David sought out and watched.

was shrouded in shadows, and the brightest of hopes were concealed behind multitudes of secrets. Had not Isaiah written a little disconcerting phrase that, following the evangelist St. Matthew, the whole Catholic tradition has translated as, "A virgin shall conceive, and bear a son" (vii:14)?

Even when He had come, would it be possible to recognize Him by the manner in which He would exercise His reign? Not even in this way, for on this point, there were two opposing versions which Jewish intelligence, great as it was, could not succeed in reconciling. According to some, the Messiah was to be a king in the temporal sense of the term. He would reign effectively. And the Jewish mind, without doubt in the great majority of cases, imagined Him under the appearances which tradition had given to sovereigns. A characteristic passage of the *Targums*—the commentaries of the rabbis—describes Him thus: "How fair he is, the king Messiah who shall arise from the House of Judah! He girds his loins, he advances into the plain, he engages in combat against his enemies, and puts kings to death!" The apocryphal psalms of Solomon give no other image, and it must be admitted that the psalms of our Bible leave us disconcerted when they insist on presenting the Messiah in the guise of a monarch who "breaks the nations with a rod of iron," who dashes them in pieces "like a potter's vessel"—"He shall fill the places with the dead bodies; he shall wound the heads over many countries"—whose "arrows are sharp in the heart of the king's enemies" (Psalms ii, cx, xlv).

Such images are perfectly comprehensible if we take the trouble to replace them in their historical setting, and remember who the people were who elaborated them. It is now three thousand years since Israel first carried them in her heart! The evolution of the image of the Messiah is one of the most striking proofs of that "progressive revelation" of which we have seen many examples. It was already a great thing that to these brutal visions of future domination was often added the hope of justice, the image of the equitable king, for example, elaborated in Psalm lxxii. Little by little, Messianism, without entirely detaching itself from an earthly vision, grew away from it. It became more and more interior in Jeremiah and Ezekiel. And Nahum, one of the minor prophets, exclaims, "Behold upon the mountains the feet of him that bringeth good tidings, that publisheth peace!" (1:15).

It was, in fact, another image of the Messiah that grew upon the immense presentiment of Israel. As a man, he would be near men. He would be humble; "lowly and riding upon an ass, and upon a colt the foal of an ass" (Zechariah ix:9), but yet He was in fact the king, under divine protection. Still more extraordinary, this envoy of the Almighty was to know that commonest of all human destinies, sorrow. In an astonishing and wonderful passage, the greatest of the prophets, Isaiah, surely announced the sorrowful Messiah, the suffering Christ:

"He is despised and rejected of men; a man of sorrows, and acquainted with grief: and we hid as it were our faces from him; he was despised, and we esteemed him not.

"Surely he hath borne our griefs, and carried our sorrows: yet we did esteem him stricken, smitten of God, and afflicted.

"And he was wounded for our transgressions, he was bruised for our iniquities: the chastisement of our peace was upon him; and with his stripes we are healed. . . .

"He was oppressed, and he was afflicted, yet he opened not his mouth: he is brought as a lamb to the slaughter, and as a sheep before her shearers is dumb, so he openeth not his mouth.

"He was taken from prison and from judgment . . ." (Isaiah LIII).

This image, so precise and so moving that no Christian can contemplate it without emotion, was this the true Messiah that Israel was to recognize? Was it he of whom David had written in advance that Psalm xxii, whose first verse Christ was to murmur in His agony? Was it of him, "the transpierced," that Zechariah had prophesied that Israel should "mourn for him as one mourneth for his only son" (Zec. xii:10)? Does not the author of the Book of Wisdom show in the same perspective that the sacrifice of the "just, the son of God," outraged and tortured by the crowd, condemned to a shameful death, enters into the purposes of God, when he enables him to overcome evil, the devil by whom "came death into the world" (Wisdom II:24)?

We see, then, that this progressive revelation tended to develop more and more the inner meaning of Messianism. Pursuing this meditation on sorrow and its meaning from which David, Jeremiah, and the Book of Job had already drawn such profound conclusions, the Jewish mind was to carry it to its supernatural consequences. The idea of redemptive suffering opened the way for the dogma of the Incarnation, as did also the philosophic reflections of Wisdom that tended, more and more, to represent it under a concrete form, with a personal character, "the breath of the power of God, and a pure influence flowing from the glory of the Almighty" (Wisdom VII:25), announcing the Gospel of St. John. Messianism thus found its third foundation; it no longer reposed only on the certitude of the Mission of Israel and on images of the end of the world; into it had penetrated, imperiously, the hope of one who, by his suffering, was to redeem the faith of men, and who was, upon earth, to be the human expression of the infinitely wise will of God.

Herein lay the dilemma. Between these two images of the Messiah, that of a glorious king who should re-establish Israel in her power, and that of a suffering Christ, a saviour dying to expiate the sins of the world, the Jewish community believed that there was an opposition. Christianity, in an ultimate revelation, was to realize the union of these two so widely separate theses. And, it must be admitted, it was natural that the chosen people could not, alone, succeed in doing so.

In the time of Christ, many symptoms prove to us that it was rather in the temporal form as powerful and glorious that the Messiah was envisaged. "But we trusted that it had been he which should have redeemed Israel," the disciples at Emmaus were to say (Luke XXIV:21), and, on the day of the Ascension, at the moment when Jesus was about to ascend into heaven, the Apostles were still asking Him, "Lord, wilt thou at this time restore again the kingdom to Israel?" (Acts I:6). It was very understandable, it was human.

This nation had lived in a stubborn hope. Attached to their land, to the hill on which the Temple stood, their memory was full of texts which told them of the glory of their ancestors; they had only been able to survive and preserve their message by their savage exclusiveness. Pride had long been their weapon, from the time when Abraham in his tent despised the Canaanite idolaters, until that other time, very recently, when the Jewish community had rejected the Hellenic civilization of Antiochus Epiphanes. There had been a tendency in human nature for pride to become vainglory from the time when there were, acting upon the visions of the future, two of the sentiments that move the hearts of men most strongly: the desire for vengeance, and the bitterness of lost happiness.

Therefore they preferred to see in the Messiah, the restorer rather than the saviour; without supernatural graces, all men reason in just the same way. "They shut their eyes," Father Lagrange writes, "to the texts that foretold the sufferings of the Messiah." From this they came to ask whether those that spoke of his humble coming were not susceptible of more noble exegesis; one rabbi even suggested that the ass of which Zechariah speaks, as the mount of the King Messiah, should be replaced by a white horse!

The radical incomprehension that the Jewish people opposed to Christ was therefore definitely being prepared. He who was to teach the spirit and not the letter, who was to defend the idea of universal religion against Jewish particularism, was already a scandal for the Jews; but much more so was this unhappy Messiah, this destitute, this condemned man who, instead of restoring Israel in her glory was to suffer the agony and shame of the Cross.

The roads here were to divide. On the one hand, there is that which was followed first by a very small number of holy souls who, in the message of the Crucified, heard the response to all those aspirations, desires, and sufferings that the human heart contains. On the other, those who, not always basely, to be sure, and sometimes with greatness, awaited in the release of the Kingdom, the glorification of a nation that God had alone selected for

His service. And it is this second route that was, in the seventieth year of our era, to lead Israel to catastrophe. Josephus has very truly said, "What excited them to war against Rome was an ambiguous prophecy, found in the Holy Scriptures, announcing that a man of their country was to dominate the universe."

Until our own day, Israel has remained in the second way. Marked with so much blood, wetted with so many tears, its history bears the mark of that decision. But we must not forget that the other road also leads from Jerusalem, nor forget the cry that arises from their book, "I knew that my redeemer liveth" (Job xix:25).

A "SACRED" HISTORY

From the time when Abraham, in Ur of the Chaldees, received the summons to a new destiny, until that when the great presentiment of a nation was filled with the hope of a saviour, many centuries had passed over the earth. Two thousand years separated these two equally mystical events, but the thread of an impeccable logic undoubtedly unites them. No history gives in a greater degree than does that of Israel the impression of having obeyed an internal development, of having borrowed from circumstances only the means of being the more completely itself. And the weight of this small nation is so great, the influence of themes that have sprung from it so considerable, that we are driven, as it were, to investigate the causes of that spiritual fecundity, and in that sequence of events we endeavour to find a meaning.

This would be to go beyond the scope of history and to pass into the region of theology. Bossuet, in his most important work, the *Discours sur l'Histoire universelle*, has proposed a logical explanation for it: if "that long series of particular causes that make and unmake empires, depends on the secret orders of divine Providence," so to an even greater extent must the destiny of a people that carries within itself the certitude of the divine Promise be supernatural. These men of Israel, in spite of all their faults, were the privileged witnesses of a unique truth; "their whole history, all that befell them from day to day was but a continual unfolding of the oracles that the Holy Spirit had given them." They jealously guarded a great illumination, but "it was in the light of the Messiah that that great light was to appear uncovered."

To keep within the terms of history, three observations may be made which bear out Bossuet's theory. The first bears on the indestructibility of Israel. It is more than astonishing, indeed it is rationally incomprehensible that this nation, so small, has survived the centuries without ever disappearing. Where are the Hittites, the Hyksos, the Assyrians, the Parthians? Yet all these nations possessed great empires, ruled over vast territories. It happened on more than one occasion that Israel was reduced to a handful of men, but neither Egypt, nor Assyria, nor the blows of Babylon, nor the seductions of Greece were able to make that seed, always ready to germinate anew, disappear. And, to our own day, uprooted from its country, dispersed throughout the world, the inheriting race continues its indestructible existence, like a prickle in the living flesh of nations that disturbs them and compels them to self-examination.

The very development that this history has followed gives rise to a second observation. We have often pointed out its progressive character. It is beyond question. A deepening of truths already known, an addition of new certitudes; ceaselessly, by these two methods, Israel became spiritually enriched. Abraham laid, irremoveably, the corner-stone of monotheism; Moses formulated the Law, proclaimed the essential principles; the Prophets, by associating faith definitively with morals, gave a model to all the religions of the world; following them, the community, returned from exile, discovered in the immensity of its distress and its hope a metaphysics and a morality that no nation had ever equalled before Christ. Now this characteristic of progressive development is a unique fact; if we were to consider other civilizations, we would say that the human spirit followed a very different curve. After a period of attempts, it attains its highest development, and then comes decadence, and a more or less rapid decline. Israel has scaled the successive stages, and when, in the end, her spirit was caught in the impasse that does not permit her to recognize Jesus, it was not by betrayal of her essential fidelity but by virtue of a preponderance of certain of her own spiritual elements, as if to leave to the Christian message its character of mystery and revelation.

The third observation that one might make is this: this witness of Israel, great as it may be, seems to us incomplete. On many points, as we receive it, we have the impression that it might be more complete, more decisive. To be sure it would be altogether unjust to judge it in comparison with Christianity which is, precisely, its fine flower; and in order to give it its full weight, we must weigh it in the same balance as other contemporary societies of antiquity; and to these it is infinitely superior. But this impression of incompleteness suggests in an irresistible fashion Bossuet's conclusion. The spirit must find its logical conclusion. This logical conclusion exists. *"Finis enim Legis, Christus,"* we say with St. Paul; or with Pascal, "Jesus Christ, whom the two Testaments envisage, the Old as its hope, the New as its model, both as their centre" (*Pensées*, 740).

It is, then, not only a solid tradition rooted at the heart of our Western and Christian culture, it is also the most objective consideration of these facts that justifies us when, in summing up this long series of significant events, we give them for title these two words: sacred history.

January 1941–June 1942.

CHRONOLOGICAL TABLE

Dates (B.C.)	Principal Events in Sacred History	Correspondences in Date
About 2000	Abraham's vocation and his departure from Ur	Reign of Hammurabi in Babylon 12th dynasty in Egypt, that of Senusrets (Sesostris) First palaces of Knossos in Crete Aryan infiltrations in Asia Minor: the Hittites
About 1800	Jacob	Hyksos invasion of Egypt, the consequence of a new Aryan wave. Simultaneous decline of Mesopotamia
1740? 1630?	Joseph's Egyptian adventure	Hyksos domination in Egypt
About 1580		Pharaohs of the 17th dynasty drive out the Hyksos kings In Crete, reign of Minos of Knossos
16th to 13th centuries		18th and 19th Egyptian dynasties (*See* Table on p. 89) The Queen-regent Hatshepsut (1500–1450)
1440?	The Exodus (on the hypothesis of the longer chronology)	Amenophis II (1450–1420) The revolutionary Pharaoh Ikhnaton and the documents of El-Amarna (1375–1360) Rameses II (1290–1225) fights against the Hittites

407

CHRONOLOGICAL TABLE—continued

Dates (B.C.)	Principal Events in Sacred History	Correspondences in Date
1225?	The Exodus (on the hypothesis of the shorter chronology)	Minephtah (1225–1215)
From 1400 for the next four centuries		Great Aryan invasion, fall of Crete (1400) and the Hittite empire (conquered by King Midas at the end of the 12th century). The Achaeans: Mycenae, Tiryns
1180	Joshua enters Canaan	
About 1100		The Trojan war and the voyages of Odysseus Philistines on the coast of Canaan Tiglath-Pileser I in Assyria
12th and 11th centuries	Period of the Judges (Deborah, Gideon, Jephthah, Samson); Samuel about 1080 Conquest of the Promised Land; wars against the Canaanites, Bedouins and Philistines	The great empires of Egypt and Mesopotamia remain dormant Beginning of the Aramaean expansion Tyre, in Phoenicia, rises to great importance
End of the 11th century		Terrible wave of Aryan invasion; the Dorians; fall of Mycenae and Tiryns; the Achaeans set out for Asia Minor
1040–1012 1012–975	Saul, King of Israel (wars against the Philistines) David (conquest of Jerusalem in 1005)	Phoenician maritime empire

408

	Northern Kingdom (Israel)	Southern Kingdom (Judah)	
975–935	Solomon (building of the Temple: the whole of Canaan pacified)		Hiram, king of Tyre (979–946)
935	Division of Israel into two kingdoms		Egyptian revival (22nd dynasty) In the 10th century, Assyrian power becomes formidable
		Rehoboam (935–915)	The Pharaohs (Lybians) make expeditions into Canaan
	Jeroboam (925–911) (1st dynasty) Nadab (911–910) Baasha (910–887) (2nd dynasty) Elah Zimri (3rd dynasty) Omri (4th dynasty) Ahab (875–853), Jezebel and the Prophet Elijah	Abijah (915–913) Asa (913–873) Jehoshaphat (873–849)	Assur-nazir-pal II, king of Assyria (884–859); Assyrian expansion as far as the Mediterranean
9th century	Ahaziah of Israel Jehoram of Israel (852–842) The Prophet Elisha Jehu (842–815) (5th dynasty) Jehoahaz	Jehoram of Judah (849–842) Ahaziah of Judah (842–836) Athaliah (842–836) Joash (836–797)	The legendary king Lycurgus of Sparta Foundation of Carthage by the Tyrians (825)

CHRONOLOGICAL TABLE—continued

DATES (B.C.)	PRINCIPAL EVENTS IN SACRED HISTORY		CORRESPONDENCES IN DATE
8th century	Jehoash of Israel (799–784)	Amaziah	
	Jeroboam II (784–744); the Prophet Amos	Uzziah (789–738)	Homer?
	King Zachariah; Jonah(?)		Foundation of Rome: April 21, 758 (legendary date)
	Shallum (6th dynasty); the Prophet Hosea	The Prophet Isaiah (from 738)	
	Menahem (744–735) (7th dynasty)	Jotham	Tiglath-Pileser III, king of Assyria (745–727)
	Pekahiah		
	Pekah (733–731) (8th dynasty)	Ahaz (733–718)	Beginning of Greek colonization
	King Hoshea		
	Fall of Samaria (722)		Sargon II (722–705): apogee of Assyria
7th century		Hezekiah (718–689); the Prophet Micah. In 701 the Assyrians raise the siege of Jerusalem	In Iran, Zoroaster, the religious reformer Sennacherib (705–681), revolts of Merodach-Baladan
		Manasseh (689–641)	Esarhaddon (681–668)—The Ethiopian Pharaohs Assur-bani-pal (668–626) in Assyria; in Egypt, Psammetichus inaugurates 26th dynasty
		Amon	

	Josiah (639–609); "discovery" of the Law	New Aryan invasions; the Medes (Cyaxares, 625–585); the Scythians (625)
	Jehoahaz, Jehoiakim. The Prophets Nahum, Zephaniah, Habakkuk; beginning of Jeremiah Zedekiah (597) Fall of Jerusalem (586)	Cylon and Dracon in Athens Babylonia revolts against Assyria; fall of Nineveh (612) Nebuchadnezzar II (604–562) Apogee of neo-Babylonian civilization
6th century	Exile of the Israelites in Babylon The Prophets Ezekiel and Daniel	The Buddha in India Solon in Athens Development of the Greek cities in Asia Minor, and the kingdom of Lydia under Croesus In the West, the empires of Carthage, of Marseilles and of the Etruscans
About 570	Tobias?	Achaemenes the Persian proclaims his independence of the Medes
552 539 538	Cyrus conquers Babylon Decree of Cyrus authorizing the Israelites to return to their own country	Cyrus achieves Persian unity under his domination and conquers the whole of the Fertile Crescent
	Palestine henceforth a dependent state of the Persian empire	In Greece, Pisistratus and his sons, tyrants of Athens (540–510) Cambyses, son of Cyrus (529–522), conquers Egypt Darius I (522–485); Clisthenes in Athens (507)

CHRONOLOGICAL TABLE—continued

DATES (B.C.)	PRINCIPAL EVENTS IN SACRED HISTORY	CORRESPONDENCES IN DATE
5th century	The Prophets Zachariah and Haggai: rebuilding of the Temple	Rome throws off the Etruscan kings, the Tarquins, in the revolution of 509
		First Medic war: Marathon 490
	Judith?	Xerxes (485-465)
	The Prophet Malachi	Second Medic war: Salamis, 480
		Rome struggles against the Latins, the Aequi and the Volsci (episodes of Cincinnatus and Coriolanus)
445	Nehemiah rebuilds the walls of Jerusalem	The Law of the Twelve Tables (450, The Greeks force the Persians to sign a peace treaty and to liberate the coast of Asia Minor (448)
		The Parthenon is dedicated to Athena (440)
		Rome captures Veii (under Camillus, 406)
		Peloponnesian war (431-404): fall of the Athenian maritime empire (404)
4th century	Esdras and the editing of the Law (398). (The text of the Old Testament was established during the four succeeding centuries)	Death of Socrates (399)
		Spartan domination in Greece
		Rome captured by the Gauls (387)
		Pelopidas, Epaminondas, Theban supremacy in Greece: battle of Mantinea (362)
		Philip of Macedonia subjects Greece, following his victory at Chaeroneia (338)
334	End of Persian domination: Alexander passes through Canaan	Alexander lands in Asia
332		Fall of the Persian empire of Darius III

323		Death of Alexander
		War of Rome against the Samnites (Caudine Forks, 321)
		Destruction of the Etrusco-Samnite league by Rome
		The empire of Alexander is divided between his generals (306): Egypt under the Lagidae, Syria under the Seleucids
		War of Rome against Pyrrhus (281-275)
3rd century	Palestine under the domination of the Lagidae. The Oniades and the Tobiades contend for power. At Alexandria the Bible translated into Greek (Septuagint version)	First Punic war (264-244)
		Antiochus III the Great, of the Seleucid Dynasty (223-187)
		Ptolemy IV of the Lagidae (221-203)
		Second Punic war (218-201), Hannibal
200	Jewish resistance to the influence of the Lagidae. Battle of Panion: Palestine passes under Seleucid control	Antiochus III destroys the army of the Lagidae
2nd century		First war between Rome and Macedonia (200-197): Roman victory at the Cynoscephalae (197)
		Antiochus III defeated by Rome at Magnesia (190)
		Seleucus IV (187-175)
		Antiochus IV, "Epiphanes" (175-163)
		Second Macedonian war, Pydna (168)
166-165	Heliodorus driven from the Temple. Jewish resistance to Seleucid influence: the Maccabees. Mattathias	
165-160	Judas Maccabeus succeeded by Jonathan (160-143), and Simon (148-134)	Greece a Roman province (149-146). Third Punic war, end of Carthage (146)

CHRONOLOGICAL TABLE—continued

Dates (B.C.)	Principal Events in Sacred History	Correspondences in Date
134-104	John Hyrcanus	Rome colonizes Provence (125)
1st century	Alexander Jannaeus (103-76)	The Gracchi, Tiberius (133) and Caius (123)
		Marius defeats Jugurtha (105), the Cimbri and the Teutons (102-101)
		War between Sulla and Mithridates (87-84)
		Sulla dictator (82)
	Alexandra Salome (76-67)	Pompey subjects the Pirates and Mithridates (69-63)
63	Conquest of Jerusalem by Pompey	Pompey in the East
		First triumvirate: Pompey, Caesar and Crassus (60)
		Conquest of Gaul by Caesar (58-52)
47	Caesar passes through Palestine, and is saluted by Antipater	Caesar in Egypt: Cleopatra
		Death of Caesar (44)
		Second triumvirate: Octavius, Antony, Lepidus (43)
40-4	Herod	Battle of Actium (31); Octavius, master of the world, takes (in 30 B.C.) the name of Augustus
20	Reconstruction of the Temple	
6?	Birth of Jesus Christ	

INDEX

415